PLYMOUTH DISTRICT LIBRARY

D1595830

242.74 M

The mystery of the rosary :
Marian devotion and the
reinvention of Catholicism /

Plymouth District Library
223 S. Main St.
Plymouth, MI 48170

Jan 2010

242.74
m
BaT 13109
75

The Mystery of the Rosary

Madonna del Rosario (The Madonna of the Rosary), by Caravaggio, circa 1606–07 (Vienna, Kunsthistorisches Museum, Gmäldegalerie).

The Mystery
of the Rosary

Marian Devotion and the
Reinvention of Catholicism

Nathan D. Mitchell

NEW YORK UNIVERSITY PRESS
New York and London

NEW YORK UNIVERSITY PRESS
New York and London
www.nyupress.org

© 2009 by New York University
All rights reserved

Library of Congress Cataloging-in-Publication Data

Mitchell, Nathan.
The mystery of the rosary : Marian devotion and the
reinvention of Catholicism / Nathan D. Mitchell.
p. cm.
Includes bibliographical references and index.
ISBN-13: 978-0-8147-9591-0 (cloth : alk. paper)
ISBN-10: 0-8147-9591-9 (cloth : alk. paper)
1. Mary, Blessed Virgin, Saint—Devotion to. 2. Rosary. 3. Catholic
Church—History—Modern period, 1500– I. Title.
 BT645.M58   2009
 242'.74—dc22   2009013547

New York University Press books are printed on acid-free paper, and
their binding materials are chosen for strength and durability. We
strive to use environmentally responsible suppliers and materials to
the greatest extent possible in publishing our books.

Manufactured in the United States of America
10 9 8 7 6 5 4 3 2 1

To Demetrio S. Yocum
in solitude, for company

Contents

Acknowledgments

Although writing is often seen as solitary work, authorship is a complex communal activity. It is my happy task, therefore, to acknowledge the many individuals and groups whose assistance made this book possible.

Thanks are due first to editor Jennifer Hammer at New York University Press, not only for her initial interest in this project but for her sustained follow-up, wise counsel, and keen eye. Her astute editorial recommendations helped me focus and reorganize the book's chapters at critical moments in their development. Gratitude is also due to Ms. Hammer's able assistant, Gabrielle Begue.

To all my colleagues and students in the Department of Theology at the University of Notre Dame I owe a deep debt of gratitude. Their advice, wisdom, and generosity made my work a pleasure, not a burden.

To the staff of the Theodore M. Hesburgh Library at Notre Dame—and especially to Susan A. Feirick and her colleagues at the circulation desk—many thanks for their assistance, patience, and sense of humor.

Finally, to Demetrio, *mille grazie* for daily inspiration, insight, and encouragement: "Aquæ multæ non potuerunt extinguere caritatem, nec flumina obruent illam. Si dederit homo omnem substantiam domus suæ pro dilectione, quasi nihil despiciet eam" (Canticum canticorum 8.7).

Introduction

Since its appearance in the fourteenth and fifteenth centuries, the rosary of the Virgin Mary has remained such a familiar practice among Catholics in the Latin West that its popularity has not been eclipsed even during periods of seismic social upheaval, cultural change, and institutional reform. Through successive historical epochs—from the late Middle Ages, to early modernity, to the "reflexive" modernity of our own times—the rosary, a ritually repeated sequence of prayers accompanied by meditations on episodes in the lives of Christ and Mary, has varied little in form (round beads strung on cord or wire), structure, or content. This is a remarkable fact when one considers that during these same centuries the official *liturgy* of the Roman Catholic Church underwent profound changes—most notably in 1474 (publication of the first *printed* edition of the *Missale Romanum*, which contained the material said or sung during Mass); in 1570 (publication of the so-called Tridentine *Missale Romanum*, revised after the Council of Trent); and again in 1970 (publication of the *Missale Romanum* of Paul VI, as mandated by the Second Vatican Council). Today, significant numbers of people who pray the rosary daily may be found on every continent (with the possible exception of Antarctica). As a popular devotion, moreover, the rosary appeals to a broad spectrum of believers, from traditionalists such as Mother Angelica (founder of the Eternal Word Television Network) to liberal Catholic critics such as Garry Wills.[1] Rosaries may thus be found in the hands of popes, professors, protesters, commuters on their way to work, children receiving the Eucharist (Holy Communion) for the first time, or homeless persons seeking shelter and safety from hostile passersby.

How does one account for the rosary's ubiquity, durability, and resilience? This question—and a proposed answer—are the subject of *The Mystery of the Rosary: Marian Devotion and the Reinvention of Catholicism*

Recent scholarship on the rosary focuses primarily on its medieval origins or on the devotional milieu (*devotio moderna*) that framed its initial appearance. But positivist histories leave many questions unanswered. History, after all, is less the science of retrieving the past than the exercise of a complex hermeneutic or method of interpretation. Its ultimate quest is not simply to determine "what happened" but to understand how what happened continues to shape human experience. *The Mystery of the Rosary* argues that to understand the rosary's adaptability and survival across chronological periods, cultures, and continents, one must examine more closely the changes Catholicism itself began to experience after the Reformation—the movement initiated by Martin Luther to reform Catholicism, which led to the eventual development of Protestantism—and the Council of Trent, convened in response to the Reformation to clarify Catholic faith and doctrine in the sixteenth century. These changes resulted, I will maintain, from a series of "reframings" that reshaped how Catholics understood church reform. We will explore these reframings in chapters that will consider the visual representation of sacred subjects, the relation between devotion and the liturgy's ritual symbols, religious identity, and the rosary itself as devotional prayer with a strongly sacramental subtext. A final chapter will "read" the rosary in light of present-day perceptions of Catholic faith and piety.

This book, then, will not reconsider the medieval origins of the rosary, except for a brief initial overview, but will begin in earnest with the enhanced status and popularity of the rosary among Roman Catholics, particularly after the Christian military victory over Ottoman forces at Lepanto, off western Greece, in 1571. In the aftermath of this perhaps unexpected change of fortune, the Roman Church began to redefine itself not only in relation to Islam but also in relation to the changing landscape of European Christianity. During a crucial quarter century, from roughly 1585 to 1610, early modern Catholicism began to emerge as no longer a church defensively preoccupied by "Counter-Reform" but as a proactive community of renewal ready to reinvent itself.

A moderate version of such reform had already begun during the Council of Trent (1545–63). Yet despite widely accepted assumptions to the contrary, Catholicism after Trent did not become a fossilized, monolithic institution immune to change. True, the early modern church did not suddenly shed its authoritarian structures or its habit of controlling and supervising members while regulating their beliefs and behaviors. Writing about Rome as a "renewed religious capital" in the late sixteenth century, historian Jean Delumeau notes perceptively that the "prestige of a city once more conscious of its potential increased the authority of the popes in the Catholic world and thus completed the activities of Trent which, against all expectation, had strengthened the position of the Holy See."[2] This rather unexpected result led an early historian of the Council of Trent, Paolo Sarpi (1552–1623), to note that "the court of Rome, which feared and avoided this council as the most likely instrument to modify the excessive and limitless power it had acquired over the years, so hardened its grasp on the party that remained faithful to it that its authority has never been so powerful and so secure. The moral is to surrender everything into God's hands, and not trust in human prudence."[3]

Early modern Catholicism was thus a deeply ambivalent reality, at once humble(d) yet grandiose, eager for renewal yet resistant to change. Despite these ambiguities, the character of Catholic thought and religious practice did shift perceptibly as the Roman Church moved from Counter-Reform to "early baroque," and from European to "global" community. This shift was nowhere so noticeable as in church art and devotional life. For as I hope to show, a reform of church life is inevitably a reform of its images as these are framed in its icons, its rites, and its written narratives. While post-Tridentine church leaders like Carlo Borromeo and Gabriele Paleotti discussed what was theoretically appropriate in "sacred art," innovative painters like the Carracci and Caravaggio were relandscaping the Catholic imagination with canvases that both shocked and amazed their viewers. Similarly, while theologians discussed the fine points of dogmas about Christ and his Mother, a visionary writer like Sor María de Jesús (Mary of Ágreda) was able to reimagine the human relationship with God in a novelistic narrative that incorporated the early modern self as subject in the history of salvation.

The Mystery of the Rosary argues, in sum, that the rosary survived and flourished because it was able to absorb the reframings of reform, representation, ritual, religious identity, and devotion that came to characterize early modern Catholicism and that have continued to shape Catholic piety and practice to the present day. For while the core of Jesus' own message may have been relatively brief and direct—repent, believe, love, serve, make peace, welcome God's reign among you (see, e.g., Matthew 5)—Christianity has a long, tangled, and sometimes troubled history. One of the attractions of the rosary—as both a devotion and an object of study—is its ability to focus attention on the central meanings and mysteries of Christian faith, as seen and experienced through the lives of a man (Jesus Christ, God's Word made flesh [John 1.14]) and a woman (Christ's Mother, Mary). Without getting too sidetracked with peripheral matters of belief or behavior, the rosary has enabled praying Christians to contemplate the "basics" of human existence as seen from God's angle.

Take, for example, the so-called joyful mysteries of the rosary, five episodes derived from Luke's gospel: (1) the angel's announcement of Jesus' birth (Luke 1.26–38); (2) Mary's visit to her cousin Elizabeth (Luke 1.39–45); (3) Jesus' birth (Luke 2.1–14); (4) Jesus' presentation in the Jerusalem Temple (Luke 2.22–38); and (5) Jesus' being lost and found in the Temple (Luke 2.41–52). Embedded within these events are profoundly human—and accessible—motives, conflicts, and emotions. They deal with the raw material of the human drama: a young woman suddenly confronted with an intruder whose improbable "message" leaves her stunned, confused—and pregnant. There follows a panicky trip to a trusted, older relative who, though surely postmenopausal—also becomes pregnant, leaving her aged husband literally speechless. Then we hear of parents in flight, a birth on the run in a stinking, unsanitary shed. After that, the drama continues with an old man's promise that the kid will run into deep trouble and the mother's heart will be broken (Simeon's prophecy, Luke 2.34)—followed by the scary episode of a missing child.

From the perspective of Christian faith, these scenes ("joyful mysteries") reveal a God passionately in search of humankind, trying by every means—including the edgiest and most unexpected—to get our attention long enough to reveal the divine presence. On a simpler level, they remind us of the grandeur and misery of human life, challenging us to make sense of our personal histories, even if they are littered with interruptions, failures, doubts, and disasters. The rosary gave (and continues giving) many Christians an opportunity to register, review, and (when necessary) revise their relations with God. Understanding the history of this devotion will help us see how, paradoxically, Catholics have maintained traditions of belief and behavior not through single-minded intransigence but by embracing flexibility and change. Here our principal lens for interpreting that history will be reinterpretations of Mary and the rosary in visual art, in ritual words and actions, in personal narratives, and in that expanding interiority and self-awareness that shaped early modern Catholic women and men.

1

Reframing Reform

On a late winter day in 1615, the young Jesuit priest John Ogilvie was led to his execution in Glasgow as the sun dropped toward the horizon. Present at the proceedings was John Eckersdorff, a Hungarian Calvinist who left a vivid account of what happened as Ogilvie was about to be hanged: "Just before he went up the ladder, he flung his rosary from the scaffold as a last souvenir for the Catholics who were near him. This rosary, flung at random, hit me in the chest, so that I had but to put out my hand to take it. There was however such a rush and crush of the Catholics to get hold of it that unless I wished to run the risk of being trodden down, I had to cast it from me."[1] Eckersdorff's report bears witness to the emblematic status of the rosary among early modern Catholics especially, though not exclusively, in the British Isles. Rosary beads had become characteristic markers of recusant Catholic identity and were among the devotional items whose possession was prohibited by Protestant reformers in both Scotland and England. Such beads—made of a variety of materials, from knotted string to precious coral—embodied what it meant to be a practicing Catholic in a time of religious strife and persecution.

The rosary did not, however, originate in the early modern period. Its roots are medieval, and its name derives from the Latin *rosarium* (literally, "rose garden"), which in fourteenth-century Europe had also come to signify a collection of devotional texts ("roses") offered in praise and petition to Christ and/or the Virgin Mary. Knowledge about the rosary's origins received an enormous boost in 1997, when Anne Winston-Allen's indispensable study, *Stories of the Rose*, appeared. Winston-Allen subtitled her book "The Making of the Rosary in the Middle Ages," and while she does devote some space to the early modern era—to Martin Luther's reaction to the "marketing of the rosary," for example—her principal concern is how the devotion evolved in the formative fifteenth century and what its possible antecedents may have been in fourteenth-century "life of Christ" rosaries such as the one used by Cistercian nuns at the monastery of Saint

Thomas on the Kyll.[2] (The "life of Christ" rosary focused on events in the life and career of *Jesus* but seems to have involved repetition of the prayer known as Ave Maria or Hail Mary.) Importantly, Winston-Allen also chronicled the crucial transition from medieval "Marian psalters"—modeled on the biblical psalms but composed of 150 Hail Marys, with the words of the angelic salutation (Luke 1.28 + 1.42) sometimes surrounded by rhyming tropes—to the cyclic "life of Christ" meditations that eventually became central to the rosary as prayer and practice. For those unfamiliar with Winston-Allen's important book, I will provide a very brief overview of the early development of the rosary here, in order to lay the foundation of what is to come.

The use of beads as counters to help a praying person keep track of repeated petitions is a practice far older than Christianity itself.[3] Like their ancient predecessors, rosary beads (usually numbering fifty-nine in modern rosaries) were used to count devotional repetitions of the Ave Maria (Hail Mary), the Paternoster (Our Father), and the Gloria Patri ("Glory be to the Father"). The Hail Marys were prayed in groups of ten ("decades"), each group separated by a single bead (often larger in size) on which the Our Father was recited. To this circle of beads, a pendant was eventually attached, consisting of a medal (often engraved with an image of Christ and/or the Virgin), from which hung five additional beads and a crucifix. Use of the pendant permitted the addition of a brief introduction to the decades of the rosary. The Creed ("I believe in God") was recited while holding the crucifix; there followed an Our Father, three Hail Marys, and a Gloria Patri. Then came the rosary's five decades (one Our Father, ten Hail Marys), recited while meditating on Christian "mysteries" (scenes or episodes drawn from the lives of Mary and Christ).[4] The five-decade rosary was commonly called a "chaplet"; a *complete* rosary consisted of fifteen decades, totaling 150 prayers, equal to the number of psalms in the Bible. Thus, Christians often called the rosary "Our Lady's Psalter" (or collection of psalms) even though, technically, medieval Marian psalters constituted a distinctive devotional and literary genre that reworked the language of the biblical psalms into poetic texts and rhyming tropes in praise of the Virgin.

From its inception, it seems, the rosary was a popular success. It was portable, it appealed to both laypeople and clergy, its prayers could be easily memorized and recited in either Latin or the vernacular, and its meditations required not literacy but simply the exercise of one's imagination. Almost from the start, too, the rosary was linked both to art and material culture and to the emerging print culture of the late fifteenth century. Rosary books with woodcut illustrations abounded. Indeed, Winston-Allen shows how the rosary—which imaged Mary herself as a *rosarium*—helped to blur the distinction between sacred and profane art, since the rose garden imagery, found in both visual images and popular song, combined sacral and erotic impulses (drawing upon the biblical Song of Songs).[5]

Moreover, the rosary's popularity helped reshape social structures, especially through the confraternities ("brotherhoods") that soon began arising among persons attracted to the devotion. These voluntary, pious associations grew rapidly and were in principle open to all, including women. There was no fee for membership, making them accessible to the poor as well. In fact, as we will see, the rosary confraternities became preeminent instruments of social transformation within both late medieval and early modern Catholicism. Yet they also became bones of contention among reform-minded Christians in early sixteenth-century Europe. For one thing, the benefits promised to members were sometimes unwarrantedly extravagant—for example, reciting the rosary could protect the devotee, convert a pagan nobleman, or release a soul from purgatory.[6] For another, members were expected to assist not only the living through prayer and charitable works, but the dead as well. Typically, a confraternity member was expected to say a specified number of rosaries on behalf of deceased members and their families. Like other prayers in the later Middle Ages, the rosary was enriched with indulgences (a remission of the temporal punishment for sin). Pope Sixtus IV, in 1476, had explicitly extended these indulgences so that confraternity members could apply them not only to themselves but to "souls already suffering in purgatory."[7] Martin Luther, who in principle had no objection to devotion to the Virgin Mary, did react vigorously against the merchandising of indulgences attached to the rosary because such arrangements seemed to privilege an individual Christian's "good works" above the uniquely efficacious act by which Christ redeemed humanity through his suffering, cross, and death. What Luther despised was not the rosary as such but the confraternities' novel marketing techniques, which encouraged members to "earn indulgences" through a prayer that was less expensive and far more convenient than pilgrimages, since it "could be said anywhere and at any time."[8]

Winston-Allen's work provides a necessary prelude to this book because we will focus here not on the late medieval origins of the rosary or its continued evolution in the early Renaissance but on what I think is an equally momentous transition that began to unfold *after* the Council of

Trent (1545–63), during an epoch commonly called the "Counter-Reformation" or "Catholic Reformation," but better designated as "early modern Catholicism."[9] Our goal here is to see how the rosary and Marian piety became emblematic of an innovative, renascent Catholicism, especially in the late sixteenth and early seventeenth centuries;[10] how the image of Mary and the rosary began to be reinterpreted in the early baroque era; how the rosary's post-Tridentine evolution was directly connected to *both* liturgical *and* devotional customs; how Marian devotion survived and flourished even (or especially) in circumstances where the public practice of Catholicism was prohibited; and how and why the rosary has continued to play a vital role in the lives of modern and postmodern Catholics.

Reforming a Reform: 1585–1610

For the rosary to flourish in the new atmosphere that followed the religious and political upheavals of the early and middle sixteenth century, it was necessary for Roman Catholicism not only to pursue a reform among its leaders and members but also to "reform its reform." Until the mid-twentieth century, Counter-Reformation Catholicism was commonly viewed as a defensive, monolithic reaction against reformers (especially Martin Luther, Ulrich Zwingli, and John Calvin) that resulted from decisions made at and after the Council of Trent. Counter-Reform was identified with a rigid authoritarianism embodied in papal absolutism, exercised through repressive institutions such as the Inquisition and the Index of Forbidden Books, and exemplified by harshly punitive measures against dissent in any form. It was assumed, moreover, that "Counter-Reformation" ideology dominated Catholicism from the mid-sixteenth century until at least the age of the Enlightenment and the French Revolution (1789–99). Yet these views may owe more to popular caricature than to hard historical data and scholarly consensus. Ever since the German church historian Hubert Jedin made his now-famous distinction between "Counter-Reformation" and "Catholic Reform" in 1946, scholars have had to confront the fact that while these two periods may share some elements of a common history, they neither are equivalent nor can be reduced to a univocal religious culture.[11]

Our study must begin, then, by examining some of the ways early modern Catholicism struggled to reframe the dynamics of reform, to "reform the (Tridentine) reform" during a crucial quarter century that lasted from roughly 1585 to 1610. A pivotal moment in this attempt to reinvent itself was Catholicism's retrieval of Marian devotion after the Council of Trent. Devotion to Mary had, in fact, been a hallmark of later medieval Christianity in the Latin West, as art, iconography, literature, liturgy, and music all attest. The famous frescoes that Giotto (1267–1337) created on the walls of the chapel commissioned by the powerful Scrovengi family in Padua, for example, contain a complete "life of Mary" cycle, as well as a "life of Christ" series. Those who prayed and worshiped in that space would have been surrounded at every moment by brightly colored iconography that drew visual attention to Christ and his mother. Similarly, medieval Christian poetry and prose abounded in collections of popular material focused on the person and power of the Virgin Mary—for example, the versified *Miracles of the Virgin Mary* by Nigel of Canterbury (ca. 1130-1200).[12] Most notable of all, perhaps, were the Hours of the Virgin Mary, a cycle of prayers assigned to specific times of day and modeled on the Divine Office (the church's official daily prayer). The Hours of the Virgin had become popular additions to the daily prayer of many monastic communities by the end of the first millennium, and they gained enormous popularity among literate lay Christians through the medieval books of hours.[13]

In the early sixteenth century, however, challenges to popular medieval perceptions of Mary's place in the life of faith and prayer had begun to surface among both humanists (like Desiderius Erasmus 1466/9–1536) and reformers (like Luther). Erasmus was not opposed to daily prayer in honor of Christ's Mother, but "he seemed to regard as excessive the many daily offices that constituted the Hours of the Blessed Virgin Mary, the staple of the medieval Books of Hours."[14] Moreover, he preferred the use of more explicitly *scriptural* language for Marian prayer. Similarly, Luther's *Personal Prayer Book* (Betbüchlein; 1522) had concluded that Christian prayer "should include the Mother of God" (through recitation of the Hail Mary, for example), but urged believers not to let their hearts "cleave to her, but through her penetrate to Christ and to God himself."[15]

We will discuss the views of Erasmus in greater detail later. Here we need only note that the question of if, when, and how to address Mary in Christian prayer was an issue already on the table for debate in the early sixteenth century, and that in the aftermath of the Council of Trent, it became an increasingly urgent topic among promoters of the Catholic "Counter-Reform." In fact, the first Marian sodality (a devout association of laypersons similar in structure and purpose to the late medieval confraternity) appears to have been established at the Jesuits' Roman College in

1563, just as the bishops at Trent were concluding their deliberations.[16] It appealed to an elite corps of pious students upon whom it imposed "minimum requirements of devotion: prayer meetings, frequent communion, and observation of feast days of the Virgin."[17] Such sodalities "sprang from the same soil that had nourished the *devotio moderna*, as well as the rosary confraternities in the Low Countries and the Oratory of Divine Love in Rome, thus linking late medieval Catholic reform to the spirit of Tridentine Catholic renewal."[18]

Yet there was the rub. Just as debate continues within contemporary Catholicism about the meaning of "the spirit of the Second Vatican Council," so a similar debate developed during and after the Council of Trent. The phrase most commonly used to describe Trent's agenda is "reform in head and members," and the fundamental framework for such a reform had already begun to emerge in the fifteenth century.[19] Faced with an explosion of protest in early sixteenth-century Europe, many Catholic ecclesiastics agreed on the *urgent need* for reform, but not necessarily on the *methods* for achieving it. Such disagreement is one reason why the Council of Trent falls into three distinct phases or "periods," some of them separated by nearly a decade.[20] This separation into periods reveals not only the external political pressures facing Catholic bishops in a Europe increasingly polarized between old-religion loyalists and newly forming Protestant factions but also uneven support for reform from the papacy.[21] For example, the election of the papal legate (emissary) and committed council supporter Marcello Cervini as Pope Marcellus II in 1555 was perceived as a clear victory for the forces of reform; but the new pope died after only three weeks in office, and his successor, Gian Pietro Carafa (Pope Paul IV), though "unmistakably a reformer," was "not a conciliar one."[22] As historian Michael Mullett notes, "Paul IV was by nature an autocrat and was suspicious of Trent. He replaced conciliar with papal reform and set up a commission of reform, made up of sixty prelates, which was seen as an alternative to the Council."[23] To speak, then, of an early modern Catholic renewal that included among its major elements a Marian piety increasingly attached to the rosary requires some caution.[24] At least five factors about this period of history need to be considered:

First, the "Catholic Reformation" was not, as historian Louis Chatellier remarks, "a new construction" emerging suddenly "from the insight of a few exceptional men."[25] Reform had been in the air for well over a century prior to Trent, and the postconciliar renewal of Catholicism (what some have called "Triumphant Catholicism") is best perceived as "the organising and harmonising of a number of initiatives which had appeared, in some cases several centuries earlier, in a disconnected way in various parts of Europe, in the apostolic and pastoral sphere."[26] As we will see, for instance, the "Christian optimism" of innovators within the "Oratorian orbit"—for example, Saint Philip Neri, Gabriele Paleotti, and Federico Borromeo—exemplifies but hardly exhausts the broad spectrum of approaches to reform that emerged in Trent's wake.[27] What came to be known as the "Oratory of Saint Philip Neri" began in Rome about the year 1575 (its constitutions were approved by Pope Paul V in 1612, after Neri's death). A similar "French Oratory" was established in 1611 by Pierre de Bérulle and given papal approval in 1613. Stressing the need for cooperation between Catholic clergy and laypeople, both these groups believed that Catholicism could best meet the challenges of the Reformation not by reacting negatively and "circling the wagons" but by proactively embodying the freshness and vigor of faith ("Christian optimism"), at it was being lived among ordinary laypeople, including both rich and poor, gentry and street people, the devout and the skeptic. Neri's Oratory was a community of secular (i.e., diocesan) priests who lived and worked together without vows, taking their message out of the churches and directly into the streets. De Bérulle's was a more centralized congregation of priests who focused on education, especially on preparation of seminary students for ordination. Gabriele Paleotti and Federico Borromeo were not "Oratorians" as such but career churchmen (eventually cardinals) who knew, admired, and supported Philip Neri's work

The simple fact was that many Catholic bishops at—and after—Trent had no intention of conceding that Lutherans or Calvinists had a monopoly on reform ideas. Even though the initial phase of Catholic renewal after Trent may have emphasized direct episcopal (especially papal) control over church life, alternative visions of reform (like those of Neri, Paleotti, and Borromeo) also managed to assert themselves [28] Among these were innovative proposals for implementing Trent's decrees on the reform of church art and religious images, especially the iconography of Christ and the Virgin Mary.

Second, the history of early modern Catholicism, especially as represented by what some historians call "Catholic renewal," is actually the history of a prolonged oscillation between accommodation and flexibility on one hand and fierce struggles for control on the other. "Threatened in its European homeland by the advance of Islam on the borders of the Holy Roman Empire, and in its very heart by the Lutheran and Calvinist

'Reformation,'" the Roman Church "had with all urgency to take the measures necessary to confront this new situation."[29] Meanwhile, preachers and pastors like Philip Neri recognized that new times demand new, even radical, methods in preaching, catechesis, prayer, and study. Catholic Christianity had to be made attractive as well as disciplined and truthful. "Tridentine Catholicism succeeded in the long term," writes Hsia, "not by suppressing 'superstitions,' but by grafting orthodoxy onto traditional and popular spirituality."[30] This point will be particularly relevant for our discussion of the preeminence that Marian devotions such as the rosary achieved among Catholics during this period.

Third, the encounter between European and non-European civilizations also had a significant impact on the evolution of early modern Catholicism. During the so-called age of discovery, European Christians not only met new peoples and cultures in Asia, Africa, and the Americas but also had to redefine the way they understood the church's mission everywhere the world.[31] This meant, among other things, recognizing that Europe itself had become "mission territory."[32]

In this climate, what was seen as central to missionary activity was subject to diverse interpretation. Chatellier points to the appreciable differences of approach that had already emerged, for example, between Franciscan and Jesuit missionaries in the sixteenth century. The reformed branch of the Franciscan order known as the Capuchins, for instance, saw the missionary as engaged in a kind of counterpoint related to the biblical figures of Martha and Mary (see Luke 10.38–42; John 11.1–44).[33] Martha and Mary (the two sisters of Jesus' friend Lazarus, according to John 11.1) were seen as representing two distinct orientations within Christianity. Martha—the busily active woman concerned about household chores and "getting the work done"—was contrasted with the quietly contemplative Mary, who "sat beside the Lord at his feet listening to him speak" (Luke 10.39). Successful missionary preaching meant "doing the work of Martha—useful, indispensable, but by its nature inferior in value to listening ·to the Truth, the choice made by Mary."[34] Thus the greater part of the Capuchin missionary's time was to be spent "in silence, retreat and privation"; then, renewed by these ascetic practices, he would "descend from 'the mountain' to address the people" with the truth of the scriptures.[35] Jesuit missionaries, on the contrary, were to rely less on personal inspiration and more on authoritative direction from those persons whose own experience could serve as models and guides to good living, and who knew how to conduct apostolic activities with "discernment and political sense."[36] Moreover, in the mission strategy of Jesuit founder Ignatius Loyola, preference was given "to 'persons of high rank,' such as princes or prelates," and "'great nations' like India, or important towns, are to have priority. . . . [T]hese rules allowed of no exceptions and were applicable equally to Christian Europe and the 'infidel' Indies."[37] Education, preparation, talent, and political savvy were paramount. Only the best men available were to be sent as missionaries, especially if the place were politically or culturally important (e.g., India, China, Japan, Naples, the Republic of Genoa).[38] Despite such differences of approach, missionary activity—in Europe, in Asia, in the Americas—was generally seen as a providential expansion of God's grace through the gospel, leading the Catholic Church to acquire "a world-historical dimension" and making the "centuries of Catholic renewal" after Trent "the first period of *global* history."[39]

Fourth, the work of historians like John Bossy cautions us against assuming that the Catholic strategy of "Counter-Reformation," in which church life and practice were authoritatively reorganized from the top down, represented a simple repudiation of earlier medieval parish-based piety. The Catholic "social miracle" (which Bossy describes as a vision of society based on peace, reconciliation, and communion among its members) happened—or at least worked itself out most effectively—at the micro-level of local parish practices rather than at the macro-level of nation, region, or centralized seat of power (e.g., Rome).[40] This should not be taken to mean that Trent's reform program affected only career ecclesiastics (bishops and priests) and theologians or that local parishes were largely immune to the Council of Trent's impact and aftermath. On the contrary, for the "ordinary population," especially in places such as France and Italy, the Tridentine Counter-Reform meant the enforcement of

a system of parochial conformity similar in character to that which the contemporary Church of England was seeking to impose [e.g., through the Book of Common Prayer], though much more comprehensive in its detail. The faithful Catholic was to attend Mass every Sunday and holyday in his parish church. He was to receive the Church's sacraments, other than confirmation, from the hands of his parish priest, who would baptize him, marry him, give him extreme unction on his deathbed, and bury him. He would receive the eucharist at least once a year, at Eastertide, and with the same regularity the priest would hear and absolve his sins in the sacrament of penance.[41]

It goes without saying that Trent invented neither these practices nor the religious beliefs and expectations that supported them. Yet the council had left Counter-Reformation bishops and pastors much better equipped than their late medieval or early Renaissance predecessors to compel uniform parochial practice, especially in matters of religious ritual. What was revolutionary about Trent's reforms was not that they sought to rouse Catholic Christians from inertia to action, or from nonparticipation to participation in the church's life and liturgy. Rather, Trent's primary innovation consisted of making the local *parish* the primary venue for the practice of religious faith, worship, and devotion.[42] At the beginning of the sixteenth century, the church had been largely a conglomerate of more or less "autonomous communities" based mainly on bonds of "kinship and the solidarities which presupposed them."[43] For the average rural layman in the pre-Reformation church, Bossy suggests, moral living and regular (if infrequent) participation in sacraments were "part of a machinery for the regulation and resolution of offences and conflicts otherwise likely to disturb the peace of a community."[44] That is, the pre-Reformation church's goal had been to impose "Christian ethics on social behaviour"; after Trent's reforms, the focus shifted toward "conformity in religious observance."[45] To say this, Bossy argues, is not to suggest that Counter-Reformation Catholicism lost interest in the moral significance of social relations among its members in favor of a more individualized, "interior" Christianity. It is simply to note that Trent took the focus *off* family and kinship systems and instead made *participation in parish life* the mainspring of Catholic identity.[46] By "imposing a regime of ritual conformity on ordinary Catholics" and by making the *parish* the center of that conformity, the Counter-Reform "excluded laypeople from autonomous religious action."[47] This also explains why Trent was rather suspicious of family-centered piety and private devotions like the rosary, for these seemed to share, with the reformers, a preference for *personal* (as opposed to sanctioned, ecclesiastical) interpretation of scripture and doctrine. Trent understood that a reform of church in head and members was best controlled by a papacy with power to impose uniformity in vital matters of belief and behavior, ritual and doctrine. Variation in ritual observance, for example, was seen as tantamount to heterodoxy; hence the liturgical reforms that followed Trent and governed the public prayer and sacramental celebrations of Catholics for the next 400 years were assigned to commissions formed and regulated by the pope, and were imposed with rare exceptions on all parishes worldwide.[48]

In sum, Bossy's research helps to show how Catholicism made the transition from a late medieval, kinship-based society that derived its energy and influence from family friendships and local connections to a truly "global" Christianity whose organization—political, spiritual, administrative, and theological—worked from the top (pope and bishops) down, with the local parish (not the family) as a focus of religious activity.

Finally, in spite of vigorous papal supervision over the process of reform, early modern Catholicism cannot simply be identified with papal autocracy, institutional reform, intellectual history, socioeconomic change, or even with its guiding agents—aristocratic, self-disciplined males and missionary zealots. Despite its obvious connections with all the aforementioned, Catholicism after Trent was surprisingly innovative. It not only developed new methods of achieving acculturation, social control, ritual conformity, and parish-centered piety but also fostered novel ways of imagining the complex relationship between God, human persons, and an expanding world of cultural diversity and religious pluralism.

Early Modern Catholic Spirituality

In this connection, the work of historian H. Outram Evennett remains important for understanding the Counter-Reform and its outcomes. Counter-Reformation Catholicism was, in his view, "first and foremost a powerful religious movement" that represented spiritual renewal more than institutional reform.[49] It was a "positive and creative" development "stimulated in all its aspects . . . by the challenge of Protestantism."[50] Unquestionably, this "coming into existence of new and competing forms of established Christianity in Europe" had both positive and negative outcomes for the Roman Church. It produced "a new and modernized efficiency in catechismal [*sic*] and controversial methods, and a new impulse to the serious study of Church history," but it also intensified "those habits of caution, suspicion, intransigence, and the appeal to force which are the hallmarks of the anxious defensive, involved in the elaboration and safeguarding of more rigorous definition."[51]

Yet it was the inventiveness and originality of Counter-Reformation Catholicism that interested Evennett most. As he argued, the fifteenth century "was full of reforms and reformers who between them could not make a Reformation; either in the Catholic or in the Protestant sense. . . . The essential sterility and ephemerality . . . of all reform movements between the Council of Constance [1414–18] and the pontificate of Paul III

[1468–1549] proceeded in the last analysis from the tiredness of generations which seemed to have lost the art of creation, or re-creation, in so
many spheres of human activity; which could produce neither a Loyola
nor a Luther."[52] Evennett's claim about spiritual stagnation in fifteenth-century Catholicism was surely exaggerated, especially if one moves beyond
institutional history to consider the work of well-known artists of the pre-
Tridentine period like Leonardo da Vinci and the young Albrecht Dürer.
Moreover, Evennett seems not always to have recognized the potentially
misleading nature of the categories he uses to describe the attitudes of
churchmen (e.g., Philip Neri, Ignatius Loyola) who emerged as Catholic
reformers during and after Trent. Evennett spoke of "spirituals" versus "in-
transigents," using these labels to delineate the differences between "open-
minded reformers" and "closed-minded reactionaries" within Tridentine
Catholicism. As noted earlier, a figure like Marcello Cervini (elected as
Pope Marcellus II in 1555)—whom modern historians might identify as
an "intransigent" because of his firm support for papal power—was perceived as a "spiritual" progressive by many of his contemporaries (e.g., the
English cardinal Reginald Pole). Yet this polarity is misleading for historians today because Cervini and his coreligionists "exemplified the standard
ambivalence, if not the inherent contradiction of reformers throughout
Christian history: [they] sought to move the institution forward by—at
least in part—looking backward."[53]

One may thus admit that Counter-Reformation Catholicism was first
and foremost a religious movement while maintaining that its *spiritual*
character must be seen in relation to larger patterns of social, cultural,
and institutional history. Such a contextualization does no damage to the
real innovations that emerged in the church after Trent. For instance,
recent studies of art and literature in early modern Italy show that "the
often-assumed cultural handcuffs applied by a disciplining church were
seriously, but not completely, constricting."[54] Competing visions of Christian life could and did survive encroachments from papal power. The art
of Caravaggio, which we will consider as a visual example of "reforming
reform" in chapter 2, well illustrates this point. So do the contributions
of early modern lay confraternities, despite repeated efforts to rein them
in by popes like Gregory XIII (d. 1585), who "recognized the potential for
control in confraternities and saw them as a means of extending papal
control over lay devotional practices."[55]

Evennett was thus justified in arguing that Catholicism after Trent
witnessed both the birth of new devotions (e.g., the practice of the Forty

Hours devotion to the consecrated eucharistic elements in imitation of the forty hours Jesus lay in the tomb prior to his resurrection) and the renewal of older ones (such as the rosary). He was also right to note that Catholic devotions after Trent were strongly influenced, in structure and content, by that council's teaching on grace, justification, and the importance of "good works" (e.g., relief of the poor, care of orphans).[56] The doctrinal clarifications hammered out by the Tridentine bishops were spurred partly by the Roman Church's encounter with the reformers' theology—especially Luther's insistence that God's justification of sinners could never result from meritorious human works—and partly too from what Stephen Greenblatt calls "self-fashioning."[57] Yet the kind of self that began to emerge during the early modern era was not simply, as Evennett suggested, a "sixteenth-century man" who reflected the "bustle and energy and determination" of the age and felt "at last that he had a power over himself and over things."[58] First, one of the early "masters" of such self-fashioning was Queen Elizabeth I, a monarch who clearly understood the role of theater in the construction of self and in the creation of a "public character."[59] Second, the creation and deployment of the early modern self was not simply—or even principally—an assertion of personal autonomy ("power over self and things"). Self-fashioning, as Greenblatt observes, began not "from within" but in "submission to an absolute power or authority situated at least partially outside the self—God, a sacred book, an institution such as church, court, colonial or military administration."[60] It was achieved "in relation to something perceived as alien, strange, or hostile," a "threatening Other" who must be "discovered or invented."[61] In sum, "self-fashioning occurs at the point of encounter between an authority and an alien," and since what is produced by this encounter "partakes of both the authority and the alien that is marked" for resistance or opposition, "any achieved identity always contains within itself the signs of its own subversion or loss."[62]

Seen from this perspective, Tridentine or "Counter-Reformation" spirituality was a far more fragile and vulnerable project than may at first meet the eye. It is in light of this vulnerability, too, that one should evaluate Evennett's conclusion:

> The revival of the sacramental life, the spread and development of powerful new techniques of meditative prayer and eucharistic devotions, the driving urge towards outward activity and good works as a factor in personal sanctification, all deployed . . . within the framework of Tridentine doctrine: here . . . are the essential elements of Counter-Reformation

> spirituality, as formulated and taught by a succession of spiritual ge-
> niuses . . . throughout the sixteenth and seventeenth centuries, transform-
> ing and enormously quickening the spiritual life-blood of Catholicism,
> eventuating in a new creative efflorescence of institutions, and new reor-
> ganizations of the practical working and administration of the Church, in
> a word the beginnings of modern Catholicism.[63]

Spirituality is not, after all, an idea or an elixir, but an outcome produced
by practices performed by human agents, by personal "selves." It is entirely legitimate, for instance, to observe a "driving urge towards outward
activity" as characteristic of Catholicism after Trent, and there are plenty
of examples to support the observation.[64] Yet this same urge has to be
seen in relation to efforts by church authorities to make sure the poor
were off the streets and out of sight in cities increasingly threatened by
rampant homelessness, vagrancy, and violence. Innovations in charitable
activity were accompanied, in other words, by attempts to shield society
from the threat posed by an "other" perceived as alien, strange, or hostile. Similarly, innovations in eucharistic piety (such as the Forty Hours
devotion mentioned earlier) were certainly an aspect of early modern Catholicism, but they did not always result in more frequent reception of
Holy Communion by laypersons, probably because Jansenism, especially
in seventeenth-century France and the Low Countries, influenced both
lay and clerical attitudes toward the sacraments, as Evennett himself admits. (Early Jansenists, such as Antoine Arnauld [1612–94] blended moral
rigorism with pessimism about human nature to argue that close scrutiny of the individual's conscience should always precede the reception of
communion.)[65] The Christian approaching communion was expected to
define his or her self over against the "alien" authority of conscience.

Generalizations about "Counter-Reformation spirituality" can thus
be hazarded only with extreme caution.[66] Perhaps the best one can do
is point to certain traits or characteristics that appear with some frequency and consistency. Some of these traits seem genuinely new; others are renewals or reinterpretations of older practices. Among the "new"
are popularizations of systematic methods of meditative prayer based on
the *Spiritual Exercises* of Ignatius Loyola; an emphasis on private sacramental penance (made increasingly anonymous after the construction of
"confessionals," as mandated by the Council of Trent); and a remarkable
expansion of "nonliturgical devotions" centered on the reserved eucharistic species (i.e., portions of the consecrated bread kept, after Mass, in

a "tabernacle"—a locked compartment on the altar—and used to bring communion to the sick or dying). These latter included private "visits" to the Blessed Sacrament (i.e., visiting the parish church to pray before the consecrated eucharistic bread kept in the tabernacle, which for Catholics signifies the real presence of Christ), as well as periodic celebrations of the Forty Hours devotion.[67] Among traits rooted in older practices were prayers and meditations derived from the late medieval *devotio moderna*, focusing on the sacred humanity of Jesus, especially his passion and death. The rosary was among these "older devotions," but it was reinterpreted, after Trent, in relation to the imaginative mise-en-scène meditations popularized by the Ignatian *Spiritual Exercises*.[68]

The expanding role of the rosary in the lives of early modern Catholics is especially noteworthy, not because the devotion itself was a novelty but because it came to be seen as compatible with—and closely connected to—so many other dimensions of the "devout life," public and liturgical, as well as private and meditative. At the beginning of the twentieth century, for example, Jesuit historian Herbert Thurston's research shed light on the links between public recitation of the rosary and choral recitation of the Divine Office. From the beginning, almost certainly, the rosary was regarded as a form of prayer that blended both vocal (out-loud recitation) and mental (interior meditation) aspects. Thurston's research revealed that in the sixteenth century the public and vocal character of the rosary was further enhanced, in some places, through recitation in the choir of the church—as though the rosary were itself an "hour" (like morning or evening prayer) belonging to the daily liturgical offices. Basing himself on a rare work of Alonso Fernandez, entitled *Historia de los insignes Milagros* and published in Madrid in 1613, Thurston outlined "the manner in which the Rosary [was] said publicly in choir in the Dominican church of the Minerva at Rome."[69]

The parallels between this ritual form of the rosary and principal parts of the Divine Office such as vespers (evening prayer) are remarkable. (The Divine Office, the daily prayer of the church, is divided into eight distinct "hours" or "offices": matins [vigils, nocturns], lauds [morning prayer], prime [6:00 a.m.], terce [9:00 a.m.], sext [noon], none [3:00 p.m.], vespers, and compline [prayer before going to bed]. Today the Divine Office is officially known as the Liturgy of the Hours.) Like the latter, the rosary began with the standard introductory versicle, *Deus in adjutorium meum intende* (God, come to my assistance), followed by a hymn.[70] "After that," Thurston's description continued, a point of meditation on one of the mysteries was read aloud and an antiphon was intoned. [The antiphon was a short verse, usually taken from the Bible, sung before and after a psalm or as a refrain between verses of a psalm.] Then followed the *Pater* [Our Father] and ten *Aves* [Hail Marys], which were either said or sung, the one side of the church answering the other side exactly as the psalms are sung in choir. Then to maintain the analogy of the psalms there was added the *Gloria Patri* ["Glory be to the Father"], followed by the antiphon in full, with versicle and prayer. This process was repeated for each of the five mysteries, and the whole service concluded with another versicle and prayer, and with the anthem of our Lady varying according to the season.[71]

As Thurston pointed out, this description is significant for two reasons. First, it helps explain how the doxology (Gloria Patri) began to be added at the end of each decade of the rosary, with the Salve Regina (Hail, [Holy] Queen) as a final anthem for the whole prayer.[72] Second, Fernandez's words reaffirm the ritual roots of "Our Lady's Psalter," long a preferred term for the rosary, *in the public liturgy of the church.* In short, the rosary was not perceived, among all early modern Catholics, as merely a "private and personal" devotion having little or nothing to do with the church's public prayer. For that reason, Catholic spirituality after Trent cannot necessarily be characterized as a dominant preference for "individual rather than corporate or liturgical expressions."[73] On the contrary, some of the most notable representations of this new spirituality appear in Christian art explicitly intended either as part of a church's iconographic and architectural program or as altarpieces that accompanied the liturgical celebrations themselves.

A Revolution in Images

Sixteenth-century Europe, in sum, experienced a revolution not only in beliefs and ideas but also in ritual and images. Yet these revolutionary changes did not result in a complete break with the medieval past. It is well known that medieval Christians prayed in church spaces that were highly ornamented inside and out with brightly painted frescoes, elaborately colored walls and facades, polychrome statues, carved capitals, and stained glass that created curtains of colorful light to surround worshipers at prayer. Such spaces shaped both Catholic attitudes toward ritual performance of the liturgy and the structures of imagination that fed personal devotion. As already noted, Winston-Allen's *Stories of the Rose* points not only to the connection between vernacular *texts* and the origins of the rosary but also to the vital link between the rosary and *visual culture* (print, painting, woodcuts).

Early modern Catholicism, for all its innovations, did not forsake this long-standing relationship between worship, devotional piety, and the visual arts, as these influenced portrayals of the Virgin Mary. The Council of Trent, in fact, insisted on the continued value of the visual, even as it sought to reform church art through its decree on the "invocation and veneration of saints' relics and on sacred images" (1563).[74] The council seems to have understood that a revolution in images is more radical and far-reaching than debates about nuances proper to Christian doctrine. A devotion like the rosary was, I argue, extraordinarily sensitive to changes in Catholic iconography. Visual art landscapes the human imagination. It thus makes a profound difference whether, when praying the rosary, a Christian's meditations are colored by Giotto's frescoes in the Scrovegni Chapel or by images like those in Caravaggio's edgy painting *Death of the Virgin Mary*.

At the same time, early modern Catholicism found it necessary to alter its own self-image not only within Europe, under pressure from the Reformation, but also in relation to newly discovered peoples in the "New World" and to the Islamic presence represented by military and political strength of the Ottoman Empire. Jesuit historian John W. O'Malley notes that Renaissance Rome, prior to the Reformation, had already been preoccupied by the notion of reform and also by an optimism attached to the perception that the "Eternal City" had a God-given "mission to unify mankind."[75] This optimism eventually came to characterize significant aspects of Catholic thought and practice after Trent, particularly in the quarter century from 1585 to 1610. It was to become the driving force behind the innovative religious reforms proposed by Saint Philip Neri and the Oratorians.

Yet that optimism had suffered a serious setback in 1527, when Rome was sacked and the pope (Clement VII) imprisoned for several months by troops loyal to the Holy Roman Emperor, Charles V. Roman optimism and its self-congratulatory rhetoric had also been shaken by the reformers' successes in central and northern Europe, as well as by "a deep and persistent fear of Turkish advances" toward the Continent.[76] This latter fear had both ethnopolitical and religious roots (reflected in the church's long and largely unsuccessful campaign against Islam in both the Holy Land and the Iberian Peninsula). Church documents of the early sixteenth century thus betray a claustrophobic fear that the Ottoman Empire might soon overrun and annex a significant portion of Europe, with Christians confined to a tiny corner of the Continent.[77] This fear of failure and confinement lent support to the notion that part of Rome's program of reform should involve the defeat (or forced conversion) of the Turks. Given this atmosphere, one can understand why the victory of Christian coalition forces over the Ottoman navy at the Battle of Lepanto (October 7, 1571) quickly became emblematic of a "renewed and triumphant" Catholicism as the century drew to a close.[78]

This renewal was not, however, merely theological, sociopolitical, or military; it also produced a concomitant revival in art and architecture, that is, in the way Catholic belief and practice were imagined, built in brick and mortar, ritualized, and represented in church art. Rome, rebuilt, became a showcase, especially after the election of Pope Sixtus V in 1585. A list of "new or rebuilt churches and palaces in Counter-Reformation Rome" reveals that in the half century between 1549 and 1600, thirty-four new or renovated structures contributed to the prestige of the "Eternal City."[79] Of these projects, at least eight were initiated during Sixtus's short reign (1585–90). The defeat of the Ottoman forces at Lepanto had also helped consolidate the Catholic reformist view that Rome was indeed the *patria communis* (common homeland) of all humanity, and that the ultimate destiny of all peoples was to share the "peace and solidarity" brought about by Christ's incarnation and redemption.[80]

The Christian coalition's victory at Lepanto is also one of the principal reasons why the rosary became so prominent in an early modern Catholic reform program that sought to unite all human persons in "peace and solidarity" (guided and governed, of course, by the Roman Church). Prelates like Pope Saint Pius V (d. 1572) were quick to assert that Christian military success at Lepanto had resulted from direct intervention by the Blessed Virgin Mary, because during the battle, members of the rosary confraternity in Rome had gathered at the basilica of Santa Maria sopra Minerva "to pray for victory."[81] A fateful link was thereby forged between the political and military fortunes of Christian armies and Mary's powerful intercession. Not only was she Christ's gentle mother and "mistress of heaven" (popular medieval images); Mary was also a fiercely aggressive warrior queen who guaranteed an emboldened, militant Christianity victory over "alien others" (especially Islam). The liturgical feast of the Holy Rosary (still celebrated on October 7 each year) owes its origins to this military victory at Lepanto.[82] Yearly celebration of this feast helped not only to reshape the image of Mary along more militant lines but to reinforce the links between praying the rosary, enlisting the Virgin's protection in perilous situations, and securing her assistance in the pursuit of the post-Tridentine church's sociopolitical agendas.

Imagining Mary: The Genre of Rosenkranzbilder

Rosary confraternities, like the one in Rome whose members prayed for a Christian victory at Lepanto, were a prominent feature of the physiognomy of sixteenth-century Catholicism, especially—though not only—in Italy.[83] Especially after Trent, and in line with its preference for *parish-centered* activity, these confraternities sought to develop in their members a strong parochial allegiance through prayer, participation in public worship, and upkeep of the church's altar and sanctuary.[84] Chapels belonging to these confraternities, often located within larger churches, were well designed and decorated, and many of them "possessed major paintings on the theme of the Rosary."[85] Such paintings—emphasizing the personal benefits of praying the rosary and fostering frequent participation in the devotion—proliferated after Lepanto.[86] In fact, the confraternities became primary patrons of rosary art, commissioning painted altarpieces that were placed on or just above the altar table itself so the images could be readily seen by priest and people alike during the celebration of the Eucharist. A case in point, Caravaggio's well-known *Madonna del Rosario* (1607), will be discussed in greater detail in chapter 2. Here, however, it will be useful to consider an earlier example of *Rosenkranzbild* (a painting that focuses on the relation between Mary, her Child, and the rosary)— Giuseppe Cesari's *La Madonna del Rosario*, "commissioned in 1589 by the Rosary confraternity of Cesena."[87] Caravaggio himself seems to have been one of Cesari's pupils, for the early art historian Giovanni Pietro Bellori (1613–96) tells us that after arriving in Rome, probably in 1592, Caravaggio was forced to live for a time "without lodgings and without provisions."[88] Cesari put him to work painting

> flowers and fruit, which he imitated so well that from then on they began to attain that greater beauty that we love today. He painted a vase of flowers with the transparencies of the window of the room, rendering flowers sprinkled with the freshest dewdrops; and he painted other excellent pictures of similar imitations.[89]

In other words, Caravaggio had gained an early and enviable reputation in Rome as a master of the still-life genre. And while almost none of Caravaggio's still-life work has survived, it does continue to show up in details of his larger paintings (e.g., in the first of his two paintings of the supper at Emmaus). The importance of this *Rosenkranzbild* genre within Caravaggio's work will become clearer as we proceed.

Flowers figure prominently as well in Cesari's own *Madonna of the Rosary*, but there they do not belong to the still-life genre.[90] Cesari shows Mary in glory, seated on a heavenly cloud and holding her Child, who hands a circlet of roses to Saint Dominic (d. 1221). In the lower half of the painting, several men, women, and children lift their hands toward the heavenly scene; meanwhile, a woman stoops to collect roses from several that lie scattered on the ground. Dominic, the medieval mendicant who founded the "Order of Preachers" (Dominicans), is prominent in the painting because most Catholics in sixteenth-century Europe accepted without question the legend that the rosary originated when the Virgin Mary presented the beads to him in a vision.[91] Yet the object itself—that is, the *rosary*—does not seem to be represented in Cesari's painting. This is probably because, in late sixteenth-century art, the iconography of the rosary had not yet achieved a standard form—so instead of receiving a rosary, Cesari's Dominic gets roses instead.[92] In short, Cesari shows a suppliant populace clamoring for *roses*, just as in Caravaggio's later *Madonna del Rosario* they will clutch after *rosaries*.[93] Still another rosary Madonna from this period, painted by Guido Reni just before 1600, might strike viewers today as more "traditional," since it shows Mary *alone* with Saint Dominic, giving him a rosary (not roses).[94]

These post-Tridentine *Rosenkranzbilder* show us Marian images in transition. Prior to the Reformation, it was perhaps not so important to root the devotion in an act (Mary giving the rosary to Saint Dominic) that demonstrated the divinely sanctioned origins of the prayer. Few Christians prior to the early sixteenth century seem to have challenged the legitimacy of the devotion, since it was deeply rooted in the late medieval piety of *devotio moderna*. Similarly, visual representations of a divine etiology for the rosary helped to make the case—increasingly important after the Battle of Lepanto—that God's plan was to unite all humankind in a fellowship of faith and prayer that either excluded Muslims or included them by way of (forced) conversions made with Mary's help.

This does not mean that painters like Cesari and Reni ignored the work of pre-Tridentine artists. An important antecedent of their rosary paintings was a famous work of Albrecht Dürer, *Feast of the Rose Garlands*, painted in 1506.[95] It too appears to have been an altarpiece created for a rosary confraternity, one connected with the German community in Venice. Some commentators suggest that Dürer's *Feast of the Rose Garlands* demonstrates how aspects of Italian Renaissance art (Venetian painting in particular) made their way into northern Europe.[96] That may be too ambitious a claim, but there can be little doubt that Dürer himself was pleased by his accomplishment, since he boasts of it in a letter written from Venice on September 8, 1506 to his old friend Willibald Pirckheimer: "My picture [*Feast of the Rose Garlands*] . . . is well painted and beautifully colored. I have earned much praise but little profit by it."[97] Notably, Dürer's painting not only celebrated Mary and the rosary; it celebrated the artist himself. In the upper right corner the viewer can see the artist's ostentatious self-portrait: Dürer stands proudly, clad in a sumptuous fur-trimmed cloak, sporting long blond curls, and gazing out at the spectator. In his hand, a parchment sheet (also visible to the viewer) proclaims: "EXEGIT QUINQUE MESTRI SPATIO ALBERTUS DURER GERMANUS MDVI" (Within a space of five months, the German Albert Dürer produced [this work], 1506).

Yet perhaps the most striking thing about Dürer's *Feast of the Rose Garlands* is its contribution to the specific genre of religious painting under discussion here, the *Rosenkranzbild*.[98] *Rosenkranzbilder* made use of an iconographic scheme closely connected to what Anne Winston-Allen describes as the "new model" for praying the rosary, a method that combined meditation on Christ's life with repetitions of the Hail Mary prayer. An older model had understood the rosary in relation to the ancient Christian monastic custom of repeating the biblical psalms (daily or at least weekly) in response to Saint Paul's injunction to "pray without ceasing" (1 Thessalonians 5.17).[99] This more ancient model may have persisted among some Christians, even after the "newer" rosary (blending meditation on Christ's life with repetition of the Hail Mary) came into vogue. The rosary confraternities, for which the paintings by Dürer, Cesari, and Caravaggio were created, permitted—and even promoted—considerable variation and flexibility in the way "the rosary devotion was to be recited."[100] Indeed, as Winston-Allen notes, the success of these brotherhoods "was at least partly due to this flexibility and to the absence of punitive regulations. Members were allowed to say the devotion when and as they wished."[101] This kind of freedom and flexibility made the rosary quite appealing to early modern Catholics.

Rosenkranzbilder often reflected this freer approach espoused by the rosary confraternities. The scenes are broadly inclusive and intergenerational, with figures representing divine and human, rich and poor, clergy and laity, women and men, old and young, arts and crafts, politics and religion. Indeed, critic Erwin Panofsky argues that the *Rosenkranzbild* evolved precisely in order "to illustrate the idea of a universal brotherhood of Christianity."[102] These pictures show a rich diversity of persons "offering—or receiving—garlands of white and red roses, the whole composition often surrounded by a larger garland of roses where ten [or more] medallions [engraved ornaments], shaped like cinquefoils, depict the five Joyful and five Sorrowful Mysteries."[103] Actually, though Panofsky does not mention it in his discussion of *Rosenkranzbilder*, the convention of medallions showing scenes from Christ's life in relation to prayer beads (possibly paternosters [beads for counting repetitions of the Our Father], not Marian rosaries) appears fairly early in the fifteenth century. Jan van Eyck's renowned "Arnolfini portrait," to which we will return later, offers an example. The portrait, dating from 1434, includes a series of life of Christ medallions encircling a convex mirror that hangs on a back wall behind the standing couple. Hanging to one side of the mirror is a set of prayer beads.[104]

In the background of the iconographic conventions connected to the *Rosenkranzbilder*, therefore, are not only the images found in the popular rosary books of the late fifteenth century but also links between prayer beads, *vita Christi* images, and ordinary events in human life (a betrothal or a marriage, as in the case of the Arnolfini portrait).[105] Something new, however, begins to emerge in Dürer's *Feast of the Rose Garlands*, for in addition to "surpassing the earlier '*Rosenkranzbilder*' in naturalism and individualization," Dürer also endeavored to strengthen the impression of movement. "The rose garlands . . . are actually placed upon the heads" of the worshipers by Christ, Mary, and Saint Dominic, "and this action is represented with as much liveliness and variety as possible."[106] Figures in motion are, of course, *living* figures; they suggest a direct interaction between the persons represented in the painting and the viewer who gazes at it. Lively painting of this kind implies that the human subjects the artist has portrayed and those who gaze upon them have become contemporaries. They are directly involved in one another's lives. For Christians looking at images of the Virgin Mary, such natural human movement made it clear that Christ's Mother is not some remote historical figure consigned to the irrelevant past but a living presence involved *now* in the faith, life, and prayer of those who seek her protection and intercession through the rosary. These same qualities—naturalism, individualization, movement—are reprised, as will be seen shortly, in Caravaggio's *Madonna del Rosario*.

As the word *Rosenkranz* itself implies, a wreath, garland, or crown (in Latin, *corona*) of roses became the standard iconographic convention in rosary paintings, not only in the sixteenth century but later as well, in the early baroque and later baroque periods. In fact, the word corona was sometimes used to signify the rosary itself as a material object for counting. The Dominican house of Saint Andreas in Cologne, for instance, contains a *Rosenkranzbild* painted by an anonymous artist in 1621 that combines both rose garlands and medallions representing the fifteen mysteries of the rosary (a series that was, by then, well established).[107] This painting also portrays the conventional connection between the heavenly zone, where Mary and the Child Jesus appear in glory, and the earthly zone, with its typical assortment of clergy, religious (women and men), imperial potentates, military personnel, peasants, and simple folk. Similar iconographic conventions continued into the eighteenth century as well, as Tiepolo's *Institution of the Rosary* (1737–39) reveals.[108] This painting, a fresco, is the largest rosary painting found in European art, and it combines two distinct iconographic traditions. The picture's upper section, focusing on the figure of Mary, shows her giving the rosary to humankind; the lower section, focusing on Saint Dominic, depicts the multiple benefits the rosary has brought the world. In the earthly zone, moreover, all kinds of people are represented: "the Doge, a Turk, a nun, . . . a mother and child, a symbol of Christian charity—so that the viewer, whether rich or poor, could identify with them."[109]

In this book, however, the *Rosenkranzbild* that will receive greatest attention is Caravaggio's *Madonna del Rosario*, because it embodies a momentous shift—a visible rewriting—of iconographic traditions related to the rosary. *Madonna del Rosario* was painted near the conclusion of the period (1585–1610) that I have described earlier as a "reform of the (Tridentine) reform." In this work, Caravaggio capitalized on certain conventions common to the *Rosenkranzbild* genre: Dürer's naturalism (already adumbrated in van Eyck's Arnolfini portrait); the intimate connection (even blurring) between "heavenly" and "earthly" zones; and the pervasive theme of human solidarity. Caravaggio represented, I argue, a new understanding of the complex relation between artistic image and Christian life. In his hands, images were no longer potent visual *reminders of* the real;

they were indispensable *portals to* the real, even when their subject matter was not explicitly religious. Art, Caravaggio seemed to believe, is access; it *gives* presence and does not merely describe it. Like the new sensitivity to human movement seen in Dürer's *Feast of the Rose Garlands*, Caravaggio's painting displays subjects (the Virgin Mary, Saint Dominic) and viewers within a shared living space—the *present*. Mary is not present to those who pray the rosary merely as historical memory, but as immediate reality.

Hence, Caravaggio's art often evokes the density of ancient icons that simultaneously draw us *to* the image and invite us to go *beyond* it. Icons, Jean-Luc Marion maintains, are not objects we see and seize but an *other*'s gaze that meets our own and subverts it.[110] What is at stake in the icon, therefore, "is not the perception of the visible, nor aesthetics, but the intersection of two stares."[111] The viewer is not a voyeur whose target is the icon. On the contrary, the icon, far from succumbing to our attention, empties itself, renounces itself. Icons are "not there to be seen," but to be "[c]rossed over by . . . my gaze, responding to a gaze which preceded it."[112] One may say, then, that the icon is "the product of the image's kenosis [self-emptying, self-surrender]"—the opposite of the "modern logic of imaging," which relies on "auto-sufficiency, autonomy, auto-affirmation."[113] Iconic images renounce themselves so they may be "crossed" (as a frontier is crossed); they beckon toward a "land of unlikeness." Far from being mirrors that reflect back our own image, icons produce a tear in the fabric of space and time that lets the light of another's gaze reveal itself. Icons thus reorient "light from illumination of the present to the suggestion of the infinite," and "by using light and shadow no longer to define but to dissolve visible forms . . . as in Caravaggio and Rembrandt," they disclose something decisively new and perhaps threatening.[114]

Trent and the Reform of Iconography

Art historian Helen Langdon thus seems entirely justified in speaking of the "harsh vernacular" of Caravaggio's art.[115] A search for the source of such vernacularism in paintings intended for use in church—*Madonna del Rosario* was, after all, commissioned as an altarpiece meant to hang in full view of the congregation as the priest celebrated Mass—leads one back to the Council of Trent and the quarter century of "reforming the reform" that followed it between 1585 and 1610. In its final session (XXV), on December 3, 1563, the Council of Trent had promulgated a decree on the "invocation and veneration" of saints' relics and on "sacred images."[116] While this document summarized "for the first time the whole of medieval Catholic doctrine on images," it was short on specifics, and so "it remained for self-appointed commentators" to elaborate further the principles Trent had presented in brief outline.[117]

One of the first churchmen to take up the challenge of Trent's decree on church art was Cardinal Gabriele Paleotti (1522–97), who became archbishop of Bologna. In his *Discorso intorno alle immagini sacre e profane*, first published in 1582, he urged Christian painters to render justice to the visible universe, God's creation, by creating figures and images that are real, tangible, human, and "naturalistic."[118] The roots of his "Christian naturalism" were already present in the late medieval *devotio moderna*, and perhaps even earlier, as historian André Wilmart's studies demonstrated more than seventy-five years ago.[119] For centuries, a vigorous cross-fertilization had enriched Christian prayer, public and private, and as a result medieval texts often blended, almost seamlessly, both liturgical and devotional images. A case in point is a troped (interpolated) Credo from the late eleventh or early twelfth century.[120] Though a modest text, this Credo is, in Wilmart's words, "a faithful image of Christian belief and piety in the first eleven centuries, to such a degree that a believer of the fourth or fifth centuries could have recited it without encountering anything strange or unaccustomed."[121] A sample section from this Creed reveals images that are vivid, tangible, human, and naturalistic:

> I believe, Lord, that you were betrayed by Judas, . . . questioned . . . convicted . . . led before [Pilate], . . . beaten . . . handed over to soldiers, smeared with spittle, hammered with blows, crowned with thorns, stripped of your clothing, lifted onto a cross, offered vinegar to drink, pierced with a lance.[122]

Such concrete images are derived, of course, from the Christian scriptures, but in this interpolated Credo they form part of a personal prayer rather than narrative or reportage. The text's "minute enumeration of circumstances in the life of the Savior that would come to be called 'the mysteries,'" wrote Wilmart, already contains, in embryonic form, images that later medieval piety would emphasize in its devotion to Jesus' humanity, especially his suffering—images that were also linked "to the meditative practice of the Rosary."[123]

Trent had itself reaffirmed this ancient Christian ideal of *imitatio Christi* by recommending frequent meditation on his sufferings and death, since Christ himself had become the supreme exemplar of patience, humility, exalted charity, meekness, obedience, and unshaken firmness of soul not only in suffering for justice' sake but also in meeting death. That such meditative practices not only survived but flourished in the period under discussion in this chapter is evident from contemporary accounts. *Roma Sancta*, a description of religious life and organized charity in that city written in 1581–82 by the English priest and Bible translator Gregory Martin, devoted an entire book to church buildings, preaching, public worship, and devotional life.[124] In a pertinent passage of Book One, Martin drew attention to the work of the "pope's preacher," a Spanish Jesuit by the name of Father Toledo (Toleto).[125] The style of Italian preaching struck Martin with special force. He wrote:

> And to heare the maner of the Italian preacher, with what a spirit he toucheth the hart, and moveth to compunction (for to that end they employ their talk and not in disputinge matters of controversie which, God be thanked, there needeth not) that is a singular joy and a marveilous edifying to a good Christian man. Wherein they doe so excel, that upon good fryday, when they doe al preache upon the whole passion for three or foure houres, they doe so lively and lamentably represent the nailing of Christ to the crosse, and other circumstances, that the hardest hart melteth into dropping teares, and craveth mercie for his sinnes by the merits of that bitter passion.[126]

Such preaching happened not only in the Roman churches

> but in every such place of the citie where the people assemble upon Sundayes and holy dayes, either idely or unfruitfully occupied, namely countrye men of al ages, that stand there in troupes to be hired into vineyards, and otherwise. Among them and such like there are that preache upon such dayes continually, in every such Piatsa or market place, wherof Rome is ful. And these [preachers] be commonly Jesuites, which desire leave of their superiors so to be occupied, and then going every one with his fellow, and deviding them selves into these forsaid assembles, make the verie stal or bulke of some window their pulpet, and without al other ceremonies, only a Crucifixe in their hand or ready aboute them, they beginne some good matter of edification, agreeable to their audience,

with ful streame of the plainest scriptures . . . most sweetly exhorting to good life, . . . often setting before them the paines of hel, and the joyes of Heaven.[127]

Gregory Martin's first-person narrative notes that Roman preachers of the late sixteenth century directed their messages toward persons coming from very diverse socioeconomic circumstances, including groups of migrant workers—"poor labourers and country men" hanging out "in troupes" and hoping for hire, especially during grape harvest.[128] The venues for this preaching also varied, from street and square ("Piatsa") to market stall and windowsill. And the preachers' clientele included not only the devout Catholic elite but beggars, "bankers, and secrete usurers," as well as "harlottes, curtisanes, and Ribbaldes."[129] The effect of such preaching moved some hearers to extreme acts of repentance, including voluntary flagellation; hence preachers came to their task well equipped with props. "Once . . . I fel upon such a sermon as now I speake of," wrote Martin,

and staying to the end, I saw him after earnest exhortation to penance and chastening of their bodie, so to conform them selves to Christ Crucified, which there he shewed them, I saw him (I say) withal bring forth a little bagge ful of whipcord, there comen for discipline and voluntarie penance, and they held forth their hands as thicke and as greedily to take every man a Whipcord to use afterward in his chamber, as if he offer them old angles or pretious stones.

If *Roma Sancta* testifies to the early modern continuation of *devotio moderna*'s focus on Jesus' sufferings as central to the Christian's *imitatio Christi*, it also witnesses to a notable expansion of rosary confraternities and rosary meditation in the late sixteenth century, not only in Italy but also within the community of Catholic exiles in France.[130] These confraternities expanded, in part, because they served an important social function in a world perceived as increasingly dangerous (as Gregory Martin's account of London life suggests). Confraternity members believed that cities would become safer if they (the members) sought not only to *pray* for the needy but also to alleviate poverty and lawlessness through positive action (e.g., feeding the hungry, providing shelter for vagrants). Still, the primary focus of the rosary confraternities continued to be prayer and mutual support. "The Companie of the *Rosarie*, is spred from Rome through the world, specially where the Jesuites are," Gregory Martin tells us.[131] Membership in the Roman confraternity exploded during the Holy Year (Jubilee) of 1575, when "above 30,000 persons . . . entered into the Company of the holy Rosarie."[132]

It is significant that members of the confraternity concentrated primarily on prayer "for each other and for all the world" in "the very Communion of Saincts," rather than on their private needs and individual concerns. Because the world itself seemed to be expanding (sixteenth-century exploration had acquainted Europeans with "new" peoples in Asia, Africa, and the Americas), many early modern Catholics sensed a need to move beyond the largely individualist, inward-looking piety of the *devotio moderna*. Catholicism's "social miracle"—which in its medieval expression focused on one's immediate blood relatives—was being reinvented in the period after Trent. The creation of community *outside* the limits of family ties and kinship systems became newly important. Thus, each month, each member of the rosary confraternity received a "paper for that moneth," which included "some fest or holy day of the moneth, a moral sentence out of the [biblical books of] Proverbes or Ecclesiasticus [Sirach]; a general title [or intention, e.g., prayer for prisoners], and special names [of individuals] for whom . . . [to] specially pray."[133] The list of intentions Martin mentions closely resemble the solemn intercessions of the Roman Catholic liturgy for Good Friday, as found, for example, in the reformed *Missale Romanum*, published in 1570 by Pope Pius V, to whom liturgical reform had been entrusted by the Council of Trent.[134]

Links to Christian liturgy also shaped Gregory Martin's discussion of the "Rosarie . . . our Ladies Psalter."[135] After explaining to his readers how the "Beades of five tennes said thrise" make a cycle of prayers "correspondent in number to Davids Psalter," Martin remarks that repetition of the angel's salutation to Mary (the *Ave Maria, gratia plena*, based on Luke 1.28, 42) not only salutes "the greatest benefite that ever was and highest mysterie wrought for mankind" but also links those who pray "with the Angel, and S. Elisabeth, and with S. James, S. Basil, S. Chrisostom in their Greeke Lituriges," which "praise and magnified the Mother of God, calling her blessed."[136] In this passage, Martin was almost certainly alluding to the ancient and privileged place of the theotokion in Greek liturgical traditions. (The theotokion was a liturgical hymn in praise of Mary, the Mother of God [*Theotokos*, in Greek]. These hymns were used in public worship in the Christian East with increasing frequency after the ecumenical Council of Ephesus [431], convened by Emperor Theodosius II in the hope of settling the Nestorian controversy. Nestorians were generally willing to address Mary as Christotokos [Mother of Christ], but not as Theotokos.)[137] Martin also connected recitation of the rosary—"our Ladies Psalter"—with the custom some "lay Persons" had of praying each day the hymns and biblical psalms of "our Ladies Mattins . . . an abridgement of the longer Breviarie."[138]

Martin's *Roma Sancta* not only connects the rosary to larger patterns of Catholic public prayer (e.g., general intercessions, the canonical hours, especially the Office of the Blessed Virgin Mary), but also provides a list of "fifteen Meditations, . . . five Joiful points, five Dolorous or sorrowful, and five Glorious," that are "to be meditated by one and one, either in saying the Rosarie, or before, or after, as every man feeleth it most commodious."[139] Martin's list is, of course, the familiar set of "mysteries"—he calls them "Meditations"—attached to recitation of the rosary.[140] These points of spiritual meditation, Martin alerted his readers, are "much used" not only in Rome but in "al the better Cities of Italie," and are the subject of helpful rosary books written by authors such as "Lewis of Granata."[141]

Martin's travelogue shows that the rosary survived the upheavals that followed the Reformation and was becoming a staple of Early Modern Catholic piety, in part because of the vigorous activity of the confraternities in Rome and throughout Europe. And although Martin himself was not a Jesuit, he was a fervent admirer of Ignatius Loyola and a champion of the new meditative style the latter had proposed in his *Spiritual Exercises*. That style involved the vivid exercise of one's imagination to "paint the scene" of an episode in Christ or Mary's life and so fix it firmly in one's mind. In this, Loyola's method of meditation strongly resembled what has been noted about Dürer's innovative *Feast of the Rose Garlands*, which brings living movement into the painting of sacred subjects in order to show the contemporaneity between what is represented and the viewers' lives.

The Return of Christian Optimism

Gregory Martin's description of devotional life in Rome was written about ten years before the painter Caravaggio began his career in that same city in 1592. Martin had related the rosary—especially as recited by the rapidly growing clientele that belonged to the Roman confraternity—to intercessory prayer within the communion of saints, to liturgy, to meditation on a set of fifteen points "concerning our B. Ladie," and to daily contemplation of Christ's passion and death.[142] Martin also spoke admiringly of the preaching style practiced in late sixteenth-century Rome—by Jesuits, of course, since he was strongly attracted to their Society, but also by figures such as Philip Neri and his companions at the Church of San Girolamo.[143] The group of (originally lay) preachers that formed itself around Philip Neri eventually came to be known, as we have seen, as Oratorians, but they were called by their contemporaries Reformati, "Refourmed, or rather in deede Reformers of the rest by example and doctrine."[144] Martin's description of this strangely assorted group is both charming and informative. Every day after dinner, he tells us, four Reformati preached for two hours to whomever might gather to listen. This they did "not in pulpet, but upon a benche somewhat higher then [*sic*] the audience, sitting as it were among them," and making

> familiar discourses . . . of diverse godly matters in great varietie of utterance and wittes, but one divine spirit moving al their tonges to winne infinite souls to life everlasting. Neither are they curious in this case or solemne, but every one as he seeth cause, taketh this text of Scripture or that, this Ecclesiastical storie or that, the life & example of this Sainte or that: every one a diverse thing, and many of them every day play their part with singular grace, amiable speeches, Zelous spirit, often inculcating Confession, Receaving, Visiting prisons, visiting Hospitals, and serving also the sicke and sore, which in Rome is no rare thing.[145]

These lively and informal preaching sessions thus included not only instruction and exhortation but also outreach to the needy. Often they concluded with "the finest and gravest musicke to the honour of God . . . in the praise of God."[146]

In sum, the *ragionamenti spirituali* (meditative discussions) of the Roman Reformati attached to the Church of San Girolamo were lively, innovative, inclusive, imaginative, informative, and musical. "The outstanding originality of the place," writes twentieth-century Oratorian and theologian Louis Bouyer, "sprang from the almost complete independence enjoyed by the priest there so that each of them worked in an entirely personal sphere, beginning any new enterprise that appealed to him and gathering about him his individual disciples; San Girolamo was in fact a regular colony of small assemblies each with its own meeting place in one of the Fathers' rooms."[147] During these impromptu discussions, Philip Neri avoided "doing all the talking," instead encouraging the group that gathered around him each day to "work things out for themselves."[148] These sessions were conducted in truly peripatetic fashion, since participants typically went outside for the "customary Roman saunter in the cool of the evening" and continued their discussions as they walked along the streets. Bouyer observes that the pattern and pastoral methods employed by these Reformati strongly resembled the techniques used later within Protestant evangelical revivalism.[149] The Roman confraternity known as *SS. Trinità dei Pellegrini*—a forerunner of the later Oratory—sponsored youth hostels that were nothing like "present-day hostels provided for well-to-do pilgrims to Lourdes or Lisieux"; they were similar to "a Salvation Army hostel, and the pilgrims themselves . . . resembled tramps rather than the devout tourists whom we call pilgrims today."[150] In style and appeal, Neri's peripatetic *ragionamenti* were more like the later Quaker prayer meeting or Methodist worship on the American frontier than like traditional Catholic *colloquia spiritualia*.[151] The almost conversational style of prayer and reflection represented by Neri's innovative technique reminds one of the freedom and flexibility that the rosary confraternities encouraged among their members. In contrast to the ritual rigidity and rubricism of the post-Tridentine church's official liturgy, flexible devotions like the rosary—or meditative discussions like Neri's *ragionamenti*—gave early modern Catholics greater freedom to "customize" their prayer life.

We will return to Philip Neri and the Reformati, but here I call attention to the probable connection between these sixteenth-century street preachers and the approach to religious faith and practice we will see represented in the art of Caravaggio. Philip Neri himself was unquestionably a charismatic preacher, but his behavior also bordered on the bizarre.[152] When communicating himself at the Eucharist, he could not refrain "from biting the chalice, so that he left the mark of his teeth on the gilding," and he trembled so violently while attempting to distribute communion to others that he often had to stop and "pause for a little while."[153] He was sometimes so overcome by emotion when reciting the rosary that he could not get past the first Our Father.[154] His personal appearance also raised eyebrows. Sometimes Neri wore his clothes turned inside out or "arrayed himself in a cassock with large white shoes."[155] He seemed to relish his "fool for Christ" image, once parading about Rome in a "magnificent fur of marten skin" given him by Cardinal Gesualdo and, while maintaining an "air of recollection . . . casting an admiring glance at his fine dress" from time to time.[156] As Helen Langdon notes, Neri loved to shock and embarrass "a courtly world with insistent reminders of the religion of the streets; he strove to revive a pure sense of the poor in spirit, and a spirituality that should reunite the literate and sophisticated with the lowly and simple."[157]

The Oratorian preference for *sermo humilis* (lowly speech)—a form of discourse that largely rejected Renaissance humanist retrievals of classical oratory and style—not only shaped Philip Neri's personal method of preaching but also contributed to a burgeoning "Christian optimism, a second wave of Counter-Reformational thought."[158] This optimistic second wave within early modern Catholicism, especially in the quarter century between 1582 and 1610, surfaced not only in nonconformist figures like Philip Neri but also, as will be seen, in far more compliant career ecclesiastics such as Cardinal Federico Borromeo, archbishop of Milan and guiding genius behind the extraordinary art collection at Milan's Pinacoteca Ambrosiana.[159] It surfaced, too, in the art of Caravaggio, most particularly in those canvases where the Virgin Mary is a central subject. It also helped to popularize even further the already cherished devotion of the rosary, which focused on joyful intimacy between the Christian, Mary, and Christ through meditations and prayers using the *sermo humilis* of scripture and everyday life. A trajectory that began, arguably, with the innovative "figures in motion" technique of Dürer in *Feast of the Rose Garlands* continued in Neri's *ragionamenti* and Caravaggio's canvases. In each of these we see contemporary Christians brought into intimate conversation with Mary and her holy Child through the medium of vividly imagined meditation and repeated prayers (the Hail Marys of the rosary).

Moreover, Neri's "plain speech" style of preaching and catechesis did not represent a rupture with humanist tradition but revealed his preference for simpler, more accessible speech—the "harsh vernacular" of the streets—over the techniques of classical rhetoric.[160] Though most proponents of *sermo humilis* were accomplished Latinists, they were also determined reformers who strongly believed that the salient purpose of the Council of Trent had been to *reform the church*, and not merely to resist Protestantism. They were well-educated, ecclesiastical loyalists who were nevertheless imbued with a humanistic liberalism that both valued "pagan letters and . . . the Gospels" and stoutly repudiated autocratic papalism.[161]

Another example of how churchmen in the final two decades of the sixteenth century began reframing the Tridentine reform by reinterpreting Christian humanism in light of Philip Neri's *sermo humilis* may be seen in the life of the previously mentioned Gabriele Paleotti, a liberal-minded man who "never passed a day without reading some Greek," and who, in an age of increasing papal absolutism, maintained "the right of the Cardinals to take part in the councils of the Pope."[162] Earlier in his career Paleotti had earned the reputation of being a rigorous reactionary, a zealot *sans pareil*. Yet his work as a reform-minded bishop intent on implementing Trent's mandate for a renewal of pastoral life tempered that reputation.[163] Paleotti proved himself to be not only a capable administrator in Bologna but also a skilled and flexible interpreter of Trent's teaching on sacred images. His *Discorso* was both a commentary on Trent's decree and a veritable "catechism of images."[164] Paleotti's *Discorso* is also important because it shows us a post-Tridentine Catholic bishop taking "the first step toward internal reform of his diocese" precisely through *a reform of its art*.[165] Images, Paleotti believed, are the first and most powerfully formative preaching Christians encounter when they assemble in church. Hence art is an embodiment of *muta predicazione*—"silent preaching"— using *unwritten* signs to condense God's work as Creator within the stuff of this sensible world.[166]

Paleotti had a hunch that the Christian's understanding of faith comes as much from images—found in art or the natural world—as from formal preaching and catechesis. It was a hunch shared by artists like Caravaggio, who depicted Mary not in inaccessible glory but in poses anyone might have encountered on a Roman street. His *Madonna di Loreto* (also known as *Madonna dei Pellegrini*), for example, shows Mary standing on tiptoe in a Roman doorway, one knee crossed over the other. Her posture makes her seem almost weightless, yet at the same time she is so real and substantial that her body casts a heavy shadow on the doorpost. This artistic combination—heavenly weightlessness and earthbound tangibility— helped shape a new image of Mary in the minds of early modern Catholics. These images constituted a new, nondiscursive kind of preaching, just as Neri's *sermo humilis* and Paleotti's *muta predicazione* did. Faithful devotion to Mary did not have to involve fluttering angels and crowns of roses. One could pray the rosary and meditate on its mysteries while imagining an appealing, sexy young woman, baby in arms, standing in the doorway of the house across the street.

Paleotti's *Discorso* thus differed in tone, content, and emphasis from earlier commentaries on Trent's decree on church art such as Charles Borromeo's 1577 *Instructionum fabricae et supellectilis ecclesiasticae libri duo* (*Two Books of Instruction concerning Church Building and Furnishing*; 1577).[167] Precision in the rules for the building and design of churches, as well as conformity with liturgical legislation enacted by popes after the Council of Trent and embodied in reformed books such as the *Missale*

Romanum of 1570, were paramount for Borromeo. His *Instruction* did of course include a chapter titled "On Sacred Images and Pictures," but his premier preoccupation seemed to be strict compliance with church dogma: "First of all, let no holy image be produced for the church or any other place that may contain false dogma, or may foster dangerous error among the uneducated, or may contradict Sacred Scripture or the tradition of the Church. [Let there be only art] that agrees with the truth of the Scriptures, traditions, ecclesiastical histories, and the custom and usage of mother Church."[168] Superstition, falsity, and inaccuracy have no place in church art, Borromeo insisted, nor does anything "profane, trashy or obscene, indecent, provocative, or merely titillating."[169] Even nature itself is suspect; "representations of beasts of burden, dogs, fish, or other irrational animals ought not be allowed in church or any other sacred place."[170]

In contrast to Charles Borromeo's concern for rational control and conformity, Paleotti's *Discorso* took another direction. It emphasized the transformation of Christian life and vision—or, more precisely, of life *through* vision—that is the ultimate aim of church art. Dogma alone, however precise or well supervised, would not produce real change, and the church could not be reformed unless its images were.[171] In words reminiscent of Thomas Aquinas, Paleotti argued that because human persons are created, they have a *tendenza naturale verso il Creatore* (a natural tendency toward their Creator), and hence the radical source of all iconography resides within *nonverbal* "rules of language" rooted deeply in the human spirit itself.[172] It is this that gives images their power and truth, their ability to draw viewers beyond themselves toward the disclosure of transcendent mystery. In his *Discorso*, therefore, Paleotti hinted at an optimistic Christian humanism grounded in what was most common to all persons, high or low, rich or poor, famous or obscure—namely, their human condition and its ineradicable orientation toward God.

Paleotti knew Philip Neri well and admired his innovative use of *sermo humilis* and *ragionamenti*. He belonged to that "Oratorian orbit" that helped reframe the Counter-Reform in the light of "Christian optimism." The final quarter of the sixteenth century, when churchmen like Paleotti and Neri were active, thus proved to be a critical moment in the evolution of early modern Catholicism. It was a time when the church's obsession with *reacting to* the reformers began giving way to innovations in both religious life (Neri's Oratorians) and church art (Paleotti's *Discorso*). It was also a decisive period for the reinterpretation of the Virgin Mary and for devotion to her through popular prayers such as the rosary—reframed, now, within the vivid imaginative techniques of Ignatian meditation. "The quarter century from 1582 . . . to 1608," writes Ian Verstegen, "was indeed an active period in Roman church history. These were the years of what is called the Church Triumphant, the post-Tridentine church full of confidence. There is good reason to regard the papacy of Sixtus V (1585–1590) as a turning point of the Catholic Counter-Reformation and therefore a new attitude to religious imagery."[173] Even though one might quibble with the phrase "Church Triumphant," Verstegen makes a valuable point. It is entirely plausible to view this quarter century as a time when Roman Catholicism confidently seized the offensive and stopped defining itself principally in relation to the (Protestant) Reformation.

Assertions like these must of course be made with care. For one thing, there was no universal consensus that church art should be reformed in line with the proposals of Paleotti's *Discorso*, which took a deliberately optimistic view of human nature and emphasized what was common to *all* persons, high or low, rich or poor, famous or obscure (their vulnerable human condition and its ineradicable orientation toward God).[174] Nor did the spirit of innovation embodied in Neri's pastoral work—especially his efforts to make Christian faith intelligible and attractive to "street people"—necessarily imply a wholehearted acceptance of avant-garde art. In fact, Neri's interests were quite broad and included not only contemporary art but early Christian imagery as well, especially Byzantine iconography. Art historian Constanza Barbieri suggests that the Oratorian emphasis on Christian optimism and joy was based not on then-fashionable movements in art but on the much deeper "revalorization of the visible and of sacred icons" that had followed Trent's decree on church art.[175] This renewed Catholic emphasis on the utility and legitimacy of images was fed by some of the same springs that were renewing devotion to the rosary among early modern Catholics. Barbieri identifies four such sources (all of them outlined in principle in Trent's decree): (1) a renewed interest in images that belong to the church's communal memory (*memoria*); (2) a renewed appreciation of art as a Bible for the poor (*Biblia pauperum*); (3) a renewed emphasis on sacred art's legitimate arousal of religious affectivity, emotion, and imagination (*excitatio*); and (4) a renewed confidence that Christian art, well made, could arouse delight and joy (*gaudium*) by showing believers *invisibilia per visibilia* (the unseen through the seen).[176]

These four elements helped restore the *human* to post-Tridentine Catholic iconography, especially its images of the Virgin Mary. It became increasingly possible to imagine *Mary in her own right*, as a young woman and mother, standing in the doorway of her house, without the sacralizing presence of adoring angels or crowns of roses. Such a natural, believable humanness is what we see in Caravaggio's *Madonna di Loreto*. Thus painted images that reframe sacred stories can report back to memory *all* the implications connected to a particular theme, *including the essentially human ones* (*memoria*). At the same time, images (like Caravaggio's *Madonna*) could palpably embody a story (about Mary and her divine Child) that viewers might grasp without reading, simply by letting their *eyes* take in the story (*Biblia pauperum*). In effect, these images make all our senses "readers," since figurative arts function anagogically, expanding both the human sensorium and the human capacity for fantasy so as to arouse thought, reflection, and, finally, contemplation (*excitatio*). Such an expansion of pleasure results in joy (*gaudium*).[177]

Ideas of this kind were not utterly new in the latter part of the sixteenth century, but they did gain renewed currency in a time when the complex relation between art and Christian belief was being renegotiated within early modern Catholicism.[178] The urge to make art report visible reality, to create figures that were truly human—real and tangible—is evident not only in the work of ecclesiastics such as Paleotti and Philip Neri but also in painters like Caravaggio.[179] Helen Langdon's use of the term "vernacularism" to describe this particular moment in the renegotiated relation between art and faith seems especially apt.[180] It was not simply that by the end of the sixteenth century Neri's *sermo humilis* had found its way into church art. Plenty of painters in this period had created "religious pictures with humble figures, but they tend to be dull and timorous works, where the poor, devotionally idealized, are the clean and grateful recipients of charity."[181] Yet Caravaggio made this vernacularism harshly visible by thrusting the poor—unsanitized and perhaps ungrateful—directly into the viewer's face without explanation or apology. "Caravaggio, like Filippo Neri, is creating a shock of humility, pushing the world of the poor before an elite audience, and using a language that seems rough and vernacular, and available to everyone."[182]

More will be said in the next chapter about the impact Caravaggio's rewritten icons had on the ways early modern Catholics viewed Mary and the rosary. Here our focus is on the idea that the connections between the rosary and visualization—already being made at the earliest stage of the devotion's development—intensified with the arrival of early modern Catholicism, as embodied, for example, in Paleotti's conviction that our very humanness is itself the source of our connection with God.[183]

Thus a *human* Mary giving her rosary not merely to inaccessible saints and angels, not simply to the wealthy and powerful, but to humble people with dirty feet and ragged clothes became a potent demonstration of how God chooses to connect to the human world. (We will see this very point made in Caravaggio's famous and controversial altarpiece, the *Madonna del Rosario*.) Increasingly the rosary was perceived not just as scripturally based prayer but as a portable *Biblia pauperum*, a series of striking scenes that speak in strong vernacular to educated and unlettered Christians alike. These scenes were not just incorporated into the early printed "rosary books" discussed by Winston-Allen; they were also linked to newer, visually imaginative methods of meditation, especially in the wake of Ignatius Loyola's *Spiritual Exercises*, completed circa 1541.[184] The relationship between rosary and church art was thus strengthened not only by external events in late sixteenth-century history (e.g., the Christian armies' victory at Lepanto) but by new proposals about how to meditate on mysteries long linked to the rosary (the Ignatian *Exercises*). These proposals, in turn, were connected to principles, reaffirmed at Trent, that supported the use of images in Catholic prayer and worship: *memoria, Biblia pauperum, excitatio, gaudium*.

Religious innovators like Philip Neri and painters like Caravaggio did not invent these principles but sought new ways of integrating them into Christian life. Both men found methods for rethinking biblical stories "in intensely human terms."[185] Helen Langdon notes that Caravaggio's vernacularism created an "intensely personal" version of biblical narratives by using scenes and figures drawn "from the contemporary secular world."[186] Thus, despite its general rejection of vernacular *languages* for use in celebrating the church's liturgy, the Council of Trent had implicitly endorsed a *visual vernacularism* in its 1563 decree on sacred images.[187] If everyday speech, with its "shock of humility," could not be used in the church's public ritual, it could certainly insert itself into the spaces and visual images that surrounded those celebrations (altarpieces, paintings, glass, sculpture). Whether one accepts or rejects Walter Friedlaender's well-known thesis about the presence of Oratorian piety in the work of late sixteenth-century Italian artists such as Caravaggio, the latter's paintings speak for themselves.[188] "Again and again in his paintings," wrote Friedlaender, "Caravaggio shows a deep sympathy for people who are materially poor—for example the poor peasants kneeling before the *Madonna di Loreto* or the simple people at the feet of the *Madonna del Rosario*."[189] Only the most obtuse viewer could fail to grasp the point that by depicting the downtrodden in this way, Caravaggio was *reinterpreting the image of Mary herself*, making her "Mother of the Poor," "Friend of the friendless," "Shelter of the homeless." Within post-Tridentine Catholicism, Mary and her rosary were becoming not merely aggressive, militant allies of Christian armies (the Battle of Lepanto) but champions of the have-nots, marginalized by a society (and sometimes a church) that preferred to keep the poor invisible.

Such innovative art witnesses eloquently to a visual vernacularism in which the objects, persons, works, and actions of an everyday world "are steeped in echoes of biblical reality."[190] It is hardly an exaggeration to claim that

> Caravaggio's was a new and profoundly Catholic art which rejects the ideal beauty of Raphael and Michelangelo, and whose brooding and tragic darkness conveys the terror of broken humanity at man's alienation from God. His earth-bound figures are travelers or pilgrims, mired in the prison of this world, and unconsoled by any vision of Paradise.[191]

In the words of the Salve Regina, the medieval Marian antiphon still used at the conclusion of the rosary, especially when prayed in common, this is a vernacularism in which we meet "poor, banished children of Eve, mourning and weeping in this vale of tears.[192]

Conclusion:
The Rosary's Role in the Diffusion of Early Modern Catholicism

The rosary—reframed as a devotion particularly dear to the Virgin Mary as "Mother of the Poor"—played a vital role in reshaping piety within an early modern Catholicism that was eager to present *itself* (rather than Protestant communities) as the cutting edge of a revitalized Christianity genuinely global in its mission and catholic in its membership. Some historians today prefer to link devotions like the rosary to the beliefs and practices of traditionalist "rural piety," as opposed to the more reformist interests of urban elites.[193] Yet such oppositions must be handled with caution. Historian Keith P. Luria points out that the use of binary opposites—"popular versus elite, unofficial versus official, collective versus individualized, rural versus urban"—to characterize religious belief and practice in early modern Europe is "far too simplistic to describe the dynamic of religious change."[194] An apt illustration of Luria's point comes from the proliferation of religious confraternities throughout Western Europe during the sixteenth and seventeenth centuries. These played an essential role in the continuing success of what Bossy calls the Catholic "social miracle."[195] The confraternities fostered "social emotions," a climate that contributed to the creation of relationships within "the social universe as a whole."[196] This was a particularly important development after the Council of Trent shifted the vital center of Catholic piety from family to parish. The rosary confraternities, as we have seen, not only survived the Reformation but flourished well beyond it. These were not exclusively urban organizations; they were found in villages and rural areas as well.[197] In fact, one of the remarkable aspects of the rosary confraternities was their inclusivity. They were voluntary associations that appealed beyond boundaries based on territorial, socioeconomic, gender, or generational factors.

One cannot claim, then, that the rosary represented "rural traditionalism" as opposed to urban "progress, innovation, and cultural sophistication."[198] Nor can one argue that because it was often said privately, the rosary encouraged an isolating individualism in contrast to the communal piety that characterized the church's liturgy.[199] The rosary was seen instead as a powerful incentive to associational life among the Catholic faithful, and the projects of its confraternities (e.g., feeding the poor, commissioning artworks for the parish church) were likewise understood as communal enterprises.[200] Luria thus seems justified in concluding that when viewed from the perspective of the associational life (the "social miracle") fostered among the rosary's devotees, the

> Catholic Reformation program was not . . . simply imposed on the faithful as a means of instilling within them an interiorized and spiritualized form of piety. New religious ideas entered communities as much, if not more than, from lay as from clerical initiative. The people who joined Rosary confraternities did . . . associate themselves with what Catholic reformers hoped to achieve. . . . Individual prayer coexisted with collective engagement. But the devotion also provided a means for families to further social rivalries. The practice of rural piety did not exclude one or the other of these objectives; it allowed for both.[201]

Luria's point about the complex role rosary confraternities played within early modern Catholicism is amply confirmed by the research of Louis Chatellier. In *The Europe of the Devout*, Chatellier studied what he calls "Marian congregations," associations of laymen and clerics "established by Jesuits in their colleges from the end of the sixteenth century" to act as a "leaven" that might "reform the world," shaping it into a "Catholic society."[202] These congregations formed an impressive network across most of Western Europe.[203] Their members, called *sodales* (companions, fellows, comrades), were diverse; they included "young men alongside the adults . . . merchants, burgesses and sometimes nobles and clerics alongside the artisans."[204] *Libellus sodalitatis* (*Little Book of the Fellowship*), published in 1576, encouraged members of these Marian sodalities to perform daily religious exercises that included both liturgical (Mass) and devotional elements (e.g., rosary and recitation of the Litany of the Blessed Virgin Mary).[205]

The importance of these sodalities should not be underestimated. R. Po-Chia Hsia summaries the point well:

> With the revival of Marian devotion after Trent, a cult that took on militant and triumphant traits, Rosaries [*sic*] confraternities became signs of the spread of Counter-Reformation vigor. Marian sodalities represented the third and most important type of Counter-Reformation confraternity . . . [and] came to embrace large sections of the urban population in Catholic Europe.[206]

Unquestionably, too, devotion to Mary in early modern Catholicism sometimes took on traits of militancy and triumphalism, as witness the Catholic reaction to the victory at Lepanto and the attribution of its success to the devout prayers of the rosary confraternity in Rome. Hsia highlights this aspect of Marian piety by pointing out that the sodalities often "looked upon themselves as the spiritual elite in the fight for orthodoxy."[207] Yet Chatellier is surely right to say that "fighting for orthodoxy" was not always the central focus of such groups. Their chief goal is better described as a broad "transformation of society."[208] Catholics who participated in Marian congregations or rosary confraternities may well have had elitist proclivities, but their brand of "elitism" aimed at producing social inclusivity rather than exclusivity. Their aim was nothing short of a new social order. Chatellier writes:

> The model presented to Christian families from the middle of the seventeenth century diverged considerably from that of the patriarchal family. It was even its exact opposite. The direction of the household belonged to

the father and mother jointly. . . . Similarly, if the rigid barriers separating the different social groups (Gentlemen, burgesses, artisans and journey-men) began to weaken . . . it was perhaps not only because of the development of the economy, but also because of the wishes of the Catholic associations which had sprung from the [Marian] congregations. The family came before the individual, the Christian community of the parish was preferred to the old socio-professional hierarchy. And already a new society seemed in the process of formation. An elite much larger than before, and much more mixed in its social origins and functions, emerged.[209]

We should be on guard, then, against two oversimplifications. The first assumes that "Counter-Reformation" Catholicism was single-mindedly intent on reconsolidating ecclesiastical power and controlling the parameters of orthodoxy. These motives were surely present, but they were tempered by other concerns—for example, the "religion of the poor" and the promotion of a "devout life" among "ordinary people" (based on Neri's *sermo humilis*, "a Christian sublimity that rejects pagan subtleties and the blandishments of the fine style.")[210] The second oversimplification assumes that from the late sixteenth century onward, Catholicism was preoccupied almost exclusively with the encroachments of Islam, of Protestant heterodoxy and/or of secularizing "de-Christianization" within Europe. The phenomenal expansion of religious confraternities throughout Western Europe between 1600 and 1800 suggests that Catholicism during this period was more than a lockstep, rearguard reaction against its enemies (within or without). Early modern Catholicism cannot be claimed as the direct forebear of the rigid, ultramontanist ideology later associated, in the early nineteenth century, with the pontificate of Pope Gregory XVI. In fact, as Chatellier points out, the "renewal of the [religious] congregations at the turn of the eighteenth and nineteenth centuries calls into question a received idea, that of the de-Christianisation at work in the Europe of the Enlightenment."[211]

The "reform of reform" that occurred within the quarter century between 1585 and 1610 involved, therefore, not only a reassessment of early modern Catholicism's relation to Islam, Protestant Christianity, and the newly discovered worlds of Asia and the Americas but the fashioning of a (re)new(ed) Catholic identity shaped by the factors we have been discussing in this chapter: the Christian optimism represented by Philip Neri and the Oratorian orbit; a sometimes shocking visual vernacularism that saw Christ's presence throughout the created world, but especially in the poor; the social miracle wrought by "rituals of participation" that included "greeting, meeting and eating"; and the socioreligious networking embodied in rosary confraternities and other similar "congregations."[212] What was truly unique about this period, however, was the way changing images of the Virgin Mary contributed to a reshaping of the church's own self-identity. Catholics had long believed that Mary was not only "mother of Christ" but "mother of the church," since the church is itself Christ's body (Ephesians 1.22–23). A shift in the way Mary was perceived was inevitably registered in a shift of self-understanding on the part of the church. We have seen that these shifts produced a somewhat curious constellation of images: "aggressive militancy" (Mary as warrior who fights for the church in its struggle against the Ottoman Empire in the Battle of Lepanto) combined with tender regard for the poor and marginalized; an obsession for control from the top down (concentrated in the hands of male clerics), coupled with the proliferation of associations (Marian sodalities and rosary confraternities) characterized by flexibility, freedom, open membership, and equal participation by women and men.

2

Reframing Representation

The piazza in front of the Church of Saint Dominic in Bologna has been a public gathering place since medieval times. Paved with pebbles, it served as the spot where the townspeople could stroll, shop, listen to outdoor sermons, gather to gossip, or bury their dead. Inside the church lies the body of Dominic Guzman, founder of the Order of Preachers ("Dominicans"), who died there on August 6, 1221. Also inside is a spectacular Cappella del Rosario, featuring a historic organ on which young Mozart played in 1769, and festooned with art by some of the leading painters and sculptors of the middle to late sixteenth century. The Cappella del Rosario is a maze of color and form, with works in multiple media—painted murals, marble, stucco, and carved, gilded wood. Among the chapel's most prominent features are fifteen paintings of the mysteries of the rosary, arranged as a framing altarpiece and completed in 1601. Among the notable painters represented is Ludovico Carracci (1555–1619, who depicted the first two "joyful mysteries," the Annunciation and the Visitation), and the female artist Lavinia Fontana (1552–1614, who contributed the paintings of the "finding of Jesus in the temple" [the final "joyful mystery"] and the "coronation of the Virgin Mary" [the final glorious mystery]).[1]

The Madonna at the center of these fifteen painted panels is wearing two rosaries around her neck and with her free hand seems to be dangling a rope of rosary beads to a waiting world below.[2] The Christ Child whom she holds in her other arm also seems to dangle a long rosary "and does so, like the Child in many a painting of the previous century [the fifteenth], very much with the air of any small child solemnly absorbed in experiment."[3] Nevertheless, the early baroque exuberance of the altarpiece—with its swirling fabrics, forms, color, and light—makes viewers keenly aware that they are seeing not a late medieval *Rosenkranzbild*, nor even an early Renaissance one such as Dürer's *Feast of the Rose Garlands*, which we discussed in the preceding chapter, but a work created half a century after the Council of Trent. The chapel's altarpiece contrasts sharply with Saint Dominic's thirteenth-century alabaster tomb, directly opposite, which narrates the saint's life and miracles, *none of which "record anything to do with the rosary."*[4] The latter point is especially telling, since the legend that Saint Dominic was personally given the rosary by the Virgin Mary and was subsequently responsible for spreading the devotion across Europe became commonplace in the later Middle Ages and endured well into the twentieth century.

The Cappella del Rosario in Bologna thus embodies, in its sculpture, art, and architecture, a kind of thumbnail history of how the rosary evolved in the imagination of Christians from the fourteenth to the early seventeenth century. Dominic's tomb is *blank*—that is, it makes no visual reference to the rosary at all (and hence supports those who later argued that the legend about Dominic's role in spreading the devotion cannot be historically verified). Yet the baroque altarpiece focuses on almost nothing but the rosary and its mysteries. It embodies the spirit of a confident, "triumphant Catholicism" sure of its role and mission in the world, and certain that a militant Virgin Mary is herself fighting on the church's behalf (as she had done at Lepanto in 1571)—holding out to humanity an object (rosary beads) that will save the devout and punish the infidel.

Naturalism and the Reframing of Marian Iconography after Trent

We have seen that we cannot understand how the rosary and Marian devotion were reinterpreted within early modern Catholicism if we restrict ourselves to textual evidence alone—even official texts such as the Council of Trent's 1563 decree on the reform of devotions (saints and their relics) and sacred images. If Edward Muir is right to say that the (Protestant) Reformation represented a revolution in "ritual process and ritual theory," it must also be said that the subsequent Catholic renewal was a revolution in iconography.[5] As the opening vignette of this chapter suggests, we can actually document (in structures like the Bolognese) the transition from early thirteenth-century art (Dominic's tomb, which offers no visual connection between Mary and the rosary), to post-Reformation attitudes that reflect her new status as militant advocate of a Catholicism no longer obsessed with defining itself by the past (the late Middle Ages, the Reformation) but plunging confidently, even optimistically, into early modernity.

A key player in that transition was the painter Caravaggio, about whom more will be said shortly. He was not, of course, the first or only artist whose work signaled the coming of a new age in the representation of religious subjects and stories. Ludovico Carracci, Lavinia Fontana, and the other early baroque artists who contributed to the Cappella del Rosario in Bologna were also reshaping the image of Mary, presenting her not with the stiff, superhuman formalism that characterized much medieval painting and sculpture but in more natural poses based on a close observation of nature. Carracci and Fontana already alert us to a change happening to the visual representation of religious subjects during the era of Counter-Reform or Catholic renewal.[6] That period was characterized by a "seething creativity" that sought not only to retrieve and revitalize Christian humanism but also to reexamine traditional narratives and beliefs by *reimagining* them.[7] Indeed, such developments in art and architecture are a major focus of scholars who dispute the canonical concept that Catholic Counter-Reform was relentlessly "repressive, iron-fisted, [and] autocratic."[8] To challenge this concept is not to deny that the church was deeply interested and involved in controlling the political and social climate of many, if not all, early modern societies.[9] Taking a page from Michel Foucault's studies "on the disciplinary function of modern states and their subordination of subject populations," a number of historians today use the term *disciplinamento* (disciplining) "to describe post-Tridentine efforts to establish regularity and order in ecclesiastical institutions and devotional behavior."[10] Those devotions included the rosary, which, despite the freedom and flexibility Christians had in praying it, could also be controlled by church authorities through the parish-centered rosary confraternities.

Yet *disciplinamento* did not stifle creativity; it often stimulated it. Such was the case in Bologna, for example, during the episcopal tenure of Gabriele Paleotti, a member of the Oratorian orbit whose *Discorso* on church art we discussed in chapter 1. In 1576, a few years before his treatise appeared and Bologna was raised to the rank of an archdiocese, Paleotti wrote his people a pastoral letter in which he thanked God not only for making the city wealthy and peaceful but for lending it luster through its advances in the arts and sciences.[11] Yet the very moment the bishop was praising scientific progress and applauding the persistent and lively flowering of the arts in Bologna, the church's rigorist, post-Tridentine offensive was beginning to make itself felt throughout Italy. Bologna was by that time part of the papal states, and one might well suspect that Paleotti's glowing encomium was smoke and mirrors, a deliberate attempt to disguise the real situation.[12]

The records of the Bologna archdiocese do, however, support the "strongly innovative nature" of Paleotti's initiatives, as well as the spiritual and social reforms he advocated, even if the first flush of reformist fervor after Trent had begun to fade and Paleotti's optimism and originality ran into opposition from "clergy, lay confraternities, and city authorities."[13] Two points in Paleotti's reformist program of pastoral action deserve special mention. The first of these, embodied in a Christmas letter to the clergy and people of Bologna in 1575, was Paleotti's promotion of "new initiatives in the field of public assistance" that involved closer collaboration between church and city. In this, the bishop's proposals built on earlier experiments with "comprehensive municipal poor relief" initially sponsored during the first half of the sixteenth century by Bolognese lay confraternities.[14] These initiatives indicate that "spiritual and material assistance to the sick, imprisoned, vagabonds, and orphans . . . to the weakest and most neglected members of society" was a central theme of Paleotti's episcopate.[15]

Second, he fostered education by making catechism classes in Christian schools available to children of the poor and by supporting the contributions of Bologna's ancient university to the city's cultural life. Paleotii avoided the repressive control tactics favored by the Inquisition (as remodeled by Pope Paul III in 1542), yet he considered it vital to bridge the gap between Christian piety and science, and thus he actively sought involvement by intellectuals in the church's religious life and activities.[16] Nevertheless, his deep appreciation of nature—an attitude he shared with Federico Borromeo, another member of the Oratorian orbit discussed in chapter 1—prevented him from trying to subordinate scientific research to the claims of faith and revelation. He saw the two as allies, not competitors.[17]

Paleotti's respect for natural science significantly expanded the influence of that late sixteenth-century "Christian optimism" we discussed in chapter 1. Both science and faith seemed, at that moment, to encourage a reframing of the relations between God, human beings, and the world. The representation of those relations in Catholic iconography—including images of Mary and the rosary—was affected as well. (It is significant that two of the innovative artists who contributed to Bologna's Cappella del Rosario—Ludovico Carracci and Lavinia Fontana—were working in the city during Paleotti's tenure as archbishop.) Moreover, among Paleotti's personal friends were two teachers at the University of Bologna, the historian Carlo Sigonio and the naturalist Ulisse Aldrovandi. In 1556,

Aldrovandi took over the university chair that, a few years later, was given the title *"Lector philosophiae naturalis ordinarius de fossilibus, plantis, et animalibus"* (Ordinary Professor of the Natural Study [*philosophiae*] of Fossils, Plants, and Animals).[18] Aldrovandi is known to have influenced the composition of Paleotti's *Discorso*.[19] It is painting's God-given vocation, Paleotti argued, to explore the world of nature, even if not all natural subjects belong in church art.[20] In asserting the privileged role of the natural world in artistic representation, Paleotti's *Discorso* clearly reflected Ulisse Aldrovandi's scientific attitude and approach to the natural world, for the latter believed that painting must provide "a faithful image of reality," since "art is an image and vestige of nature," while nature itself remains "the true exemplar."[21]

This is not to say that Paleotti had simply imported humanistic theories about science and history without alteration into the *Discorso*. Still, as Paolo Prodi points out, the early drafts of Paleotti's magnum opus bore the stamp of these two intellectuals, Sigonio and Aldrovandi, who, though they cannot be considered "coauthors," were certainly more than casual consultants in the composition of the *Discorso*.[22] Paleotti's youthful contact with these scholars while he was a student at the University of Bologna had matured once he returned to the city as its bishop. Based on shared interests in critical historiography and the natural sciences, the relationship between pastor and professors evolved into "a collaboration that we would today call a 'brain trust' at the service of reform in the Church of Bologna."[23] Aldrovandi had been instrumental in setting up the first botanical garden in Bologna, and his presence was palpable in Paleotti's thought about the four fundamental motives—necessity, utility, pleasure, virtue—that first led to the use of profane images and then set the stage for the creation of sacred images.[24] The pleasure aroused by images is derived from several sources, Paleotti argued, but central among them is *"their capacity to imitate the real,"* for nature itself has an innate power to produce images of things—apart from any human intervention—and then present them to our eyes in all the vitality of their colors and movements.[25]

A right reading of the relation between nature and image was thus critical, in Paleotti's view, not only for the production of "profane" or natural images—of the sort, for instance, that Aldrovandi was to incorporate in his "iconographic census of nature"—but also for the creation of sacred images, especially those of Christ, Mary, and the saints.[26] For a vexing question in the post-Tridentine debate about what is appropriate in sacred art was whether or to what degree "naturalism" has a legitimate place—or whether, instead, what is "natural" needs first to be tutored by divine revelation and Christian doctrine before it can be admitted into the church. Paleotti's contribution to this question cannot be overestimated, even if one denies a direct link between his own views about naturalism and the "Carracci reform" of painting that was shortly to follow in Bologna.[27]

This reform would have momentous consequences for the history of Counter-Reformation devotional art, and especially for the work of Caravaggio. Indeed, as Charles Dempsey shows, Ludovico Carracci and his cousins became "deeply involved in a national debate" that fundamentally reframed perceptions about the relation between nature and art. If the Council of Trent had adopted the view that the artist's primary duty was to make art "subservient to the truth, and that the inventions, ornaments, and difficulties of art should not be exalted for their own sake," then it became necessary to reconsider what means could or should be used to create "a convincing illusion of external reality."[28] The religious image, especially, "had to be verisimilar in order to convince the spectator of the higher truth it conveyed. Rather than making an open display of skill, as the art of Michelangelo and his followers was perceived to do, the Carracci reform responded to Tasso's call for "*l'arte che tutto fa, nulla si scopre*" (that art which hides all art)."[29]

Yet creating an "art that hides all art" was not as simple as it sounds. It not only demanded a reevaluation of what belongs to nature, along the lines pursued by Gabriele Paleotti and Ulisse Aldrovandi but also required "a renewed and deepened analysis of the effects of nature" and of the means and techniques by which art tries to render nature faithfully through "verisimilitude."[30] Art, after all, is always an illusion. So the artist's basic task is to coax viewers into believing that what they see is not simply paint, canvas, form, color, and brushstroke but an opening to the real. Naturalism seeks to represent the world with a minimum of distortion or abstraction, and so employs a visual rhetoric of persuasion that claims what viewers see in art is true to life. Though they are important artists in their own right, the Carracci are relevant to this chapter because of their contributions to naturalism in painting and because of their influence on Caravaggio, the "arch-naturalist."[31] It was Caravaggio, as Dempsey observes, "who made the problem of naturalism an issue by insisting on the particular truth of experiential reality," an issue that resurfaced in Counter-Reformation literature about prayer, contemplation, and meditative techniques such as those used in recitation of the rosary.[32]

The Carracci had used naturalism as a means to an end, a window opening onto the abstract truth that lies beyond experience, that is, as a way of showing in art how the world's visible realities evoke and illumine the invisible power of God.

Caravaggio, however, took naturalism to a new and controversial level. Early biographers like Gian Pietro Bellori (1613–96) complained he was an extremist who insisted on painting directly from life and hence "merely copied bodies as they appeared to the eye."[33] Yet Bellori's complaint missed the point. It can hardly mean that Caravaggio ignored or rejected everything his contemporaries were doing. His famous paintings of Saint Matthew, which may still be seen in the Contarelli Chapel of the Church of San Luigi dei Francesi in Rome, were clearly influenced by the Carracci, and "it is not coincidental that these works are the first to evince [Caravaggio's] strongly chiaroscuroed manner, spotlighting areas of bright color, for which he is preeminently famous."[34] Yet Caravaggio went much further as a representative of the early baroque style in painting. Even as he "appropriated the illusionistic conventions of the Carracci in his work," he also reframed "the reform they had effected."[35] The Carracci had based their iconographic revolution on two pillars: one scientific ("investigation of the effects of spontaneous nature"), the other art historical ("investigation of artistic and rhetorical techniques and traditions").[36] In contrast, Caravaggio "made experiential nature alone his subject" and hence "called into fundamental question the relationship of art to the truth."[37] In short, Caravaggio's paintings confronted viewers with two disturbing questions: First, does the innately illusory character of art—its obvious pretense—have anything real to do with our daily *experience*? Second, does art actually connect us to earthly and spiritual realities, or is it simply the "promise of an eternal truth beyond experience"?[38]

These questions came to a head, as we will see, in the attempts made by Caravaggio and others to reinterpret both the figure of the Virgin Mary and the rosary devotion. After all, if Mary is simply "Queen of Heaven"—as she was often depicted in medieval iconography and sculpture—how could Christians claim she was interested and directly *involved* in their earthly lives? In other words, was Mary's role as "Help of Christians" (a title used for her in the Litany of Loreto) linked to the world's real time and space—or was it simply part of the illusion embodied in art itself?[39] Similarly, does meditating on the mysteries of the rosary actually make one a "contemporary participant" in the events (e.g., Christ's crucifixion or Mary's Assumption into heaven)—or is the whole scheme of contemplative meditation little more than an exercise in autosuggestion? Is the relation between viewer and sacred icons a real one or merely an occasion for religious voyeurism? Does an artist's image of Mary and her rosary actually have the power to arouse real religious affections, or are those feelings false and bogus?

Catholic artists of the late sixteenth and early seventeenth centuries were seeking solutions for many of these problems. Charles Dempsey argues that by the year 1605, "the stylistic boundaries over which the expressive potentialities of the new baroque illusionism were to be contexts for the rest of the [seventeenth] century had been drawn: the naturalistic idealism of the Carracci, the experiential realism of Caravaggio, the rarefied idealism of [Guido] Reni [1575–1642]." Dempsey's view seems plausible, especially if one sees baroque art as a multifaceted reaction against the prevailing mannerist style that had preceded it. Arnold Hauser famously characterized mannerism as "intellectualism, spiritual aloofness, and emotional remoteness," as opposed to the "emotionalism and sentimentalism," the "pain and suffering, wounds and tears," that belong to the baroque.[40] Like most generalizations, this one falters, but Hauser is probably right to contend that in its view of church art and music the Council of Trent was "not just anti-mannerist but [was] tending towards the baroque."[41] Trent resisted mannerism in church art on two counts: formalism and sensualism. Mannerism's "virtuoso formalism" meant painters ceased to be concerned about the "content of their paintings" and grew obsessed by stylish displays of their own technical virtuosity; similarly, its sensualism led not to erotic pandering but to a persistent preference for "pleasures of sense" over "religious feelings."[42] Mannerism, in a nutshell, represented visual distraction rather than contemplative edification.

Implicitly, then, Trent's goal in its decree on sacred images had been to redefine the relation between art and affectivity, viewers and images. Gabriele Paleotti's *Discorso* was very much in line with this redefinition, as one may gather from his discussion of Christian images and their impact on the human affections in book 1, chapter 25. There, he cited the Greek notion of ζωογραφία ("live writing" or "living scripture") and claimed that a sacred image has precisely the same impact on a devout viewer.[43] There is, Paleotti asserted, ample patristic precedent for such a claim, for Augustine told us openly in his *Confessions* that a work of *pre-Christian* literature (Cicero's *Hortensius*) had changed his life: "This book changed my affections, turned my prayers and vows to you, Lord, and upended all my desires, making them different; suddenly, all my [earlier] vain hopes became meaningless."[44] Such a life-changing revolution, Paleotti went on to say, is exactly the goal of sacred images:

> To hear about a saint's martyrdom, or the devotion and constancy of a holy virgin, or especially the passion of Christ—these certainly touch us in the most immediate and lively way. But when we see before our very eyes this holy martyrdom, this suffering virgin, or Christ himself nailed to the tree, our devotion can hardly help being increased; it grips us ever more profoundly, and someone who doesn't feel these things intensely would have to be utterly bereft of human feelings.[45]

Paleotti thus aligned himself with earlier commentators on Trent's decree on church art such as Andrea Gilio, who, in his *Due dialoghi degli errori de' pittori* (*Two Dialogues about the Errors of Painters*, 1564) explicitly alluded to the "coldness of the earlier [mannerist] artistic style."[46] In calling for a more expressive artistic language, Paleotti and Gilio were certainly combating the idea that Catholic art has nothing to say to human sensibility, to the most basic feelings, emotions, affections, and experiences. Bishops like Paleotti, naturalists like Aldrovandi, and reform-minded painters like the Carracci were proposing an art rooted not in virtuosic showmanship on the painter's part but in nature, in everyday life. They understood the need for a change in the relation between viewer and image and thus supported "a simple and clear spirituality accessible to everyone."[47]

This, of course, was precisely what devotions like the rosary also aimed to do. Familiar, repeated prayers—learned by heart at mother's knee—combined with scenes of sorrow, pathos, joy, and triumph (the "mysteries") to bring Christians into intimate contact with "a God with skin on" who makes the *human* cause his own. Although neither Trent's decree on sacred art nor Paleotti's *Discorso* mentions it, early modern Catholicism was seeking to retrieve, through the *rosary*, a perhaps forgotten aspect of ancient Christian *iconography*. Ancient icons of Christ and the Virgin Mary were perceived not so much as "objects" to be gazed upon but as *living presences that looked directly at you*, the "viewer." Icons were not about our seeing but about our *being seen*, knocked breathless by the powerful glance of an Other. The icon invited viewers to "cross the visible" and enter a sacred space where Christ, Mary, and the saints gaze upon *you* with compassion, mercy, love, and forgiveness. Similarly, in the rosary devotion, repeated prayers (which functioned like mantras) served to still the mind and body so that what God does for us in Christ stands revealed to us in the joyful, sorrowful, and glorious mysteries of redemption. Post-Tridentine Catholicism was rediscovering that the rosary is not so much about how we, the praying devotees, understand or interpret the mysteries but how those mysteries interpret us, gripping us at the very roots of our being and asserting God's unique claim over our hearts and lives. The vivid use of human imagination in meditating the mysteries—embodied in art through the techniques of naturalism—was not an end in itself but aimed at opening a space for God's self-communication. Like icons, the rosary became a site of revelation where the holy is met in the homely (wood, paint, color, form) and the divine is disclosed in the daily (e.g., a mother's happiness at the birth of a child [the mystery of Jesus' Nativity, the third joyful mystery] or parents' relief at finding a lost child healthy and safe [finding Christ in the Temple, the fifth joyful mystery]).

Rewriting Icons: Caravaggio's Marian Images

Caravaggio's career took place, then, at a time when early modern Catholics were busy reinterpreting their devotions and artists were struggling to redefine the relation between image and viewer, "seeing" and "being seen." At the same time, spiritual writers like Francis de Sales (1567–1622) were encouraging Christians to embrace "the devout life." Such a life—especially as it appealed to early modern *laypersons*, and not merely to clergy or religious professionals—embraced both a renewed emphasis on participation in sacraments (especially Eucharist and penance) and innovative proposals for prayer and meditation (such as those found in the *Spiritual Exercises* of Ignatius Loyola). Devotion to the rosary was an essential part of this picture, as Saint Francis de Sales bore witness in a brief memo on "how to say Our Lady's chaplet [i.e., rosary] devoutly."[48]

It can unquestionably be argued that despite Trent's decree, early modern Catholicism could not shake itself free of mistrust in matters of church art. While late sixteenth-century ecclesiastics rejected mannerism in principle, they continued to permit its use, since in many cases "it was the only art available," and it had become an important, if imperfect, ally in the church's effort to present itself as friend of the arts, "in contrast to the Reformation, which was hostile to them."[49] The two depictions of rosary mysteries (finding Christ in the Temple, the coronation of Mary as Queen of Heaven) contributed by Lavinia Fontana to the Cappella del Rosario in Bologna were painted in the mannerist style, with its characteristically affected poses and artificial (as opposed to natural) qualities. Yet even Fontana's work avoided extreme mannerist gestures and made some concessions to naturalism. The dominant attitude of many important sixteenth-century spiritual writers, however, was that naturalism is dangerous in both literary and visual art. Such a view is evident in the thought of Saint John of the Cross (ca. 1542–91), a mannerist poet and mystic who insisted that "the devout needed no pictures."[50] Here, for example, is a characteristic passage from his work *The Ascent of Mount Carmel*, which deals with the "spiritual senses" (spiritual experience interpreted through analogies with human sensation):

> As was the case with the imaginative corporal apprehensions, we must disencumber the intellect of these spiritual apprehensions by guiding and directing it past them into the spiritual night of faith, to the divine and substantial union with God, lest the solitude and denudation concerning all things, which is a requisite for this union, be impeded by the hindrance and weakness these apprehensions occasion. These apprehensions are nobler, safer, and more advantageous than the imaginative corporal visions because they are already interior, purely spiritual, and less exposed to the devil's meddlesomeness.[51]

Yet such a text must be read in relation to John's entire work, whose supreme expressions are, arguably, the *Spiritual Canticle* and *The Living Flame of Love*. Here, for instance, are two brief excerpts from the latter work:

> O sweet cautery,
> O delightful wound!
> O gentle hand! O delicate touch
> That tastes of eternal life
> And pays every debt!
> In killing you changed death to life.

> O lamps of fire!
> In whose splendors
> The deep caverns of feeling,
> Once obscure and blind,
> Now give forth . . .
> Both warmth and light to their beloved.[52]

It may be argued that these are simply virtuosic linguistic displays in the mannerist mode, yet they do appeal directly to natural bodily sensations and to the emotionalism, the "pain and suffering, wounds and tears," that Hauser identifies with the baroque. Despite his suspicions about image and sensation, John of the Cross could not help being an early modern poet. His words may counsel imageless union with the divine, but they perform a lively, affective connection with the "traitor *touch*" that *tastes* eternal life.[53] Other early modern Catholics, such as the Jesuits, embraced art and image more enthusiastically, and even Hauser admits that eventually "the baroque was once more able to be liberal and pleasing to the senses."[54] Early modern Catholicism not only reframed reform and representation but helped create a baroque style in which "churches became, not so much places of remorse and repentance, as inviting, welcoming, friendly homes for the faithful. Once more they could be adorned and resplendent. . . . It was even possible to revert to the practice of tickling [the] senses."[55]

Whether or not Caravaggio may be called a "tickler of the senses," his art certainly contributed to the reframing of Christian icons such as the Madonna and the rosary. We have seen that as it began to be reinterpreted in post-Tridentine Catholicism, the rosary took on a number of characteristics ancient Christianity had attributed to the visual art of icons. The rosary was not simply repeated prayer (Hail Marys) and discursive meditation ("thinking" about the mysteries) but a site of sacred presence and revelation. The naturalism of the episodes that formed the heart of the mysteries—a condemned man's torture (Jesus scourged and crowned with thorns, the second and third sorrowful mysteries); the wind and flames of the Spirit's descent at Pentecost (third glorious mystery)—created a "bridge beyond" that invited those who prayed to cross the visible. By entering more deeply, through meditation, into the depths of the natural world—with its chaos, doubts, disappointments, suffering, and failure—those who prayed the rosary found themselves made sudden citizens of heaven, much as the children in C. S. Lewis's Narnia novel *The Lion, the Witch, and the Wardrobe* open the door of an old armoire and find themselves no longer in England but in the Land of Aslan (the Lion who is a figure of Christ).

It is significant that Caravaggio's mature work focused on presenting religious subjects within a naturalistic perspective. He was an unmistakably *Catholic* painter who often transgressed what Counter-Reformation ecclesiastics like Charles Borromeo regarded as propriety, decorum, and decency in church art. Yet Trent had not challenged the legitimacy of natural images; rather, it called for their retention through a critical reassessment of their use.[56]

Caravaggio's controversial art is thus a good place to start when tracing the fate of the rosary as it was being reinterpreted by early modern Catholics. Along the lines of Paleotti in his *Discorso*, Caravaggio sensed that the best way to portray God's presence and action in the world is through a faithful rendering of nature. For in nature there is nothing inherently obscene or indecent, even if human persons sometimes feel squeamish in the presence of natural bodies, behaviors, qualities, scenes, or events. His art embodied much of the complexity and contradiction that characterized Catholicism itself during this period of its history. Helen Langdon summarizes this point eloquently when she writes about the portrait of Caravaggio that emerges from recent research:

> He was a violent man, but he lived in an extraordinarily violent time, and his behaviour was governed by complex codes of honour. . . . He was a highly intellectual painter, admired and feted by poets and literary men, and many of his paintings are a sophisticated play on the nature of artistic illusion. He was also a great religious artist who created a new and passionate Catholic art, with an extraordinary ability to re-imagine the scriptures, and to relate them to his own times. . . . Caravaggio's art transcends the pietistic art of the Counter-Reformation, and makes a powerful and immediate appeal across the centuries. For his works also convey a highly individual response to the Christian mysteries; they suggest an extraordinarily direct and tragic sense of the human condition and the fate of man.[57]

"An extraordinarily direct and tragic sense of the human condition": this phrase well summarizes what Catholics hoped to experience when praying the rosary. Yet that devotion did not simply offer the devout an opportunity to mourn the sad condition of humankind; it offered itself as a site of sacred presence, of divine self-disclosure where God and God's Mother could be met. A similar experience is what Caravaggio's art aimed to achieve visually. Langdon sees Caravaggio as simultaneously a contrarian who subverted the "pietistic art of the Counter-Reformation" and a traditionalist who could not let go of the "grand Christian narrative" (a narrative that would create significant problems for later theological discourse).[58] Her assessment is accurate, I think, and aptly describes as well the forces, tensions, and conflicts that inspired both the freshness and the fears of early modern Catholicism. Already in his own time, Caravaggio's critics had mentioned not only his *naturalism* but also the pervasive *darkness* of his later paintings.[59] He had always painted directly from life, without preliminary sketching, and as he grew older, he let his models be lit only by whatever natural daylight could filter into a room from a single high window.[60] This was not merely a painterly technique; it became the spiritual linchpin of his life's work. In Caravaggio's later paintings, darkness

> hid background, panorama, distance, distractions, clouds and sunlight. It eliminated the long view, the big picture. Darkness obscured earthly crowds, mighty armies, mythological masses, heavenly hosts. It removed distant lands and celestial life from view. It fixed the gaze on the drama of the human body and held it there. Darkness therefore had its limitations as a way of pictorially transmitting heavenly glory and earthly hierarchy. . . . What darkness and intimacy *could* do was register the intensity of individual feeling.[61]

"It fixed the gaze on the drama of the human body and held it there." Peter Robb's statement could stand not only as a summary of Caravaggio's spiritual credo but also as a synopsis of Catholicism in the age of the early baroque. The body as both cabinet of wonders and chamber of horrors became "standard catholic iconography" during the Counter-Reformation.[62] Both religious art and secular literature were replete with bodies blissful and battered, limbs severed and restored, "nailed hands and rolling eyes"—and with narratives that combined a "mix of sex, death, frustration, incest, pain, voyeurism, nymphomania, . . . sadism, repentance."[63] Not insignificantly, the fifteen Christian mysteries of the rosary were also connected to the human sensorium, to human bodies and their fate. Seeing, hearing, telling, touching, tearing, walking, lifting, giving birth, dying: all these bodily acts and more figure into the rosary's meditations. Nowhere does the rosary invite speculation on abstract truths or ideas. From Christ's conception at the Annunciation to Mary's Assumption "body and soul into heaven," the rosary resolutely fixes the Christian's gaze on the drama of the body and holds it there.

As framed for meditation while praying the rosary, then, the fifteen traditional mysteries focus attention not on an abstract "humanity in general" or on disputed theological questions about sin and grace but on specific fleshly individuals and their relations with each other. Often, these persons are young and experienced (Mary at the Annunciation), or older, obscure women suddenly surprised by joy in a remote corner of the world (Elizabeth at the Visitation). Here too Caravaggio's art tutored the Christian imagination. Summarizing his role as innovator in the religious iconography of early modern Catholicism, Patrick Hunt observes that Caravaggio avoided "scenes with scores of people or masses," that he instead "highlighted the individual" and saw drama arising "as much from the character as the event."[64] His was a world of "what can—and must—be seen" within the encroaching darkness that constitutes the human condition. His canvases confront viewers with *image* as *reality*—as *access* to reality—rather than as escape into fantasy, symbolism, spiritualism, or sentimentality.

And such reality was, perhaps more often than not, discomfiting. Here one may grasp some of the reasons why scholars like Walter Friedlaender and others have drawn parallels between Caravaggio and Saint Philip Neri's "Oratorian orbit."[65] Unlike his contemporary Ignatius Loyola, Neri was not interested in creating a highly regimented and centralized religious order.[66] We discussed Neri's charitable work among street people in late sixteenth-century Rome earlier; here we may focus on Neri's rather "irregular" personality—his independence, spontaneity, and nonconformity.[67] He seemed to prefer life as a layman, spending the bulk of his time, as Ignatius himself did, "in the streets, in the hospitals, among the beggars, . . . by the beds of the sick, catechising the children, rescuing prostitutes, feeding the hungry and helping the dying."[68] In fact, many of Neri's contemporaries thought he had accepted ordination to the priesthood (at the "advanced" age of thirty-six) reluctantly and under duress, "by force."[69] His preference for life on the streets, as a holy fool among beggars, was rare and even dangerous in mid-sixteenth-century Rome, given the climate of "centralization, . . . control and repression, inaugurated by the Council [of Trent] and the Inquisition."[70] Anyone who sought to engage in public church work was under intense pressure to conform, to embrace a style of life approved by the church's authorities, especially the Inquisition, and to avoid ascetic eccentricities. Yet according to Antonio Gallonio, his associate and earliest biographer, Neri "aimed in particular at striking up friendship with the most depraved among them [poor young people in Rome], reckoning that he ought to provide the most assistance to the ones who needed it most."[71] As we have seen, Neri's career represented another side of the Counter-Reform, one whose links to Caravaggio are almost impossible to deny.[72]

Even if one disputes a direct connection between Neri's nonconformist piety and Caravaggio's unconventional paintings, one cannot doubt the
fascination that the figure of Mary had for both men. Images of Mary appear in at least nine of Caravaggio's surviving works, and each appearance is distinctive. And even great painters like to recycle. Consider, for
instance, the "great swag of knotted red curtain" pulled aside to reveal a
tight cluster of figures in Caravaggio's huge canvas *Madonna del Rosario*
(painted ca. 1607).[73] Almost identical red drapery had framed the scene in
his *Morte della Vergine* (*Death of the Virgin*), painted perhaps two or three
years earlier (ca. 1604). Both paintings focus on the Mother of Jesus; both
were probably commissioned as altarpieces; both are large, ambitious
works completed during the last four years of the artist's life; both aroused
anger and outrage; and neither piece, as matters turned out, was accepted
for use in church.[74]

Despite it innovations, Caravaggio's *Madonna del Rosario* is basically
in alignment with Trent's criteria for appropriateness in church art, especially if one considers the religious culture of late sixteenth-century and
early seventeenth-century Italy.[75] By that time, the rosary had become a
firm fixture in the devotional life of Catholics throughout Western Europe. Moreover, despite earlier opposition from Catholic humanists such
as Erasmus and reformers such as Luther, "devotion to the Rosary had
begun to revive in Italy in the second half of the sixteenth century, and it
exploded as the century drew to a close."[76] The rosary's enhanced status
was due not only to the increasingly proactive vigor of Catholic response
to the Reformation but also, as we have seen, to geopolitical factors such
as the defeat of the Turks by a coalition of Christian forces at the Battle of
Lepanto, a victory linked to "the belief that the Virgin herself had caused
favourable winds" and so had personally intervened to halt Turkish expansion into Europe and to thwart the Ottoman push to control commerce and travel in the Mediterranean.[77]

Almost overnight, as we have seen, Lepanto became a wildly popular
subject in contemporary paintings, among them works by Paolo Veronese
(1528–88) and Titian (Tiziano Vecellio, 1490–1575).[78] Veronese's work—
now in the Galleria dell'Accademia in Venice but originally installed on
the left side of the rosary altar in the Church of Saint Peter the Martyr
on Murano—highlighted popular beliefs about Mary's intervention on
behalf of the Venetian ships at Lepanto.[79] Titian's painting, in contrast,
omits any visual reference to Mary and focuses instead on the figure of
Spain's Philip II offering his infant son, Fernando, to a winged Victory;

in its foreground a bound, captive Turk crouches on the floor (on a level with the family dog), while the Battle of Lepanto is depicted on one wall of the room.[80] As Herbert Thurston pointed out almost a century ago, the Christian naval victory at Lepanto resulted not only in renewed devotion to the rosary but also to the creation of an annual feast day in its honor, to be observed by all members of the rosary confraternity in Rome.[81] Moreover, in 1573, Pius V's successor, Gregory XIII, allowed this feast to be kept "in all churches which possessed an altar dedicated to the Holy Rosary."[82] The military success of the Christian coalition breathed new life into an old devotion and brought the rosary into a closer connection with the church's liturgical calendar.

Yet, while rosary altarpieces of the late sixteenth century and early seventeenth century sometimes incorporated images of the heroes of Lepanto, Caravaggio's *Madonna del Rosario* did nothing of the sort.[83] The cast of characters in this work includes, besides Mary and the child Jesus, three Dominican saints standing upright (Dominic, Peter Martyr, Thomas Aquinas); a kneeling, "black clad white ruffed middleaged man"; and five further figures—three kneeling *lazzaroni* (paupers, especially those whose poverty pushed them into lives of petty crime), plus a nursemaid and toddler, all with their backs to the viewer.[84] Although many commentators draw attention to the way Mary's position at the top of the painting dominates the scene and anticipates the "elaborate ordering and interlocking of forms that herald the Baroque altarpiece," what is most striking in *Madonna del Rosario* are people's *hands*.[85] Almost every figure in the composition is shown stretching a hand toward something or someone. Mary points a finger at Dominic, possibly in a gesture of command or commissioning; Dominic's open hands, each carrying a rosary, extend toward the kneeling *lazzaroni*; and the latter group's uplifted hands seem to beg for the objects Dominic holds.

Viewed as a unified composition, *Madonna del Rosario* seems to be both perfectly orthodox and perfectly proper. Unlike his earlier and edgier *Madonna dei Pellegrini* of 1604, where Mary's relaxed posture and décolletage suggest "a sexy young housewife coming to the front door of what looked like a very ordinary Roman home," Caravaggio's *Rosary Madonna* seems preeminently safe and respectable.[86] Surrounded by stern saints, a wealthy nobleman, a young woman and her toddler, and the urban poor, Mary stands serenely aloft, an authoritative "mediator, uniting high and low"; she thus embodies the values of early modern Italian rosary confraternities, "hierarchical organizations" that "intended to bind together rich and poor in the devotional activity of reciting the rosary, whose cult offered hope to the poor."[87]

But then one begins to notice the details. There is, for example, that lumpy diaper, bulging below the toddler's outer garments—an innocent enough detail, but does it belong in a painting designed to hang directly over an altar where the Catholic Eucharist was to be celebrated? Then there are those three kneeling *lazzaroni* with their filthy hands and fingernails, the grime caked on the soles of their feet plainly visible in the lower part of the painting. Religious confraternities of this period routinely urged their members to devote "some money and much time . . . in philanthropic actions toward less fortunate 'neighbours,'" yet by the beginning of the seventeenth century there is also evidence for what may be called "a subculture of criminal poor," well-organized "gangs of thieves, tricksters and people intent on misusing charitable institutions and the generosity of donors."[88] This growing threat produced a backlash against the poor in large Italian cities such as Rome and Naples. For example, even as Rome was enjoying a major *renovatio* in luxurious art, architecture, and public ceremonies during the last quarter of the sixteenth century, these developments were increasingly overshadowed "by the ever more turbulent and threatening world of the poor and dispossessed."[89] Helen Langdon suggests that this happened in part because Rome had become an irresistible magnet for "a vast itinerant population":

> It was a city where men outnumbered women, and, dominated by celibate churchmen, it attracted courtesans from all over Italy, who formed a colony in the *rione* [borough] of Campo Marzio. The number of pilgrims and beggars, attracted by indulgences, and by the charitable institutions [e.g., confraternities], was huge, and in the Jubilee years outweighed the permanent population. Ruthlessly suppressed by Sixtus V [pope from 1585 to 1590], bandits nonetheless remained a constant fear beyond the city walls. And the poor, whose humility had, in the Middle Ages, been exalted as a spiritual value, were growing in numbers, in Rome as throughout Europe.[90]

Yet nuance is needed here. Modern historians generally agree that attitudes toward the poor in Europe had begun to shift in the late fifteenth and early sixteenth centuries. As a result, treatment of the poor became more oppressive throughout the Continent, and a sharp division between "deserving" and "undeserving" poor can be documented from the sixteenth century onward.[91] Nevertheless, such generalizations beg qualification. When it comes to the situation in Italy, for instance, Christopher Black writes that, while there are good reasons to maintain that "from the late sixteenth century there were increasing moves towards a harsher disciplining of the poor," one should be "wary of seeing this as the product of a clear ideology, or a consistent policy."[92] There were, he notes, considerable "variations in attitude, policy and institutions within Italy" and elsewhere.[93] Whether or not there existed—in fact and not merely as a literary fiction—a well-organized, violent, criminal subculture is perhaps debatable, but there is little doubt that "myths and realities," when mingled, could elicit a potent "repressive response."[94]

The issue of the poor and how to treat them continued to be a neuralgic subject in post-Tridentine Catholicism, and it had an impact on associations like the Marian sodalities and the rosary confraternities, which, as we have seen, were devoted not only to prayer and increased participation in the church's sacramental life but to care of the needy. In his well-known study *Bread of Dreams*, Piero Camporesi advances the argument that "penury and hunger . . . became chronic and endemic in the West during the sixteenth to eighteenth centuries," and that this phenomenon originated not simply in natural disasters (famine, drought) but "in the economy, the means of production and the political will of the rulers."[95] It was thus in the interests of those who held wealth and power to discipline and control—to *manage*—the poor through a combination of punishment, embodied in laws against vagrancy, and public assistance or charity, regulated by institutions such as hospitals, sanitariums, hospices, or mendicants' institutes.[96] It was to the advantage of the anxious and powerful "haves" to dramatize as direly as possible the threat posed by the have-nots—"the uncontrolled proliferation of the wretched"—because this helped to justify the often excessive measures used against them.[97] Yet even Camporesi admits that in reality the menace posed by the poor was often exaggerated for literary effect.

This does not mean that the upper classes—in late sixteenth-century and early seventeenth-century Italy, for example—did not detest the poor or seek effective ways of keeping them under control.[98] An example comes from the Apostolic Hospice of Saint Michael in Rome, a "composite institution which grew up piecemeal through consolidations and additions," and that originated in "some of the earliest attempts made in Rome to combat the increasing pauperism and the mendicity accompanying it."[99] There has been much debate among historians of criminology about whether Saint Michael's represents a prison, a punitive house of correction, a penitentiary focused on the inmates' rehabilitation, an orphanage, or simply a refuge, a safe haven for the needy, the aged, the sick, and the vulnerable. Helen Langdon suggests that Pope Sixtus V's interest in Saint Michael's was motivated mainly by hostility against noisy beggars whose growing presence was seen not only as a disturbance to the law-abiding faithful but as "a danger to stability and to the very fabric of society."[100]

Yet Langdon's view is not entirely accurate. Pope Sixtus V did rail against vagrants and beggars as public nuisances, but he also placed Saint Michael's under papal patronage—at his own personal expense.[101] He thereby created a comprehensive—some might say totalizing—institution that could provide for the reception, shelter, education, and sustenance of the urban poor, especially children.[102] Moreover, the hospice would be run through a cooperative arrangement involving clergy, the Roman people, and members of lay confraternities.[103] By today's standards, Sixtus's approach to charitable giving would probably be construed as controlling and paternalistic, but his contemporaries regarded it as progressive and enlightened.[104]

Still, it must be said that Sixtus (who, as we have seen, did so much to revitalize church architecture in Rome between 1585 and 1590) did in fact seek to keep the poor out of sight—and that is precisely what Caravaggio did *not* do in *Madonna del Rosario*. One might suppose that the painting's primary purpose was to show devout worshipers where and how "heaven and earth meet"; yet instead of presenting a conventional, devotionally idealized group of paupers cleaned up and made presentable for church, Caravaggio confronted his viewers with an unwashed and possibly dangerous gang of three, their importunate hands clutching for the rosaries Dominic offers. At the same time, however, Caravaggio's painting is "traditional," for it visually endorses the legend about the rosary originating in a vision of the Virgin Mary to Saint Dominic. This combination—the edginess of portraying possibly dangerous paupers in an *altarpiece*, blended with the endorsement of a familiar, pious legend—epitomizes some of the important changes that were occurring to the rosary in the early modern era. On one hand, the rosary reflected the survival of traditional prayer forms that originated in the late medieval *devotio moderna*; on the other, the rosary's flexibility (a feature promoted by the confraternities) meant that *its interpretation was difficult to control by church authorities*. Ironically, despite its diffusion throughout the post-Tridentine church, the rosary— praised by popes for its crucial role in the Christian victory over the Ottoman Turks—could never be fully regulated (or its meanings monitored) within a Catholicism increasingly centralized around papal power and the Roman curia (the pope's "cabinet").

Caravaggio's painting embodies some of these same ambiguities. He seems to have *wanted* his barefoot beggars to seem threatening "in a brutal and despairing city where the mob was feared."[105] Moreover, if *Madonna del Rosario* was intended, as many think, for the parishioners of San Domenico in Naples, then the painter's choice of figures could well have been deliberately provocative. San Domenico was "an aristocratic church, in the city's ancient centre, its sacristy lined with royal tombs, and frequented by a cultivated élite."[106] The church originated in the tenth century but later came to be associated with the Dominican order. (The Dominicans' historical connection with this Neapolitan church may help explain the presence of Thomas Aquinas in Caravaggio's painting.) Helen Langdon suggests that the wealthy clientele associated with San Domenico may have objected to *Madonna del Rosario* because its members felt the devotion was fit "only for the lower classes, for women of the people," and that the presence of Caravaggio's *lazzaroni* "gave too great an urgency to the world of the poor."[107] In other words, it may have been the wrong painting for the wrong church. Yet it seems unlikely that recitation of the rosary and devotion to the Virgin Mary were widely perceived as "class-based" issues. In fact, inventories of medieval and early modern jewelry reveal that rosaries made of silver, gold, coral, pearls, and precious stones were abundant, greatly admired and used by wealthy Christians.[108] And the famous gold rosary of Mary, Queen of Scots (executed in 1587), exemplifies Catholic royalty's use of the rosary as both an object of devotion and an item of apparel.

Still, Caravaggio did like to portray Mary as a trustworthy advocate for the oppressed and needy, as he does in *Madonna dei Pellegrini*, which links the figure of Mary with the *Roman* poor.[109] In fact, the art historian and painter Giovanni Baglione (1566–1643), wrote that Caravaggio's *Madonna dei Pellegrini* (also called *Madonna di Loreto*) had been

> painted from life [i.e., without prior drawn sketches] with two pilgrims— the man with mud-caked feet, the woman wearing a filthy, torn headdress. He [Caravaggio] trivialized the qualities an important painting should have, but the poorer classes made a huge fuss over it.[110]

Baglione complained that the enormous interest and excitement elicited by Caravaggio's work "came from all the wrong people for all the wrong reasons—reminding you it wasn't the first time dirty feet had been a problem in M's art . . . [and that] the greatest offence of these destitute pilgrims or vagrants in showplace Rome was being seen at all."[111]

We can say, then, that while the rosary and devotion to Mary were not widely perceived as "class-related" in early modern Catholicism, there was a feeling—reflected in Baglione's complaint—that the poor should be kept out of sight, at least in art intended for use in church. The chief problem posed by the poor seemed to be not their existence as such but their visibility and proximity to prosperous urban dwellers who preferred them to be invisible, distant, and anonymous. Caravaggio's "offense," in a painting such as *Madonna del Rosario*, was that he seemed to place the humble and poor on a par with the wealthy patrons who had commissioned the altarpiece in the first place. He implied, thereby, that Mary's gift of the rosary to humankind was an utterly unrestricted one—as, indeed, her Son's act of redemption had been on the cross. In other words, Caravaggio's rosary painting was a sort of visual commentary on Paul's bold affirmation in Galatians 3.28: "There is neither Jew nor Greek, there is neither slave nor free person, there is neither male nor female, for you are all one in Christ Jesus."

Caravaggio revisited this theme in other paintings where the Virgin Mary was featured, especially the *Madonna dei Pellegrini* (1604). In this work, Mary embodies an almost seductive sensuality. Caravaggio had used posture, form, and color "to mark an erotic surge, a peculiar voluptuousness of perception."[112] Here was a Madonna who not only lived and breathed among poor pilgrims but whose attitude toward their plight seemed suffused with ready warmth and acceptance. Mary gazed down on the weary travelers as a solicitous next-door neighbor might. She was very much within reach of praying people. Caravaggio's image made viewers wonder if it was proper to portray Christ's Virgin Mother leaning casually against a door frame, surrounded by beggars badly in need of bathing. "Feet," novelist Luigi Santucci once wrote, "are miles away from their possessors' smiles, feet are rough wild animals, and looking at a foot makes it harder to believe in man's soul and easier to think we're just transitory puppets whose destiny is dissolution."[113] Yet Caravaggio's Mary was not one to be put off by gnarly feet that "only a mother could love," and in both *Madonna del Rosario* and *Madonna dei Pellegrini*, she became "an icon remade."[114]

In contrast to the iconographic traditions embodied in earlier *Rosenkranzbilder*, Caravaggio's Mary had become a *mother* whose attention and affection were available to anyone in need. Still, some critics (Peter Robb among them) see the *Madonna dei Pellegrini* as a relapse on Caravaggio's part, a flirtation with unctuous religiosity and "sentimentality" whose "giveaway" gesture is "the chubby forefinger of the Christ child blessing the humble poor."[115] This "awful priestly finger-wagging from a child," writes Robb, "was M's worst—his only—lapse into counter reformation kitsch."[116] I do not concur with Robb's analysis, but his comment does raise larger questions about Caravaggio's intentions not only in *Madonna dei Pellegrini* but in *Madonna del Rosario* as well. For despite his well-earned reputation for rewriting traditional religious icons, Caravaggio was also a shrewd businessman who knew how to market his work by making friends in high places.[117] Moreover, despite his subversive style and his having had (by 1605) at least five major paintings rejected by those who originally commissioned them, Caravaggio's works sold briskly among influential collectors in Italy or made their way to artists and dealers in other parts of Europe.[118]

Yet Caravaggio's business acumen should not blind us to the fact that from the period that produced *Madonna di Loreto, Madonna dei Pala-frenieri (The Grooms' Madonna)* and *Madonna del Rosario* (ca. 1603–6) until his death (1610), his work and experience were focused almost exclusively on "the figures and images and events of the Christian drama."[119] This momentous shift in the artist's career was important not only for the history of Western art but also for early modern understandings of the Virgin Mary. It was not simply that Caravaggio chose, increasingly, to reframe her image in ever-more-naturalistic (even voluptuous) human terms, though this is quite palpable in the *Palafrenieri* altarpiece, where Mary is a dark-haired beauty whose daring décolletage might well have distracted priest and people as they stood before the altar.[120] His *Madonna dei Palafrenieri* also contains a detail that became theologically significant within post-Tridentine Catholicism. Mary is shown treading on a coiling serpent, crushing its head with her foot. Relying on the Latin Vulgate translation of Genesis 3.15, early modern Catholics held that from the beginning of human history, God had decreed the serpent's (devil's) power would be destroyed by a woman (Mary) and her holy offspring (Christ).[121] Such interpretations reinforced Mary's hawkish warrior image, already burnished by her role in the victory at Lepanto. Post-Tridentine Catholicism and Caravaggio's art were reinterpreting the relation between human beings and God by highlighting Mary's militant advocacy and by stressing the rosary as a principal means by which God's work in an expanding world was being accomplished.

In the last six or seven years of his life (1603/4–1610), therefore, Caravaggio renegotiated the *distance* that separates subject from beholder, painterly illusion from viewer's affectivity. To shorten the distance between "us" (viewers) and "them" (natural objects portrayed in pictures) had been, we have seen, a vexing problem for early modern painters and naturalists.[122] For him, drawings, etchings, or paintings were valuable only to the degree that they accurately registered reality as it *is* in nature. After the Carracci introduced their innovative paintings in Bologna, however, a shift occurred. Naturalism no longer had to mean an anatomist's obsession with body parts or a botanist's detailed rendering of roots, shoots, leaves, and flowers. It could also include natural *process*, the unfolding history of objects as they change, mature, age, or rot. Visitors to the Carracci academy in Bologna could thus see an enormous variety of "living persons, nudes entirely or in part, weapons, animals, fruits, and, in short, all things in Creation."[123] Naturalism could not be restricted to things as they presently *are*; it must include, as well, reality as it is *changing*, as it is *becoming something "other."*

We can see a similar shift, especially in Caravaggio's later work, such as *Still Life with Basket of Fruit* (1601).[124] As his paintings appeared to become more illusory and even hallucinatory—their dark surfaces illumined only by piercing shafts of light—their power intensified. Darkness pervades the *Madonna dei Palafrenieri*, for example, though the painting's three figures (Mary, Christ, and Saint Anne) are lit by a shaft of light whose source is invisible. In such works, the boundary between fiction and reality grew increasingly blurred. Yet instead of becoming less natural or less convincing, these late religious paintings explored, with ever greater precision, persons and experiences we might be inclined to miss or ignore. The *Madonna dei Palafrenieri* was, we have seen, intended as another of Caravaggio's Roman altarpieces, but it aroused vigorous protest and controversy. For one thing, he painted Mary with "large breasts thrust into a conspicuously tight and low cut dress," leaning (too) far forward "over her well muscled nude boy."[125] Nudity (or seminudity) was to be avoided in post-Tridentine church art; moreover, Caravaggio's Madonna looked a bit *too* full-bosomed to be placed over an altar where the holiest mystery of Catholic faith was to be celebrated—in, of all places, Christendom's premier church, the Basilica of Saint Peter in Rome.[126] Meanwhile, Saint Anne, instead of looking sweet and grandmotherly, was a wizened crone with bad teeth and deeply furrowed face and neck, dressed in "mouse-coloured clothing."[127] She strongly resembles not her holy daughter but the old serving maid in Caravaggio's second *Supper at Emmaus* (1606). Finally, there is the lashing snake that Mary and her child tread upon. Everywhere the viewer looks, the artist has "stripped the most sacred beings of their deserved majestic raiments. Instead of the triumphant Mother of God and infant Saviour, Caravaggio evoked a 'peasant woman killing a viper in a barn,' to quote from one modern historian."[128]

From a strictly theological point of view, Caravaggio's *Madonna dei Palafrenieri* was unobjectionable. It accurately portrayed what post-Tridentine theology affirmed (based on Genesis 3.15), namely, that the Virgin Mary, conceived without sin, cooperated with her Son in crushing the serpent's head, and so deserves to be considered the co-redemptrix of the human race. At one level, then, the painting was an "apparently impeccable illustration of Marian devotion," fully in compliance with Catholic orthodoxy.[129] Although the Immaculate Conception was not one of the rosary's fifteen mysteries, it was implied by Mary's unique destiny—her "assumption body and soul into heaven," followed by her "coronation as queen of heaven" (the fourth and fifth "glorious" mysteries). Caravaggio's painting denies none of this, yet it disturbs the viewer with its "strong whiff of nude baby-flesh, that all-too-visible, almost bare bosom, that old hag receding, wrinkled, into a deathlike darkness."[130] No wonder the painting was removed from the Basilica of Saint Peter almost as soon as it had been installed.

Yet Caravaggio's *Madonna dei Palafrenieri* was a significant step in his ongoing effort to overcome the "defect of distance," to renegotiate the physical and psychological space that separates artistic subject from beholder, painterly illusion from viewer's affectivity. He was trying to accomplish in art what the devout Catholic hoped to do when praying the rosary, namely, attain a familiar intimacy with the central figures in the history of salvation. As Catherine Puglisi points out, this Madonna painting "isolated three figures in the starkest of settings" and placed them within "a shallow foreground space" that "set them on the apron of a stage, so to speak, thrusting out towards the spectator beyond the imaginary proscenium formed by the frame." This technique substantially "shortens" the distance between subjects and viewers. Instead of compressing rather flat, insubstantial figures "into the airless space of Mannerist paintings, Caravaggio fashioned three-dimensional bodies occupying real space."[131]

Caravaggio's innovative way of reframing traditional representations of biblical scenes and Christian beliefs is an essential moment in the history of early modern Catholic devotion generally—and of the rosary specifically. The fifteen mysteries of the rosary were, after all, a *compendium fidei* (summary of faith), a narratively expanded Credo that invited contemplative review of the most fundamental tenets of Catholic belief. In such contemplation, however, *the believer him- or herself becomes a direct participant, an active agent in the mystery being meditated.* This was, perhaps, the most significant way Catholics' approach to the rosary began to change in the late sixteenth and early seventeenth centuries—the period of time we have been discussing. Caravaggio did not paint in order to instruct, catechize, or edify viewers but to provoke a (perhaps unnerving) experience of direct involvement in the painted scene itself. Similarly, the rosary—especially when prayed using the vivid imaginative techniques of Ignatian meditation—was no longer an exercise in "thinking about" divine mysteries but of participating directly in them.

The rosary was thus becoming a *medium of presence* rather than the "physical reminder" of a sacred past. The devotee's prayer and accompanying meditations aimed at overcoming the "defect of distance," much as Caravaggio's illusionistic technique created a space that *thrust forward toward the spectator* and so shortened the space between subjects and viewers. The sacred though ordinary-looking figures of a Caravaggio canvas spill out into the spectator's space and blur the line that separates the "viewers" from the "viewed." Seeing and looking become truly a two-way street, transpiring on both sides of the "imaginary proscenium" formed by the picture's frame." This is not merely a matter of making onlookers feel as if "they are there" to witness some *past* historical event. Caravaggio (and the rosary meditations) had something more radical in mind: the dynamic "real space" of the holy figures intersects the real space of the "spectators" and makes everyone, viewers and viewed alike, active participants in a human drama. Painted personages such as Mary, Christ, or the saints are no longer sacred (stereo)types; they are real individuals, with personal histories as palpable, particular, and plebeian as our own.[132] Caravaggio's rewritten icons—like the rosary's meditated mysteries—blended *our* histories with *theirs.*

Caravaggio's late religious paintings thus came to evoke, in both import and impact, those ancient Christian icons of Mary and Christ that were beloved by early modern Catholic nonconformists like Philip Neri. True, Neri used to warn penitents "not to stare too hard at images," yet his "theatrically embraced poverty," simplicity, and "one on one relationship with God" fostered a spirituality that Caravaggio also promoted and provoked by his paintings.[133] The latter's work, as we have been discussing, both reflected and resisted post-Tridentine criteria for decorum in church art. The bishops at Trent had insisted that nothing "disorderly or unbecoming and confusedly arranged, nothing that is profane, nothing disrespectful . . . [or] unusual" should be allowed in the creation of sacred images.[134] Yet while many (though not all) church leaders seemed to view art as an opportunity for *disciplinamento*, for the transmission of a set of tightly controlled messages, Caravaggio saw it as a compelling meditation on the most scandalous of all Christian mysteries—the incarnation, God's own Word becoming flesh, the same flesh shared by both the Madonna and those kneeling *lazzaroni*, with their tattered clothes and filthy feet.

Perhaps, however, neither *Madonna dei Palafrenieri* nor *Madonna del Rosario* was as transgressive as another of Caravaggio's altarpieces, the *Morte della Vergine* (*Death of the Virgin*), where Mary lies sprawled at the center of a mournful scene—discolored, bloated, her bare feet sticking out, her left arm flung to one side, awaiting (it seems) not the triumph of assumption into paradise but the final ignominy of dissolution after death. The scandal embodied in *Morte della Vergine* is perhaps plainer to see than the subtler one found in the warmly appealing images of Mary in the two paintings just mentioned. Caravaggio's portrayal of Mary, dead, confronts the viewer unsparingly with

death as the loss of physical life, death as coldness, weight, silence, immobility. Death as human emptiness. Death as pure absence. Death as the end of the road. It was death as a very fresh experience, death as that moment when everybody around suddenly realized there was nothing more to do, that the physical care and the comforting were no more use and a person was now a corpse.[135]

Obviously, the *Morte della Vergine* did not depict the sort of death that, by the early seventeenth century, Western Latin theological tradition had come to associate with Mary's Assumption.[136] By that time, Christian beliefs about Mary's uniquely privileged status, at the beginning and the end of her life, were well established in both East and West. While evidence from the first four centuries is scanty, texts purporting to describe what happened when Mary reached the end of her natural life began to circulate from the late fifth and early sixth centuries onward. Stephen J. Shoemaker has shown that thereafter, Christian hypotheses about Mary's Dormition (falling asleep) and/or Assumption proliferated.[137] Such speculation appeared first in Syria, Palestine, and Egypt but quickly spread elsewhere. "This sudden proliferation of traditions," writes Shoemaker, "calls for an explanation: something about this topic and its narrative traditions must have resonated with the issues and concerns of the early Byzantine world."[138] The explanation may lie, as Brian Daley suggests, both in the "powerful role of royal women in the fifth-century Byzantine court" and in those Christological controversies that, following the ecumenical Council of Chalcedon (451 c.e.), prompted Christian reflection on "Mary's role in the story of salvation."[139] In any case, well before the end of the first millennium, some sixty distinct narratives purporting to describe what occurred at the end of Mary's life and written in at least nine different languages had appeared. And while there was no consensus about precisely what Mary's *kathisma* (sitting down to rest) involved—whether, for example, her "entering into glory" meant that her *body* also "shared in her glorification"—pastors, preachers, and theologians agreed that Mary's death was a "moment of mystery, parallel in some ways to the death of Jesus, . . . a time of unique recognition of her holiness by her Son and the heavenly powers."[140]

Caravaggio's unsparing portrayal of Mary's death seemed, then, to fly in the face of Christian beliefs, liturgical practices, and devotions "that had been in place in churches of both the East and the West for more than a millennium."[141] Yet *Morte della Vergine* captured quite well the conviction that drove both artists and ecclesiastics to reframe representations of Mary in early modern Catholicism. As we have seen, Caravaggio's own work emerged from his struggle with the "defect of distance." *Distance*, Trent's decree on church art had maintained, breeds decorum—and decorum in Christian images is *bonum valde desiderandum* (a good earnestly to be desired). Nevertheless, Caravaggio's Marian paintings showed, as did his other religious works, that there is no decorum in nature; there is only life in its disorderly, chaotic, embarrassing fullness. Art serves life, and life-in-the-flesh is what God himself embraced not only in the filthy feet of *lazzaroni* but in Mary's womb as well.

Conclusion: Icons Rewritten

To study the rosary in relation to the art of innovators like Caravaggio is to continue a pattern already established in the fifteenth century, when the devotion was still something of a novelty. From its inception, the rosary had relied on the twin powers of interior visualization (personal appropriation of images through meditation) and exterior representation (the creation of images that would stimulate the praying Christian's imagination). Caravaggio had thus continued the tradition of late medieval rosary picture books and early Renaissance *Rosenkranzbilder*, but he dramatically redefined these genres. Although he died hardly more than half a century after the Tridentine decree was promulgated, his work already represented a significant departure from what ecclesiastics stuck in the "Counter-Reform-reaction" mode regarded as decorum and decency in church art. Trent, we have seen, had reaffirmed the legitimacy of images and called for their retention; yet the Council of Trent had also called for a thorough overhaul of Christian artwork based on a critical reassessment of the "use and abuse of religious imagery."[142] Meanwhile, theologians like Carlo Borromeo had begun discussing in detail what Trent's defense of Christian iconography might mean for the design and decoration of new or renovated churches.

Caravaggio's own late-life obsession with religious themes and subjects helped to both support and subvert the Catholic imagination as it began to reshape itself in the wake of Reformation, Counter-Reformation, and what we have been calling "reform of the (Tridentine) reform." Trent had insisted that bishops diligently instruct their flocks about the great value to be derived "from all holy images, not only because the people are thereby reminded of the benefits and gifts bestowed on them by Christ, but also because through the saints the miracles of God and salutary examples are set before the eyes of the faithful."[143] Caravaggio created images—especially of the Virgin Mary—that both reflected and resisted this Tridentine principle. He understood that when it came to questions about propriety and decorum in church art, the really dangerous element, from the political and theological viewpoint, was the *human*.[144]

We have focused in this chapter on Caravaggio's images of Mary in order to highlight the role of visual perception in shaping religious practice.[145] His work displayed a visual solution to what late sixteenth-century naturalists like Ulisse Aldrovandi called "the defect of distance" by altering the relation between subjects and spectators. Caravaggio's Marian images rewrote traditional biblical narratives with often surprising, even scandalous, results. Unlike most earlier *Rosenkranzbilder*, for example, Caravaggio's *Madonna del Rosario* (like his *Madonna dei Pellegrini* and *Madonna dei Palafrenieri*) did not portray Mary crowned as a triumphant queen surrounded by choirs of adoring angels. Nor did they show a hovering, white-bearded Father-God welcoming her as she was borne aloft on shining clouds into heaven. Caravaggio allowed Mary to be a *woman*, real and accessible, a holy woman whose unique role in the history of salvation requires us to see her as fully "carnal, human, . . . heavy with a sense of sleep, sex, birth and death."[146] Caravaggio's work showed Mary at every stage of her adult womanhood (much as the mysteries of the rosary do), yet he was not an artist obsessed only by youth and beauty.[147] He feared neither aging nor the aged and did not hesitate to direct "loving attention" to "the old of both sexes."[148] Such respect and "feeling for the realities of age" was "something quite new for a painter," for even a master like Leonardo "had turned age into a caricature."[149] Caravaggio, in contrast, showed care and affection for the diminishments and vulnerabilities of old age. Thus, he could portray Mary as youthfully appealing while depicting her old and wrinkled mother, Saint Anne, with unsparing realism.[150] No matter what his subject was, Caravaggio could see persons as they really were, without cosmetic deception or phony melodrama.

Our purpose in discussing Caravaggio is not to argue that his work set the iconographic standard for Catholic devotional art during the decades and centuries after Trent. For it is well known that early modern (or Counter-Reformation) images were characterized, more often than not, by the "rolling eyes, bleedings wounds, and cherubs' heads on wings" often associated with sentimental kitsch.[151] Caravaggio's historical importance lay in his ability to challenge this Counter-Reformation "chamber of horrors" with "freshness and frankness," with a new way of seeing, an "unimpeded directness of vision that saw the person, or indeed the thing, in and as and for itself."[152] Caravaggio's art is therefore important for us not because his portrayals of the Virgin Mary prevailed over all other images but because he showed how to reframe representation—to reform visual perception and its relation to faith—in ways that were compatible with both the real world of history and the requirements of Catholic orthodoxy.[153]

3

Reframing Ritual

'Anqasa Berhan (Gate of Light), an ancient hymn still used by Ethiopian Christians in public liturgy and private devotion, begins with a series of ecstatic salutations that acclaim "our Lady and God-bearer":

> Holy and happy, glorious and blessed, honoured and exalted, Gate of Light, Ladder of Life and Dwelling-place of the Godhead, Holy of Holies are you, O our Lady and God-bearer, Mary Virgin.
>
> You are named the Good-pleasure of the Father, the Dwelling-place of the Son and the Shade of the Holy Spirit. O blessed above every creature, you replaced the heights of heaven, for you were the heights of heaven upon earth.[1]

Gate, ladder, dwelling, holy of holies, mother, shade, heaven on earth: a rich medley of Marian images flows through *'Anqasa Berhan*. While many of these are common in the liturgical hymnody of the Christian East, others are quite unusual. A portion of *'Anqasa Berhan*, for instance, links the name of Jesus (which begins with the Greek letter iota) to the number "ten" (also represented by iota) in order to make the point that just as God spoke "iota [ten]" words to Israel on Sinai, so God speaks "iota [Jesus the Word]" over Mary, and thereby reveals her as a new Sinai.[2] The image of Mary as mountain is found in other Ethiopic liturgical texts as well. A text for daily prayer on Tuesday evokes this image explicitly: "He who came down upon you [Mary], O mountain endowed with reason in humility, the Friend of man, was made man through you."[3]

These images from the Ethiopic *'Anqasa Berhan* show how Mary was sometimes imagined and addressed in Christian liturgical practice, for in ritual performance words function in ways significantly different from their descriptive or expository role in, say, scriptural commentary, sermon, and theological treatise. The imagery of the Gate of Light intends to evoke rather than explain, to expand the praying person's imagination rather than to define doctrine or defend moral principle. In ritual contexts, words are images and images words, a point Pope Saint Leo the Great (d. 461) once made in a Christmas homily to the people of fifth-century Rome:

> *It is not only to our memory, it is to our very eyes,* so to speak, that there returns not only the astonishing conversation between the angel Gabriel and Mary, but also her conception [of Jesus] by the power of the Holy Spirit. For Mary's faith was as marvelous as the angel's announcement. Today the Creator of the world came forth from a virgin's womb, and the One who made all things became the Son of one whom he had made [Mary]. Today the Word of God appeared robed in flesh, and what had never before been visible to human eyes began to be touchable by human hands.[4]

Leo's insight was that ritual words are revelatory and iconic, condensed symbols embodying multiple meanings that repeated liturgical usage neither reduces nor exhausts. Christian liturgy enacts mystery; it does not "reenact" history.

The ritual performance of texts thus shares symbolic space with painted icons. Both are evocative media that intend to open new modes of perception rather than to arouse discursive thought or propose novel ideas. Both are sites of revelation rather than occasions for speculation and debate. Ritual words aim to perform in speech what artists like Rublev in his icon of the Trinity or Caravaggio in his *Madonna del Rosario* tried to accomplish with form, color, figural composition, and chiaroscuro (oscillation between light and darkness). Ritual, in short, is itself a species of visualization, and iconographers like Rublev or Caravaggio were as much liturgists as painters.

We have seen, moreover, how Caravaggio proved it was possible to combine a painter's love of illusion and artifice with an early modern scientist's respect for nature. More important, he showed how intensely personal beliefs and nonconformist convictions could challenge yet cherish basic tenets of Catholic faith. Caravaggio was simultaneously "modern" and "orthodox." Nowhere was this more evident than in his two paintings of an event Catholics regarded as basic to their ritual-sacramental tenets, *The Supper at Emmaus.*[5] After John's "bread of life discourse" (John 6) and the synoptic Gospels' accounts of the Last Supper, this appealing story of bewildered disciples and a Stranger who share dinner after a long day's journey (Luke 24.13–35) was central to Catholic belief about Christ's eucharistic presence "in the breaking of bread" (Luke 24.35). Caravaggio's earlier and perhaps more dramatic painting of the Emmaus scene was replete with "illusionistic devices"—the cropped chair in the left foreground, the basket perched precariously on the table's edge, one disciple's lunging, open hand—dramatic elements that make the scene appear to materialize before our very eyes.[6]

Compared with earlier Catholic iconography of the Eucharist, especially Leonardo's *Last Supper* or Titian's *Supper at Emmaus*—where decorum reigns, at least on the tabletop—Caravaggio's portrayals of the Emmaus story were unsettling.[7] In his first *Emmaus* painting, a dead roasted chicken rests on the shining white linen that tops a sumptuous brocade table covering. Its obvious lifelessness is in vivid contrast to the youthful, unbearded Risen Christ, whose right hand thrusts so far forward it seems to break the picture's plane and enter the viewer's personal space. Still, Caravaggio left viewers in no doubt about what his intentions were. "The careful arrangement of food and drink and the absence of plates and utensils," notes Catherine Puglisi, "announce that this is no ordinary tavern fare but a symbolic meal," and Christ's powerful hand gesture may be construed as an act of eucharistic blessing.[8]

All this testifies to Caravaggio's orthodox, if nonconformist, Catholicism. It also suggests a connection with something we will study more closely in this chapter, namely, the relation between the early modern attempts at reframing representation we discussed in the previous chapter and the spread of Jesuit methods of "visualization" in meditation, outlined by the *Spiritual Exercises* of Ignatius Loyola and later applied to the rosary. These *Exercises* (begun in 1522) provided Christians with a systematic, monthlong program of prayer and meditation in which the use of the human imagination in "setting the scene" and contemplating Christ's life was paramount.[9] In a well-known passage of those *Exercises*, Ignatius advised Christians who meditate that "it is profitable to use the imagination and to apply the five senses to the first and second contemplations," which deal with the angel Gabriel's annunciation to Mary and the Nativity of Christ.[10] (These two events constituted the first two of five "joyful mysteries" of the rosary, though Ignatius made no reference to this devotion in his *Exercises*). Sight, hearing, smell, taste, and touch may all be profitably utilized: "By the sight of my imagination I will see the persons" (e.g., the Virgin Mary, the angel Gabriel); "by my hearing I will listen to what they are saying. . . . I will smell the fragrance and taste the infinite sweetness and charm of the Divinity. . . . Using the sense of touch, I will, so to speak, embrace and kiss the places where the persons walk or sit."[11]

The vigorous use of the body's senses united to the mind's imagination is in fact a hallmark of the Ignatian method of meditating outlined in the *Exercises*, as the "first prelude" to the second week indicates: "*The First Prelude*: A composition by imagining the place. Here it will be to see with the eyes of the imagination the synagogues, villages, and castles through which Christ passed as he preached."[12] Such imaginative "compositions of place" were not to be generic recollections but vivid appeals to the sense of sight:

> [While meditating on the mystery of the incarnation] it will be to see the great extent of the circuit of the world, with peoples so many and so diverse, and then to see in particular the house and rooms of Our Lady, in the city of Nazareth in the province of Galilee. . . . I will see the various persons, some here; first, those on the face of the earth, so diverse in dress and behavior; some white and others black, some in peace and others at war, some weeping and others laughing, some healthy and others sick.[13]

One can almost imagine Caravaggio himself practicing such methods while painting the *Madonna di Loreto*, with its voluptuous Mary standing on tiptoe at the front door of her house to welcome weary pilgrim vagabonds.[14]

Such ways of (re)imagining persons, scenes, and events permitted praying Christians to customize each mystery of faith, to tailor it in relation to their particular needs, and thus to inscribe it onto their own personal life drama and individual history. The result was a far more intense, intimate system of meditation that respected freedom and diversity in the way each person grasped and appropriated the central mysteries of faith. This is itself a remarkable development within a church that favored *disciplinamento* and control, and that routinely censored both artworks and printed books.[15] I thus concur with Catherine Puglisi's observation that the Ignatian *Exercises* opened up a way for people to reconstruct the physical setting and circumstances of the mystery to be meditated, but I would challenge her argument that such reconstructions were primarily "didactic" and hence foreign to the "minimalist, non-descriptive settings" of Caravaggio's art.[16]

Personal prayer and mediation were not, however, the only "theater of the imagination" inviting participation by early modern Catholics. The

Council of Trent not only sought personal "reform in head and members" but also had reasserted the primacy of sacraments in Christian life and mandated a reform of all the liturgical books of the Roman Rite. Our first task in this chapter is to examine how these reformed rituals reframed the image of Mary and tried to reshape devotion to the Mother whose "fruitful virginity brought forth the rewards of unending salvation to the human race."[17]

Ritual Reform

When speaking about ritual reinterpretations of Mary and the rosary in early modern Catholicism, two points should be kept in mind: first, that the earliest Christian liturgical feasts honoring Mary originated in the East and did not appear in the Latin West much before the sixth century C.E.; second, that the Feast of the (Most) Holy Rosary had not yet been established when the principal post-Tridentine reforms of the Roman Rite—the *Breviarium Romanum* of 1568 and the *Missale Romanum* of 1570—were published under papal auspices.[18] Obviously, then, the earliest images of Mary in the Roman liturgy were in no way connected to the rosary, though they *were* linked to those mysteries (e.g., the Annunciation, Christ's Nativity and Presentation in the Temple) that, in time, formed the core of the fifteen-scene cycle of rosary meditations.

The way Mary was imagined in some of the earliest Latin liturgical texts that do mention her unique role in the history of salvation may surprise modern readers. Here, for instance, is the text of a preface found in the old Gelasian Sacramentary and intended for use in the ancient Roman eucharistic canon on January 1 (*In octabas Domini*/On the Octave [Day] of the Lord's [Birth]).[19] The prayer begins, according to the classical liturgical pattern of the Latin West, by addressing the Father, through Christ; yet in this preface, the person being addressed suddenly changes midway through the text:

> It is truly right [and just, fitting and proper, that we should give you thanks and praise] through Christ our Lord. Celebrating today the octave of his birth, we venerate your wondrous deeds, Lord, for the one who gave him birth is both mother and virgin, and the One who was born is both infant and God. Deservedly, the heavens resound, the angels rejoice, the shepherds are glad, the magi are changed, kings are troubled, and little babies are crowned with a glorious martyrdom [a reference

to the "holy innocents"; see Matthew 2.16-18]. *Give milk, mother, to our food* [i.e., Christ our food]; *give milk to the bread that came down from heaven* [John 6.41], who was placed in a crib as if it were fodder for devout beasts. For there the ox acknowledges its owner and the ass [acknowledges] the cradle of its Lord, his circumcision and foreskin. For our Savior and Lord was also received in the temple and deigned to be embraced most cordially by Simeon. And therefore, with angels and archangels [and all the power of heaven, we proclaim your glory and say, "Holy, holy, holy . . ."].[20]

This preface focuses almost as much on Mary as it does on Christ the newborn Savior. She is praised as "both mother and virgin" (*et mater et uirgo est*); she is directly addressed (*Lacta, mater*), despite the prayer's initial invocation to the "Lord" (*Domine*); and she is urged to suckle the one who is "our food, the bread that came down from heaven" (*cybum nostrum . . . panem de caelo uenientem*). In the preface passage just quoted, the Latin verb translated by the phrase "give milk," is *lactare* (*lacta* is the imperative singular form of the verb). Both Christian and classical Latin link *lactare* to the intimate relation between a mother's body and her child's, since the word literally signifies that the breasts are filled with milk and so are ready to feed a hungry infant. The text speaks too about the animals present at the manger—the ox and ass that acknowledge their "owner" and his "cradle," his "circumcision and foreskin." That all animals are given the power of speech on Christmas Eve became a popular medieval legend, based perhaps on a well-known responsory from the liturgical night office of vigils (nocturns, matins) for Christmas: "O great mystery and wonderful sacrament—that beasts should behold (their) newborn master, lying in a manger! Blessed is the virgin whose womb merited to bring forth Christ the Lord!"[21] This text was kept in the office for Christmas Day in the *Breviarium Romanum* of 1568, and although it was not repeated at vigils on January 1, five of the eight responsories in that latter office focused on the person of Mary as *mater et uirgo*. One of these, *Nesciens mater uirgo uirum* (A virgin mother who knew not man), links the fruitful virginity of Mary to the lactation theme found in the preface of the old Gelasian Sacramentary: "A virgin mother who knew not man brought forth, without pain, the Savior of the ages, the very king of angels. A virgin alone gave him milk from her bountiful breast, from a brimming heaven [*sola uirgo lactabat ubere de caelo pleno*]."[22] Mary's body is idealized (a virgin who bears a child without pain or sorrow), yet is also represented as fertile, maternal, and nourishing (it pours forth milk from bountiful breasts). Bringing the human and divine together in close—even discomfiting—juxtaposition was a hallmark of the liturgical tradition we are examining, just as it characterized the art of Caravaggio.

And there is more to be said on this subject. The Gelasian preface quoted earlier reinforces a connection between Mary and the Christian celebration of the Eucharist, a link already established by the inclusion of Mary's name in the variable *Communicantes* portion of the Roman Canon, as found in the same source: "United in one communion, we venerate, in the first place, the memory of the glorious ever-virgin Mary, Mother of Jesus Christ our Lord and God."[23] This *Communicantes*—or commemoration of saints—is a standard structural feature of many eucharistic prayers (also called "anaphoras") found in the liturgical traditions of both East and West.[24] Memory is connection. So when gathering in response to Jesus' command ("Do this in memory of me"), Christians typically named many of the holy forebears, women and men, who preceded them in faith and now form a joyful company in heaven. In that communion of saints which, the faithful believed, the liturgical assembly joins when celebrating the Eucharist, Mary had pride of place and was thus named first. Even when variants of the *Communicantes* were introduced into the Roman Canon, Mary continued to be "first among the saints."

Thus, for example, at the Easter Vigil, according to texts provided in the old Gelasian Sacramentary, the priest-presider would have prayed: "United in one communion, and celebrating the most holy night of the resurrection of our Lord Jesus Christ according to the flesh, we venerate, in the first place, the memory of the glorious ever-virgin Mary."[25] For this same vigil, moreover, the old Gelasian offered a choice of two prefaces, the first of which (possibly of Frankish origin) is significant because of the way it connects the church (as mother), Mary, Easter, and Eucharist:

It is truly right and just, fitting and salutary. . . . For the most favorable time is now present for us, and the light of the longed-for night has arrived. What greater or better act can there be than to proclaim the power of the rising Lord? For today, breaking down the barriers of hell, he received the victory banner (most dear to us!) of his resurrection, and rescuing broken humanity from the envy of the Enemy he carried [us] upward to the wondering stars! O the mystical and venerable exchanges of this night! O the kindly, everlasting benefits [given] to holy mother church! [Christ] did not wish to have something he could slay, but desired to find what he could redeem. Mary exulted in this most holy [night] of her child; the church exults in beholding the birth [in baptism] of her own children. Thus that blessed font which flowed from the Lord's [wounded] side [became] the source of sin's removal, so that at these sacred altars, everlasting Life might confer life-giving food on those reborn.[26]

The preface examined earlier (for January 1) connects Mary with "our food," the "bread that came down from heaven"; this preface for the Easter Vigil sees Mary as an image of the church. Since baptisms were typically celebrated during the night of the Easter Vigil, the Gelasian preface draws a parallel between mother Mary, who exults in her Child's triumph over death, and mother church, who exults in the baptismal birth of her own children.

In his classic study of the rites and texts of the old Gelasian, Antoine Chavasse argued that this Easter preface belongs to the more ancient layer of texts that were eventually combined to create the sacramentary.[27] This does not necessarily mean that it originated in Rome; it may well have been a composition written or redacted on Frankish soil.[28] Nevertheless, we know that the hybrid (Frankish-Roman) forms found in the Gelasian eventually influenced the evolution of the medieval Roman liturgy itself, especially that of the papal court, and that the "old Gelasian Sacramentary" deserves to be included among the contributing "ancestors" of the post-Tridentine *Missale Romanum* of 1570.[29] We know, further, that the old Gelasian book already contained liturgical prayers for four feasts honoring Mary: those of February 2 (the Purification or Presentation of Christ in the Temple); March 25 (Annunciation); August 15 (Assumption); and September 8 (the Nativity of Mary). Since the titulary themes of all these feasts except the last one came to be included among the mysteries of the rosary, and since all four of them were incorporated into the *Missale Romanum* of 1570, it will be useful to examine them a bit more closely.

As Chavasse points out, the Roman liturgy did not adopt these feasts all at once or all together; they entered the tradition gradually, by steps.[30] Moreover, the old Gelasian Sacramentary sometimes showed a discrepancy between the titles it gave to sets of prayers and the actual content of the prayers themselves. The Gelasian texts for February 2, for example, are preceded by the title "Prayers on the Purification of Holy Mary," yet they make no direct reference at all to the Mother of Christ. Instead they focus on the Lord's coming "in our flesh" (*in nostra carne*) and on his presentation in the Jerusalem Temple.[31] In point of fact, Jesus' encounter with Simeon in the acknowledged center of Jewish worship (the Temple) gave the feast on February 2 its ancient significance: it was seen as an encounter of the Lord with his people, and hence was properly a feast with Christological—not Marian—content.[32]

Still, the eucharistic liturgy for that day would have included scripture readings, and almost certainly a proclamation of the gospel text from Luke 2.22–38.[33] This Lucan pericope includes the well-known passage in which the aged Simeon says to Mary, "Behold, this child is destined for the fall and rise of many in Israel, and to be a sign that will be contradicted (and you yourself a sword will pierce) so that the thoughts of many hearts may be revealed" (Luke 2.34–35, NAB). Readers familiar with medieval Marian poetry will think at once of the anonymous thirteenth-century sequence *Stabat mater dolorosa* ("The sorrowful mother stood"), a text that eventually made its way into Roman Catholic liturgy (September 15, Feast of Our Lady of Sorrows) and popular devotions (e.g., the stations of the cross), as well as iconography.[34] It became popular to represent Mary as *Mater dolorosa*, her heart pierced by seven swords (an obvious allusion to Luke's comment, "You yourself a sword will pierce").

Of course these later devotional developments were not yet in evidence in the old Gelasian Sacramentary, nor in the liturgical books as reformed after Trent in the later sixteenth century. Of the four Marian feasts in the Gelasian, two (Purification/Presentation; Annunciation) were based on biblical narratives, and two (Assumption; Mary's Nativity) were not. This same cycle of festivals—with the addition of the feast of Mary's conception (*Conceptio Mariae*) on December 8—appeared in the *Breviarium Romanum* of 1568 and the *Missale Romanum* of 1570 (*MR 1570*).[35] However, the Tridentine books made use of prayer formulas taken not from the old Gelasian but from the later, so-called Gregorian Sacramentary, a version of which (the *Hadrianum*) had been sent by Pope Hadrian I to Charlemagne's court at the emperor's request toward the end of the eighth century.[36] The Gregorian is important because its history and diffusion across Europe were important stages in the evolution of the Roman liturgy itself (especially in its papal form).

Like the Gelasian—but to a higher degree—the Gregorian Sacramentary can be considered an ancestor of the ritual reforms that followed the Council of Trent. For example, the sets of prayers used for Mass on the four older Marian festivals in *MR 1570* (Purification, Annunciation, Assumption, Nativity of Mary) are derived, almost verbatim, from the

Gregorian. These prayers are notable not so much because of their innovative images but because they express Catholic doctrine about the relations between the Godhead, Christ, Mary, and Christians with a high degree of succinctness and precision. *MR* 1570's opening prayer for Mass on the Feast of the Annunciation on March 25, for example, reads: "God, at the message of an angel, your Word willed to take flesh from the womb of the Blessed Virgin Mary. Grant to your suppliants that we who believe her to be truly the mother of God may be helped through her *intercession* with you."[37] The prayer's strength lies in its succinct allusion to biblical narratives (Luke 1.26–38, the story of the Annunciation; John 1.14, "the Word became flesh"); its clear expression of Mary's role in the history of salvation as Mother of God (Dei Genetrix; Theotokos); and its emphasis on her powerful intercession before God on behalf of those who pray. Similarly, the opening prayer of the Mass for the Feast of the Assumption (August 15) highlights Mary's unique intercessory role. "We ask you, Lord, to forgive the sins of your servants, so that we, who cannot please you by our own actions, may be saved by the *intercession* of the Mother of our Lord Jesus Christ."[38] The same focus on intercession is found in the prayer after communion for the feast of the Purification on February 2: "Lord our God, we ask that, through the *intercession* of blessed Mary, ever virgin, you make these holy and venerable mysteries, which you have bestowed to safeguard our salvation, an effective medicine for us both now and in the future."[39]

Because her relation to God's Word made flesh was perceived as inimitable, Mary was presented in these festal liturgies of *MR* 1570 as uniquely equipped to act as go-between in the often turbulent history of humanity's attempts to draw near to God. Her role in these liturgical prayers is precisely *intercessory*; she in no way rivals or competes with "the one mediator between God and the human race, Christ Jesus, himself human, who gave himself as ransom for all" (1 Timothy 2.5–6, NAB; cf. Hebrews 9.15; 12.24). As the *Communicantes* of the Roman Canon makes clear, Mary ranks first in the communion of saints because she is the "premier member and intercessor" in a worshiping church that offers prayer "at all times, in all places, for all conditions of people," without ceasing (cf. 1 Thessalonians 5.17–18).

Yet these are not prayers rich in images. In them, we do not meet Mary as the lactating mother of "our food, the bread of life come down from heaven." Nor do we see her as radiant image of that exultant mother—the church—who brings forth newborns in baptism at the Easter Vigil.

The prayers just reviewed from *MR* 1570 appeal to scripture, to Christian memory, and to dogma (e.g., the Chalcedonian affirmation of Mary as Theotokos), but they do not elicit a strongly affective response in those who pray. In short, these prayer-texts are ritually performative—for example, they express and embody the community's faith in God and its confidence in Mary's intercession—but they do not stir the imagination or stimulate the religious affections along the lines Ignatius Loyola proposed in his *Exercises*, for example. They reflect, instead, what Edmund Bishop famously called the "genius of the Roman Rite," the sobriety of its ritual structures and the terse concision of its discourse.[40]

And there is still another matter to be considered as we explore some of the ways early modern Catholicism reframed its ritual discourse. What emerged after Trent was largely a reform of the liturgical library for use by clergy of the Roman Rite; its focus was textual and clerical. As a result, the post-Tridentine reform—especially as reflected in books such as *Breviarium Romanum* 1568 and *MR* 1570—paid little or no attention to the role of lay participants in liturgical celebration. The *Ritus servandus in celebratione Missarum* (Ritual to be observed in the celebration of Mass) of *MR* 1570 did not, therefore, specify which parts of the eucharistic liturgy, if any, properly belong to the people.[41] It indicated that the priest-celebrant should be assisted by a minister or ministers (depending on the celebration's degree of ritual solemnity), but it was silent about whether or when laypersons present at Mass are invited—or expected—to say or sing anything. In this, the post-Tridentine reform differed substantially from that of the Second Vatican Council, which replaced the *Ritus servandus* with the *Institutio generalis missalis Romani* (*General Instruction of the Roman Missal*) and clearly spelled out not just the role of the ordained celebrant who presides at Mass (priest or bishop) but of ordained deacons, officially designated ("instituted') ministers, lay ministers (e.g., cantors, organists, leaders of song), and the entire assembled people.[42]

Even more critical, perhaps, was the fact that the prayers we have been analyzing from early modern sources such as *MR* 1570 (and its early and late medieval ancestors) would not have been immediately intelligible to persons with little or no facility in Latin—if, that is, the liturgical texts could be heard at all. For while *MR* 1570 clearly assumed that the eucharistic liturgy could—even should—be sung, the recited ("low") Mass without singing prevailed as the "ordinary fare" for many Catholics in parishes. Moreover, despite *MR* 1570's inclusion of musical settings for many parts of the Mass, for example, the variable preface and the Paternoster

(Our Father), the very heart of celebration—the *Canon missae* (Canon of the Mass) or eucharistic prayer—was recited sotto voce and hence would have been inaudible to all except those in immediate proximity to the altar.[43] The post-Tridentine books pay close attention to *Latin* texts and to the actions of the *clergy* during the liturgy, but they neglect or ignore other matters that readers today would consider vital—for example, the ritual role (if any) assigned to laypersons.

To say this is not necessarily to argue that early modern Catholicism's reframing of ritual ceremony and discourse excluded laypersons from real and active participation in the liturgy. Virginia Reinburg's research demonstrates that early modern Catholics, like their late medieval predecessors, developed their own, largely gestural language of participation.[44] Familiar patterned forms of social interaction that characterized public behavior also came to shape lay involvement in the church's public prayer. It is not a foregone conclusion, therefore, that lay experience of the liturgy in late medieval or early modern times was impoverished. Reinburg argues, for example, that in late medieval France laypeople had discovered how "to participate in the liturgy in a distinctive way—a way distinguishable from the clergy's more doctrinally instructed participation, but possessing its own integrity. . . . The mass meant what it did to lay participants at least in part because it was conducted in a ritual language of gestures and symbols they knew from secular life."[45]

A discourse of social *gestures* rather than words thus constituted "active participation" for many lay Catholics in late medieval and early modern Europe. The point is crucial because this gestural discourse shaped participation in both public liturgical prayer and private devotion. In short, ritual activity could be public and liturgical or private and devotional—or both. Such activity, moreover, not only treated words as images and images as words but also made gesture—bodily posture and performance—the key to participation in all forms of Christian prayer. Reinburg has shown that in late medieval Europe, prayerful "modes of relating to heavenly persons" were based on a vocabulary of bodily gestures derived from social rituals of homage and appeal.[46] Gestures of kneeling and folding hands, for example, embodied exchanges of recognition and reverence between patrons and clients, pledges of mutual service and protection, and "intricate exchanges of favors and gifts."[47] As our brief analysis of prefaces from the old Gelasian Sacramentary has shown, even liturgical texts sometimes incorporated vivid images derived from quotidian experience. Yet it was devotional language that was most notably "rich and varied in its use of metaphor," and the "best examples of this richness of language and social metaphor may be found in prayers to the Virgin Mary."[48] Nowhere was this more evident than in the rosary, which combined bodily gesture (oral recitation, beads passing through the fingers) with evocative images that implicated those who prayed in the very scenes ("mysteries") they meditated.

Considering the status of Mary in medieval life, liturgy, and literature, it may come as a surprise to learn that many sixteenth-century Catholic reformers seemed to move in the direction of their Protestant counterparts when it came to gestural symbolism and devotional language connected with the Virgin. It is of course customary in many cultures to use a language of humility and deference when interacting with one's social or political "superiors"—and even when dealing with peers. Standardized forms of farewell that stress service and obedience, for example, characterized letter writing in many parts of the English-speaking world until well into the twentieth century: "I am, madam [or sir], your most obedient servant" (followed by the correspondent's signature).[49] Such speech expressed and embodied a cultural system of patronage and honor that encoded basic social relationships in linguistic formulas. Omission of the formula (when writing a letter, for instance) constituted a breach or suspension of the social contract.

Yet not all cultures are written (literate or literary); some are oral, and this was certainly so in early modern Europe. In traditional oral cultures, as Kristen Neuschel notes, knowledge was "what people experienced; it was what had happened to them or what family or neighbors told them of what had happened in other places at other times."[50] The reframing of ritual within early modern Catholicism, however, was a largely literary enterprise that made use of the principles of text criticism and analysis codified by experts like Erasmus, whose edition of the Greek New Testament had become a model for humanistic scholarship. Pope Saint Pius V said as much in his bull *Quo primum* (From the very first), which accompanied publication of *MR* 1570 and sketched the methods used by the scholarly commission charged with revising the missal after Trent:

> Thus, we decided to entrust the required work [of revising the missal] to learned men of our own choosing. They, indeed, diligently collated all their work with the ancient codices in our Vatican Library and also consulted well-preserved or emended codices from elsewhere. In addition, they examined the works of ancient and approved authors concerning the

same sacred rites; and so, they have restored the [Roman] Missal itself to the original form and rite of the holy Fathers. We ordered the finished product to be printed and published as soon as possible so all could enjoy the fruits of this labor, and so that priests would know what prayers to use and what rites and ceremonies they are required to observe from now on in the celebration of Mass.[51]

The ritual texts of *MR* 1570 thus reflected the language of an elite, clerical (male) culture of literacy. By making use of what was then cutting-edge technology—*printing*—such texts could be widely reproduced, diffused, and, when necessary, checked closely against an "original" (*editio typica*). *MR* 1570 also redefined the Roman Rite as "a *papal* rite—papal in its origins (the liturgy of the papal court), papal in form and norm, and papal in its promulgation and regulation."[52] Post-Tridentine ritual reframing thus constituted a radical innovation. For the first time in the Latin West, a liturgical reform had been carried out by professional experts using the methods and principles of enlightened humanist scholarship; that reform was then imposed by papal authority on a *global* church that had begun to expand beyond Europe into Asia, Africa, and the Americas.

The problem, of course, was that this reformed liturgical library did not take much cognizance of the fundamental differences between oral and literate cultures. *MR* 1570 represented, in fact, what Jesuit scholar Walter Ong called "the technologizing of the Word."[53] As happened widely, especially in early modern cultures of literacy, the Tridentine library of liturgical texts was dominated by conceptual thinking that "is to a degree abstract."[54] Oral cultures, in contrast, "tend to use concepts in situational, operational frames of reference that are minimally abstract in the sense that they remain close to the living human lifeworld."[55] In these two systems, thinking itself "was a somewhat different activity . . . representing different relationships to human experience and human agency, and different relationships between the individual and the community."[56] In oral cultures, especially though not exclusively, "knowledge about the world and knowledge about oneself" resulted from "interaction with other people . . . interaction with a community and the judgments of that community"; in such societies the "self was a different entity . . . than it is for us."[57]

As already noted, *MR* 1570 was a *printed* book, as was *Breviarium Romanum* 1568 and as would be the *Rituale Romanum* of 1614 (which included rites and prayers for baptisms, marriages, anointing the sick, "last rites," funerals, etc.). Printing, however, was a technology that altered not simply "particular ideas" but the very way people think, much as our contemporary "information revolution" does. Both perception and thinking—and hence the construction of knowledge itself—realign themselves in response to print media. For as they give access to information, printed resources simultaneously *distance* us from *das Ding an sich* (the thing in itself). Printing thus "contributed to a distancing of an objectified world from a human agent who stood at greater analytical distance from it and less in [direct, physical] interaction with it," and along with "distance from the physical world came distance from other people."[58] The result was not just a new kind of "brainwork" but a new map of social relationships.

Reframing Marian Discourse

This last point raises a question about how late medieval discourse about Mary was reframed in the era of early modern church reforms, Catholic and Protestant. Early modernity was characterized by the somewhat uncomfortable coexistence of two social systems, one based on orality and the other on literacy. Traditional oral cultures did not recognize the self as "inward space" that could be probed by reflection, reasoning, and thought; supported by "physical privacy" and "mental solitude"; and expanded by access to printed texts.[59] Yet post-Tridentine Catholics and Protestants alike promoted a "modern" (and literate) notion of selfhood based on development of a "deeply internalized and personalized conscience" within each individual person.[60] "A 'modern' individual," writes Kristen Neuschel, "would have a larger interior space where emotional life would have an objective existence independent of action."[61] Such a larger, interiorized "self" could fall far more easily under the (Roman) church's strategy of *disciplinamento*—though Catholic ecclesiastics hardly had a monopoly on the surveillance and censorship of individual behavior, as Robert Kingdon's studies of the records of the Geneva consistory show.[62]

These issues related to the emergence of the modern self helped to reframe liturgical and devotional language about Mary, particularly in popular practices like the rosary. For the rosary, like the liturgy itself, made use of ritual techniques that combined word-as-image with performative gesture. Even though it was often described as a devotion for the illiterate—a "Bible for the poor"—the rosary, with its appeal to the devotee's internal theater of characters and images, anticipated in significant ways the emergence of modern cultures of literacy associated with novel writing, a point we will explore further in chapter 4. Of course, persons belonging to a literary elite that cultivated the self as "private, inward space" might not use words denoting humility and social deference in quite the same way as praying persons who belonged to a more traditional oral culture. In short, words such as "*mercy, pardon,* and *intercede*" began to carry "double meanings" within early modernity.[63] To call Mary the "Mother of mercy" (*mater misericordiae*), as the medieval antiphon "Salve Regina" does, would surely have "emphasized her power and willingness to ask God to grant pardon to sinner;" but what such language meant to a literate noble almost certainly differed from what it meant to an illiterate peasant.[64] Literacy was, after all, a marker that mapped social location. For a noble, mercy might have been a routine matter of noblesse oblige; for a peasant it might have signaled an unforeseeable, unutterable, and miraculous act.[65] Sixteenth-century clerics (whether Protestant or Catholic) were, as Reinburg observes, wary of language that seemed to make the Virgin Mary a bit *too* familiar, too accessible, too easily swayed or persuaded by her "devotees' appeals."[66] This may help explain why devotions like the rosary, which could be recited privately—*without* clerical supervision, by laypeople in their homes—were sometimes the object of suspicion by church officials. The *MR* 1570 prayers we examined earlier in this chapter may have focused on Mary's intercession precisely in order to tame, discipline, or "regularize" the potential excess of devotional language.

Prayers that arose originally within oral cultures—where knowledge is what people *experience*—manifest predictably different characteristics. The Marian prayer *Obsecro te*, copied in many medieval Books of Hours, provides an excellent illustration.[67] From the outset, this prayer signals a relation between client (the praying petitioner) and patron (Mary) that seems to go well beyond anything the more sober texts of *MR* 1570 would countenance. The opening words salute Mary with an impressive array of titles, including "mother of orphans, consolation of the desolate, the way for those who stray, salvation for those who hope in you."[68] The prayer's petitions are prolix, confident, and effusive in their praise of Mary, "fountain of pity, fountain of salvation and grace, fountain of piety and joy, fountain of consolation and kindness."[69] The petitioner asks especially that Mary "secure for me, your servant, from your esteemed Son," a veritable treasure trove of blessings—"everything good for the spirit and the body," fulfillment of "my wishes and desires," which are then listed in some detail.[70]

Such language betrays precisely the kind of intimacy and overfamiliarity that sixteenth-century churchmen felt compelled to resist. Significantly, however, *Obsecro te* is not simply a petitionary "wish list." It is also prayer as holy memory, for it lists many of the episodes associated with the mysteries of Mary's "fifteen joys" and with the rosary.[71] The Annunciation, Christ's Nativity, Christ's passion and crucifixion, the coming of the Holy Spirit—all are mentioned in the prayer, often in sensitive detail. Similarly, a mid-twelfth-century prayer, *O intemerata*, addressed to both Mary and John, the beloved disciple—"jewels of the heavens, two lamps shining before God"—probably originated within a monastic milieu and may have been known and recited by the Cistercian reformer and preacher of the Crusades, Saint Bernard of Clairvaux.[72] It appeals to the Johannine account of the passion and uses Jesus' final words to John and Mary from the cross (see John 19.26–27) as the basis for petition: "By the sweetness of this most sacred love may you be joined by the words of Our Lord as mother and son, you two to whom I, the sinner, commend my body and soul today and every day, so that you might be, at every hour and every moment of my life, inside and outside me, my steadfast guardians and pious intercessors before God."

The religious discourse of *Obsecro te* and *O intemerata* appeals to concrete, affective experiences of joy, abundance, loss, suffering, and bereavement; it manifests the immediate, almost uncensored quality one associates with live speech in oral cultures. Petitioners who prayed *Obsecro te* were trying to establish an intimate, affective, personal relationship with Mary, the "Mother of mercy," and they used "a repertoire of sensory experiences to create this bond."[73] This is not prayer that places experience at a dispassionate distance from human agents and the material world. Rather, it is discourse up close and personal, the kind of speech the reformed Roman liturgy of *MR* 1570 tried for the most part to avoid. So, for that matter, did most of the Protestant reformers. In fact, early modern popes, the Catholic humanists who worked to reform liturgical rites in *MR* 1570, and Calvinist members of the Geneva consistory all shared a suspicion of the "strict identification between the physical or secular and the spiritual" that popular oral cultures liked to make in their prayers.[74] "Sixteenth-century [Catholic] clerical reformers," writes Reinburg, "clearly were concerned about the transmission of prayer—not only from devotees to heaven, but also the circulation of knowledge about prayer among laypeople."[75] They insisted, as Calvin and his fellow reformers had done, on "*doctrinally informed* lay participation."[76] They also resisted as superstitious prayer forms that were "rooted in intercession, mediation, pluralism, and materiality," yet "they succeeded only in creating a new model of Christian practice, not in abolishing the old."[77]

For a majority of Catholics before and after Trent, then, the liturgy remained intelligible more at the level of ritual symbol, physical gesture, and word-as-image than at the level of cognitive and doctrinal content.[78] The church's rites were intelligible through a knowledge born of the body as it is inscribed by daily physical contact with the world and other people. The liturgy was also intelligible, as our discussion in chapter 2 has shown, at the level of visual representation. Altarpieces such as Caravaggio's *Madonna dei Pellegrini (Madonna di Loreto)*—still in the Cavaletti chapel of Rome's Church of Sant' Agostino—framed both architectural space and liturgical celebration. At Mass, such art formed a potent visual hermeneutic that guided participants' perception of what was being said and done at the altar, even if the priest's *words* were inaudible or unintelligible. Hence, even if lay participants (at Sant' Agostino's, for example) could not *hear* Mary's name mentioned in the *Communicantes* of the canon, or appreciate the doctrinal precision of the discourse that framed the church's understanding of Mary's intercession in the opening prayer, say, of the Mass for the Assumption (August 15) in *MR* 1570, they could certainly *see* her connection to the Eucharist being celebrated among them. They could watch her holding out to them—as she did to the poor kneeling pilgrims in Caravaggio's painting—her holy Child, "our food, the bread coming down from heaven." Their perception of what Mass means was interpreted by a complex interplay of image and gesture, of sight, sound, and symbol. Liturgy rarely works, writes Eamon Duffy, "by simplicity as such. It works by symbolic word and gesture, and it is of the essence of a symbol, as opposed say to an allegory, that it is polyphonic, polysemous."[79]

Ritual gestures and symbols thus follow a logic of the body rather than rules established by cognitive criteria or discursive reasoning. Rituals first arise as bodily response to a revelation (person, thing, or event) that requires us to both "harness and stretch existing and inherited patterns of meaning."[80] Duffy thus seems on target when he says that liturgies are not logically arranged syllabi but untidy "palimpsests which grow by accretion, by the overlaying and juxtaposition of layer upon layer of meaning and sign, which are often in tension with each other, and held together not by a single dominant explanation but by performance, by the complex of recitation, repetition, song, prayer and gesture through which we appropriate and enter into the web of realities symbolized within the rite."[81]

Visual and acoustic stimuli are key elements in ritual performances guided by the body's logic. Of course such stimuli do not always need to take the form of painting, plainsong, or sculpture. Yet "seeing" has long been a dominant metaphor for the way Christians encounter and experience the Lord.[82] Obviously, not every early modern church possessed an altarpiece by an important contemporary artist, nor was every altarpiece Marian in theme. The Contarelli Chapel of the Church of San Luigi dei Francesi in Rome, for instance, is decorated with two of Caravaggio's paintings of Saint Matthew, one depicting his calling by Christ and the other his martyrdom. Both are closely connected to the Catholic Mass, not merely because of their spatial location within the chapel but also because the *Martirio di San Matteo* (*Martyrdom of Saint Matthew*) shows an arresting image of the apostle—clad in priestly eucharistic vestments—sprawled and wounded on the steps of a (contemporary) altar.[83]

X-ray research on Caravaggio's canvas shows that he originally planned to paint the scene of the martyrdom in a conventional manner.[84] As his work progressed, however, he turned from traditional narrative interpretations of Matthew's fate (based on the *Golden Legend*, a medieval collection of saints' lives compiled by James of Voraigne in 1265) to an utterly fresh approach that incorporated three major innovations. First, he dispensed with a clearly defined setting and created, instead, a wheel-like composition in which the scene's witnesses seem to flee "from the murderer and victim at the hub."[85] Second, he painted himself as one of the fleeing witnesses, and while other artists had done something similar in order to protest their piety, Caravaggio seemed more interested in contemporizing the event, imagining Matthew's execution "in the here-and-now" by creating a "vivid scene of reality."[86] The painting thus became, in Helen Langdon's words, "the murder of a contemporary priest, dressed in a black, short-sleeved chasuble," who has just been celebrating Mass "in a dark Roman church."[87] Third, the painting's strong chiaroscuro (oscillation between light and darkness) capitalized on the "dramatic potential of tenebrism (darkness obscuring most of the light in a painting)" and seemed to thrust the figures forward across the picture's plane into the viewers' space, thereby making those of us who "see" participant witnesses of the "murder of a contemporary priest."[88] In sum, Caravaggio's canvas contemporized an ancient event, rendering it present through a magnetic sort of visualization that drew spectators directly into the action. This was a technique already foreshadowed, though with far less sophisticated methods and media, in fifteenth-century rosary picture books and in the Ignatian meditations of the *Spiritual Exercises*.

Caravaggio's *Martirio di San Matteo* thus seemed to say that participation in Catholic prayer and worship is not only devout but dangerous—so dangerous, in fact, that we witnesses may well wish to flee the scene (as the artist himself is seen doing in the painting). The danger comes ultimately not from assaults by harassing heretics but from *within*, from that emerging "modern self" with its increasingly inward-looking, self-conscious individualism.[89] *Martirio di San Matteo* thus blends, with consummate skill, the chaotic present and the heroic past—something the mysteries of the rosary also did, if the Christian meditated on them with the vivid imaginativeness recommended by the *Spiritual Exercises*. The mixing of past and present is particularly evident in Caravaggio's use of the "language of gesture and expression," since he appeals to older representations of Christian martyrdom (by Titian and Raphael, for instance) and, at the same time, reframes those representations to make a potent point about the contemporary meaning of conversion.[90] Matthew's executioner, notes Helen Langdon, "is a handsome Roman youth, his mass of dark curls bound with a fillet; but his pagan nudity, and Leonardesque savagery, dominate the picture."[91] Still, this muscular young thug with bloody sword in hand is linked, by his nudity, to the painting's foreground figures, who (also nearly nude) appear to be awaiting baptism in a shadowy pool nearby. The painting suggests that the murderer has risen from among these *baptizandi* (those about to be baptized) and that he has been apprehended in the act of killing the very person who brought tidings of salvation (the evangelist Matthew).

Caravaggio's *Martirio di San Mattei* thus blended ritual's preliterate "logic of the body" with harrowing images of a "modern self" who is drawn ineluctably toward traditional Christian symbols of salvation (baptism, Eucharist), yet is simultaneously (and perhaps murderously) rebellious. Such a divided self seems very modern—and it is. It is precisely the sort of self that Virginia Reinburg alludes to when she speaks of reforming, early modern clerics who sought to abolish "devotional practices rooted in intercession, mediation, pluralism, and materiality" but succeeded only in "creating a new model of Christian practice."[92]

New Models for Piety and Prayer

In the preceding paragraph we noted that Caravaggio's art blends both a preliterate, body-based aptitude for ritual symbols and the consciousness of an emerging "modern self," with its rebellious assertiveness and autonomy. As Neuschel has pointed out, modern individuals have expanded interior spaces "where emotional life would have an objective existence independent of action."[93] Such subjects have the capacity to engender truly "private," highly individuated psychological states that do not rely on self-knowledge gleaned from direct interaction with the world and other people. In short, such a modern self could create its own dramas within a private theater of emotions, conflicts, and resolutions. It could feel gladness or guilt, stress or relief, not because these flowed directly from interaction with others in the community but because they were an "inside job," the consequence of an ampler interior space capable of producing real feelings independent of actions.

Early modern Catholicism was certainly interested in the emergence of such a self and, as I have hinted before, sought to control it through a strategy of *disciplinamento*. In fact, religious authorities shifted the center of Christian moral life away from family, kin, and peers (where it was focused in medieval Christianity) and toward the private sanctuary of an interior, individualized conscience—a conscience that could be controlled through the church's catechesis and its sacramental forum of penance (use of the confessional box in the parish church, increasingly popular after Trent).[94] The focus shifted, therefore, away from natural family ties or kinship systems, with their own criteria for behavior and sanctions against "irregularity," to a monitoring *external* authority represented by church and parish. Church leaders had much to gain from fostering the emergence of a "private individual" who would willingly submit to *ecclesiastical* discipline and control.[95] In sum, early modern Catholicism was engaged in a strenuous effort to reframe religious identity.

The process of inventing a modern self required at least two fundamental shifts. It first sought to revise the way people communicated with one another face-to-face, since it is precisely this kind of interaction that "unites peoples in groups, . . . creates and sustains knowledge about individuals and things by means of public processes accessible to the entire community."[96] Second, it elevated literacy over (largely preliterate) orality. Technology boosted this process by making printed texts widely available and by encouraging abstract speculation that permitted "the distancing of knowledge from lived experience and the juxtaposition and recombination of ideas and data."[97] Texts, after all, invite abstract speculation both by and about the self. For, like writing, reading is "a solitary activity that fosters awareness of the self as an independent cognitive and feeling agent. It permits direct contact with the author of the text—another isolated, self-aware individual."[98] Neuschel cites the example of early modern essayist Michel de Montaigne (1533–92), who developed his abiding awareness of mental solitude and inner space by "keeping company with books" and by becoming a "conscious explorer of his private selfhood."[99]

We turn now to an early seventeenth-century example to demonstrate not only the shifts mentioned in the preceding paragraph but also the expansive "internal theater" that accompanied the emergence of the early modern self as it reflected on the mysteries of faith, especially those of the Eucharist and the rosary. We will see that early modern Catholic devotional literature helps map the progress of a "new self" using "new models" of religious practice.

Our example comes from the French Jesuit Louis Richeome (1544–1625).[100] Richeome was neither a philosopher nor a theologian, and most of his literary output consisted of devotional treatises, written in a simple, lively, imaginative style.[101] His interests, however, were quite varied, and among his works is a 1611 treatise on religious painting, *La peinture spirituelle*, which reveals Richeome as a keen and appreciative observer of nature. The section of this work that describes the gardens of the Jesuit house of Sant' Andrea al Quirinale in Rome recalls Gabriele Paleotti's fascination with nature, as well as the research of naturalist Ulisse Aldrovandi.[102] Like them, Richeome saw "no visible thing which does not ring forth immediately with the overtones of its spiritual resonance."[103]

Our attention here, however, will focus on Richeome's *Le pelerin de Lorete* (*The Pilgrime of Loreto*), published in 1604, dedicated to the French dauphin (the future Louis XIII), and translated into English as early as 1629.[104] Considered as a chapter within the larger history of the relationship between Jesuits and print culture in the seventeenth century, *The Pilgrime* may be read as a work written to educate and edify an urban elite—an appeal, perhaps, to the order's aristocratic patrons.[105] From another perspective, however, *The Pilgrim* takes its place alongside *Le peinture spirituelle* as a work "most representative of Richeome's spirituality."[106] It is "an open-air school of prayer" in which the author guides "pilgrims" on a journey of twenty-one days, after which they arrive at the "house of Loreto" (day 22) and begin a "meditation upon the holy eucharist."[107] After an eight-day sojourn at "Loreto," on day 31, the pilgrims begin their return, a period Richeome calls "the ten dayes iourney of Lazarus."[108] The entire spiritual life of the Christian is thus framed within a pilgrimage to and from a Marian shrine, "the house of our Lady called of Loreto . . . one of the three most famous places of the Holy Land."[109]

Richeome's *Pilgrime* is notable not only for its discussion of the relation between personal prayer and the liturgy of the sacraments (especially

Eucharist and penance) but also for what it says about the rosary and the mysteries attached to its recitation.[110] By praying simply and devoutly and by opening their eyes "on the *world*," the pilgrims learn how to "find God in everything," especially in "the contemplation of creation and in historical events," for contemplation is meant to be a "fixing of the eyes' gaze attentively upon each object, upon God's grandeur, and upon the beauty of the heavens."[111] In this, Richeome continues the tradition of "Christian optimism" examined earlier in our discussions of Philip Neri and his "Oratorian orbit."

The pilgrim's journey to Loreto, Richeome tells readers, is an allegory of the human condition, for

> all men haue euer beene, and are still in their condition pilgrims, and trauailers vpon the earth, as the liues and wordes of Saints do teach vs; and these whome we call in special pilgrims, to certaine places of the world, doe no more, sauing that they doe that of a speciall purpose and desire, which all mortall men do of necessity, walking to their graue, &, if they be prudent Pilgrimes, drawing towards their heauenly country.[112]

No devout pilgrim should set out unprepared and unequipped, for he or she needs the "light and heate of the Holy Ghost," and that requires "the most familiar, and necessary instrument of a Christian . . . prayer."[113] Richeome turns immediately, then, to a discussion of prayer, meditation, and contemplation, noting that "prayer is a conuersion of the hart to God . . . an eleuation of the spirit vnto God . . . a contemplation, or talk of the holy soule with God, a contemplation of inuisible things."[114] By the discourse of prayer, he continues, "my vnderstanding is delighted in the meruailous workes of God, my will is warmed in his loue, and . . . my soule taketh a tongue to speake vnto him . . . adoring his greatness, admiring his wisedome, magnifying his bounty, casting herselfe into the armes of his holy prouidence."[115] To pray well, says Richeome, one must "learne to meditate well; for meditation, and contemplation do illuminate the vnderstanding, do heat the wil, eleuate the soule to God, and ioyneth it to his loue. . . . Fire is kindled in my meditation."[116]

Richeome's advice about prayer and meditation is clearly indebted to the *Spiritual Exercises* of Ignatius Loyola, where the senses are an ally, not to obstacle, to growth in the devout life. And it is interesting that when he discusses the distinction between meditation and contemplation, Richeome uses bodily metaphors:

Heereof we learne the difference betwixt these two actions; for meditation is lesse cleere, lesse sweet, and more painefull than contemplation: it
is as the reading of a booke, which must be done sentence after sentence;
but contemplation is like casting the eyes vpon a picture, discerning all at
once. Meditation is like eating: Contemplation is like drinking, a worke
more sweet, cooling, and more delicate, lesse labour, and more pleasure
than eating is. For he that meditateth, taketh an antecedent, doth be-
hould, weigh, and consider it, as it were shewing the meate with some
paine, and afterward doth gather conclusions one after another, as it were
swallowing downe of morsels, and taketh his pleasure by peeces; but he
that contemplateth, receaueth his obiect without paine swiftly, and as it
were altogeather, as if he tooke a draught of some delicate wine: such is
Meditation, and such is Contemplation.[117]

Note that Richeome assumes a culture of literacy (meditation as "reading"), as well as the legitimacy and truth of knowledge grasped by interior
visualization (contemplation as "casting the eyes upon a picture" and "discerning all at once").

After a brief discussion of the parts of prayer and "iaculatory" prayer—
"a sodaine excursion, and eleuation of the soule ayming at heauen, pray-
sing or praying to God or his Saints, in short tyme, and in few wordes"—
The Pilgrime turns to "the Beades and Rosary."[118] "Amongst the Prayers,
and meditations which should be frequent and familiar to our Pilgrime
of Loreto, it is good reason to reckon the Rosary, & Corone (Chaplet in
French). For seeing that all Christian Catholikes doe vse it in the honour of the mother of God, much more should her deuoted seruant &
pilgrime."[119] Noting that the chaplet or corona originally signified a "little
band of gold, folded and doubled after the manner of a crowne or garland, hauing pearles set on the outside," Richeome observes that "the
name of Corone" is now used "not to signify an ornament of the head, but
an instrument of deuotion."[120] Significantly, too, he sees the rosary as emblematic of "Christian Catholike" identity, a point reiterated at the end of
the same paragraph: "The Catholic Church vseth them for prayer, saying
vpon euery small bead an *Aue Maria*, and vpon the greater a *Pater noster*,
meditating or thinking vpon the same mystery of the Rosary."[121]

Richeome's list of the rosary's fifteen mysteries is identical to the modern one, although he does not assign each set of five to any particular day,
since "the pilgrime may choose, in saying his beads, which his deuotion
shall like best."[122] Here we see once more the flexibility and freedom which

praying the rosary permitted Catholics dedicated to the devotion. More-over, the rosary was itself "a little booke without words or letters."[123] This "little prayer-booke of our B. Ladyes Deuotes in the Catholike Church, a booke more rich, and noble if it be well vsed and said, then the crowne of Kings, not only for the simple who cannot read, but also fit for the learned, who may find inough to meditate vpon that profound and meru-ailous salutation, and vpon those heauenly prerogatiues of our B. Lady, which are therein contained."[124] Reading Richeome's description, one can-not help recalling Caravaggio's altarpiece *Madonna del Rosario*. One of the painting's noteworthy features is its inclusivity. Saints, nobles, working mothers and toddlers, *lazzaroni* with dirty feet and grasping hands, *all* are drawn into the orbit of Mary and the Christ child.

Yet Caravaggio's painting was not completely successful, not only because it initially failed to find a buyer but also because the awkwardly drawn, blank faces of Mother and Child create "an emotional void at the heart of the scene, which jars with the desperate attitudes struck by the humble devotees."[125] Other viewers may have thought the artist was implicitly en-dorsing the view that the rosary belongs principally to a particular social class (*impoverished* Catholics). Yet *Madonna del Rosario* in fact depicts af-fluent and poor, saints and sinners, *all together* clustering around Mary as she gives the rosary. In *The Pilgrime*, Richeome's interest seems not to have been social conflicts among Catholic but apostates who "haue forsaken the Church, and waged warre against this Sonne, & this Mother, at the begin-ning of their pretended reformation." These "misbelieuers," he argues,

did mocke Catholikes for this manner of prayer, saying that this were to serue God by count and reckoning, and this, because al things are done without count or reckoning, without measure, or order in their faith. They shew by this folly, that they are ignorant how all that God hath done both vnder nature, and vnder the law, is done by weight, number and measure. . . . *Dauid* song praises vnto God seauen tymes a day: Our Saui-our made the same prayer with the same words thrice in his agony; these works that were done by count, do they cease therefore to be diuine? What then doe these good fellows find fault with, accusing the Catholike Church for that she prayeth, and honoureth God, and the B. Virgin Mary with the salutation of the Angell, and the words of S. *Elizabeth*, often re-peated, and by number measured? seeing this is to imitate the wisedome of God, and of his Saints, so to serue him, prayse, and pray vnto him, and his Saints, with a certaine number of prayers and prayses.[126]

Although Richeome's comments were clearly aimed against "those who haue forsaken the Church, misbeliuers," the rosary's critics also included Catholic humanists like Erasmus, for whom the principal problem of popular Marian piety lay in its failure to appreciate the absolute centrality of *Christ* in Christian faith and practice.[127] Yet Erasmus can hardly be considered a "cultured despiser" of prayer to the Virgin Mary. In fact most of an entire volume of his collected works may be aptly described as his personal *Betbüchlein*, much of it devoted to the *Paean Virgini Matri dicendus* (*Paean in Honor of the Virgin Mother*), the *Virginis Matris apud Lauretum cultae liturgia* (*Liturgy of the Virgin Mother Venerated at Loreto*), and a devotional commentary on the seven petitions of the Lord's Prayer (*Precatio dominica*).[128]

The printed *Betbüchlein*—a "little prayer book" of personal and private *preces*—was certainly not a novelty in late fifteenth-century and early sixteenth-century Europe. Luther had published one of his own—possibly as "an antidote to the popular *Hortulus animae* [*Little Garden of the Soul*] and other late medieval prayer books—and it quickly became a best seller, "running through nine editions the year it was published (1522)."[129] Moreover, the Books of Hours—containing, nearly always, the Little Office of the Blessed Virgin Mary—was widely used in Catholic territories both before and after the Reformation.[130]

John W. O'Malley is unquestionably right to point out, however, that Luther's *Betbüchlein* was not really a prayer book so much as it was a little *catechism* that had more in common with what English tradition came to call the *primer* (though English primers of the medieval period always included the *Horae Beatae Mariae Virginis*).[131] A look at Luther's table of contents will reveal that it focused on the "fundamentals" of "late-medieval catechisms and catechesis—Decalogue, Creed, Our Father, and Hail Mary."[132] Though O'Malley does not mention it, these very same elements constituted the core of another late medieval tradition, namely, the Bidding of the Bedes and Prone.[133] The bedes were a "body of intercessions, generally in some kind of litany-form," that resembled, in structure and content, today's "prayer of the faithful" at Mass or the solemn "general intercessions" found in the Roman liturgy for Good Friday. These prayers, which may already have appeared in the Latin West as early as the ninth century, were from the outset offered in the vernacular languages of the people. Originally, the bedes were bidden between the homily and the preparation of gifts and table.[134] Eventually, however they became part of the late medieval Prone, a vernacular office incorporated into Sunday

Mass after the offertory (now called "preparation of the gifts").[135] Prone included popular prayers (e.g., Ave Maria), as well as catechetical instruction on the Creed and Lord's Prayer, public notifications (e.g., ensuing festivals, banns of marriage), preaching, and announcements.

Both the Bidding of the Bedes and the larger service of Prone seem to have influenced the structure and content of Luther's first German liturgy, the *Deutsche Messe* of 1526: "First, the German service needs a plain and simple, fair and square catechism. Catechism means the instruction in which the heathen who want to be Christians are taught and guided in what they should believe, know, do, and leave undone, according to the Christian faith."[136] Luther then proceeds to offer questions and answers on the Lord's Prayer, Creed, and Decalogue as elements of such instruction, mentioning along the way that pastors might wish to "take these questions from our *Betbüchlein*, where the three parts are briefly explained."[137]

Erasmus did not simply reproduce the *Betbüchlein* or *Hortulus animae* genres in his own prayer books. In 1523, when his *Precatio dominica* appeared, and again in 1535, when *Precationes aliquot novae* (*Some New Prayers*) was published, he introduced innovations.[138] Following his own advice—namely, that Christian prayers should consist primarily of the words of scripture—Erasmus commented on the prayer taught by Jesus by weaving together a catena (a linking chain) of biblical allusions.[139] When commenting on the petition "Thy kingdom come," for example, he begins: "Heavenly Father, source, creator, preserver, renewer, and ruler of all things in heaven and on earth, from you alone flows all authority, power, kingship, rule over things hidden and not hidden, over things 'visible and invisible.' Your throne is heaven, your footstool is earth, your scepter is your eternal and immovable will."[140] Two sentences yield two scripture quotes, one taken from Colossians 1.16, and the other conflated from Matthew 5.34–35 and Isaiah 66.1.

When composing prayers in honor of the Virgin Mary, too, Erasmus could sound not only "humanist" or "early modern biblical" but also "late medieval devotional." Addressing Mary in his *Obsecratio ad Virginem Matrem Mariam* (*Prayer of Supplication to Mary, the Virgin Mother*), he wrote: "I invoke the sighs of motherly love, the holiest feelings of longing, the purest of prayers, the blessed tears that you, a mother who had survived her son, shed copiously on earth."[141] Erasmus imagined Mary reflecting, in her old age, on objects and events that reminded her of her child: "'This is the cradle in which he first cried as a baby,' . . . 'This was the temple where I found him with those who were learned in the Law.

This was the dining room in which he brought joy to the banquet when water was changed into wine."[142]

One of the most beautiful of Erasmus's prayers was the *Paean in Honour of the Virgin Mother* (*Paean Virgini Matri dicendus*), a richly imaginative text that applied biblical images to Mary. The *Paean* invites comparisons with the Byzantine Akathist hymn and the Ethiopic "Gate of Light" with which this chapter opened.[143] Like the *Precatio dominica* and the *Obsecratio* quoted earlier, the *Paean* shows us both Erasmus the humanist and Erasmus the devout late medieval/early modern Catholic. The *Paean* hails Mary in terms like these:

> You are the virgin who has restored the golden age. You are the true Diana. . . . You are the fertile shoot sprung from the stock of Jesse [Isaiah 11.1]. . . . You are the celebrated house that the Son of God himself, the wisdom of the eternal Father, the wonderful architect, built for his own use [cf. Proverbs 9.1]. . . . You are the new Eve of the new Adam [cf. 1 Corinthians 15.45]. . . . You are the mountain, hard as adamant, from which was hewn, without the work of human hands, the cornerstone that makes two into one [cf. Daniel 2.34–35; Psalm 118.22]. . . . You, a rose-bush of Jericho, have given birth to the flower of the field [cf. Sirach 24.14; Song of Songs 2.1]. . . . You are the holy city of Sion [cf. 2 Kings 24.10; 25.4]. . . . You are the mirror of life [cf. Wisdom 7.26]. . . . You are the new earth, so often promised by God [cf. Isaiah 65.17; 66.22].[144]

The *Paean* reveals Erasmus's extraordinary learning and piety, as well as skill as classical scholar and humanist biblical critic. These same qualities emerge in his own *Liturgy of the Virgin Mother Venerated at Loreto*, written at the request of Thiébaut Biétry, a parish priest in the diocese of Besançon, published in 1523, the year Luther's *Betbüchlein* appeared.[145] This *Liturgy*, though intended as a devotional piece, strictly followed the structure of the Mass (introit, opening collect, scripture reading, gradual, alleluia, sequence, gospel, homily, offertory, prayer over the gifts, communion, postcommunion). Like the *Paean*, moreover, it was redolent with images for Mary taken from the Bible but embellished with classical references. Thus, for instance, the introit (opening chant) of the Liturgy began: "The laurel gives delight with its aroma; it is beautiful with its perennial verdure. So too, Virgin Mother, will your praise bloom throughout all the ages. [Verse:] Draw us after you, Virgin Mary descended from Jesse. We will follow in the fragrance of your perfumes."[146] Erasmus's Latin version

took the form of a couplet in a classical Latin poetic meter (dactylic hex-
ameter), and his reference to Mary as the "laurel" owed much to Pliny's
Naturalis historia (15.127, 133–37).[147] The opening prayer (collect) of the
Liturgy deftly maneuvered through a thicket of Christological and Mario-
logical themes, showing the relation between Christ and Mary and her
special role in the history of salvation, but avoiding exaggerated doctrinal
claims:

> O God, creator, renewer, and ruler of all things, who are glorified, in-
> deed, in all your saints but in a special manner in Mary, the mother
> of your Son, and who rejoice in the glory brought to you by the innu-
> merable miracles wrought through her both in the world at large and
> especially at the shrine of Loreto: grant, we pray you, that those who
> with piety worship you in the Son and the Son in you, and venerate the
> Son in the Mother and the Mother because of the Son, may by heavenly
> protection be freed from all evils. Through the same Jesus Christ, our
> Lord.[148]

Here we see Erasmus steering clear of language that suggests Mary is
"mediatrix" or "co-redemptrix" with Christ, while affirming her powerful protection, her intercession, and the "innumerable miracles wrought
through her."

It is difficult to say whether an early seventeenth-century French Jesuit like Richeome was familiar with Erasmus's prayers in honor of Mary.
Richeome certainly saw the rosary or corona of the Blessed Virgin as itself
a "little prayer-booke . . . a booke more rich, and noble if it be well vsed
and said, then the crowne of Kings, not only for the simple who cannot
read, but also fit for the learned."[149] But the Marian prayers of Erasmus
that we have just been considering never allude to the rosary, even though
the *Liturgy* does mention "the innumerable miracles wrought through her
both in the world at large and especially at the shrine of Loreto." By the
same token, *The Pilgrime* appears to share neither Erasmus's often irrever-
ent humor nor his humanistic enthusiasm for classical models of literature
and learning.[150] Erasmus's *Paean* and *Liturgy* display a lyrical elegance and
eloquence that are not always evident when Richeome wrote about Mary
and the rosary. The Jesuit seemed more at pains to defend the rosary as a
devotion "also fit for the learned" and to deny that it is merely a religious
exercise for the illiterate. Furthermore, as we noted earlier, Richeome's
Pilgrime was dedicated to the French dauphin and, in fact, the English

translation of 1629 was offered to Louis XIII's daughter Mary (Henrietta Maria), by then queen of England (wife of King Charles I).[151]

It seems impossible to deny, then, that despite its character as a devotional guide, *The Pilgrime* was aimed at an educated elite. Still, even though Richeome's later works like *Le peinture sprituelle* reveal a man of considerable learning and culture, well acquainted with botany and natural history, *The Pilgrime* avoided Erasmus's humanistic embellishments (his allusions, in the *Paean* and *Liturgy*, to Virgil, Ovid, Catullus, Horace, and Pliny). For example, *Le peinture sprituelle* carefully itemized the "extensive Jesuit flower collection" in Rome, yet *The Pilgrime* clearly sought to subordinate learning to piety and devotion:[152]

> Let therefore not only the Pilgrime, but euery good Christian, as well the learned, as the simple, say his beades as often as he can in the day, assuring himselfe that his deuotion herein shall not be without reward in full count and measure: and let him also account himselfe much honoured, that he may so often pronounce those wordes, which one of the chiefe celestiall spirits pronounced to the praise of the B. Virgin [i.e., "Hail, Mary, full of grace"], bringing vnto her the most noble embassage, and most important, that euer was, or can be made for men: and he may hold himselfe happy that he may pronounce that blessing, which that great Lady S. *Elizabeth*, great of so great a Saint, vsed vnto her when she was visited, blessed, and sanctified with the fruit of her womb by her first salutation, and let euery one persuade himselfe that there is spirituall profit, not only in saying them, but even in carrying them at their girdle, or otherwise, as a signe of a Catholike, against the misbelieuer, & of deuotion towards the Mother of the sonne of God.[153]

This text, which concludes Richeome's chapter "of the rosary and the manner how to say it," is important for several reasons. First, it was a cultured man's warning to a literate elite not to despise a devotion whose roots are profoundly biblical. Second, Richeome saw the central words of the prayer ("Hail Mary, full of grace . . . Blessed are you among women") as pivotal to the Christian understanding of human history. Third, *The Pilgrime* recommended that each person—learned or unlearned—should "say his beades as often as he can in the day," and that profit accrues to the prayer "*not only in saying them, but euen in carrying them at their girdle, or otherwise.*" As both biblically based prayer and devotional object, the rosary has become, in Richeome's view, "a signe of a Catholike" both in the ongoing controversy with Protestants and more positively, as an emblem "of deuotion towards the Mother of the sonne of God."

All this suggests that the rosary was in the process of becoming a means by which early modern Catholics might fulfill Paul's injunction to "pray without ceasing" (1 Thessalonians 5.17). It is noteworthy that the rosary's origins are linked to the medieval Psalter(s) of Our Lady, because the ancient monastic discipline of psalmody—especially the practice of reciting all 150 psalms each day—was intimately connected to the goal of constant prayer. A recent study by Luke Dysinger notes that the early Christian hermit Antony the Great (ca. 251–356) became, in monastic literature, "the archetype of the monk delivered from *acedia* [listlessness, ennui, spiritual boredom] through a simple practice: he is to regularly interrupt his manual labour by standing briefly for prayer."[154] If one asks what this Antonian "brief prayer" was, the answer is almost certainly memorized passages from the biblical psalms. For during the middle and latter half of the fourth century, the "continuous recitation of psalmody and the rest of scripture during ceaseless manual labour" was becoming the norm in the monastic establishments of the Egyptian desert (a favorite retreat of Christian ascetics).[155]

It is also significant that early Christian monasticism was perhaps not as interested in *liturgical* celebration as one might suppose.[156] Indeed, the eminent Jesuit liturgiologist Robert F. Taft speaks of "monastic indifference toward the liturgy," especially in the late antique East.[157] His research demonstrates that some early monastics seemed to believe the "church's liturgical assemblies were meant for the laity," along with the clergy who served them, and that there was perhaps an irreconcilable conflict between the demands of ascetic solitude and "participation in the public, ecclesial action of the liturgy."[158] Hence, both men and women solitaries in the East often reserved the Eucharist in their cells and communicated themselves from time to time within a ritual whose basic shape and content can be reconstructed today.[159]

Even in the West, the early sixth-century *Rule of Benedict* spoke at length about the daily monastic *opus Dei* (literally, "work of God," meaning the daily Divine Office)—whose core was psalmody—but says virtually nothing about Mass, though it alludes in a couple of places to the reception of Holy Communion.[160] Later history, especially that of medieval Benedictinism in the Latin West, sometimes conveys the impression that communities of monks and nuns were established primarily for the sake of performing—and even solemnizing—the church's daily round of prayer and praise (principally the daily Divine Office and Conventual

Mass). That impression, however, is largely the result of a romanticizing myth promoted in the nineteenth century by, among others, Abbot Prosper Guéranger and the "resumption of the Cluniac *monachus propter chorum* ideology."[161] This ideology argued that monasteries (of both monks and nuns) existed above all "for the sake of the choir" (*propter chorum*), that is, their chief duty was the solemn celebration of the daily office in church. Benedictines, especially, were understood to be "professional liturgists" whose service to both church and world consisted primarily of praying for others by performing the church's official liturgy.

It is much closer to the truth, however, to say that monasticism's focus was on meeting Christ in prayer, especially through constant repetition of the psalms.[162] The purpose was both anamnetic ("remembering" by turning the mind constantly back to God, its source) and apotropaic ("turning away" from demonic temptations). In short, the "recitation of the psalms and other biblical texts was supposed to drive out memories of the past and replace them with holier thoughts," and thus the psalter became a "workbook" for the monk's "whole course of life," feeding him by a "remarkable variety of images" that provided "direction for human life in all its complexity."[163]

The rosary as Richeome promoted it in *The Pilgrime of Loreto* might thus be seen as representing an early modern retrieval of ancient Christian practice—that of uninterrupted prayer through constant repetition of biblical texts throughout the day. And yet by the early seventeenth century, this tradition had become "laicized" and much more inclusive than it was in the late antique world. *The Pilgrime*, after all, was written with a lay (if elite and educated) clientele in mind; it was not aimed primarily at religious professionals (those in holy orders or members of vowed religious communities). Richeome's work thus exemplified what Stéphane Van Damme has described as "the emergence of *scriptores* [writers] inside the [Jesuit] Order in France" whose goal was to "offer the urban elite a proper cultural environment" through their production of literary and scientific works and by making their colleges "public centers of knowledge."[164] Works like *The Pilgrime* thus belong to the larger seventeenth-century Jesuit initiative of creating an "intellectual apostolate" that could capitalize on the "culture of the print market."[165]

To say this is not to deny that Richeome's *Pilgrime* rightly belongs to the early modern genre of *devotional* literature. While it did represent Jesuit literary activity, and its author did belong to an increasingly identifiable group of Jesuit scholars and *scriptores* connected with the "intellectual apostolate" and book production, *The Pilgrime* was also a persuasively humane "introduction to the devout life" for lay women and men. In its pages, the practice of constant prayer was no longer perceived as the exclusive province of nuns, monks, or clergy but was recommended to *all* Christians in a form that was simple, portable, easily memorized, and conducive to contemplation on the fundamental mysteries of Christian faith. That form was the rosary. Richeome's counsel to "say [the] beades as often as [one] can in the day" was both an exhortation to ceaseless prayer and the emblem of a transformation that was happening to Catholic identity in the early modern era. Carrying Our Lady's beads on one's person was not only a pious practice; it became the sure sign of a true "Catholike."

It was not, however, the only such sign. Liturgical and sacramental participation—especially in the Eucharist—was also emblematic of early modern Catholic identity. It is significant that just as Richeome's interest in the rosary harkened back to the earlier Christian tradition of unceasing prayer, so his meditations on the Eucharist focused on ancient themes of unity and communion. In speaking of "the effects of this Holy Sacrament," in the second part of *The Pilgrime* ("His Abode"), Richeome wrote that the fourth effect is

> to *Vnite* the soule with God, and with our Neighbour, and to dissolue all enmity and discord; so teacheath our Saviour: *He that eateth my flesh, and drinketh my bloud, remaineth in me, and I in him.* An effect which did manifestly appeare in the first Christians, who receaued euery day, of whome it is sayd, that they were one hart and one soule. The fifth, to *Enkindle* deuotion, and Charity towards God and men, euen as bread and wine doth increase the vitall spirits, and heate the body.[166]

A prayer that immediately follows Richeome's discussion of the effects of the Eucharist, however, seems less intently focused on the theme of unity among all the communicants and more insistently centered on the personal, individual benefits of communion:

> O my soueraigne Lord, and sweet Redeemer, I behould in all thy diuine workes, and especially in the Sacrament of thy Blessed Body, that thy power is infinite, that thy wisedome is a depth, thy bounty a sea without bottome or bounds. . . . What shall I wonder at in this mystery, and guift? Thy almightinesse? Who hast so wonderfully changed this common and mortall bread, into thy glorious and immortall Body. . . . Shall I admire

thy wonderfull wisedome, which in the heavenly Table of this thy body, dost teach vs Faith, Hope, and Charity, Humility, Obedience, Prudence, Chastity, Fortitude, Piety, Meeknes. . . . And whereas other bodyes could not nourish ours but for a tyme, this Body duly receaued doth feed, and fat the soule with spirituall riches. . . . Shall I admire thy infinit bounty, in making vs this present of thy Body . . . for with the same Body thou gauest vs thy soule and deity, which are inseparable companions, and therefore in this holy Table, we haue a liuely figure, and pledge of the future felicity, which shall be to liue in heauen of thy selfe, and to enjoye the immortal food of thy selfe: what shall I then say of this banquet, O my Redemmer. . . . Do me, sweet Iesus, this fauour, thus to eate and receaue thee, and to see my selfe always drowned in the depth of thy infinite charity.[167]

We have considered Richeome's prayer at some length because its language and content are important indicators of early modern Catholic eucharistic piety, at least as it was being promoted to an educated elite by Jesuit writers in the early seventeenth century. The prayer alludes to the Council of Trent's famous formula about Christ's eucharistic presence (present in the bread and wine is the whole Christ, "body and blood, soul and divinity"), but shuns the language of substance, accident, and "transubstantiation," preferring instead to say simply that "common and mortall bread" are "wonderfully changed" into "thy glorious and immortall Body."[168] The language of a "substantial conversion" of the elements of bread and wine into Christ's body and blood did, in fact, occur in the Roman liturgy as reformed after Trent, specifically in the Office of Corpus Christi, composed by Thomas Aquinas.[169] But in Richeome's catechesis, at least, this more technical theological argot is avoided.

In a manner that evokes the style of Erasmus discussed earlier, *The Pilgrime*'s prayerful thanksgiving for the Eucharist is imbued with *biblical* imagery, especially that of Wisdom personified, for example, in Proverbs 9.1–5: "Wisdom has built her house, she has set up her seven columns; she has dressed her meat, mixed her wine, yes, she has spread her table. . . . Let whoever is simple turn in here. . . . Come, eat of my food and drink of the wine I have mixed!" Richeome's prayer, in short, is dominated by discourse linked to God's wisdom, power, and liberality, all of which coalesce in the gifts of the "heauenly Table," the "holy Table" whose banquet consists of "the immortall food of thy selfe." Such discourse is derived primarily from the Bible rather than from the Roman liturgy as reformed after the Council of Trent.

In sum, the reframing of liturgical rites and texts in early modern Catholicism after Trent has to be interpreted in relation to the reframing of representation we have been considering and the reimagining of devotional life as exemplified in texts such as Louis Richeome's *The Pilgrime of Loreto*. The "devout life" as it was being explained and promoted in the early seventeenth century—by followers of Ignatius Loyola, no less than by reform-minded bishops like Saint Francis de Sales—was certainly not "antiliturgical." In a prayer addressed to the Virgin Mary just two days before arriving at the house of Loreto, Richeome's pilgrim was to say this: "Perfect and finish to my good, O gracious and faithful Aduocate [a verbal allusion to the liturgical antiphon *Salve, regina*], that which thou has begun in me, and procure, that to the prayse of thy deere Sonne my Lord and Redeemer, I may cleanse my soul from all sinne and so holily bestow my dayes in this holy Temple."[170] After finishing this prayer, the pilgrim was to "heare Masse and Matines [lauds, from the Divine Office] of that morning."

It cannot be said, then, that by encouraging daily devotions such as the rosary, exponents of early modern Catholicism deliberately sought to loosen the bonds that connected ordinary lay believers to the church's public sacramental worship. Indeed, the "social miracle" of the Eucharist was, in the opinion of John Bossy, one of the great and enduring achievements of medieval Catholicism, and this achievement survived the Reformation of the sixteenth century, at least for a time.[171] Still, from about the year 1600 forward, decisions about the Roman liturgy began to be made, especially by the church's Congregation of Rites, that may have compromised the effectiveness of the Mass as a "social institution" promoting peace and reconciliation within families and social groups (such as town or village).[172] A case in point is the fate of the liturgical rite known (and restored today) as the "sign [or kiss] of peace."

The *pax* (peace), to use its old Latin title, was and still is a ritual greeting exchanged among participants and meant to signify mutual peace and charity (*pacem et caritatem sibi invicem*) before all approach Holy Communion. In medieval practice, this rite involved use of a "*pax* brede" or "*pax* board," an object made of metal, wood, or ivory, engraved with a religious image, kissed and passed by its handle from one person to another among the clergy and laity at Mass. Significantly, this practice began to decline in the aftermath of the Reformation, in part because the Roman Congregation of Rites began to treat it as "a form of honour due to rank to be restricted to the clergy and confined within the choir; it might be allowed to the most worshipful among the laity, to princes, magistrates and lords, but only by means of the pax [board]; it was never to be given to women."[173] What for centuries had been experienced as an essential sign of peace, reconciliation, and charity that transcended barriers created by gender or socioeconomic difference had slowly become a rite affirming the celebrity status of privileged individuals within the assembly. As a result, by the early eighteenth century, the exchange of the pax among lay participants was largely abandoned "because, it was alleged, of the trouble about precedence it caused."[174]

Yet the old medieval rite of the *pax* had been a vital ingredient in what Bossy calls "the social miracle" of Catholicism, its uncanny ability to unite adherents across generations by focusing on family and kinship ties. The decline of this ritual after the liturgical reforms mandated by the Council of Trent meant that Catholics had to look elsewhere for ways to express intrachurch unity. Receiving communion at Mass was one such way, but that practice too was in decline (in both medieval and early modern Catholicism). Trent, as we have seen, proposed the *parish* as the new center of Catholic unity, but this was to substitute an *institution* for bonds that had formerly been based on more intimate, interpersonal interactions. Within such an atmosphere, the rosary offered Catholics a new way to express unity without recourse to either official liturgy or sacramental participation (e.g., through eucharistic communion). It was a devotion that could be prayed individually or in groups, in the vernacular or in Latin (the church's preferred language of prayer), by laypersons or clerics, by women as well as men, by young and old alike. It was intergenerational, transcending barriers of gender, ethnicity, and socioeconomic condition.

The rosary was thus on the way to becoming an "alternate site" of quasi-sacramental presence for early modern Catholics. For post-Tridentine Catholicism had not only lost sight of the social role of the *pax* rite during Mass; it had also (perhaps unintentionally) detached the act of receiving communion from the premier rite of reconciliation (viz., the eucharistic *liturgy*).[175] This detachment took devotional form in what Bossy calls an "asocial mysticism of frequent communion," which separated the act of communicating from the liturgical celebration of Mass itself, making it possible for communicants to receive "before or after or outside Mass entirely."[176] The result, Bossy argues, was that the "socially integrative powers of the host [consecrated eucharistic bread]" were transferred from a specifically religious site—public celebration of Mass—to specialized occasions (e.g., the Feast of Corpus Christi) or to secular persons and institutions (monarchs, civil magistrates, local governments). Whereas previously, the responsibility for maintaining "peace, reconciliation, and charity among all" was seen as a primarily liturgical and eucharistic task (embodied in rites such as the *pax* and communion *during* the liturgy), it came to be seen, during early modernity, as largely a function of civil authority. Such a displacement helped pave the way for the exercise of modern statecraft, including the maintenance of law and order among citizens. Significantly, it also opened the way for other forms of prayer, especially the rosary, to be perceived as alternative, "socially integrative" media of presence. After all, had not Christ himself promised to be present "wherever two or three gather" to pray in his name (Matthew 18.20)? Saying the rosary—especially with other lay Catholics, whether at home or in church—was surely an effective means of securing Christ's presence "among his own."

The following chapter will explore these themes further by focusing on the reframing of religious identity in early modern Catholicism. We will discuss what kind(s) of religious subjectivity emerged in early modernity, especially, though not only, in Europe, and consider the role played by Marian devotions such as the rosary in the reshaping of Catholic identity.

4

Reframing Religious Identity

Rome is a city built on hills, each of which has a unique relation to Roman history—from its position as a Western "center of empire" in late antiquity to its role as "capital of Christendom" in the Middle Ages. The Aventine Hill—today a rather prosperous, upscale area—boasts one of Rome's most notable churches, Santa Sabina, a basilica built in the early fifth century shortly after the tenure of Pope Innocent I (d. 417). Its alabaster windows and carved wooden doors (featuring one of our earliest surviving depictions of Christ's crucifixion) are matched, inside, with an monumental fresco in the church's apse—a scene of Christ enthroned in majesty, surrounded by saints and lambs drinking from a flowing stream at his feet. Based on an original fifth-century mosaic, the fresco was painted by the artist Taddeo Zuccari in 1559, a few years before the conclusion of the Council of Trent (1563).[1]

Like the Church of Saint Dominic in Bologna, where the saint is buried, Santa Sabina boasts a long connection with the Dominican order and contains, not surprisingly, a rosary chapel containing a Madonna del Rosario altarpiece painted by the baroque artist Sassoferrato (1609–85). His depiction of the Virgin Mary holding her Child and giving the rosary to Saint Dominic will strike most contemporary viewers as very familiar.[2] Yet Sassoferrato's painting seems to inhabit a world quite different from the one imagined by Caravaggio in his *Madonna del Rosario*. Sassoferrato's Mary sits enthroned, clad in a sumptuous blue mantle and framed by fluttering angels. At her feet, a crown of roses and long-stemmed lilies (a symbol of chastity) lie strewn. There are no *lazzaroni* with dirty feet, no toddlers with sagging diapers in Sassoferrato's painting, as there were in Caravaggio's. The rosary chapel in Santa Sabina shows us a perfectly sanitized sacred world, formally composed, each element perfectly in place. Saints kneel, angels hover, flowers are ever-fresh. Mary is serenely seated as she delivers the rosary to Dominic and her son Jesus gives one to Saint Catherine of Siena. In the words of two twentieth-century pilgrims to

Rome, the whole scene is characterized by a baroque sensibility that is "rather ridiculous and embarrassing."[3]

A less caustic interpretation might see Sassoferrato's painting not as vulgar baroque excess but as an exemplification of the "precious and glittering" style favored by Counter-Reformation Catholicism, especially (but not only) in southern Germany.[4] Though Sassoferrato's theme is the rosary and his painting hangs in a famous old Roman church, he represents not only a new kind of artist but a new kind of Catholic, one whose identity is shaped, increasingly, by the "sensuous worship" championed by the Jesuits and by the vivid use of the imagination in the meditative techniques espoused by the Ignatian *Spiritual Exercises*.[5] The relation of such spiritual "sensuousness" to the image of Mary and devotion to her was exploited, as we saw in the previous chapter, in the work of Jesuit writers such as Louis Richeome, whose thought about the lively truths embodied in the mysteries of the rosary was shaped by the use of vivid pictures, both mental and material.

Reinventing the Early Modern Self

The reframing of reform, visual representation, and ritual was not, then, simply an institutional process that gave the post-Tridentine Roman Church a new public persona. Such a reframing, as we have seen, also signaled the emergence of an "early modern Catholic person" possessed of a new notion of selfhood that resulted from an expanding "awareness of the self as an independent cognitive and feeling agent," an "emotional and motivational center with a personal history."[6] The early modern French essayist Michel de Montaigne, for example, was "a conscious explorer of his private selfhood," a man well aware that he inhabited "a private space of reflection and conscience" that were his own independent creation; yet the self he prized was also the result of Catholic and Protestant moralists eager to foster a "deeply internalized and personalized conscience."[7] Conscience, after all, is a mechanism of discernment and censorship that can readily be formed, monitored, and, when necessary, disciplined.

We are inclined today to interpret Montaigne's interiority and self-reflection—his "detached, skeptical persona"—as perfectly natural and rational responses to a turbulent time in human history.[8] Yet this kind of consciousness might never have been possible had not both words and the Word entered what Stephen Greenblatt aptly calls "the age of mechanical reproduction."[9] Historian Elizabeth Eisenstein has observed that an early modern belle-lettrist like Montaigne "could see more books by spending a

few months in his Bordeaux tower-study than earlier scholars had seen after a lifetime of travel."[10] Nor did the advent of print culture simply make
more material available to readers; it also changed how readers perceived
and interpreted those materials. In other words, printing affected not only
access to information but hermeneutics. "More abundantly stocked book-
shelves," writes Eisenstein, "obviously increased opportunities to consult
and compare different texts. Merely by making more scrambled data
available, by increasing the output of Aristotelian, Alexandrian and Ara-
bic texts, printers encouraged efforts to unscramble these data."[11] Humanist scholars like Erasmus were quick to perceive the potentially subversive
consequences of mechanical reproduction for both the biblical Word and
Christian theology. Eisenstein summarizes the situation well:

> Contradictions became more visible; divergent traditions more difficult
> to reconcile. The transmission of received opinion could not proceed
> smoothly once Arabists were set against Galenists or Aristotelians against
> Ptolemaists. Even while confidence in old theories was weakened, an en-
> riched reading matter also encouraged the development of new intellec-
> tual combinations and permutations.[12]

Print culture thus helped an essayist like Montaigne develop an early, if
unstable, "cult of the self"—volatile, unpredictable, and very much at odds
with the "fixed norms and forms" of behavior promoted in other printed
books of the period.[13] Yet other early modern writers, especially those eager to enforce church discipline or advance politics and statecraft, were
hard at work promoting a conscience-sensitive interiority that fostered
consistent behavioral ideals for all classes of persons—clergy, rulers, husbands and wives, children, teachers and pupils, merchants and laborers.
Indeed, a new species of literature espousing Christian idealism began to
emerge and spread with the help of print culture. An example is French
Jesuit Philippe D'Outreman's treatise *The True Christian Catholique*, translated into English by John Heigham and published in 1622.[14] In the first
chapter of the first book of his treatise, D'Outreman appealed to Saint
Augustine—a good choice, since the latter's *Confessions* were arguably the
first attempt at self-exegesis in the Latin West—and raised the unsettling
possibility that we may not be who we think we are:[15]

> Sainct Augustin explicating the name of a Christian, saieth, He who ma-
> keth him selfe a Christian only to escape the fier of hell, and to come to

heauen with Iesus Christ, countergarding him selfe against all tentations, and not suffering him selfe to be corrupted by prosperity, nor beaten downe with aduersity, and who arriueth to this perfection, that he more loueth God, then he feareth hell, Who though God him selfe should say vnto him, vse and enjuoy the pleasures of the world, commit all the sinnes thou wilt, thou shalt not be damned, would not for all this commit sinne, for feare of offending almighty God, such an one is truly Christian. . . . Acknowledge thy dignitie, o Christian (saith S. Leo) and take good heede that thou returne not by a degenerate and vnworthy conuersation, to thy wonted vilenes and basenes.[16]

Note that the word "self" (for the Christian or for God) appears four times in a short passage that stresses the role of self-censoring conscience in achieving the Christian ideal. D'Outreman's brief exposition was followed immediately by a series of "examples," beginning with that pious prince, "S. Lewis kinge of France," who often visited the site of his baptism, and "was wont to say, that he had receiued more dignitie and honor in that place, than in any other in the whole world."[17] *The True Christian Catholique* then offered readers a short catalog of moral precepts: "Now to be a true Christian, one must first flie and detest all sinne . . . keep him selfe from swearing . . . lying, vttering dishonest songes or wordes. . . . [P]arents ought . . . be not negligent both to instruct and correct their children. . . . Aboue all, the sinne of Pride, Couetousnes, Luxurie, Enuie, Gluttonie, Drunknes, Anger and Sloth, is to be auoided."[18] After these cautions, D'Outreman recommended the "exercise of virtues and of good workes," including daily prayer "to inuoke the assistance of our B. Ladie," the frequent reception of "the holy Communion," and "a singular devotion to our B. Ladie."[19] These, D'Outreman concluded, "are the most necessarie points, to liue and die a good Christian, whereof I pretend to treate, through all the chapters that doe ensue."[20]

The True Christian Catholique counseled self-censorship and self-discipline in moral formation, stressing the importance of conformity to the ideals of Christian belief and behavior found in Christ and the saints, especially "our Blessed Lady." A soldier's consistency, "making profession to follow Christ whersoeuer, with his weapons in his hande," will overcome "the worlde, the flesh, and the diuell."[21] But for skeptical early moderns like Montaigne, the dissonances within human knowledge exposed by the proliferation of printed texts engendered not only expanded interior space but a troubled conscience beset by self-doubt and anxiety. The early

modern legacy, for skeptics like Montaigne, was a self simultaneously assertive and anxious.

Eisenstein is surely right, then, to suggest that print culture helped produce a double effect on the early modern self. The wide dissemination of
literature promoting ideals of belief and behavior presented life "in terms
which made readers ever more aware, not merely of their shortcomings in
their assigned roles, but also of the existence of a solitary singular self—
characterized by all the peculiar traits that were unshared by others—
traits which had no redeeming social or exemplary functions and hence
were deemed to be" of little or no value.[22]

In short, the proliferation in print of standardized ideals for human life
and activity added still another dimension to early modern self-awareness:
guilt. I do not mean that early modernity invented guilt or that Christians
had been blissfully immune from it prior to the Counter-Reformation.
After all, the Jewish and Christian scriptures are replete with references to
sin and guilt, and the canonical obligation for Catholics to "confess their
sins once a year to the priest" goes back to church legislation enacted at
the IV Lateran Council in 1215. Moreover, the use of this obligation "as
an incentive for the systematic interior monitoring of the individual of
his own life" was already widespread in the fifteenth century.[23] Still, the
post-Tridentine appearance and spread of the confessional as a private
site where penitents could unburden their consciences anonymously may
have contributed to a shift from the earlier medieval perception of morality based primarily on the *corporatism* of "objective social relations"
among family and friends to "a field of interiorized discipline for the
individual."[24]

This enhanced awareness of the individual's singularity was also
strengthened by early modernity's emergent print culture. Expanded interior space and a detached (perhaps skeptical) consciousness of oneself
as a private center of emotion, motivation, and history are also qualities
we commonly ascribe to cultures of *literacy*. It may be objected, then, that
such qualities are useless in situations where preliterate cultures of orality prevail. Indeed, the persistence of such a premodern, oral consciousness was one of the factors that led historian Jean Delumeau to speak of
the persistent "folklorization" of Christianity in Europe, even (or perhaps
especially) after the Catholic "reformation in head and members" that
followed the Council of Trent.[25] Delumeau argues that Christian festivals (e.g., Christmas) were "folklorized" not so much because they had
pagan roots (e.g., the Roman festival of Sol invictus) but because "they

were addressed to a populace that was in general uneducated, and concretized in a civilization impregnated until a relatively late period by an animist mentality" that warped the specifically Christian content of the celebrations.[26] Similarly, Delumeau maintained, the "popular mind" unconsciously folklorized Christianity through devotion to the saints.[27] Although they were meant, officially, to be exemplars of virtue and models for imitation by devout Christians, they became "and have sometimes remained up to our own day, almost specialized divinities in the cure of a particular disease or the warding off of a possible misfortune" (e.g., Saint Jude, patron of hopeless cases; Saint Anthony, helper of those searching for lost objects).[28]

Yet cultures of literacy did not exclude the illiterate (any more than computer culture excludes everyone except "techies" and "geeks"). As we saw in the previous chapter, it is quite possible for people belonging to cultures dominated by orality to think "literately" and vice versa. As anyone who has ever looked at a page of the Gutenberg Bible knows, print is itself technology-assisted calligraphy; words on a page are first of all *images*, and only secondarily ciphers for referent "meanings." It was one of the reasons why, even in the age of manuscripts, the liturgical Book of the Gospels (known as the *evangelarium*) was an illuminated ritual object lifted high, carried in procession, saluted with song, honored with lights, and suffused by an incense cloud of fragrant smoke. Christians believed not only that the Word was made flesh (John 1.14) but that the Word had become *writing* and so took its place among the world's proliferating images.

The invention of printing was not only, then, a *textual* revolution that could both delight and disturb an early modern skeptic like Montaigne, but a revolution in *images* that fundamentally reshaped relations between self and other. This revolution profoundly affected members of both literate and oral cultures in early modernity. Consider, for example, the connection between early print media and interreligious controversy. The "first dated printed product," observes Elizabeth Eisenstein, "was issued in response to a request made of Gutenberg by an agent acting on behalf of the defenders of Cyprus against the Ottoman invaders."[29] The product in question was an indulgence, printed in Gutenberg's workshop about 1454–55, a good sixty-plus years before Luther challenged their propriety in 1517.[30] Western Christianity, then, had already made use of print technology to define itself against a "hostile other" (the "Turkish menace") in the middle of the fifteenth century. Printers like Gutenberg were enlisted to help in the "crusade against the Turks," and church leaders "hailed the new technology as a gift from God—as a providential invention which proved Western superiority over ignorant infidel forces."[31] "Wars of words," even (or especially) after the invention of printing, were wars of images, and this point is crucial if we are to understand how and why print media shaped early modern consciousness well beyond the bounds of literacy. It is also crucial to recall that an equally potent source of images and image-making was to be found in Catholic liturgy and in devotions such as the rosary, with its repeated, imaginative review of the basic episodes (the "foundation narratives") of Christian belief and behavior. Finally, as we have seen, the rosary was closely linked to the Christian "triumph" over Islam in the aftermath of the Battle of Lepanto.

Vernacular Religion

It is important to recall that already in the late fifteenth century, print culture was both illustrating and promoting devotion to the rosary. Anne Winston-Allen's research demonstrates that the early rosary books were in fact "picture texts" that appealed to "readers" who were often unlettered, just as those who possessed and used luxury Books of Hours (prayer books for lay Christians based on the daily Divine Office and sometimes lavishly illustrated) sometimes were. For example, the book known as *Vnser lieben frauen Psalter* (*Our beloved Lady's Psalter*), published at Ulm and reprinted at least seven times prior to 1503, "was the first picture rosary, fifteen woodcuts depicting a sequence of events in the lives of Christ and Mary."[32] The use of images for narrative purposes was, of course, as ancient as Christianity itself, as the tradition of painted ritual spaces (e.g., the baptistery of the early third-century Syrian house-church at Dura Europas), calligraphic gospels books (e.g., the Book of Kells), and illuminated Books of Hours shows.

Even before the picture texts of medieval rosary books became popular, there seems to have been a connection between Marian devotion and narrative image, as Jan van Eyck's famous Arnolfini portrait (1434) suggests.[33] As we discussed earlier, this painting features a convex mirror surrounded by a wooden frame decorated with ten medallions depicting religious subjects. These subjects appear to be scenes from Christ's passion, death, and resurrection, a majority of them linked later on with the sorrowful and glorious mysteries of the rosary.[34] And indeed, just to the left of the mirror (as the viewer sees the painting) are two sets of crystal beads with tassels—quite possibly prayer beads (e.g., paternosters). But of greater significance, perhaps, is the mirror itself. Ever since Erwin Panofsky published his study *Early Netherlandish Painting,* symbolic and mystical meanings have been ascribed to it.[35] Panofsky believed the mirror represented Mary as *speculum sine macula* (mirror without spot or blemish), an image found in the biblical book of Wisdom 7.26, and applied in medieval liturgy and exegesis to the Virgin Mother of Christ.

As we saw in our discussion of Louis Richeome's *Pilgrime of Loreto,* the tradition of appealing to texts from Wisdom remained popular in Catholic devotional literature of the early seventeenth century. Yet more recent art critics like Edwin Hall dispute Panofsky's interpretation of the mirror in the Arnolfini portrait, in large part because "the *speculum sine macula* as an allusion to Marian purity was not current in the 1430's."[36] Moreover, the mirror in van Eyck's painting is not spotless; it is crowded with reflected figures, including the betrothed couple and an anonymous passerby walking in the corridor outside their bedroom. Thus, "the association of the mirror with the Virgin's purity or sinlessness arose only with a new composite iconography of Marian symbols early in the sixteenth century."[37] After that, in both Catholic theology and devotion, the "mirror without blemish" imagery "was appropriated as a symbol of [Mary's] Immaculate Conception."[38]

Although Jan van Eyck is usually considered an early northern European proponent of realism in painting, Craig Harbison points out that his depictions of Mary, with their "massive formality and regality," exude "an aristocratic or courtly ethos," and that the Virgin herself seems "drained of ordinary humanity in order to embody a social ideal of courtly decorum and presentation."[39] As we have seen, this tradition of Marian imagery was significantly reframed by early baroque painters like Caravaggio and the Carracci at the beginning of the seventeenth century. Caravaggio's Madonnas are notably unregal; not even his *Madonna del Rosario* wears a crown. What did continue even in baroque art, however, was the tradition of devotional images of Mary as objects of individual worship and prayer. Moreover, the focus shifted, as it did in Caravaggio's *Madonna di Loreto* and *Madonna del Rosario,* to a woman who "stoops to conquer," whose grandeur is revealed not by the accoutrements of wealth but by loving care for the *lazzaroni* who crowd about her.

The point in relating the visual and imagistic impact of print media to the reframing of Marian iconography is to show that the invention of printing did not replace visuality with texts or concreteness with abstraction. It may very well be true, as noted earlier in this chapter, that the ever-increasing availability of texts in the early modern era "encouraged abstract speculation by permitting the distancing of knowledge from lived experience," and that literacy favored "abstract speculation about the self" through the very act of reading.[40] But from another perspective, printed books simply gave early modern viewers more pictures to look at—*portable* pictures that made the self-aware individual's expanding inner space a screen on which to project images that the page encoded as abstract black lines.

In other words, the technology of printing, coupled with the early modern individual's expanding interiority, *heightened* rather than diminished the visual potential of *all* texts, including sacred and devotional ones. Within such a climate, the boundary between cultures of orality and cultures of literacy became far more fluid and porous than it had been before. Chances are a majority of theatergoers who saw and heard Shakespeare's plays at the Globe in early seventeenth-century England did not belong to a literate intelligentsia; their primary culture was an *oral* one. But they were not rude fools. They seemed quite capable of following and appreciating drama that was verbally and emotionally complex, and of a very "elevated" artistic caliber. It seems absurd to think they found *King Lear* or *A Midsummer Night's Dream* appealing simply because they featured folkloric elements (witches and fairies).

For similar reasons, Jean Delumeau's characterization of post-Tridentine Catholicism in Europe as "folklorized" is problematic. Almost inevitably such descriptions suggest that what unlettered, religious nonprofessionals say or do is innately inferior to the more "normative" and "nuanced" beliefs and behaviors of the literate. Perhaps a more useful category than "folklorization" is "vernacular religion," a phrase that focuses primarily on how adherents *practice* their religious faith, whether they are educated or unlettered, male or female, rural or urban, rich or poor. "Vernacular religion" does not deny that there are significant differences between the practices of, say, the rural poor and educated elites, nor does it exclude women's voices and paper over real conflicts and divisions. It fundamentally endorses David Aers's argument about late medieval Catholicism in England—that "Christian tradition and Christian orthodoxy" were the result of "complex processes involving social, political, and military networks."[41]

The category of vernacular religion thus has the merit of embracing a wide diversity of practice without reducing individual differences to an

artificial religious or cultural "type." It makes room for what Louis Chatellier calls "the religion of the poor" (depicted powerfully in Caravaggio's
Madonna di Loreto), for the prayers and meditations of devout but criti-
cally self-aware humanists (e.g., Erasmus), and for the almost hallucinatory speculations of religious visionaries with minds of their own (e.g.,
the seventeenth-century Spanish nun Mary of Ágreda).[42] It also avoids
reducing popular religious practices—for example, saying the rosary or
making the stations of the cross—to the status of a "parallel universe" that
exists apart from, and even in opposition to, officially approved beliefs
and behaviors.

For in point of fact, vernacular religion has itself contributed powerfully to the development of doctrine, devotion, and ritual within the Roman Catholic Church. Chatellier cites the example of the feast of the Sacred Heart, for which Pope Clement XIII gave limited authorization (to
the Polish bishops and to the Roman Archconfraternity of the Sacred
Heart) in 1765.[43] Promoted especially by the Jesuits, though its roots lie
in the writings of medieval women mystics such as Mechtild of Magde-
burg and Gertrude of Helfta, devotion to the heart and humanity of Jesus
focused on "a God close at hand," a God whose immense love for human beings could never permit "their destruction, their damnation."[44]
More "enlightened" Christians were prone to regard practices based on
devotional attention to a body part (even if Christ's) as aberrant. In 1731,
in fact, a writer in the Jansenist periodical *Nouvelles ecclésiastiques* fumed
that the Jesuits exalt this devotion "above that of the Blessed Sacrament
[Eucharist], assuring salvation for those who communicate or sacrifice,
on that day, to *this* Sacred Heart, in their Church."[45] Despite such objections—and despite the fact that the Jesuits themselves were suppressed by
Pope Clement XIV in 1773—devotion to the Sacred Heart not only survived but flourished. Pope Pius IX made it a feast for the whole church in
1856, and his successor, Pope Leo XIII, went so far as to "consecrate" all
humanity to the Sacred Heart in 1889.

Devotion to the Sacred Heart illustrates my point about how vernacular religion contributed to church doctrine, liturgy, and theology—often
to such an extent that what enlightened elites regarded as suspect or retrograde came to be seen as an essential ingredient of Catholic orthodoxy
and praxis. In his essay "Behold This Heart!," twentieth-century German
theologian Karl Rahner (d. 1984) used the notion of "primordial word"
(*Urwort*) to uncover the deeper significance of this devotion among Catholic people.[46] "There are words," wrote Rahner, "which divide and words

which unite; words which explain the whole by breaking it up, and words
which at once conjure up that whole and produce it in the listening person (not only in his intellect)."[47] These latter words, Rahner argued, do
not "define" or "explain"; they create bonds between us and God and arrive in our midst as a gift. Among such words is "heart." By applying this
word to God, Christians affirm that what is most profound, unique, and
interior to human beings also belongs to God's own life:

> In primordial words of this kind, spirit and flesh, meaning and its sym-
> bol, concept and word, object and images are still originally one (which
> does not mean they are simply the same). Blossom, night, star and day,
> root and source, wind and laughter, rose, blood and earth, boy, smoke,
> word, kiss, lightning, breath, stillness: these and a thousand other words
> of the original thinkers and of the poets are primordial words . . . more
> profound and more true than the worn-out verbal coins of daily intel-
> lectual exchange which one often likes to call "clear concepts." In each
> of such primordial words a piece of reality is connoted, in which a door
> is mysteriously opened into the unfathomable depths of true reality in
> general; it is a word in which the transition from the individual to the
> infinite, in which infinite movement is already part of the content of the
> word itself. . . . Such a word is "heart."[48]

Rahner recognized, of course, that the discourse of devotion could
sometimes become theologically imprecise, unrefined, and intemperate.
Take, for instance, an early modern prayer to the Sacred Heart of Jesus
entitled "Actus reparationis et consecrationis" (Act of reparation and consecration), still found in a 1950 edition of the Vatican Press's *Enchiridion
indulgentiarum* (*Handbook of Indulgences*).[49] The prayer laments the daily
"contempt, ingratitude, blasphemies, insults, outrages, and negligences"
directed against God, the saints, and the church (especially its leaders),
and goes on to say:

> Would that we could wash away such crimes with our own blood! Mean-
> while, to make reparation for the divine honor that has been violated,
> we offer you the very satisfaction you once offered to your Father on the
> cross and which you continue to renew daily on [your] altars. We offer
> it in union with the expiations of your Virgin Mother, of all the saints,
> and of the devout faithful. We sincerely promise to make recompense,
> as far as we are able with the help of your grace, for all the injuries and

negligence against such great love that our own past sins and those of others have caused.[50]

Commenting on the language of this prayer (still posted on many "traditionalist" Catholic Web sites), Rahner noted that what may be theologically defensible is not always "religio-pedagogically" advisable.[51] The language of prayer in the Christian's daily life, he notes, "should be not merely dogmatically correct, but also as simple and comprehensible as possible," so that the basic "lines and fundamental perspectives" of Catholic faith (outlined, e.g., in the Creed said every Sunday at Mass) are neither obscured nor obliterated.[52] He notes, for instance, that while it is dogmatically correct in Catholic theology to say that the human man Jesus (God's Word made flesh) can and does pray to God's eternal Word, it is nevertheless entirely "out of place in everyday speech to talk of Jesus praying to himself."[53]

Rahner's words offer astute guidelines for gauging the theological adequacy of devotional texts. But our principal purpose here is not to defend or deny the theological acumen of such prayers but to understand their *popularity*. We have been discussing the emergence of the early modern self, with its expanding inner space, its self-awareness as an independent cognitive and feeling agent, its self-perception as an emotional and motivational center with a personal history. Louis Chatellier makes the perceptive observation that by opening itself to devotions like the Sacred Heart, the Roman Church was opening itself to the full range of human affectivity, including its sometimes intemperate language and emotionality.[54] In fact, of course, Christians had been doing this almost from the beginning through their use, in both public and private prayer, of the psalms of the Hebrew Bible. These biblical poems are a complex record of human emotions, ranging from sorrow, despair, violence, and almost paranoid fear to gladness and ecstatic jubilation. They chronicle not only serenity and gratitude (e.g., Psalm 133) but sudden and dramatic mood swings as well (e.g., Psalm 22). By continuing to recognize the legitimacy of such emotionally charged language and welcoming its use in prayer, early modern Catholicism opened the door to the possibility that a "new image of the Church" might emerge.[55]

That new ecclesial image made room for the beliefs and practices of what I call vernacular religion precisely because, during the seventeenth and eighteenth centuries, pastoral outreach to *lay* Catholics, especially laborers, greatly intensified. As we have seen, initiatives of this kind had been launched in Rome near the end of the sixteenth century by Philip Neri and the Oratorians at the Church of San Girolamo, where new styles of preaching (*sermo humilis*) and improvisatory catechesis (*ragionamento*) prevailed. Neri's Oratory was a meeting for prayer, scripture reading, and free-wheeling discussion—often on the streets or out in the open—rather than in a designated place or institution. The speakers at Neri's *ragionamenti* were largely laymen. Their "speaking on the book" (*ragionamento sopra il libro*) was improvised and charismatic, uttered spontaneously *in spiritu et veritate et simpliciate cordis* (in spirit and truth and simplicity of heart), rather than as a result of "profound study, premeditation," or scholastic analysis in the mode of university professors like those from the Sorbonne.[56]

Neri and his colleagues recognized that Europe itself had become mission territory for the Roman Church, and this recognition continued to shape the work of priests like Alphonsus de Ligouri a century and a quarter later. Ligouri's *cappelle serotine* (evening chapels), begun in Naples in 1727, were similar to Neri's Oratory and *ragionamenti*.[57] Both sought to develop the "inward life" of *lay* Catholics through prayer, study, and conversation. The "chapels" were not religious sites but places of work or recreation, such as "a barber's shop or an inn."[58] There, workers and tradesmen gathered of an evening to learn how to pray under the guidance of a layperson. Typically, they began "by reciting the rosary" and other familiar prayers, after which the lay leader gave a homiletic lecture on a gospel text, catechism lesson, or subject related to Catholic practice, for example, the Eucharist or veneration of the Virgin Mary).[59]

Devotion to the rosary, an emphasis on eucharistic piety and the reception of Holy Communion, devotion to the Sacred Heart, and beliefs about the unique prerogatives of the Virgin Mary in the history of salvation became, in fact, central themes of vernacular religion within early modern Catholicism. This was not, perhaps, quite the "new image of church" humanist reformers like Erasmus had hoped for at the beginning of the sixteenth century. As we have discussed, Erasmus sought a renewal of Catholic piety that was devout but shaped by humanist scholarship, a devotionalism classically eloquent but fluent in the speech of scripture. He was, as Hilmar M. Pabel observes, a person whose piety represents a unique "confluence of humanism and Catholicism."[60] John W. O'Malley suggests that Erasmus favored a *rhetorical* (not a scholastic) theology in the mode of the Bible and church fathers, whose chief intent was to persuade and enlighten, to "cultivate a sense of divine mystery," and to promote "peace and concord among all people of good will."⁶¹

This Erasmian approach to theology certainly contributed to early modern Catholicism (and, in the twentieth century, to the theology of the Second Vatican Council), but it would be difficult to argue that Erasmus became the dominant force in what Chatellier calls the formation of a modern "Catholic ideology."⁶² That force, I contend, was vernacular religion and its "new practices."⁶³ Among these new practices was the Pactum Marianum (Marian Pact), which seems to have originated in Lucerne about the middle of the seventeenth century.⁶⁴ The purpose of these religious pacts was to renew or strengthen bonds among members of a sodality or confraternity. Each participant pledged to have a Mass said whenever any other member died, so that there would be as many Masses offered for the deceased person as there were living persons in the pact. "Services for the dead," writes Chatellier, "constituted their main preoccupation."⁶⁵ Yet these pacts were not obsessed by morbidity and death. Their idea was to strengthen Catholic identity and social bonding by caring for other members at moments of family crisis or great personal stress. In pursuing this goal, the Pactum Marianum represented another aspect of what Bossy calls the "social miracle" of Catholicism. Eventually the popularity of these devout associations declined, and many of them disappeared. Yet what was left in their wake was not necessarily a failed mission and a "de-Christianized" Europe but the roots of a distinctively "Catholic society" for which early modern laypeople and associations (sodalities, confraternities, the Pactum Marianum) had laid the groundwork. "At the heart of the old Christianity," writes Chatellier, "a Catholic society was born, in whose formation the Marian congregations had played a major role."⁶⁶ So while membership in these congregations may have declined, many of their practices—including recitation of the rosary—became staples of European Catholic piety.

Vernacular religion did not, of course, erase "Counter-Reformation" Catholic identity—with its emphasis on *disciplinamento*, rigid control of belief and behavior, "reform in head and members," doctrinal orthodoxy, and ritual conformity—but it did alter and adapt "institutions and devotional groups" in the hope of transforming society more from the ground up rather than from the top down.⁶⁷ A checklist of characteristics found in vernacular religion and the early modern Catholic identity it reframed would include the following items:

First, "the project conceived after the Council of Trent by devout men [e.g., Philip Neri]" to (re)establish a Christian Europe on a new basis gradually shifted attention away from clerical life and morals to *lay* Catholics and their "interior lives."[68] This focus on laypeople's interiority (grounded in an expanded personal self-awareness) has to be seen in relation to Christianity's larger institutional agendas. For as we saw, both Catholic and Protestant leaders after Trent saw an opportunity to reinforce "correct" belief and impose conformity in moral behavior through technologies of control (e.g., use of the confessional in post-Tridentine Catholicism) and surveillance (e.g., the Geneva consistory's monitoring of the behavior of Reformed Christians in that city).[69] Vernacular religion may have drawn its energy from the grass roots, but it was closely monitored by church authorities.

Second, the goal of vernacular religion was to "reform the world," but to do this "it was necessary to *adapt* to it."[70] This motif was already present in the activity of new religious orders after Trent, such as the Jesuits, whose project was to reshape all aspects of human life and endeavor: education, cultures, sciences, and the arts.[71] Yet it became clear that another—and *nonclerical*—strategy was needed if such a social and cultural adaptation were to succeed: it was by good example and the word of others (spouse, son or daughter, fellow student, coworker, neighbor, or friend) that Christian belief and behavior would leaven the world. "Like preached to like," writes Chatellier, and "it was no longer appropriate for the Church to speak a different language from that used in the family or at the workplace."[72] In this, post-Tridentine vernacular religion paved the way not only for twentieth-century pastoral initiatives such as "Catholic Action" or the French "priest worker movement" but also for the Second Vatican Council's affirmation of "the laity's special and indispensable role in the mission of the Church."[73]

Third, vernacular religion reframed Catholic identity primarily through *practices* rather than through theological argument or homiletic persuasion. Specific religious *behaviors* identified Catholic populations, among them practices such as Sunday Mass, daily prayer (upon rising, at bedtime), the rosary, frequent confession and communion, meatless Fridays, special devotions during Lent (e.g., Way of the Cross), membership in Catholic societies (sodalities, confraternities, the Altar Society, the Holy Name Society), novenas, retreats, and pilgrimages.[74] Many of these "characteristically Catholic" practices have continued into the twenty-first century. They constitute, in some respects, a throwback to *premodern* perceptions of prayer, ritual, and sacramental activity. For as anthropologist Talal Asad argues, medieval theologians regarded sacraments not as representative symbolic events requiring interpretation but as disciplinary practices, "parts of a Christian program for creating in its performers, by means of regulated practice, the 'mental and moral dispositions' appropriate to Christians."[75] Seen from this angle, ritual is not a medium for communicating or sustaining Christianity's "root metaphors" but a practiced performance that enacts and embodies belief. Belief flows from concrete behaviors, not from cognitive speculation on the significance of symbols and root metaphors. In sum, ritual is written on the body before its implications are grasped by the mind.

Fourth, vernacular religion shows a marked preference for social and corporate unity over "personal rights," for the family over the solitary individual, and—increasingly in the post-Tridentine environment—for local parish over larger "socio-professional hierarchy."[76] It also promoted a significant alteration in the way family life was perceived. Chatellier notes that

> the model presented to Christian families from the middle of the seventeenth century diverged considerably from that of the patriarchal family. It was even its exact opposite. The direction of the household belonged to the father and mother jointed. The role of the latter . . . was considerably elevated, even, as regards the education of young children, exalted. The father was no longer the all-powerful repository of authority. He and his spouse together sought to take account of the legitimate aspirations of their sons and daughters, their choice as to vocation, trade and marriage. Relationships based on love took the place of the old relationships based on authority.[77]

Patriarchalism may not have been vanquished by vernacular religion, but at least its absolutist claims to power were exposed and challenged. Women's voices became far more audible, especially in the reframing of early modern Marian devotions.

Fifth, early modern vernacular religion shaped the development not only of Catholic devotion but of Catholic doctrine. A case in point is the Western dogma of Mary's Immaculate Conception, whose roots are ancient and patristic, but whose formulation owes as much to popular devotion and belief as it does to theological argument.[78] The belief that Mary, in virtue of her unique role as mother of Jesus (and thus Theotokos

[Mother of God]), was *conceived* "without original sin" from the very first moment of her existence was not the opinion of important medieval theologians like Thomas Aquinas. For Thomas, to say that Mary had never been touched at all "by the contagion of original sin" was to detract from the dignity of Christ, insofar as he is the "universal Savior of all" (Mary included).[79] Eastern Christians had celebrated a feast of Mary's conception from at least the end of the seventh century, even though the churches of the East never formally defined a doctrine of the Immaculate Conception.[80] In Western Christianity, this feast made its way to southern Italy, then to England and France, where the focus shifted from Saint Anne's role as mother of Mary to Mary's "being conceived immaculately."[81]

For our purposes, the important thing to note is the immense popularity of both feast and doctrine, particularly in medieval England. Devotion to the Immaculate Conception of the Blessed Virgin Mary became "a most typical aspect of late mediaeval English piety."[82] Later—and elsewhere—in Europe, painters like Jan van Eyck presented a visual "rationale for the doctrine of the Immaculate Conception," not only through specific details within paintings (e.g., the shining crystal carafe in his *Lucca Madonna*) but in his habit of presenting the Virgin Mary in striking ways that inflate her status and power.[83] One is struck, especially in van Eyck's *Lucca Madonna*, with "the care and calculation taken in its composition, and the sense of ceremony" it conveys.[84] Harbison is not being flippant when he calls van Eyck's painting a "puffed-up image," a bit of "blatant visual propaganda," whose size and shape do "more to convince us about the Virgin's power" than any theological argument.[85] By insisting that Mary was conceived immaculately and hence preserved from sin from the first instant of her life, vernacular religion was making an astonishing claim for "one of our own." For unlike Christ, Mary is not a single person existing in two natures, human and divine; she is strictly and solely *human*. To claim this singular privilege for *her*, "the fairest boast of *our* race," is to assert something radical about humanity's capacity for grace and intimacy with God. It is to claim an extraordinary potential for human identity as such.

Meditating the Marian Mysteries

Perhaps nowhere in seventeenth-century Catholic literature were these claims pressed with greater vigor than in the work of the Spanish nun Sor María de Jesús de Ágreda (1602–65). Her life, writing, and activity confront us with a fascinating coalescence of both vernacular religion and an emerging early modern self-awareness that sees the human person not "in terms of dependence and rebellion but of interaction or dialogue" with "the powers that be," both church and state.[86] Before turning to Mary's meditations on the mysteries of the rosary, a brief introduction to her career as a religious leader and author will be useful.

Mary of Ágreda was and remains a controversial figure. During her lifetime, she became abbess of a monastery at the age of twenty-five, gained a great reputation for personal holiness among her fellow citizens, and was sought out for advice by King Philip IV of Spain.[87] Yet less than thirty years after her death, her magnum opus, *The Mystical City of God*, was condemned by the Roman Congregation of the Inquisition (August 4, 1681), and in our own day her private "revelations" have been linked to the anti-Semitic subtext of Mel Gibson's film *The Passion of the Christ*.[88] Among many objections to *The Mystical City of God* (hereafter, *MCG*) were those mentioned on a condemnation by the Sorbonne on September 17, 1696:

> It gives more weight to the revelations communicated [to Mary herself] than to the mystery of the Incarnation; . . . alleges new, hitherto unknown revelations which the Apostles themselves could not have witnessed; . . . uses the term "adoration" in reference to Mary; . . . refers all her graces to the Immaculate Conception; . . . ascribes the government of the Church to her; . . . identifies her as Mother of Mercy and the Mediatrix of Grace in all respects . . . pretends that her own mother Ann remained stainless in her [i.e., Mary's] birth, and adds several other fictions and offensive tales.[89]

As Thomas Kendrick noted more than forty years ago, it was not Mary's claim of visionary experiences that raised eyebrows, or her assertion that Christians may possess information about Christ's Mother from sources other than scripture. The church had, after all, routinely "permitted a fuller picture" of the Blessed Virgin, a portrait both "tender and glorious, to be cherished in the hearts of her devotees."[90] Among those devotees, however, "were many who had decided, at that time without the Church's authority, that the crucial doctrine of the Immaculate Conception was true. To such readers Sor María's book came as triumphant news. There was no doubt any more. Through Sor María by God's will came a declaration that the Virgin Mary was everything that her most ardent devotees had already determined that she was."[91] As a matter of fact, in its decree on the universal human condition that results from original sin (*peccatum Adae*, the sin of Adam), the Council of Trent had explicitly exempted the Virgin Mary.[92] After Trent, moreover, the Roman Church, without formally defining the Immaculate Conception as a dogma, had continued to include the Feast of Mary's Conception in its liturgical calendar on December 8, and texts for this liturgy were printed in the *Missale Romanum* of 1570.[93]

Mary of Ágreda's *MCG* appeared in print exactly a hundred years later, in 1670—five years after its author's death.[94] The opposition it aroused has already been mentioned, but the Sorbonne's reaction has to be read within the larger context of late seventeenth-century controversies inside the Roman Church, some of them linked, as noted earlier, to questions about the Virgin Mary's role in the history of salvation, particularly her freedom from sin at the moment of her conception. By the early seventeenth century the Immaculate Conception had become enormously popular as a theme in both vernacular religion and Christian art.[95] Already foreshadowed in van Eyck's paintings of Mary, especially the *Luccan Madonna*, it became even more popular among early baroque artists, especially in Spain.[96] Among the most notable of these was Guido Reni's *Immaculate Conception*, painted for the Spanish Infanta in 1627, the year Mary of Ágreda (Sor María de Jesús) became abbess of the discalced (literally, "barefoot") Conceptionist Franciscan nuns at Ágreda, and the year, as well, when she began writing *MCG*.[97]

Reni's painting was simultaneously the solution to one problem and the creation of another.[98] His *Immacolata* showed that it was possible to remain within the bounds of Catholic orthodoxy while representing the Virgin *in her own right without her Child*. Reni painted Mary in bright colors, "poised on a crescent moon," a crown of twelve stars hovering above her head, and surrounded by a penumbra of assisting angels as she "floats into a radiance of light."[99] The picture made an obvious appeal to scriptural imagery (Revelation 12.1) and to Trent's "Great Exception" that exempted Mary from Adam's sin. The biblical image of a "woman clothed with the sun" had for centuries been applied to Mary by church fathers, East and West, but in the late sixteenth and early seventeenth centuries, it achieved new prominence, especially in the work of the Capuchin friar and theologian Lawrence of Brindisi (1559–1619).[100] A central theme of Lawrence's *Mariale*, a collection of eighty-four sermons on the Mother of God, was Mary's role as "Godbearer, the truly natural Mother of the Only-Begotten Son of God . . . the predestined Mother of Christ, having been predestined before all creatures together with Christ, the firstborn of every creature."[101] Mary's singular predestination was often linked in Franciscan theology to her utter sinlessness and hence to her Immaculate Conception. Commenting on a verse of Palms 8 ("You have put all things under his feet"), Lawrence of Brindisi wrote that "this passage may be accommodated to Mary," for "by this divine mystery is portrayed the Virgin's wonderful exaltation above every creature."[102]

Reni's visual formula in the *Immacolata* capitalized on this theological theme. It presents the Virgin Mary as "physically present, albeit out of reach," thereby asserting her privileged triumph over sin.[103] His "definitive solution" to the problem of representing the Virgin in her own right without her Child

> was to present a vision of Mary alive amidst the heavens, crowned and triumphant over sin, and eternally young. This type could avoid contentious issues like the Immaculate Conception while hinting at Mary's Assumption and Glorification. This visionary image fulfilled all the requirements of the post-Tridentine church; an image with impeccable biblical references, an image of the Virgin in her own right without the attribute of the Child, heaven-borne yet humanly accessible, triumphant over sin.[104]

Reni's image helped establish a "consistent iconography for the main tenets of Marian devotion" in early modern Catholicism.[105] He had created an icon that could be widely circulated "in prints, in illustrated texts as well as large-scale altar paintings as weapons of conversion and persuasion."[106] Whereas Caravaggio's Madonnas seemed to shrink the distance between viewer and image, Reni's seemed to embody a "sacred distance" that removed Mary from earth and set her apart in a celestial sphere.[107] In fact, Reni's *Immacolata* was widely imitated and continued to influence Catholic devotional art in the eighteenth, nineteenth, and twentieth centuries.[108]

Mary of Ágreda may or may not have known Guido Reni's *Immacolata*, she may or may not have read the sermons of Lawrence of Brindisi, but her *MCG* was unquestionably influenced by Franciscan thought, especially by Bernardine of Siena's opinion that the existence of the Virgin Mary had been in God's mind from the very beginning, and by Duns Scotus's view that the mystery of Christ's Incarnation would have happened even if there had been no Fall.[109] Her familiarity with the apocalyptic imagery of "the woman clothed with the sun" (Revelation 12.1) as applied to the Virgin Mary is evident in the very first chapter of the first book of *MCG*.[110] And her long subtitle for book 1 tells us she will describe "the Sacramental Mysteries wrought by the Most High in the Queen of Heaven from the Time of her Immaculate Conception until the Incarnation of the Word in her virginal Womb."[111] The heart of the matters discussed in *MCG* was, in the author's view, "that all the divine blessings and privileges enjoyed by the Virgin Mary have their origin and explanation in her Immaculate Conception."[112]

Yet *MCG* cannot be read simply as theological treatise or devotional exhortation. It includes elements of each, but its specific genre, if it has one, is more difficult to determine. Sor María's text oscillates frequently between the author's narrative and the "Queen's" homilies; its language darts from expository prose to ecstatic prayer. Still the work has a complex structure and well-defined plan, which the author develops systematically over the course of eight books, from Mary's Conception to her Coronation.[113] A good deal of the material in *MCG* is derivative, making use of patristic and apocryphal sources that may have been "known to Sor María since childhood."[114] For example, the details surrounding the lives of Mary's parents Joachim and Anne, which occupy significant portions of books 1 and 2 in *MCG*, have their roots in the second-century apocryphal gospel known as the "Protevangelium of James" (Protevangelium Jacobi).[115] Legends from this work were popularized in Latin medieval literature, especially in Jacobus de Voraigne's *The Golden Legend*, and a Latin version of the Protevangelium itself had been published at Basel in 1552, so it is entirely possible that its contents were known to literate Spanish women like Mary of Ágreda in the seventeenth century. Moreover, from the Middle Ages onward, these legends about the Virgin Mary's life had become popular subjects in Christian art.[116]

Despite the derivative character of many of *MCG*'s narratives, there is also much in Mary of Ágreda's book that will strike the reader as original. For instance, *MCG* narrates the Virgin Mary's presence at the Transfiguration of Jesus, speaks of the presence of Enoch and Elijah at the Last Supper, and asserts that Christ's Mother accompanied him to heaven on the occasion of his ascension.[117] As a writer, Sor María was well aware that such assertions took her into uncharted, perhaps dangerous, territory. Her comments on the Transfiguration story reveal such an awareness:

> The Evangelists do not say that most holy Mary was present at this Transfiguration, nor do they say that She was not there; this did not fall within their purpose, and they did not think it proper to speak of the hidden

miracle by which She was enabled to be there. For the purpose of record-
ing this event here, I was given to understand that at the same time in
which some of the holy angels were commissioned to bring the soul of
Moses and Elias from their abode, others of her own guard carried the
heavenly Lady to Mount Tabor, in order to witness the Transfiguration of
her divine Son, for without a doubt She really witnessed it. . . .

     She began to ponder . . . what She had seen and heard; exalted praise
of the omnipotent God welled forth from her lips, when She considered
how her eyes had seen refulgent in glory that same bodily substance
which had been formed of her blood, carried in her womb and nursed at
her breast.[118]

Sor María carefully alerted the reader that she did not wish to set the
gospel record aside but simply to *supplement* it from her own personal
meditations and private revelations. She was quite conscious, too, of her
status as beneficiary of "special gifts of enlightenment," as the "words of
the Queen" made clear to her:

My daughter, as thy soul has been furnished with special gifts of enlightenment, I call and invite thee anew to cast thyself into the sea of mysteries contained in the passion and death of my divine Son. Direct . . . all
the powers of thy heart and soul to make thyself at least somewhat worthy of understanding and meditating upon the ignominies and sorrows
of the Son of the eternal Father in his death on the Cross for the salvation
of men.[119]

It is easy to dismiss Sor María's speculations as preposterous, especially
at those points where she literally puts words into the mouths of Christ
and Mary. Yet this strategy of "imaginary conversations" or dialogue is an
ancient one, and in the Christian East it even helped shape the language
of the church's liturgy. For example, the deacon-poet Ephrem the Syrian
(306–83), a contemporary of Latin church fathers like Ambrose of Milan,
portrayed the Theotokos speaking these words to her Son when the Magi
brought him gifts of gold, frankincense, and myrrh (Matthew 2.1–12):
"O Son of the Rich One, Who abhorred the bosom of rich women, who
led Thee to the poor? For Joseph was needy and I also am in want, yet
Thy merchants have come and brought gold, to the house of the poor."[120]
Ephrem then added a further comment on the scene: "The King before
Whom the angels of fire and spirit tremble, lies in the bosom of a girl, and

she cuddles Him as a baby. The heaven is the throne for His glory [Isaiah 66.1], yet He sits on Mary's knees."[121] Like their Syriac-speaking counterparts, Byzantine hymnographers freely put words in Mary's mouth, as this passage from the liturgical Canon of the Forefeast of the Epiphany, composed by Romanos the Melodist (fl. ca. 540), reveals:

> Receive the three gifts [of the Magi], my child, and grant three prayers for her who gave Thee birth. I beg Thee in behalf of the heavens above and the fruits of the earth, and them that dwell thereon, be reconciled to all for my sake. I supplicate Thee in behalf of all men. Thou hast made me the pride and boast of all my race [Judith 15.9–11]; for the universe considers me as a powerful protection, rampart and stay. May them that were cast from the joys of Paradise look to me that I may direct them. Save the world, O Saviour; for its sake Thou didst come. Establish Thy Kingdom; for its sake Thou hast let Thy light shine on me and the magi, and all creation.[122]

Mary of Ágreda may not have had the lyric gifts of Ephrem or Romanos, but there can be little doubt she had both a fertile imagination and the courage to use it. Thomas Kendrick seems justified in calling *MCG* "an original, lively, and powerful book," even if "part of its contents . . . reads as truly unbearable nonsense."[123] For readers today the nonsense is probably most evident when Mary speculates about Joachim's virility or imagines Jesus and John the Baptist communicating with one another from within their mothers' transparent wombs.[124] These were surely among the passages of *MCG* that theologians at the Sorbonne had in mind when, in 1696, they objected to the book's "indecency" and "scandalous language."[125]

Perhaps, then, Mary of Ágreda could have used a good editor. Still, her book demonstrates many of the qualities we have been examining as aspects of early modern self-awareness, with its expanded "interior space" and inward-looking imagination. She wrote, acutely conscious of the peril surrounding a woman author in a man's world and a man's church. Repeatedly, in *MCG*, Sor María protests that she is writing "not as a teacher but as a disciple, not as one instructing, but as one trying to learn, knowing that it is the duty of women to be silent in the holy Church, and to listen to the teachers (1 Corinthians 14.34)."[126] These considerations did not, of course, prevent her from writing a massive work of nearly 800,000 words, a feat that hardly attests the reticence one might expect to find in a compliant, contemplative abbess. As a matter of fact, however, in the very same breath she uses to announce her role as that of "disciple, not teacher," Mary makes it quite clear that *compliance* is not her aim. "*But*," she adds to the words previously quoted, "as an instrument of the Queen of heaven I will declare what She deigns to teach me and whatever She commands me; *for all the souls are capable of receiving the Spirit, which her divine Son has promised to pour out over men of all conditions* (Joel 2.28)."[127]

It is significant that Mary of Ágreda appeals to a famous passage from the prophet Joel, because this text affirms that in the coming age, the Lord will pour out the spirit abundantly and indiscriminately on both women and men, "servants *and handmaids*," so that "sons *and daughters*" will prophesy and "old men *and young* . . . shall see visions" (Joel 3.2, NAB). Joel looks, in other words, to a time when the Lord's spirit will take equal possession of all alike, regardless of gender or generation. Written when Mary was a mature woman in her early fifties, after serving her community as abbess for twenty-eight years, the "Introduction" for the revised *MCG* of 1655 can hardly be said to embody the impetuosity of youth.[128] It shows us a writer well acquainted with her craft and well acquainted, too, with her own interiority as an early modern woman. Her writing has itself become the performance of an expanded self-awareness. "I am now convinced," she asserts, "that the Church has authorized this history through my superiors. That I should err is possible [NB: she does not say "likely"], and to an ignorant woman, natural; but then I err, while obeying and not acting of my own free will."[129] She clearly recognizes the worth and value of herself as a writer and of what she has written, for she imagines the Lord saying to her: "Do not . . . show thyself thankless for my mercy by burning what thou shalt have written, lest my indignation deprive thee of the light which . . . thou hast received for the manifestation of these mysteries."[130]

In short, *MCG* "presents a story that Sor María had composed within herself by means of meditation, prayer, and, she would insist, her privileged visions."[131] She worked, as we have seen, within an imaginative tradition whose roots reach back to ancient Christian liturgical and devotional texts. At the same time, she wrote as an early modern woman whose claims of "weakness" and "ignorance" mask yet encode an abiding confidence in her own powers as thinker and writer. Church and state in the seventeenth century were interested in regulating behavior through "private mechanisms of conscience and guilt," and they were ready to reward those individuals who complied with such strategies of control and conformity.[132] On the surface Mary of Ágreda was such an individual. Yet Sor María knew quite clearly who *she* was and what she was capable of doing. Especially notable was her conviction that while her writing was undertaken with the approval of her "superiors" and in submission to "correction" by the "holy Catholic Church," *her personal* commission *had come directly from the "Queen of heaven" and her Son*. In Mary's case, conformity merely "cleared the ground" for far more important, internal work—that of self-fashioning, the deliberate shaping and expression of an identity forged in private mediation and publicly performed in writing.[133] In *MCG*, Mary of Ágreda inscribes herself as an early modern woman who embodies the changes in "intellectual, social, psychological, and aesthetic structures" that had begun to govern the generation of new identities.[134]

As a result, Mary of Ágreda's *MCG* does not easily fit the genre of post-Tridentine devotional literature. It is neither exhortatory in the style of Louis Richeome's *The Pilgrime of Loreto*, whose purpose is to inspire lay Christians to follow "the devout life," nor quietly meditative in the monastic mode of Dom Gaspar Gorricio de Novara's *Contemplaciones sobre el Rosario de Nuestra Senora Historiados. Un incunable Sevillano*, an incunabulum (early specimen of European books printed from movable type before 1501) published at Seville in 1495.[135] Dom Gaspar's work is an important witness to the development of rosary devotion in Spain, since in that country Carthusians were commonly known as *hermanos rosarieros* (rosary brothers), renowned for making and distributing prayer beads.[136] If an early engraving of her is accurate, Sor Maria's own community— the discalced nuns of the Immaculate Conception—was also devoted to the rosary, since it appears to have formed part of each nun's monastic habit.[137] Yet Mary of Ágreda's own meditations on the mysteries that formed the heart of the rosary are far more complex than those of Dom Gaspar. For instance, in his own series of reflections on each "Ave" of the joyful mystery "The Presentation of the Lord in the Temple," Gaspar writes: "Let us contemplate how this great Lady was much consoled . . . and how she rejoiced and marveled at the blessings and prophecies of the just Simeon. . . . And beyond this . . . let us consider that prophecy of Simeon who said '*Et tuam ipsius animam pertransibit gladius* (and your own soul a sword will pierce) . . . and in memory of these words let us say '*Ave Maria*.'"[138] Gaspar's sober reflection sticks closely to the biblical text, which he is content to summarize, adding slight embellishments.

But Sor María's remarks on the scene of Jesus' Presentation in the Temple occupy an entire chapter of *MCG*.[139] She explains the significance of Simeon's prophecy about the sword that will pierce Mary's soul in these terms:

> At the moment when the priest Simeon mentioned the sword and the sign of contradiction, which were prophetical of the passion and death of the Lord, the Child bowed its head. Thereby, and by many interior acts of obedience, Jesus ratified the prophecy of the priest and accepted it as the sentence of the eternal Father pronounced by his minister. All this the loving Mother noticed and understood; She presently began to feel the sorrow predicted by Simeon and thus in advance was She wounded by the sword, of which She had thus been warned. As in a mirror her spirit was made to see all the mysteries included in this prophecy; how her most holy Son was to be the stone of stumbling, the perdition of the unbelievers, and the salvation of the faithful. . . . At the same time She also saw the glory and excellence of the predestined souls. Most holy Mary knew it all and in the joy and sorrow of her most pure soul, excited by the prophecies of Simeon and these hidden mysteries, She performed heroic acts of virtue.[140]

Mary of Ágreda's expansive meditations are not simply evidence of an early modern writer's prolixity. They are a key to the "the genre of this enormous and remarkable book."[141] We have already seen that Sor María's account of the life of the Virgin moves back and forth between narrative and homily, scriptural exegesis and devotional commentary, expository prose and ecstatic prayer. Like Guido Reni's painting of the *Immacolata*, *MCG* begins by letting us see the Virgin Mary "in her own right," as a woman with her own personal history, her own unique relationship to God, her own perils and privileges, her own motivational and emotional life. As Sor María tells it, the Madonna is not a cartoon based on the Bible but a real character of flesh and blood in a story that has plot, dramatic action, surprise and reversal, development and telos.

In my view, then, Mary of Ágreda's *MCG* is best read as an early modern novel. Its author writes with a novelist's eye for the telling detail, a novelist's affectionate interest in the "characters" she creates. Plot, scene, sequence, and character development are all important. Moreover, *MCG* is structurally complex. It employs not only multiple forms (history, biography, homily, prayer, exegesis, encomium, psychological analysis) but multiple narratives. Ostensibly, *MCG* tells the Virgin Mary's life, her origins and family, her destiny, her ordeals—an embellished, even fictionalized, chronicle of her joys, sorrows, and eventual triumph. Yet the book gives readers something more than a seventeenth-century Spanish version of *Jane Eyre*. *MCG* also documents Sor María's personal religious experiences, the visions and revelations she received over the course of her career as nun and abbess between 1619 and 1665. So there is simultaneously an autobiographical narrative at work in *MCG*, but it is autobiography of a distinctly early modern sort. Sor María becomes a character in her own novel; in writing *MCG*, she also writes herself. By opening up the interiority of her characters (their thoughts, motives, emotions), she reveals to us her own expanding self-awareness, her struggle toward "self-fashioning," self-definition. She becomes not only the *novel's* narrator but *our* "psychopomp," guiding us through an interior landscape, a geography of the soul.

There is therefore a certain ventriloquism in the "words of the Queen" (the Virgin's homilies) that conclude almost every chapter of every book in *MCG*. Christ's Mother is imagined as the person speaking, but the voice actually belongs to Sor María. Mary the Theotokos becomes Sor María's own "persona," the mask through which she performs her identity as woman, nun, abbess, spiritual seeker, "daughter of the Church." I say this not to diminish the spiritual significance of Mary of Ágreda's work for Catholic readers but to illustrate the degree to which *MCG* is—and could only be—the work of an early modern novelist. Novels, as we understand them today, became in fact the literary icon of modernity. Their condition of possibility as literature lies in an expanding human capacity for self-conscious articulation, for shaping the private—often isolated and anguished—individual self.[142] Mary of Ágreda lets us eavesdrop on this process and thereby lets the reader's voyeuristic eagerness intrude upon her novel's plot and action. Readers become interactive "characters" in *MCG*, as they do in any novel capable of making us care deeply about its content, characters, plot, and action.

There is a connection here between Sor María's novelistic technique in *MCG* and the work of imagination as explicated in the Ignatian *Exercises* and applied to meditation on the mysteries of the rosary. The Ignatian method involved not simply "setting a biblical scene" in one's mind but expanding and enriching that scene through application of one's "spiritual senses." The meditation on hell, for example, insists that the first point will be to see with the eyes of the imagination the huge fires and, so to speak, the souls within the bodies full of fire. . . .

I will hear the wailing, the shrieking, the cries, and the blasphemies against our Lord and all his saints. . . .

By my sense of smell I will perceive the smoke, the sulphur, the filth, and the rotting things. . . .

By my sense of taste I will experience the bitter flavors of hell: tears, sadness, and the worm of conscience. . . .

By my sense of touch, I will feel how the flames touch the souls and burn them.[143]

Mary of Ágreda's posthumous magnum opus retold scriptural stories in a similarly vivid way, with some of the verve and edginess that Caravaggio employed in rewriting traditional icons. Caravaggio's pictures often seem to push beyond the picture's plane into the viewer's space, drawing us into the painting—or better, perhaps, bringing the scene, the story, the figures directly into the physical and psychological space of our own lives. The result was enhanced intimacy between viewer and subject. It was surely not a simple flair for self-advertisement that caused Caravaggio to paint his own portrait in several of his works (*David with the Head of Goliath*; *Self-Portrait as Bacchus*; *Musicians*; *Martyrdom of Saint Matthew*; *Raising of Lazarus*). We have considered connections between the reformist humanism of the Oratorian orbit and Caravaggio's own religious sensibilities as these are reflected in his paintings. Catherine Puglisi goes so far as to say that "essential elements" in Caravaggio's religious works—"the sensory realism, humble types, and absence of heavenly visions"—embody aspects of Philip Neri's personality, including his down-to-earth humor, his habit of lampooning "pretentious ceremony," and his "suspicion of mystical experiences."[144]

On the surface, this might seem to suggest that the work of an early modern painter like Caravaggio was the direct antithesis of what Mary of Ágreda was attempting in *MCG*. Sor María's universe, after all, teemed with apocryphal lore, revelatory visions, effusive oratory, and majestic figures bearing royal titles ("Queen," "Your/His/Her Majesty"). Yet the Virgin Mary never wears a crown in any of Caravaggio's paintings, so it is difficult to identify *MCG*'s royalist imagery with Neri's *sermo humilis*, with the fetching young woman leaning in a humble Roman doorway in *Madonna di Loreto*, or with the grasping, dirt-crusted *lazzaroni* in *Madonna del Rosario*. Still, the principal character whom Mary of Ágreda created in her monumental novel is a voluble, assertive woman with a mind, a personality, a room, and a story of her own. For instance, in her account of the circumcision of Jesus (a ritual for Jewish males in which Mary would almost certainly have had no direct involvement), Sor María tells us that the "holy Mother perceived and in her heavenly wisdom penetrated the mystery of this sacrament."[145] She understood that her Infant's "delicacy and tenderness would make this ceremony more painful to Him than to other children," and thus insisted that she hold him throughout the procedure, weeping "like the guileless sheep which raises its voice in unison with the innocent lamb," making sure the officiant had at hand "the soothing medicine ordinarily applied at circumcision," wiping her baby's tears, and catching his blood in her own supply of linen.[146] And as noted earlier, Sor María's *Madonna* reveals an almost embarrassing concern for the fate of Jesus' foreskin.[147]

Nevertheless, Caravaggio and Mary of Ágreda did occupy common ground—in their symbolic use of light to signal God's presence and grace, for example, and their shared emphasis on the legitimacy of each individual's personal encounter with God.[148] Just as *MCG* used novelistic techniques to create real "inner lives" for its characters, so in a number of paintings, Caravaggio "attempted to give expression to his figures' inner sentiments," and to unleash these same *affetti* "in the spectator as well."[149] Commenting on the earlier of Caravaggio's two versions of *The Supper at Emmaus*, Bert Treffers remarks that in it "Christ makes an almost physical appeal to the viewer" with his right hand, while "blessing the broken bread with his left," and that the apostle's outthrust hand (on the viewer's right) "seems to span the entire pictorial space."[150] Caravaggio had used similarly vigorous and dramatic gestures—hands and arms flung out—in other religious paintings, notably *The Martyrdom of Matthew*, *The Conversion of St. Paul*, and *The Crucifixion of St. Peter*. These gestures, Treffers notes, embodied Christ's call to follow him into both suffering (cross) and victory (Eucharist, foretaste of heaven's banquet).[151] By inscribing powerful emotions on the bodies of his painted subjects, Caravaggio created visual dialogue between subject and viewer, eliciting similar affects within the early modern spectator.

As different as their personal lives were, Caravaggio and Mary of Ágreda also shared a common spiritual source: Franciscanism. The late sixteenth century had witnessed a remarkable resurgence of interest in the thought of St. Bonaventure (1217–74). This medieval Franciscan had been declared a doctor of the church by Pope Sixtus V in 1588, and several of his works were printed or reprinted at Venice between 1593 and 1609.[152] In treatises like *Itinerarium mentis in deum* (*The Mind's Journey to God*),

Bonaventure wrote theology in the language of the heart, as the following well-known passage illustrates:

> Consult grace, not doctrine; desire, not understanding; prayerful groaning, not studious reading; the spouse, not the teacher; God, not man; darkness, not clarity. Consult, not light but the fire that completely inflames the mind and carries it over to God in transports of fervor and blazes of love. This fire is God, *and His furnace is in [the heavenly] Jerusalem* [Isaiah 31.9]. . . . Let us die, then, and pass over into the darkness; let us silence every care, every craving, every dream; with Christ crucified, *let us pass out of this world to the Father* [John 13.1].[153]

Bonaventure's emphasis on the religious affections—desire, not reason; fire, not light—belonged to his larger program for Christian living in imitation of Christ. Treffers's research demonstrates that Bonaventure's mystical interpretation of the Franciscan ideal of following Christ impinged directly on Caravaggio's painting of religious and devotional subjects, especially his *Francis in Ecstasy*, painted in approximately 1595–96.[154] In this painting, where a prone, swooning Francis could almost have been an early self-portrait, Caravaggio "relays a pointed message. With his powerfully foreshortened left hand the saint entreats us to follow his example, but what this actually entails is indicated by his right hand, which touches the wound at his side. The imitation of Christ, he seems to be saying, is a matter of the heart."[155] The painter's concern was not "doctrine but grace," not theology but the Christian's interior personal journey with Christ crucified from this world to the Father. Caravaggio created not a historically faithful illustration of the miracle but an affective probing of its spiritual meaning—for Francis, the artist, and the viewer.[156]

Caravaggio's art thus portrayed visually what, a few decades later, Sor María's *MCG* would accomplish verbally. Both were early modern appeals to an expanded self-awareness, with its private, internal mechanisms of conscience and consciousness. Both inscribed emotion and affectivity on subjects and viewers, characters and readers. And both adopted this strategy under the influence of a revitalized Franciscan (Bonaventuran) theology which recognized that "physical formal language is necessary in order to express the innermost workings of the soul."[157] In Caravaggio's work,

> all those vehement gestures, full-blooded angels and semi-tangible visions [are] nothing less than a summoning up of their exact opposites:

the more material the body, the more ethereal the spirit. External agitation is the result of internal processes; it is the palpable translation of deeply felt emotion.[158]

Caravaggio came to the spiritual by way of extreme naturalism, and so, on her own terms, did Sor María. For all their mystical, almost hallucinatory, intensity, *MCG*'s visions and revelations are anchored in the concrete, the palpable, the real, the quotidian. Meditating on the mystery of the Visitation (the second of the rosary's five "joyful mysteries"), for example, Sor María did not fail to focus on the Virgin Mary's "humility and self-abasement in serving her cousin Elizabeth" by "washing dishes" and tidying up the house.[159] The "Queen" herself explained that such naturalism is no vice, since "no occupation or exterior act . . . no matter how lowly it may be . . . can impede the worship, reverence and exaltation of the Creator of all things."[160] So deeply does Christ love humility, the Virgin continued, that she herself would readily have "suffered the torments of the world" to have a chance to "sweep the floor or kiss the feet of the poor."[161]

Here once more we meet a Franciscan spirituality that was being retrieved during the early modern era, especially in late sixteenth-century and early seventeenth-century Europe. Its robust naturalism is another aspect of vernacular religion, and in artists like Caravaggio and Mary of Ágreda, such naturalism served a specific goal. For them, salvation was not "an abstract concept, but was to be sought in the practice of everyday life."[162] In Caravaggio's *Madonna di Loreto*, naturalism "completely accords with the type of devotional practice the painting seems to enjoin."[163] Pilgrimage was "not the best way to keep one's feet clean," and those who undertook it had to do so in "complete humility," embracing poverty and forgoing "all earthly pleasures during the journey."[164] Pilgrims arriving at the holy site of Loreto were expected to circle the house three times "on their knees," and "with a humble heart."[165] Moreover, as *MCG* suggests, the Virgin Mary herself became an obscure and lowly pilgrim when she visited her aged cousin Elizabeth, who had unexpectedly conceived a child late in life.[166] The larger message, of course, was that life itself is a pilgrimage, and only the humble poor can hope to enter heaven.

Naturalism in art both shocks and compels, and the work of Caravaggio and Mary of Ágreda is no exception. Yet naturalism in the early modern mode was not only a result of vernacular religion and self-reflective interiority; it was also a consequence of the reassessment of the

Catholic Church, which we have seen took place in the second half of the sixteenth century and was consolidated around 1600. This reassessment was not simply a product of new religious movements such as Neri's Oratorians or Ignatius Loyola's Jesuits, which emerged before or after the Council of Trent.[167] Older orders, like the Franciscans and Carmelites, also experienced a renewal of their distinctive charisms and a retrieval of their theological roots. The "affective perception of faith" championed by Saint Bonaventure in works such as his *Itinerarium mentis in deum* and the "devotional mysticism of the Song of Solomon" were also indispensable for the reframing of Catholic identity and devotional practice.[168] The act of meditating on the mysteries of the rosary, for example, took a decidedly new turn when one applied the imaginative techniques of Ignatian meditation to biblical scenes or treated sacred figures like the Virgin Mary as characters with lives of their own in an early modern novel.

Reinventing Religious Identity in Early Modernity

The rosary was not the only pious practice that was reshaped in early modern Catholicism, but it was perhaps the most popular and widespread one. Part of that popularity flowed, we have seen, from the connection between devotion to the rosary and the success of Catholic coalition forces against the Turks at Lepanto. In the minds of many, Mary's intervention— her powerful response to the prayers of the Roman rosary confraternity— had in effect saved Europe from a dread "other" (the Ottoman Empire, the religion of Islam). At the same time, the rosary appealed to the human imagination in ways that the church's official liturgy (in Latin and often inaudible) did not. Moreover, the Ignatian *Exercises* and Mary of Ágreda's *MCG* demonstrated—in the media of literature and print—that the contemporaneity Caravaggio sought in his art (shrinking the distance between sacred subjects and viewers) could be achieved through other means as well.

The reframing of Catholic identity was, therefore, a complex process with multiple features. It included the expanded interior space, self-awareness, and personal autonomy that are hallmarks of early modern subjectivity, yet it also involved a retrieval of those "affective perceptions of faith" found not only in medieval theologians like Bonaventure but in humanist reformers like Erasmus, in early baroque artists like Caravaggio, and in early modern mystics and devotional writers like Mary of Ágreda. Still, the affective devotionalism we find in Caravaggio's *Madonna di Loreto* or Sor María's meditations on Christian mysteries in *MCG* was more than a nostalgic throwback to medieval precedents. It was an affectivity born and bred among the early modern mechanisms of interiority, self-discipline, and self-control. Unlike their premodern predecessors, early modern persons regulated behavior not so much through "public rituals and shaming" but through "internal, private mechanisms of conscience and guilt."[169]

The twentieth-century cultural historian Norbert Elias (d. 1990) used the concept "threshold of shaming" to chart changes in the ways people have created boundaries between behaviors deemed acceptable in public and those meant to be kept private.[170] The threshold of shame thus measures the limits of acceptable social behavior in a specific historical period and shows how the scope of human affectivity was either expanding or shrinking.[171] In Elias's view, the degree and amount of unscripted, unexpected, or spontaneous behavior people in the West were willing to tolerate in public steadily *diminished* over time. This shift is evident especially in manuals of etiquette. A fifteenth-century book of table manners, for instance, advised individuals that "it is unseemly to blow your nose into the tablecloth" (suggesting, of course, that diners often did just that).[172] The first chapter of Erasmus's *De civilitate morum puerilium* narrowed what was acceptable in public, noting that to blow the nose on one's hand and then "smear the snot on your garment" is grossly impolite, and that "it is proper to wipe the nostrils with a handkerchief and to do this while turning away, *if more honourable people are present*."[173] But by the late seventeenth century, blowing the nose in public was barely tolerated at all: "You should avoid yawning, blowing your nose and spitting. If you are obliged to do so in places that are kept clean, do it in your handkerchief, while turning your face away and shielding yourself with your left hand, and do not look into your handkerchief afterwards."[174]

In the sixteenth century, the transition from public to private, internalized criteria for evaluating and controlling public behavior was still in process, so when reading advice like Erasmus's, we are liable to feel it is both "medieval" and "exactly the way we feel today."[175] Table manners—like food and seating arrangements—showed the degree to which meals were social maps, and in the early modern era those maps were changing. Prominent Europeans of the early sixteenth century like St. Thomas More found themselves caught in the middle of this transition—drawn inexorably toward modernity yet resisting it. This is the argument Stephen Greenblatt advances in the first chapter of *Renaissance Self-Fashioning*.[176] More understood, writes Greenblatt, that there was "an essential relationship between private property and private selves," and in his *Utopia*, therefore, *nihil usquam priuati est* (nothing that is private exists anywhere).[177] Hence too, More's emphasis on the utopian *reduction* of the self: "In place of the anxious striving of the [modern private] individual, the Utopians share a powerful sense of relatedness."[178] Social order and proper norms for public behavior are guaranteed by the individual's "absorption into the community and indoctrination in its patriarchal values," while "disorder is checked not by fines or seizure of property [as in modern states] but chiefly by *shaming*."[179]

Unfortunately for More, the England of Henry VIII was not Utopia, and willy-nilly, he found himself a utopian Christian struggling against an early modern monarchy. Moreover, More himself was agonizingly aware of the degree to which he was the result of his own self-fashioning and not of that self-cancellation to which he may have aspired. His mode of being was

> genuinely perplexing and uncomfortable, the more so in the context of early sixteenth-century England, which it represents as something quite exceptional. For his life seems nothing less than this: the invention of a disturbingly unfamiliar form of consciousness, tense, ironic, witty, poised between engagement and detachment, and above all, fully aware of its own status as an invention. . . . For one consequence of life lived as histrionic improvisation is that the category of the real merges with that of the fictive; the historical More is a narrative fiction. To make a part of one's own, to live one's life as a character thrust into a play, constantly renewing oneself extemporaneously and forever aware of one's own unreality— such was More's condition . . . his project.[180]

More's position was not unlike that of Sor María, whose *MCG* reveals as much about how a seventeenth-century Spanish nun fashioned her private persona as it does about divine revelations. But there is a crucial difference between the two. More was troubled and torn by the self he had created, while Mary of Ágreda seems quite comfortable with her identity as a self-aware *individual* singled out for *private* revelations, quite apart from her relationships with others. Sor María seemed to love being a character in her own novel, while More feared the "narrative fiction" he had become.[181] Consequently, despite the picture of him drawn in modern dramas like *A Man for All Seasons*, "the defiance of the crown which cost

More his life was far from being the heroic act of private conscience of a modern individual, but rather was a deliberate effort at nonmodernity; it was an attempt to relink internal conscience and external behavior in a way that More sensed was being lost."[182]

Caravaggio and Mary of Ágreda were thus early modern Catholics in a way that Thomas More was not. And ironically, the very church More died defending soon saw that it, like the state, would be better served not by utopian Christians but by private, inward-looking, self-conscious, "modern" individuals.[183] The nonmodern view of selfhood that More died asserting was based on a view of the human person as "constituted within ritual, as existing in a matrix of relations (friend/enemy)," in which the "central mediating institution was communion."[184] Within such an arrangement, it was "the ritual [e.g., of Eucharist] that constituted the social order" and defined its boundaries and tensions.[185] Moreover, well into the sixteenth century, as David Sabean writes, "moral discipline remained officially a matter for the state," and "civil punishments for religious infractions also belonged to secular authorities."[186] In sum, it was the state's responsibility to curb public dissent and enforce compliance. But the alliance between religious and secular authorities took a new turn during the early modern period. Both "sought to give the *individual* the burden of his or her guilt as a *private psychological state*, and to have him or her turn to the church . . . for psychological care by means of catechism, confession, and so on."[187] The authority to regulate behavior, limit dissent, and control compliance no longer resided within that interpersonal network of family and social relationships that Sabean calls the "village," but within institutional structures of church and state working in alliance with one another. In the early modern era, both these institutions needed to reframe Catholic identity by fostering the emergence of private, individual persons who would be subject to such control and hence independent of the "village" community. It is no exaggeration to claim that church and state together invented the "private individual."[188]

The realism of Caravaggio and the imaginative devotionalism of Mary of Ágreda embody the emergence of such an identity. In both cases we meet gifted artists who are aware of both their uniqueness as creative individuals and their distinctiveness as Catholics. Stephen Greenblatt has argued that such "faith in the centrality of the self" was "justified in a quasi-theological sense by the inwardness that Protestantism held to be one of the signs of truth."[189] He goes on to say that—at least in the English court poetry of Thomas Wyatt—this interiority served not simply "histrionic self-manifestation" but a *"revelation* of the self in discourse."[190] Our concern in this chapter, however, has been to explore how the early modern emphasis on *inwardness* characterized not only Protestantism but also Catholicism, and that writing as a *"revelation* of the self in discourse" was precisely (if somewhat disingenuously) Mary of Ágreda's goal in *MCG*. She too sought not to manipulate her audience but to render her inner life in painstaking detail, to invite readers to witness the movements of (her) mind "through assurance, doubt, dread, and longing."[191]

In Caravaggio's rewritten icons and Mary of Ágreda's visionary account of the Virgin Mary's life, we see early modern Catholicism turning *away* from its premodern, medieval, and "rural/village" roots. An example from the church's penitential discipline can help confirm this point. In the early tenth century (ca. 906), chronicler and canonist Regino of Prüm included in his *De synodalibus causis et disciplinis ecclesiasticis libri duo (Two Books on Synodal Cases and Ecclesiastical Disciplines)* a description of how Christians guilty of public sins were enrolled as public penitents by the diocesan bishop at the beginning of Lent.[192] The penitents appeared at the church door "clad in sackcloth, with bare feet, with their faces downcast toward the earth, by their very garb and countenance proclaiming themselves guilty."[193] (Here, of course, we find a pattern of ritualized "shaming" behaviors.) The bishop led these guilty ones into the church, where they prostrated themselves on the floor while he chanted "with tears the seven penitential psalms."[194] Then the bishop sprinkled ashes on their heads and "with groaning and frequent sighs" told them that, "just as Adam was cast out of paradise, so they also for their sins are cast out from the Church" for the duration of Lent.[195] They were reconciled to the community on Holy Thursday and readmitted to the "sacred Supper of the Lord."[196]

The system of penance Regino described was obviously not a "private" process in the modern sense of that word. Nor was his description of how bishops or presbyters should hear confessions private by post-Tridentine standards. There was of course no mention of a confessional box; the penitent's confession was itself "relatively open and would have been audible (and no doubt interesting) to those waiting their turn to confess."[197] The intense inwardness and sorrow for sin emphasized by the penitential psalms were mediated by *public* rituals that the whole community could see and witness.[198] What John Bossy calls a "social universe" of sin is still quite palpable in Regino's description.[199] While it is legitimate to argue, as Bossy does, that the interiorization of penance was under way well before the Counter-Reformation, what changed significantly after Trent was the sacrament's *ritual* profile. What had once been a matter of public ceremony whose venue was the entire space of the church building became not merely private but anonymous and *secret*, concealed by the confessional. Lost was the ancient notion that Christians are reconciled to God by being publicly reconciled to the church community. Regino of Prüm's account of penance thus registers that premodern view of selfhood mentioned earlier, a perception that sees human persons as constituted within ritual and existing within a network of interpersonal relations in which the central mediating institution was the church's liturgy of reconciliation and communion.

In conclusion, it cannot be said that the early modern reframing of Catholic identity resulted simply from a dramatic expansion of self-awareness and interiority, or because "self-fashioning" began to reshape not only social elites but the rural poor, or because authorities in church and state began working together to control behavior and enforce conformity. It is a matter of record that the Counter-Reformation Church did in fact promote a "code of religious practice" based on a "system of parochial conformity" and regulated by bishops "empowered by the council of Trent to enforce it."[200] It is also true that this system did foster (and even compel) a religious identity based on public practices that were already largely in place within pre-Reformation Catholicism. Yet one must also note the persistence in early modernity of a religious affectivity (with remote roots in medieval theologians like Bonaventure) that surfaced in ways ecclesiastical authorities often disliked and disapproved, and sometimes destabilized the very structures of conformity the early modern church was at such great pains to promote and preserve.

We see the innovative, potentially destabilizing impact of religious affectivity and vernacular religion inscribed on the images of Caravaggio and the novelistic narratives of Mary of Ágreda. True, the post-Tridentine church was intent on regularizing all aspects of "popular religion," especially the popular confraternities, and to a large degree it succeeded in neutralizing the threat these sometimes posed to conformity in religious practice.[201] But how could the church handle a "problem" like Sor María de Jesús? After all, the alleged damage her astonishing revelations in *MCG* did to devout Catholics surfaced well after the author had died. Moreover, the linchpin of her mystical "novel" about the Virgin Mary's life—belief in the Immaculate Conception—finally made its way into official Catholic dogma, much as Margaret Mary Alacoque's affective devotion to the Sacred Heart finally found acceptance in the Catholic liturgy. Bossy seems justified in saying that "a transition from medieval Christianity to modern Catholicism meant, on the popular front, turning collective Christians into individual ones," and "the attempt to achieve this transition was very commonly a failure."[202]

Dogma and discipline may therefore have been the lung through which church authorities expected all the faithful to breathe, but as we will see in the next chapter, hard-to-regulate devotions, especially the rosary, were early modern Catholicism's powerful "other lung." We can, in fact, speak of the "subversive potential" of the rosary in both its historical origins and its early modern reinterpretation. In spite of seventeenth-century paintings such as Sassoferrato's canvas in the rosary chapel of Rome's Church of Santa Sabina—which repeat the legend that Mary gave the rosary to Saint Dominic—the devotion did not, in fact, originate in any historically verifiable act of God or the church. It began as a popular, vernacular devotion "from the ground up," rather than as a result of decrees "from the top [church authority] down." And because, from at least the fifteenth century onward, the rosary had connected repeated prayers with *private meditation on the Christian mysteries*, the rosary gave scope to the human imagination in ways the church's more closely regulated rituals did not. Add to this the expanding self-awareness and interiority of early modern figures like Ignatius Loyola (*Spiritual Exercises*) and Mary of Ágreda (*MCG*), and you have a potentially volatile devotion whose "acceptable boundaries" church authorities had difficulty determining. Affinities between the rosary and medieval religious affectivity (evident in the writings of theologians like Bonaventure) also reinforced a Marian piety that sometimes surfaced in ways ecclesiastical authorities disliked and disapproved (e.g., Sor María's private communication from the "Queen"), destabilizing the very structures of conformity the early modern church was at such great pains to promote and preserve.

5

Reframing the Rosary

In a letter written to his brother in 1591, the Florentine painter Giovanni Battista Paggi (1554–1627) commented that "the hand is the instrument of the intellect, and without intellect, nothing good can be created."[1] By connecting hand and intellect, Paggi was pointing to the physical roots of human knowledge, a position that would probably have pleased Aristotle, who had argued that hand is to the body what intellect is to the soul.[2] The human hand—with its opposable thumb—is not only a marvel of creation and evolutionary engineering but also a rich source of metaphors. What is the hand itself, after all, but a five-pointed star opening at the end of a wand (the arm)? Moreover, as we know from the prehistoric cave paintings at sites like Lascaux and Altamira, images of the hand were among the most ancient forms of human signature. The artists who created pictures of bison and horses at those sites "signed" their works by including their handprints. The English monk Bede the Venerable (d. 735) taught his students how to count and compute sums by using their fingers as calculators.

Praying by hand is one of the things that distinguished the Catholic rosary from other forms of popular devotion in the early modern period. For even in the absence of a string of beads, one's ten fingers could serve as prayer counters and physical reminders that one's whole body and being were focused on God as one meditated on the mysteries of Christ and the Virgin Mary. We possess, in fact, an early sixteenth-century printed book called the *Chiropsalterium* (literally, "hand psalter"), which instructed readers how to use their hands as a mnemonic device for praying and meditating on the biblical psalms (the text of which had previously been committed to memory). (The rosary itself, we recall, was also called "Our Lady's Psalter.") There is evidence that the *Chiropsalterium* was widely known in religious communities, and that its material could include Marian elements, since Christians used many of these same psalms in the popular Hours of the Blessed Virgin, which reinterpreted passages from the biblical psalms in relation to the mysteries of Mary's life (e.g., her visit to Elizabeth, the birth of Christ).[3]

Such evidence attests to the rosary's innate adaptability. It was a devotion that could literally be "prayed by hand" or linked to a portable object (beads, knots on string) accessible to persons high and low, literate and unlettered. The rosary appealed across boundaries of class, culture, and gender. As Caravaggio's *Madonna del Rosario* vividly demonstrates, it was a devotion as easily linked to sophisticated theologian-saints like Thomas Aquinas as it is to beggars, nannies, and toddlers with sagging diapers. A handy illustration of this adaptability may be found in the rosary's popularity in England during the sixteenth and seventeenth centuries, a period during which Catholics saw themselves reduced to minority status, routinely penalized for practicing their faith, and denied access, often, to the comforting assurance of their traditional liturgy and sacraments.

Writing about the situation of Catholics in England and Wales during the period between 1558 and 1640, Michael Mullett remarks that "it was late medieval piety that fed the devotional life of the Catholic remnant in Elizabethan England."[4] Originally formed within a late medieval, urban ambience, this piety centered on—though it did not confine itself to—the eucharistic liturgy and popular prayers such as the rosary. The ethos of this piety, Mullett writes, was "formed in the medieval Netherlands that had produced the *devotio moderna* and the *Imitation of Christ* (whose influences were disseminated in England by the Carthusians)" and "was still being fostered a century after its implantation in the country."[5] The persistence of this piety, Mullett maintains, is astonishing. It continued to be a source of "post-Reformation English Catholic spiritual life," even outside private urban households, for in cities such as York the Corpus Christi dramas that embodied "a distinctively Catholic eucharistic theology" survived for at least ten years after the 1559 Elizabethan Religious Settlement (or Elizabethan Reform).[6] Moreover, allusions to the old religious practices (and possibly implicit endorsements of them) found their way into Shakespeare's dramas during the late sixteenth and early seventeenth centuries.[7]

Yet Lisa McClain observes that while historians have studied the persistent popularity of devotional practices in England both before and after the Elizabethan Reform, little attention has been paid to "*alternative* roles for the rosary" or to the "*changing* interpretation and practice" of such devotions.[8] Failure to study this issue, McLain argues, overlooks the Catholic Church's "centuries-old *modus operandi* of accommodating itself to different, often hostile environments in its efforts to perpetuate the Roman faith."[9] She goes on to observe that in a time when public practice of the "Old Religion" in England was subject to intense scrutiny and severe sanctions, it became necessary for Catholics to redefine or reinterpret the use and meaning of familiar prayers and devotional objects.[10] Under these conditions, the import and significance of popular prayers like the rosary shifted. When English Catholics were confronted by the loss of public spaces for worship, their prayer beads became, in effect, miniature shrines—private sanctuaries for worship that were tangible, yet portable and easily hidden. Surrounded by a state church whose royal head was officially hostile to them, Catholics—bereft of their traditional sites and supports (churches, clergy, liturgy, saints, relics, images)—could still claim to possess, through the rosary, a potent and ever-present intercessor in the figure of Mary.[11] Moreover, since the public celebration of sacraments was increasingly sporadic, infrequent, and dangerous, the rosary offered Catholics both the solace of meditating on the central mysteries of faith and the soteriological benefits of sacramental grace even in the absence of liturgical rites.[12]

McClain does not believe that the shifting significance of the rosary among English Catholics following the Elizabethan Reform was primarily the result of gender-based differences "between male and female use of the rosary"; on the contrary, her evidence suggests that the rosary was popular among both women and men and did not simply exemplify "a private, household religiosity shaped predominately by women."[13] For example, in his *Instructions for the Use of the Beades*, published at Louvain in 1589, the exiled English priest John Bucke recommended the rosary as a devotion beneficial to all "true and good Catholics" of whatever "trade, occupacion or qualitie . . . you are, whiles you goe about your necessarie businesse in your vocation, or whiles you are traualing by the waye; or in tilinge or plowinge the ground."[14] Even if they continued to live and work in "darke Egiptiacal England (the verie sea of heresie)," every Catholic, Bucke believed, could remain an active participant in "the wider, multidimensional society of which he or she was a part," struggling to balance "their families' social and financial well being . . . with their fears for the fates of their souls."[15] Remaining in a homeland where they no longer controlled church practice or property, English Catholics were confronted with the need to renegotiate their identity as citizen-subjects, workers, and communicants loyal to both the pope and a queen whose titles included that of "supreme governor of the Church in England."[16]

It is of course true that reinterpreting, reimagining, or reconceptual-izing Catholic identity and devotions (including the rosary) was hardly a phenomenon limited to English Catholics after the Elizabethan Reform. On the contrary, such a reframing of reform, representation, rites, and re-ligious identity reflected a process broadly at work among early modern Catholics throughout Europe. Here, however, we will focus on how the ro-sary itself became a principal medium through which these Catholics re-negotiated their relationship to sacred places, persons, objects, and events. The British Isles between the sixteenth and eighteenth centuries are a good place to begin, in part because laypeople and their piety played a key role in the "continuing persistence and survival of Catholicism in England after 1559," and in part because praying the rosary became a way to par-ticipate in the Roman liturgy itself.[17] For example, in early seventeenth-century Ireland, where Catholicism was a "penalized majority faith," the Roman Congregation of the Holy Office allowed the superior of the Irish Dominicans to permit priests "to conduct very basic, unceremonious ad-ministration of the Sacraments and reservation of the Host, as well as to substitute the Rosary for the Office [Divine Office, Liturgy of the Hours], and to celebrate Mass outdoors, underground, or in the early hours, or in the afternoon, or in front of Protestants and excommunicates."[18] These permissions represented Rome's response to an emergency situation, but they were also, in fact, transferable to diocesan priests throughout the British Isles. So it is not surprising that in seventeenth-century Scotland, "the Rosary, rather than the Mass, with its accoutrements, may have come to be recognized by its foes as the visible expression of Catholic profes-sion."[19] As we will see, the rosary not only became a way for lay Catholics to pray and participate *during* Mass; it also, in a sense, *became* the Mass when public liturgical spaces (churches, chapels, shrines) were no longer readily accessible.

Seeking Survival and Sacramental Access

In discussing how the rosary was reframed by early modern Catholics in the British Isles, several factors need to be considered. First, as Christopher Haigh writes, "the English Reformation was not a precise and dramatic event, it was a long and complex process."[20] Even though, under Eliza-beth, Catholicism went from being "prescribed orthodoxy to prohibited deviation," the reformation of the church in England proceeded slowly.[21] It began not with grand gestures by a newly empowered majority but as the work of small yet vocal minorities.[22] Second, the traditional faith, piety, and practices of the Old Religion—briefly restored under Mary Tudor (1553–58)—persisted despite Parliament's 1559 Act of Uniformity requiring English Christians to resume use of the Book of Common Prayer in force at the time of Edward VI's death in 1553.[23] Elizabeth's accession and restoration of the Edwardine prayer book did not immediately revolutionize the ritual and devotional life of English parishes. Many of the churches in her realm continued adhering to the conservative traditions of the Old Religion. For example, nearly a decade into her reign (1567), "the Bishop of Bangor reported that Catholic altars and images were still being used in Protestant churches and that parishioners still worshipped with relics and rosaries."[24] Even among London's 106 parishes, there was wide diversity and variation in religious practice, even though the conservative presence in the city had been reduced to "a hard core of Catholic recusancy" by about the year 1580.[25]

In short, the Old Religion did not simply or suddenly disappear in England. The geography of Elizabethan Catholicism, John Bossy notes, included pockets of vigorous "seigneurial Catholicism" that survived among the landed gentry: "Nobles or gentlemen who felt the insufficiencies of the new-found religion more strongly than the inducements of [Elizabeth's] court could retire to their 'estates;' to the seigneurial household, its buildings, lands, and the village or villages which it dominated. Within this unity the rites and observances which had disappeared from public view could be preserved."[26] Among Catholics in such circumstances, the Old Religion could continue relatively intact, even if some public displays like processions or pageants had to be pared back or discontinued entirely. The customary Catholic cycle of fasts and feasts could be more easily maintained within a seigneurial household, especially if its personnel included a priest who "could at the same time act, or be disguised, as tutor, steward, or something similar."[27] This was the situation in many larger houses, where liturgy and hospitality blended so smoothly that on greater feasts like Christmas and Easter, a large contingent might be present for Mass—the musicians doing double duty as liturgical choir and entertainment for the guests.[28] Such an "integration of religion into the household accounts for a fact which has been universally observed as characteristic of Elizabethan Catholicism, the importance of the position occupied in it by women."[29] Within such families, moreover, even important sacramental rites like baptism and marriage—for which the proper venue was the local parish—could be melded into the private life of a country estate.

In some ways, then, the survival of the Old Religion within the seigneurial system exemplified the principle of "live and let live." These
Catholic households, in effect, revived the proprietary churches of an earlier epoch. Since Catholicism of this kind was largely a "complex of social
practices rather than a religion of internal conviction, it offered no barrier
to the degree of attendance at the parish church required to preserve the
integrity of the household; a sufficient dissociation could be expressed by
not communicating, by keeping one's hat on or talking during the sermon."[30] In other words, nobles and gentry could conform to the new religious arrangement while continuing to practice Catholicism privately at
home—and this, without any excruciating crisis of conscience or moral
scruple. "All that was implied," writes Bossy, "was a distinction in the order of society between what was the Queen's and what was one's own;
freedom of conscience meant the free decision of the mode of existence
of one's household. The government, at least provisionally, accepted the
distinction, and conflict either interior or exterior was minimal."[31]

During the first ten to twelve years of Elizabeth's reign, therefore, lay
Catholics of the upper classes remained quite numerous, public, and truculent in their opposition to the new religious polity.[32] In his study of the
evolution of the English reformation between 1530 and 1570, David Loades
offers an example from the autobiography of Thomas Hancock, a reformed
parson who was confronted while giving a required sermon against the
Roman Mass by one Thomas Whyte, an angry seigneurial Catholic:

> I being minister of God's word in that town of Poole, preaching the word
> upon some Sunday . . . inveighed against Idolatry and covetousness . . .
> [for] if it be so that no man hath seen God, nor can see God with these
> bodily eyes, then that which the priest lifteth over his head [at the eleva-
> tion during Mass] is not God, for you do see it with your bodily eyes: if
> it be not God, you may not honour it as God, neither for God. Whereat
> old Thomas Whyte, a great rich merchant and a ringleader of the papists,
> rose out of his seat and went out of the church saying, "Come from him,
> good people; he came from the devil and teacheth unto you devilish doc-
> trine." John Notherel, alias John Spicer, followed him, saying, "it shall be
> God when thou shalt be but a knave."[33]

"These were typical voices of early Elizabethan lay Catholicism," writes
Mullett, "loud, aggressive, unafraid, fluent and abusive, and above all confident in the imminent vindication of tradition and continuity."[34]

Nevertheless, Catholicism in Elizabeth's England was far more complex than its survival among the seigneurial classes may suggest. Despite their truculent tone, Old Religionists like Thomas Whyte and John Notherel represented something more subtle than unthinking traditionalism, "obstinate habit," superstition, or "rural rejection of all change."[35] These "religious traditionalists were liturgically and ecclesiologically knowledgeable, consciously Roman in their allegiance to the pope and insisting on the retention of the Mass; they were to be found amongst the laity in town and country."[36] Moreover, their intellectual heritage was humanistic; it had been fed and fueled by university professors teaching at prestigious sites like Oxford—scholars in the Erasmian mold for whom "the sense of criticism and intellectual renovation was not distinguished from the idea that the unity of Christendom was the only preservative of truth."[37]

In short, the Old Religion's survival—whether in public or underground—was not simply a result of seigneurial resistance against the queen's estate (which Catholic nobles would have admitted was entirely her own business, not theirs). Nor did it result simply from the class-based conflicts that caused many landed Catholics to despise adherents of Elizabethan Protestantism as low-life "basket-makers and beer-brewers."[38] Unquestionably, class distinctions and social prejudices were at work in shaping these attitudes, but Bossy is also right to suggest that the radical basis for Catholic resistance to the events of 1559 was scholarly humanism.[39] The initial reaction of Catholic humanist intellectuals to Elizabeth's new order was to relinquish their posts at Oxford and Cambridge and cross the sea to Louvain. In June 1559, for example, when the Royal Commissioners arrived at Oxford to "undo the work of Cardinal Pole [during Mary Tudor's short reign] and to tender the oath of supremacy," sixteen priests withdrew from Trinity College alone, while similar numbers left other colleges to "cross the sea" or live with friends.[40] Yet this move did not necessarily represent a major shift in thinking. Gradualism was the watchword among a majority of the English scholars who relocated to Louvain; they believed there was no pressing reason to panic over Elizabeth's religious settlement. They were not

> unduly worried about the present, or concerned for the future; the traditional structure of church order, of belief and practice, seemed to them part of the order of the universe; there had always been heresies and schisms, but as a violation of this order they could not finally prosper. In the meantime they must get on with their work as clerks, examining

and purifying traditional doctrine with the best techniques available, and defending it against the attacks of heretics. At the worst, they would have to see that this work was safeguarded and carried on by successors who, when the time came, would be ready for the task of restoring true religion in England.[41]

These expatriate, humanistic gradualists thus represented views quite similar to those of the Catholic gentry that remained in England. They were not innovators bent on radically reinterpreting Catholic tradition to meet the unprecedented new conditions of the time, but preservationists who sought a gradual refinement and purification of traditional doctrine and practice while looking forward to an eventual restoration of the Old Religion in their homeland. Queen Elizabeth could do what she wished in her own estate; meanwhile, Catholicism could continue to flourish among traditionalist nobles and propertied gentlemen, albeit with a much lower public profile. After all, the queen herself seemed to expect little more than external conformity to her Settlement, for she had tolerantly insisted in a 1569 speech that none of her subjects were to

> be molested either by examination or inquisition in any matter either of faith, as long as they shall profess the Christian faith, not gainsaying the authority of the Holy Scriptures, and of the Articles of our faith contained in the creeds Apostolic and Catholic, or for matter of ceremonies, or any other external matters appertaining to Christian religion, as long as they shall in their outward conversation show themselves quiet and conformable and not manifestly repugnant and obstinate to the laws of the realm, which are established for frequentation of divine service in the ordinary churches.[42]

In many respects, Elizabeth's words simply summarized the deliberate, decade-long policy of her government, namely, that "any public, professional or ecclesiastical career was to be contingent upon the taking of an oath which denied implicitly Papal Supremacy concerning *cura animarum* (pastoral care of souls)" while nonconformist Catholics unconcerned about career advancement could continue the "quiet enjoyment" of their property and family provided they attended "the newly arranged liturgy of the State Church."[43] But this policy of religious toleration did not survive the Northern Rebellion of 1569 or the papal bull of 1570, *Regnans in excelsis*, which formally excommunicated Elizabeth and freed her subjects from allegiance to her authority. The Northern Rebellion, also known as the "Earls Rebellion" or the "Rising in the North," was a short-lived insurgency that arose in the shires of Durham and York among Catholic nobles who hoped to restore the ancient faith and liturgy and (probably) to replace Queen Elizabeth with Mary Queen of Scots. Its chief instigators, the Earl of Northumberland and the Earl of Westmoreland, protested from the outset that they were loyal subjects whose only goal was to rescue Elizabeth from bad advisers and to restore truth and good order throughout the realm. As they told their sympathizers and supporters:

> We, Thomas [Percy, seventh] Earl of Northumberland, and Charles [Neville, sixth] Earl of Westmoreland, the Queen's true and faithful subjects, to all the same of the old Catholic faith. Know ye that we, with many other well-disposed persons, as well of the nobility, as others, have promised our faiths, in the furtherance of this our good meaning.
>
> Forasmuch as divers disordered and evil-disposed persons, about the Queen's majesty, have, by their subtle and crafty dealing to advance themselves, overcome, in this our realm, the true and Catholic religion towards God, and by the same abused the Queen, disorder the realm, and now, lastly, seek and procure the destruction of the nobility. We, therefore, have gathered ourselves together, to exist by force; and rather by the help of God and you, good people; and to see redress of these things amiss, with restoring of all ancient customs and liberties to God's church, and this noble realm; lest, if we should not do it ourselves, we might be reformed by strangers, to the great hazard of the state of this our country whereunto we are all bound.[44]

Setting out in early November with an "undisciplined, badly armed" force of between 5,200 and 12,000 soldiers, the insurgents managed briefly to restore Catholic liturgy to Durham Cathedral, where they knocked down the new Communion Table, restored two altars (where the old high altar had been), burned or ripped up the English Bible and Prayer Book, and ransacked the (Elizabethan) bishop of Durham's property.[45] They maintained control of the cathedral for about ten or twelve days, then marched south to restore the ancient Catholic services at churches in Staindrop, Darlington, Richmond, and Ripon. By December 16, 1569, the rebel army had been disbanded. Charles Neville escaped to the Netherlands, while the Earl of Northumberland was eventually captured. It had been a largely bloodless insurrection, but its aftermath was far grislier.

Elizabeth executed about 500 of those involved in the "Rising of the North," including Northumberland.[46]

Nevertheless, a policy of religious toleration might still have prevailed in England had it not been for the circumstances that surrounded the publication in 1570 of Pius V's bull excommunicating Elizabeth. Pius's original intention had been to pursue a policy like the one Clement VII used when dealing with King Henry VIII. Clement formally excommunicated Henry on July 11, 1533, but deferred implementing his decision until the "secular arm" (in this case, the Holy Roman Emperor and King Francis I of France) was ready to enforce the papal bull.[47] Since, however, the secular arm "never got ready, the bull remained permanently unpublished, and consequently [was] of no effect as far as [Henry VIII's] subjects were concerned."[48] In the aftermath of the failed "Rising of the North," Pius V's plan seems to have been quietly to circulate—among Catholics in England who had not supported the rebellion—his decision to excommunicate Elizabeth. Through such stealth diplomacy, the pope hoped to solicit broad Catholic support without, at the same time, risking a public confrontation that would tip the queen off to his ultimate intention.[49] The papal plan was thwarted, however, when John Felton, a seigneurial Catholic from an old Norfolk family, jumped the gun and, in the spring of 1570, rashly affixed a copy of the bull, *Regnans in excelsis*, to the palace doors of the bishop of London.[50] Felton may have believed his action would spur Philip II of Spain to support the Catholic cause in England, but in fact Philip was annoyed, complaining in a letter to Don Gueran de Spes (the Spanish ambassador to the English court) that "His Holiness has taken this step without communicating with me in any way, which certainly has greatly surprised me, because my knowledge of English affairs is such that I believe I could give a better opinion of them, and the course that ought to have been adopted than anyone else."[51] The result of making Elizabeth's excommunication public, Philip warned, would be "the more to oppress and persecute the few good Catholics still remaining in England."[52]

Once *Regnans in excelsis* was publicized, the situation of Catholics in England was bound to change. Quiet dissimulation and outward compliance with the Settlement of 1559 were no longer sufficient. Between 1559 and 1570, it had been possible for many Catholic laity to attend the Prayer Book services in their local parishes while retaining traditional practices of piety. "While the Protestant service was in progress," writes historian Conrad Swan, "some directed their attention to . . . saying their beads, or reading Our Lady's Primer [containing the Little Office of the Blessed

Virgin Mary], while others read secular works such as those on *Materia
Medica* or the Humanities."[53] The casuistic basis for such nonconformity
was the notion that oaths obligate those who swear them only if administered by persons acting under legitimate (i.e., papal) authority. Since the
1559 Acts of Supremacy and Conformity were administered under royal
(not papal) authority, they are neither legitimate nor binding, and Catholics may ignore them.

Renegotiating Sacred Space

After 1570, then, Elizabeth's government became much more aggressive
in punishing religious nonconformity.[54] In 1571, for example, the English
Parliament passed tougher penal laws against the practice of Catholicism,
which, among other things, "made it a treasonable offence to question
the validity of the monarch's religion, to challenge her right to the crown
on religious grounds, or to aid those who did so"; it also became illegal
(and treasonous) to "bring or receive papal bulls [recall John Felton's ac-
tion], crucifixes, rosaries, or an *agnus dei* [a small, usually circular, devotional item, made of wax and imprinted with an image of a lamb representing Christ]."[55] The prohibition against tangible symbols of Catholic
devotion—the rosary in particular—is significant, and we will return to it
shortly. First, however, a few comments are needed about the sacramental
situation of English Catholics during their transition from "monopoly to
minority status."[56]

Catholicism is, after all, a sacramental faith that relies on the ministry
of priests (and bishops) for everything from rites of initiation (baptism,
confirmation, Eucharist), to services for marriage and burial, to liturgies of
reconciliation (penance) and healing (anointing of the sick, "last rites"), to
the ordination of new ministers. In a word, sacramentalism lies at the core
of Catholic identity, and sacraments grow scarce in the absence of ordained
clergy. The crisis English Catholics faced after the accession of Elizabeth
was above all a sacramental crisis, both because a majority of them believed
the new Prayer Book liturgies were not faithful to the Old Religion and because after the settlement of 1559, Catholic priests who withheld their ministry from the Church of England often could not safely minister among
their people.[57] Still, this hardly meant that all or most Catholic clergy fled
the country, as many humanist dons from Oxford and Cambridge had
done. On the contrary, a large contingent of the so-called Marian or "Massing" priests—those ordained before or during the Catholic restoration

under Mary Tudor—survived and succeeded in keeping the Old Religion alive in many parts of Elizabethan England until (and even after) missionary priests trained on the Continent began arriving in 1574. As Michael Mullett points out, part of the reason for the Marian priests' success

lay in their relative legal immunity. The Act of Parliament of 1585 making it high treason for a priest ordained abroad even to be in England exempted priests ordained within the realm—the "Marians"—who thus operated with a comparative freedom of action denied the seminarians. They enjoyed operational advantages: they were safer for lay people to harbour; they knew their way around their terrain; and they could consecrate marriages which might be recognized by the Church of England. It is true that as a result of the dominant martyrological concerns of post-Reformation English Catholic historiography, the seminarians have always enjoyed the cachet of heroism. The assets of the "Massing" priests in Elizabethan England lay rather in the appeal, especially the popular appeal, they exercised as touchstones with a familiar past, and as former parish priests who had refused to conform to a novel religious dispensation and who covertly provided a liturgy well loved by many.[58]

When English priests and seminarians stealthily began returning to England after 1574, they did not immediately succeed in creating a new kind of "fugitive" Catholicism. Their presence may simply have sustained the loyalty of largely wealthy English Catholics whose families had managed to continue practicing the old faith (with the help of the Marian priests) even after Elizabeth's Settlement. Thus the English Catholic community that managed to maintain itself for almost three centuries, between 1570 and 1850, was not "the successful product of a missionary triumph in the face of Protestantism and persecution," but a "rump community."[59] The deeper question is how this rump community of Catholics survived in a climate that made sacraments scarce and sacred spaces (churches, shrines, liturgies, devotional objects) hard to come by. For the fact is that English Catholics did eventually create, over the course of nearly three centuries, "a comprehensive devotional structure which maintained the continuity of tradition while it renewed and adapted its data into forms appropriate to the situation."[60] Their story is not simply one of transition from "monopoly to minority status" or of mere survival in the face of failure and decline; it is also a story of renewal in which devotions such as the rosary came to play a central part.

Over the course of Elizabeth's long reign, therefore, Catholics in England came to be, in McClain's fine phrase, a "church without churches," a sacramental community forced to live without sacraments. In the absence of church buildings and public shrines, the challenge was to find sites to accommodate ritualized actions that "physically, ritually, or imaginatively separated the space from ordinary use."[61] These spaces might be natural (fields, forest, orchards), domestic (private homes or estates), forensic (courts of law, where Catholics, lay and clergy, were arraigned, tried, and sentenced), penal (prisons, execution sites), or mental and physical (mind, heart, and human body as sacred shrines). Under such circumstances, *portable* spaces—represented by devotional objects like rosary beads—became simultaneously signs of a distinctive religious identity and sites that fostered social gatherings for prayer and mutual support. For, wrote Richard Broughton in 1617, even if "we can not goe to the Church" for common prayer "because of misbeleuers" and the "wicked [who] occupy the place" and "prophane" it, let "the true beleuers . . . euery one by them selues, singe, reade, pray, or two or three gathered together. For where there be two or three gathered together in my name, there am I in the middest of them. Let not the godly pray neither at home with an heritike, for what society is there betwene light & darknesse?"[62]

The reinterpretation of the rosary by Catholics in Elizabethan England resulted largely from the fact that adherents of the Old Religion were required to seek new forms of sacred space for the practice of their faith. Their traditional venues—public churches staffed by validly ordained Roman priests celebrating the sacraments in liturgies approved by the pope—were no longer available. What this entailed, of course, was a need to find new, unsuspected spaces that could become privileged sites of God's self-communication to human persons—even in the absence of sacraments or priestly ministers. Those "spaces" might not be public and visible but private and interior. They could, for instance, be the prayerful sanctuary of one's own heart—or a set of rosary beads concealed in the sleeve of one's garment. Such newly imagined spaces did not deny the primacy of sacraments or the role of ordained clergy in the economy of salvation, but they did insert a wedge, however slight, between private act and public cult.[63] It seemed to loosen the bond between what later theology would call "sacramental efficacy" and the ritual enactment of the sacramental sign.

Still, the conviction that a believer's body is itself sacred space reaches back to the very origins of Christianity (see John 2.19–22; 1 Corinthians 3.16–17). "Offer your bodies," wrote Paul to the Romans, "as a living sacrifice, holy and pleasing to God, your spiritual worship" (Romans 12.1). From Paul's perspective, every Christian's body is ritual space—altar and sacrifice, a site of transformation where Christ manifests his presence. In the literature of Christian martyrdom, particularly, the body as "altar" or "holocaust" became a common trope. We find it, for instance, in the second-century *Martyrdom of Polycarp*, which describes an early Christian bishop's death by fire. Polycarp, we are told, "put his hands behind him and was bound, as a noble ram out of a great flock, for an oblation, a whole burnt offering made ready and acceptable to God."[64] As he was dying, he uttered a prayer whose structure and contents closely resemble those of an early Christian eucharistic prayer:

> O Lord God Almighty, Father of thy beloved and blessed Child, Jesus Christ, through Whom we have received full knowledge of thee, . . . I bless thee, that Thou has granted me this day and hour, that I may share, among the number of the martyrs, in the cup of thy Christ, for the Resurrection to everlasting life, both of soul and body in the immortality of the Holy Spirit. And may I, today, be received among them before Thee, as a rich and acceptable sacrifice, as Thou . . . hast prepared beforehand and shown forth, and fulfilled. For this reason I also praise Thee for all things, I bless Thee, I glorify Thee through the everlasting and heavenly high Priest, Jesus Christ, thy beloved Child, through whom be glory to Thee with him and the Holy Spirit, both now and for the ages that are to come. Amen.[65]

As witnesses looked on, the fire that was consuming Polycarp took on "the likeness of a room" in which the bishop's body was seen "not as burning flesh, but as bread that is being baked," a suggestion, surely, that suffering makes the martyr resemble a loaf of eucharistic bread.[66]

The Rosary as a Eucharistic Site

Given the antiquity of such traditions, it comes as no surprise to hear Christians of later centuries appeal to similar tropes that identify the body as sacred ritual space. Under pressure of persecution and often denied physical access to the sacraments, especially the Eucharist, English Catholics of the late sixteenth century and seventeenth century were encouraged to acknowledge their own bodies as sacred space, the material means, "similar to the unconsecrated [eucharistic] bread," of transformation into

Christ's own body and blood.[67] For example, in their mid-seventeenth-century devotional treatise, *Jesus, Maria, Joseph*, authors Arthur Crowther and Thomas Vincent, both Benedictine monks, offered meditative texts ("elevations") to suggest Christians can, by prayer, transform themselves—their own bodies—into eucharistic offerings:

> By your Incarnation, you establish a new manner of gracious favor in the world, which makes me in the Order of Grace, not only existent by you, but existent in you. So that by this manner of Grace . . . I am not only yours, not only by you, but I am in you; I live in you, I make a part of you; I am bone of your bone, and flesh of your flesh, let me also be spirit of your Spirit, let me live by your life, let me participate of the Interior, of Grace, of the Estate, of the Spirit of your Mysteries.[68]

In another "elevation," the authors write, "Love puts you on the cross, and placeth us in Glory; and, finally, this Love transforms us into you, not only a communication of qualities, but even by a communication of substance, O Son of God! . . . I adore you in this love, in this annihilation, in this powerful transformation."[69]

McClain suggests that what Crowther and Vincent proposed in these and similar texts amounts to a veritable transubstantiation of the "believer's substance into Christ's," and this proves that at least some seventeenth-century English devotional writers were proposing "alternatives to traditional experiences of the Mass" within a sociopolitical situation where regular attendance at the liturgy was impossible for many Catholics.[70] She also argues that the treatise *Jesus, Maria, Joseph*—though designed, by the authors' own admission, to "promote worship upon the rosary"—proposed prayers (like the ones just quoted) that embody what could be called a revisionist theology of the Eucharist, in which the individual believer assumes "both the role of priest and of the Eucharistic host within his own person, sacrificing his own body as if upon an altar."[71] Elsewhere in her study, McClain is at pains to point out that such revisionist interpretations distinguish *English* Catholic thought about sacraments, devotions, and the intercessory power of revered figures like the Virgin Mary from contemporary, post-Tridentine *continental* perceptions.[72]

McClain makes a valuable point, but she may be underestimating factors that suggest significant affinities between early modern Catholics in England and their coreligionists on the European mainland. For instance, the missionary priests who in the 1570s reentered England after training on the Continent (as opposed to Marian priests who had never left the country) were imbued with a distinctive brand of Catholicism that owed as much to their training in Jesuit spirituality as it did to the perils of a now-persecuted religious minority. We have seen, for example, that the Ignatian *Exercises* profoundly affected how many early modern Catholics used their imagination while meditating on the mysteries of the rosary. Englishmen (like Gregory Martin) who trained as seminarians on the European continent were often educated in Jesuit institutions and were imbued with Ignatian spirituality, even if they did not belong to the Society of Jesus.

These missionaries, who worked primarily in the south and east of England, quickly turned from itinerancy to residential chaplaincies, that is, from the dangerous enterprise of moving from place to place to more secure conditions within the manor houses of Catholic gentry. In the Continental seminaries these missionaries "had shared the intense spirituality of an institutional spiritual life, and the Jesuits and their friends had taken the '*Spiritual Exercises*': in England, many of them tried to recreate their student experience in the religious round of the reformed Catholic gentry household."[73] Literature like Jesuit poet Robert Southwell's *Short Rule of a Good Life* proposed an ideal of devotional piety and sacramental practice that presupposes a resident chaplain. Moreover, the missionaries often worked in households distinguished by a pattern of family-centered religious practice that reflected the piety of Catholic gentry living in relative security on their hereditary estates. By this time, too, Continental reinterpretations of biblical narratives, liturgical rites, and devotional objects were well under way, especially in the visual arts. Furthermore, influential English Catholics like the Bible translator Gregory Martin (1542–82) spent significant time in Rome and left appreciative accounts of what they saw and experienced there (including devotional practices such as the rosary).[74] Martin and his friend the martyr Edmund Campion had been young scholars at Oxford in 1557, had spent time at the English college in Douai (1571–73), and were very much under the spell of Jesuit life and spirituality.[75]

In sum, Catholicism in England, like its counterpart on the Continent, retained a good deal of diversity both during and after the Elizabethan era. No single designation ("traditionalist," "reformist") does justice to its diversity and pluriformity, especially if one takes into account the socioeconomic differences between Catholic gentry and the working poor. Nevertheless, there is good reason to think that the rosary was being reinterpreted among some seventeenth-century English Catholics as a "eucharistic site" in which laypersons, "praying by hand" and presenting their own bodies as "a living sacrifice" (Romans 12.1), could obtain *sacramental* grace. To put it another way, the rosary was being reframed as a new form of "spiritual communion" through which lay Catholics might experience the ultimate effect (Latin, *res*) of the Eucharist (i.e., the real, personal presence of Christ, which in turn creates the unity of his body the church), even in the absence of liturgical rites, sacramental signs, and priestly ministry. What was new about such interpretations was not the notion of "spiritual communion" as such but *the link between it and the rosary*. Through the contemplative participation of prayer—by "telling their beads" and "praying by hand"—Catholics could experience in their own bodies the real sacramental effects of the Eucharist, a union with Christ and his church so real, intense, and intimate that it made believers "bone of his bone, flesh of his flesh, and spirit of his Spirit." Reframed in this way, the rosary, concealed in the hands of praying Catholics required to attend the Prayer Book "Holy Communion" in an English parish, could be seen as connecting them to the grace of Eucharist. Under such conditions, adherents of the Old Religion could "hide in plain sight," using devotional media like the rosary to gain access to *sacramental* grace.

One finds hints that such a reinterpretation was gaining ground in John Bucke's *Instructions for the Use of the Beades* (1589), published under the auspices of the English College at Louvain and containing, in the author's words, "many matters of meditacion or mentall prayer, with diuerse good aduises of ghostly counsalye."[76] Bucke began by proposing points for meditation on each of the fifteen mysteries of the "Rosaire, Psalter, or Crowne of our Laidie . . . upon the beades."[77] "Fyrst set before the eyes of your soule," Bucke advised, the first "secret" or mystery ("the annunciation of the blessed virgin Mary") offered to the imagination, while saying the Our Father and ten Hail Marys *"attentiuelie, distinctlie, and deuoutlie."*[78] Bucke's deliberate choice of these three adverbs ("attentively, distinctly, and devoutly") is significant, because they echo the three-word formula that describes how the priest should pronounce the words of eucharistic consecration ("Hoc est enim corpus meum" [This is my body]) in the Mass rubrics of the 1570 *Missale Romanum*.[79] In Bucke's comments on mystery after mystery, this same language—closely linked to the priest's actions during the central prayer of the Mass—is repeated. Indeed, in his recommendations for the fourth joyful mystery, he made an explicit connection between the mysteries of the rosary and the "great mysteries" of the Mass. Meditating on the words of "olde Simeon the Byshop" while holding the child Jesus, Bucke encouraged whoever prays the rosary to "learne to present thy selfe oftentimes in the Churches withall *diligence, reuerence and deuocion,* specially at the holy sacrifice of the Masse: that thou mayest be partaker of great mysteries."[80] Of course Bucke knew full well that a majority of his intended readers (Catholics in Elizabethan England) could not regularly participate in "the holy sacrifice of the Masse." Their participation in "great [sacramental] mysteries" would necessarily have to take an alternative form, and this seems implied by Bucke's words in the sentence that immediately follows his allusion to the Eucharist:

And think how just and faithfull persones by deuout prayer, and godlie patience, haue at last obtained their holie desires, as this man [Simeon] dyd. And here also marke how our Sauiour in his infancie, being but eight dayes olde, shed his bloode for thee at his holie Circumcision: and learne for his sake to suffer from thy childhode what aduiersitie so euer fall vpon thee.[81]

Language like this sounds as if it were explicitly tailored to the situation of Elizabethan Catholics who, being a church without churches, were forced to seek sacramental grace in the absence of priests and liturgies. The shedding of Christ's blood at his circumcision—which is *not*, in fact, connected with the "fourth joyful mystery" (Christ's presentation in the Temple)—is surely alluded to because it fits both the perilous condition of Catholics in England (facing death because of their faith) and the sacrificial nature of the Mass. This impression was further reinforced by comments Bucke makes a few paragraphs later. "And thinke not," he warned,

to finde him with worldely affection towarde thy kinred, nor among the delites of flesh and bloude: but in the Church of God, by often hearing the word of God, and frequenting the Sacramentes. Allwayes prouide to thy vttermost power that thou kepe him in the cabinet of thy harte: and leese him not after thon [sic] hast founde him. This order thou must obserue in reciting the Rosarie.[82]

Again, such language seems coded precisely for people who, in a time of danger and persecution, might not always "finde him [Christ]," even among their closest kin. Bucke urged his readers, moreover, to stay faithful to the "Churche of God" by frequenting the *sacraments*, though he certainly knew this was often impossible. For that reason, it would appear, he urged each Catholic to "kepe him [Christ] in the cabinet of thy harte and leese him not" after finding him—an oblique allusion that compares each true believer's heart to a tabernacle where the reserved eucharistic sacrament is kept.[83]

Another interesting example emerges from Bucke's commentary on the third glorious mystery ("the coming of the holie Ghost").[84] When describing the effects of the Spirit's presence, he lists "six speciall causes of the comyng of the holy Ghost," namely, "to reioyce the pensiue; to reuiue the deade in synne; to sanctifie the vnclean; to confirme his Disciples in loue: to saue the just: to teach the ignorant."[85] Bucke then proceeds to list the "speciall meanes" by which the Spirit's "guyftes and graces are preserued and encreased in vs."[86] Heading Bucke's list of means is "prayer with humilitie," followed by "diligent frequenting the Sacraments with hearing diuine seruice," and the "continual exercise of the woorkes of Charitie." These, the author assures his readers, will provide "strength against all assaultes and tentacions of ghostlie and bodilie enemyes," and "no peril nor persecucion can annoye that persone whiche hath the holy Ghost." Traditionally, of course, Catholics held that persons "have the holy Ghost" in virtue of their *sacramental participation* in Christ, because the "water and blood" that flowed from Christ's side (John 19.34) became, as medieval theologians taught, the radical source of Christian sacraments.[87] Yet Bucke puts "prayer with humilitie" at the top of his list, thereby suggesting that his readers are people under pressure of persecution who must find an alternative means of sacramental access in order to "receive the benefits of the Mass without the performance of the sacrament itself."[88]

In short, Bucke's *Instructions for the Use of the Beades* seemed to transfer the medieval trope connecting Christ's passion and the sacraments to the *rosary*. Perhaps the strongest evidence for such an implied transference is visual rather than verbal. A woodcut accompanying Bucke's meditation on the fourth glorious mystery ("the Assumpcion of our Ladie") shows Mary holding the child Jesus while standing on a sliver of moon— a typical image based on Revelations 12.1–5. Surrounding these figures is a rosary of five decades whose Our Father beads seem to recall the five wounds of the Crucified (side, two hands, two feet). Devotion to the five wounds of Jesus' passion hearkens back to the high Middle Ages, but it persisted in early modern Catholicism, in England and elsewhere in Europe. A primer in Latin and English, printed at Antwerp in 1599, about ten years after Bucke's *Instructions* were published at Louvain, includes "a

prayer vnto the woundes of Christe.”[89] Significantly, too, Bucke's meditations on the mysteries of the rosary are followed, a few pages later, by a
series of meditations on the passion and another series on the benefits of
receiving Holy Communion.[90]

All this does reinforce the impression that the rosary was being reframed as a “eucharistic site” within a largely lay Catholic population that
no longer had free access to sacraments and thus had to search for sacramental grace by using their own bodies as altars, their own hearts as
tabernacles, and their own devotional prayers as “eucharistic thanksgiving and communion.” At the same time, however, we have to remember
that the picture of English Catholic life during and after the Elizabethan
era is not a uniform one. The history of English Catholics between the
late sixteenth and eighteenth centuries is a checkered pattern of retreat
and advance, recession and revival. That history must be interpreted not
merely on the basis of sociology (a religious majority becomes a minority), or on the basis of religious conflict (resulting in persecution and
turning England into “mission territory” for Catholics), but also in relation to larger patterns of socioeconomic development in Europe.[91] At one
level, what happened to Catholics in England seems to have been unique,
and would lead one to affirm that English Catholic reinterpretations—of
sacraments, devotions, and lay involvement in church life—differed dis-
cernibly from what was happening on the Continent. Yet on another level,
as Bossy notes, Catholics in seventeenth-century England may have been
suffering not from systematic deprivation (of clergy and sacraments) but
from a “social crisis of consumption.”[92] He means that the sheer numbers
of missionary priests entering the English mission—inspired by the renewed Christian activism embodied in the careers of Ignatius Loyola and
Philip Neri—threw English Catholicism into an imbalance of supply and
demand. “The English mission,” Bossy writes, “was indeed afflicted with a
social crisis in the consumption of its products, and confined with in the
narrow possibilities of a luxury trade. If the seminaries had been facto-
ries they would have gone bankrupt through over-production; the price
of priests, like the price of everything else, must have been at rock bottom
between the 1640s and the 1670s.”[93]

The Rosary and Print Culture

Caution is needed, then, in evaluating the impact of lay Catholics and
their devotions—most notably the rosary—on reinterpretations of piety

and doctrine. It can hardly be said, for example, that the rosary represented "lay Catholic piety" as opposed to the "liturgical-sacramental piety" of the clergy and religious professionals. For one thing, many of the rosary's most vocal proponents in seventeenth-century England were clergymen like John Bucke, Henry Garnett, and Gregory Martin. Furthermore, the rosary itself, as we have seen, could sometimes be interpreted in quasi-sacramental terms as a "eucharistic site." Nor was this linkage between Mass and rosary found only in England. The doors of the Jesuit Chapel of Our Lady of Doctrine in Lisbon's Church of Sao Roque, for example, are inlaid with precious woods that "show the iconography of the Confraternity of Christian Doctrine, namely *a missal and a rosary*."[94] The Confraternity of Christian Doctrine (CCD) was the largely *lay* arm of a catechetical movement that originated in Italy during the first half of the sixteenth century and was given official recognition in 1571 by Pope Saint Pius V, who encouraged bishops to establish it in every parish.

The CCD's principal aim was to enlist the active collaboration of *laypeople* with clergy in the faith formation of children and adults. Devotion to Eucharist and rosary—two fundamental foci of Catholic doctrine and practice—lay at the heart of such formation, just as they did in John Bucke's *Instructions for the Use of the Beades* and in Henry Garnett's *Societie of the Rosary* (1624), a treatise for members of a lay rosary confraternity. Bucke had explicitly linked meditation on the mysteries of the rosary to the "great mysteries" of the "holy sacrifice of the Masse," while Garnett made a similar connection more indirectly, by commenting about Mary as an embodiment of the "Wisdom of God."[95] "How trew it is of her," wrote Garnett, "which is spoken of the Wisdome of God, with which she was so abundantly endowed, that she preuented those who desire her, for to shewe her selfe first vnto them."[96] An even more explicit link between Mary, Wisdom, and the Eucharist appeared in Louis Richeome's treatise *The Pilgrime of Loreto* (1629), where the Christian's inward journey to Mary's house (believed to have been miraculously transported to the Italian town of Loreto) embodied both the mystery of God's new Temple in Christ and of the "heavenly Table" of Christ's body and blood.[97] The building of Solomon's Temple, wrote Richeome, alerts us "to meditate a mystery of a future Temple, which Jesus Christ the true Salomon, and true Dauid both, triumphing in his heauenly kingdom in abundance of euerlasting peace shall build of his chosen liuely stones [the Christian faithful], which he causeth to be hewed and polished in this world at the cost and charges of his owne precious bloud"; meanwhile, God's Wisdom draws those "liuely stones," Christ's members, to the "heauenly Table of [his] body," which does "teach vs Faith, Hope and Charity, Humility, Obedience, Prudence, Chastity, Fortitude, Piety, Meeknes, and all other goodly Christian uertues."[98]

Bucke, Garnett, and Richeome focused on Mary as model of Wisdom and faith. Their works exploited a relationship between the rosary and print culture whose roots reach back to the fifteenth century.[99] What was innovative in the thought of these three Englishmen, however, was the reframing of sapiential (spiritual wisdom), sacramental, catechetical, and devotional themes by relating them to the *rosary*. Print culture was an invaluable ally in this process of reinterpretation, even though priest-missionaries and English recusant literature were hardly the first to make use of it. For example, G. L. Barnes has studied the impact of the role of early English printed primers on the religious formation of lay Catholics from 1529 onward.[100] He concludes that the relationship between the primer tradition and lay Catholics was paradoxical, since on one hand, "primers enabled the laity to hold to the elements of traditional piety while at the same time they responded, and even contributed, to innovative changes in the books of popular devotion."[101]

In short, print culture—at least as represented by the primer tradition in England—spurred both innovation and conservatism, change and resistance to change (a phenomenon we have encountered earlier in the evolution of early modern Catholicism). This meant, among other things, that primers could be used to shape or reshape belief and practice among traditionalist and reform-minded Christians alike. Formation of the laity, Barnes observes, "demanded a subtle balance of the old and the new," and many of the printed primers in England during the sixteenth century reflected precisely such a balancing act. For example, a primer published in 1539 by John Hilsey—Dominican friar, bishop of Rochester, and close ally of Thomas Cranmer—printed a version of the Hours of the Virgin Mary traditionally found in primers (just as they had been in medieval Books of Hours). But Bishop Hilsey carefully pruned his texts to remove much of the explicitly Marian material found in the medieval form of those hours. Thus, for instance, the repeated response used for the invitatory psalm (94 in the Latin Vulgate numbering, 95 in the Hebrew) at the hour of matins (i.e., vigils) was no longer "Ave Maria, Dominus tecum" (Hail, Mary, the Lord is with you), as it was in the medieval form of the hours, but "Come unto me all ye that labour and are laden, and I shall refresh you" (Matthew 11.28).[102] Often, then, though not always, Hilsey avoided hymns, prayers, or phrases addressed to the Virgin Mary herself. His version of the famous Marian antiphon, "Salve Regina" (Hail, [Holy] Queen), still used at night prayer in the Roman liturgy throughout most of the year, was revised to read, "Hail, heavenly *King, Father* of mercy, our life, our sweetness, our hope, all hail."[103]

Hilsey's reformist sympathies are also clear from comments he made to justify the changes to the "Hours of our Lady" introduced in his 1539 primer. These daily prayer hours, he remarked, were attached to Mary's name not because, as "some unlearned hath both feigned and taught . . . she should use to say it" herself, but because "all the Anthems, Hymns, Lessons, Reponses, Chapters, and Collects, were thought to be of our Lady." Yet if we "let the learned judge," Hilsey asserted, this impression will prove "false and foolish," for

> there were many Scriptures distorted unto our Lady, which in their own native sense are nothing meant of her, but of Christ, the Wisdom of the Father. . . . For this cause have I thought it my bounden duty towards God's true and sincere honour to set forth such a manner of Primer, wherein might be no such distorted Scripture or false honour of that most immaculate Mother of God, lest the youth should . . . take such Scriptures to be of our Lady, which are of God, and to give such praise to her as should only be given to God.[104]

Here, Hilsey reflects Christian humanism of the kind encouraged by Erasmus, who also thought devotion to Mary should be brought into better alignment with the biblical texts. Hilsey's goal was not to dispute "the honour that belongeth to that blessed Virgin Mary" herself but to avoid distorting the Bible's words, especially when educating the young.[105]

Moreover, the highly traditional nature of the primer genre itself kept the temptation to make radical changes firmly under control.[106] It is not surprising, then, to find that Hilsey retained a number of traditional Marian antiphons, prayers, and hymns in his printed version of the "Hours of Our Lady." At the hours of lauds (morning prayer), for instance, both the rhyming antiphon that accompanied the psalmody and the metric hymn that followed the short biblical reading (Ephesians 2.8–9) highlighted traditional Catholic understandings of Mary's unique role in the history of salvation and of her powerful intercession: "Holy Mary, most pure of virgins all, / Mother and daughter of the King celestial, / So comfort us in our desolation, / That by thy prayer and special meditation, /

We may enjoy the reward of the heavenly reign, / And with God's elect there for to remain" (lauds, antiphon); "O Virgin Mary most gracious; / O mother of God incomparable, / To thy Son pray for us, / That he after death be favourable" (lauds, hymn).[107] Perhaps, as Barnes suggests, the primer's ability to accommodate innovation and tradition simultaneously made them as valuable to reform-minded prelates like Hilsey or Cranmer as to adherents of the Old Religion. "Remarkably," he notes, "there were no innovations in Reformation theology itself that could be described as distinctively English. Especially up until 1545 [when Henry VIII's primer appeared], it was the primers themselves that contributed the distinctive element: the creativity with which they assimilated foreign theology to the native digestive system."[108]

Creativity also characterized the primer tradition as it continued in recusant literature produced for English Catholics offshore. An example is *The Primer, or Office of the Blessed Virgin Marie, in Latin and English*, printed at Antwerp in 1599.[109] In addition to the usual material, this volume included short votive offices ("of the Holy Cross" and "of the Holy Ghost"), as well as an ample selection of devotional prayers; the narratives of Christ's passion from all four Gospels; the "antiphonaes, verses, and prayers of the principall feastes of the whole yeare"; prayers for various occasions (e.g., before and after confession, before and after receiving Holy Communion); the "manner how to serve the priest as Masse"; the Office hymns for each liturgical feast and season; and the proper prayers for Sundays and saints' days through the year.[110] It is thus a veritable "encyclopaedia of devotion," to borrow Barnes's apt phrase.[111] Despite its fulsome content, however, this primer contains no "instructions for use of the [rosary] beads," nor does it provide any other form of the "psalter of Our Lady," though it does include a short sampler of devotional prayers addressed to Mary in Latin, with English on facing pages.[112]

More significantly, though, this recusant primer of 1599 incorporates elements that had originally been added to the genre seventy years earlier, in 1529, by the "ardent Protestant" reformer George Joye.[113] Joye's primer—entirely in English—had appeared under the title *Ortulus animae* (*Garden of the Soul*) and was modeled on a popular German devotional book whose main purpose had been to form laypersons in scripture-based, Lutheran piety.[114] Among the innovative elements Joye added were Martin Bucer's narrative of Christ's passion, a harmonized version of the four gospel accounts. As noted previously, the 1599 recusant *Primer* also included the passion narratives (not harmonized) in Latin and English.

More startling still, Catholics eventually adopted Joye's title, *[H]ortulus animae*, for their own purposes. In fact, it became the standard moniker for Catholic versions of the primer from the eighteenth to the twentieth century, chiefly because of the popularity of Bishop Richard Challoner's publication *The Garden of the Soul* (1740).[115]

Other vernacular devotional manuals—earlier than Challoner's and similar to the primer, though without the latter's emphasis on liturgical prayer—had appeared in sixteenth- and seventeenth-century recusant literature, among them the *Manual of Prayers* (1583) and Richard Broughton's *A New Manual of Old Christian Catholick Meditations* (1617). It is to these and to the works of writers like Bucke and Garnett that we must look to see how material related to the rosary came to be incorporated into the primer tradition, thereby continuing the alliance between the rosary and print culture as sources of laity formation. The 1583 *Manual*, divided into thirteen chapters, did not mention praying the rosary but did devote a brief chapter containing devotional "prayers to Saintes and citizens of the glorie of heauen," beginning with the Virgin Mary.[116] (What little liturgical material the *Manual* contains is found in chapter 2, a series of meditative prayers to be said privately during Mass.) Similarly, Broughton's *New Manual* claimed to be a collection of texts "for the most part taken forth of holy Scriptures, or the holy Fathers within the first four hundred yeares of Christ."[117] This disclaimer, plus the curious phrase "Old Christian Catholick" in the title, reveal an author trying to "beat the Reformers at their own game," choosing scripture and the authority of antiquity as the safest guides for Catholic prayer. "To make al secure in these unfortunate dayes of dissention in Religion," Broughton wrote, "I have collected this manual of old Catholick deuotions, such . . . as the title thereof enformeth you: And such as by the best testimony of God him self, his holy Primative Church, and best learned Saincts thereof . . . neither wil, nor can deceave you."[118] The *New Manual* therefore omitted all medieval devotions, including the rosary, although it printed meditations on both "our Lord's praier" and "the salutation of the Blessed Virgin, commonly called the *Aue Maria*."[119] As we have seen, moreover, not even the expanded bilingual *Primer, or Office of the Blessed Virgin Marie* (1599) contained "instructions for the use of the beads."

If, then, the rosary had become a central site of "sacramental space" among persecuted English Catholics who were trying to "reconceptualize the type of aid provided by the Virgin Mary," why is it not mentioned in many of the late sixteenth-century and early seventeenth-century devotional sources printed for their use, especially since rosary picture books had flourished since the late fifteenth century?[120] To answer this question and to understand better the relation between rosary and print culture, we have to consider what happened to English devotional literature between the period of the primers and the appearance of books such as Challoner's *Garden of the Soul*. As we have seen, the primers themselves emphasized laypeople's connection to *liturgical* prayer, especially the "hours of the Blessed Virgin," the Office of the Dead, and the psalter (especially the penitential and gradual psalms). In post-Tridentine Catholicism, additional material was added to the primer—prayers before and after sacramental confession and communion, for instance, as well as devotional meditations on Christ's suffering and the passion narratives from all four Gospels.[121]

But books like Bucke's *Instructions for the Use of the Beades* and Garnett's *Societie of the Rosary* represented an innovation in seventeenth-century English devotional literature.[122] Unlike the earlier primers, these books made use of meditation techniques popularized by Ignatius Loyola's *Spiritual Exercises*, and they presumed readers with an expanding self-awareness of the sort we met when discussing *The Mystical City of God*, by Mary of Ágreda (a younger Spanish contemporary of Bucke and Garnett). The rosary's chief advantage over the more liturgically oriented Books of Hours and primers was that it could be as public or as private as devotees wished or circumstances permitted. It could be prayed secretly while Catholics attended services of the Established Church, or with friends gathered in the communal—yet essentially private and intimate—spaces of a home. Nor did the rosary presuppose literacy as a condition for effective participation. It was, above all, a prayer of the body, available to anyone who could clutch a string of beads—or count on their fingers. The rosary could thus become a sacred site that sustained and extended the "social miracle" of Catholicism.

In short, the rosary began to occupy not only sacramental (eucharistic) space but also the "print space" previously occupied by primers, with their more "liturgically correct" psalms, Hours of the Virgin Mary, and Office of the Dead. It could do so because it fulfilled so many of the devotional and formational goals of the printed primers themselves, especially what Barnes calls their "sense of immediacy and humanity" in prayer.[123] Meditating on the mysteries of the lives of Christ and Mary, Catholics who prayed the rosary could experience—within the expanded interiority of their early modern selves—an intimate communion not only with God, the Blessed Virgin, and the saints but with the whole human community in its daily round of joy and birth, maternity and childhood, loss, grief, death, and ultimately triumph. And they could do this without recourse to the ancient liturgical forms that were rooted in the daily canonical hours of the church's public prayer. Early modern Catholics were able to retrieve through the rosary significant aspects of late medieval piety linked to *devotio moderna*, with its emphasis on personal intimacy with Jesus and Mary in their joys and sorrows. Paradoxically, this Catholic retrieval happened under the influence of Protestantizing primers like those published in the 1520s by George Joye and William Marshall.[124]

Yet it should not be assumed that the rosary—or devotional books written about it—simply replaced primers among English Catholics from the seventeenth century onward. In many respects Challoner's *Garden of the Soul*, which appeared only after many of the more draconian restrictions against the public practice of Catholicism had eased in England, represented a return to sober "liturgicism" in the primer tradition. For Challoner's goal was to provide Catholics with "a handbook of daily Christian living in the world."[125] His intent was to equip people to live *public* lives of faith and devotion supported by liturgy, sacraments, and the bedrock basics of Catholic doctrine. Eighteenth-century editions of the *Garden* thus offered users "a liturgical guide to attendance at Mass and the reception of the sacraments, much of it in Latin."[126] In these matters, Challoner's views probably coincided more closely with what the Council of Trent had in mind for the faith formation of lay Catholics. Many Catholic writers after Trent were fundamentally suspicious of domestic or "family-centered" piety because it seemed to favor what was perceived as a Protestantizing privatism.[127] Trent preferred a *parish-centered* piety focused on communal and public devotions, since these were far easier to monitor, correct, and control.[128] The rosary itself fit into such a program, in part because of the success Jesuits had with their Marian sodalities. The "Societie," which was the title of Henry Garnett's 1624 work on devotion to Mary and the mysteries of the rosary, was precisely such a sodality. In fact, during the second half of the seventeenth century, the Jesuits "increasingly supported sodalities of women and mixed confraternities," many of which were "confraternities of the rosary."[129] Nevertheless, as German Jesuits in the eighteenth century began to advocate a still "greater role for parents in teaching children their catechism," they met with stiff resistance from the clerical establishment.[130] Such resistance arose chiefly because the post-Tridentine church had but a limited, and not very enthusiastic, interest in domestic devotions and "family piety."

It is inaccurate therefore, to claim that what is commonly called baroque Catholicism was dominated by individualistic piety and nonliturgical devotionalism of the sort often associated with the rosary.[131] The *pietas
Austriaca* that shaped court life among the Austrian Habsburgs, for instance, emphasized a "public, ostentatious Marian and Eucharistic piety,"
yet it left room for figures like Maria Theresa to pray the rosary daily,
"referring to Mary as a protector or intercessor, not as ruler or empress."[132]
So while it was characterized by clericalism and a preference for public
and communal piety over private and personal devotion, baroque Catholicism was often quite flexible, leaving room for intensely individualistic
practices.[133] In its origins, Richard Challoner's *Garden of the Soul* belonged
to the public-communal-liturgical wing of baroque Catholic piety and
practice, even though later editions "suffered mutilation," veered toward
"peripheral devotions," and lost sight of the author's "insistence on the en-
trenchment of prayer in the circumstances of everyday living."[134]

The important point here is that, at least in England, print culture
sometimes supported Trent's reformist agenda (as in Challoner's late baroque *Garden of the Soul*) and sometimes militated against it (as, perhaps, in John Bucke's early baroque *Instructions for the Use of the Beades*).
Commenting on the role of print in post-Reformation English Catholicism, Alexandra Walsham writes, "It would be wrong to present print
as an effective deterrent against 'superstition': in some respects the press
provided fresh stimulus to strands of belief and practice disdained by pu-
ritan and Tridentine ministers alike."[135] The piety of recusant households,
she argues, "was primarily inward-looking and devotional in tone, a religion perhaps rooted more in prayers and self-regulated programmes of
spiritual exercise than in sacramental observances that relied on a resident chaplaincy which relatively few could afford or dared to maintain."[136]
Challoner hoped to refocus English Catholic belief and practice on the
basics of liturgy and doctrine, but he was perhaps swimming against the
tide, and what happened to later editions of *The Garden of the Soul*—especially under the influence of Cardinal Wiseman in the mid-nineteenth
century—was probably more indicative of the piety that prevailed.[137] The
Garden often became a compendium of private, sometimes sentimental,
prayers with little linkage to the sturdier stuff of Bible and psalter or to
the liturgical texts and traditions enshrined, for example, in the Hours of
the Virgin Mary.

Ironically, the rosary itself—whose mysteries are mainly biblical and
whose origins are closely connected to the psalmody and Hours embodied

in the primer tradition—came to be regarded as a kind of "devotional alternative" to participation in parish life and the sacramental liturgy. As a result, it was often difficult in places such as England to enforce the reformist policies of the Council of Trent, designed, as they were, "to reorientate the religious experience of the laity towards the Mass and private confession, and to shift the focus of religion from family and confraternity to the well-ordered parish."[138] It may well be the case, as Walsham cautiously suggests, that Catholics in England and on the Continent were moving in opposite directions during the sixteenth and seventeenth centuries, with the English traveling "along a road leading to greater lay independence and relative freedom from clerical mediation," while Continental Catholics were "diverted, with varying degrees of success, onto a track which tended towards tighter control by the priesthood and regular participation in the sacraments."[139] In England, books and print culture had become both "a partial substitute for rite" and a "bulwark of loyalty to the besieged Church of Rome."[140]

The Rosary and Visual Culture

Illuminated books of hours and late medieval printed rosary books had already encouraged what Alexandra Walsham calls "habits of visualisation," that is, "modes of mental apprehension involving the ability to 'imprint' images . . . on one's consciousness."[141] Such habits were not necessarily confined to the literate, for it was quite possible for readers to grasp (or be grasped by) images without recourse to words. "Seeing," Walsham remarks, "was a specialized form of reading."[142] Indeed, sometimes the printed text itself could achieve a visually iconic and even numinous stature. This was the argument put forward, for example, in a preface to *Holy Pictures of the Mysticall Figures of the Most Holy Sacrifice and Sacrament of the Eucharist*, by the French Jesuit Louis Richeome, an author whose work on the rosary (*The Pilgrime of Loreto*) we considered in an earlier chapter.[143] When Richeome's *Holy Pictures* appeared in English translation in 1619, the printer found himself unable to reproduce the images of the French edition because "the stamps were so ouer-worne . . . the Pictures [were] not worth the buying."[144] Seeking, perhaps, to make a silk purse out of a sow's ear, the printer justified his decision by asserting that Richeome's verbal descriptions are "so glorious, so liuely, and so compleate, as there is no need of the Pictures. . . . The Painted Table being nothing else but a visible report, or a certaine kind of speech to the eye of the beholder: as

the Description thereof againe is fitly tearmed by our Author in his Prologue, a certaine Picture deuised for the care of the Reader."[145]

In short, pictures are words ("a certaine kind of speech to the eye of
the beholder"), and words are pictures ("the Description . . . a certaine
Picture"). This symmetry was further explored in Richeome's own preface, which begins with a discussion of "what a Picture is, and how many
kindes of Pictures there are."[146] He reminds readers that images may be
natural figures (the outward form of a plant, man, or beast), artificial figures (a "thing made or framed to represent and signifie another thing"),
or "Dumbe Pictures" ("painted fables" or "the Visions framed in our
Imagination" and "represented to the sight of our inward sense").[147] But
there is as well, Richeome continued, a second category of pictures that
"serues for the eare, and for that qualitie we may call them *Speaking Pictures*."[148] In these "there is neither colour nor painting, but the bare word"
that compels us to see "the Images and Figures."[149] A third kind of picture,
Richeome concludes, are "allegoricall or mysticall pictures," which contain
"a spirituall sense, knowne to spirituall people," and have, as their "principall ende . . . to explane the things . . . instituted in the Law of Nature" to
signifiy sacramental mysteries.[150]

Richeome's "speaking pictures" invite readers to practice "seeing" with
the ear—to let *acoustic* cues consisting of letters and words on a page create *visual* images in the mind's eye. His very text thus becomes a "pensell
[pencil] of the Word" producing images that are meant to be "crossed."
By this I mean that the aim of an image is not the image itself but what
French phenomenologist Jean-Luc Marion calls "the crossing of the visible."[151] In the Christian understanding of things, he notes, religious images
or icons are radically "kenotic," that is, their "image quality is weakened,
to prevent any form of auto-sufficiency, autonomy, auto-affirmation."[152]
The icon is not a magnet that attracts and lures he viewer's sight to itself but rather an aperture, a window through which another's gaze meets
our own. The icon thus "reverses the modern logic of imaging," since it
"does not demand to be seen, but proposes that one should see or be seen
through it." The point of both "dumbe pictures" and "speaking pictures,"
as Richeome understands them, is to cross the visible and

enter into the Temple of God, there to see the holy Pictures of the Sacrament and Sacrifice of the body of his Sonne, drawne from the writings of
his holy Testament, explained by his owne Word, and that according to
the Doctrine of his Diuine Painters and Writers, the Interpreters of his

Word; the dumbe Picture shall be for your eyes, the description of them for your eares; and the exposition of one and of the other, shall serue for your spirits or vnderstandings.[153]

Richeome's view of speaking pictures is consistent with what we know about the relation between texts and images in the early modern era. Not only was seeing a specialized form of *reading*, but printed or illustrated texts themselves, even for those who had "only an imperfect grasp of the words," were often mnemonic devices reminding users of the basics of faith and practice; they could even become "a kind of intercession."[154] "Poring over a book," writes Walsham, "was an act of worship, the printed item becoming as much of an icon and object of pious reverence as an alabaster image, *agnus dei*, crucifix or string of rosary beads. . . . Like amulets, medals and fragments of the host they were sometimes perceived as sources of intrinsic holiness, of a numinous power ordinary lay men and women could tap."[155] In seventeenth-century England and New England, books themselves (especially though not exclusively the Bible) were sometimes venerated as sacred artifacts—as totems, talismans, or even tools of divination.[156] They had, in short, a cultural and religious significance extending well "beyond their mere textual content."[157]

As a material object, the rosary also took on totemic significance, linking, across generations, the worlds of the living and the dead. This may be one reason why popular Catholicism—or what we have discussed as "vernacular religion"—was so strongly anchored in the rosary. That is surely one of the reasons why the story of the Scottish martyr John Ogilvie, throwing his rosary to fellow Catholics present at his execution in 1615, became so popular.[158] Indeed, because of the well-known connection between Catholic identity and the rosary, a session of the Scottish Kirk (Church) in 1657 launched an intensive search for "Papist beids." For the beads were themselves "books," and "reading" them became "the simple man's catechism, his prayer book, and his own précis of the New Testament."[159]

Repeating prayers and meditating on Christian mysteries while using techniques of interior visualization made the rosary not only a totemic link to past and future generations but also a book of "speaking pictures" that permitted each person praying to create "his or own unique mental images while reciting the mantra of the Hail Mary."[160] As we saw in the previous chapter, the expanded interiority of the early modern self, reflected in works like Mary of Ágreda's *Mystical City of God*, permitted the creation of an internal theater that focused on both self-identity and imaginative connection with others. Within this inward environment, each person could read and write her or his own "novel" about communion with God and relations with others. In effect, the rosary became a new book of hours, a portable, material object whose tactile connection with the body and repetitive verbal script combined to create "speaking pictures" in the religious imagination.

Perhaps, then, the most striking aspect of the relation between the rosary and visual culture was the former's capacity to capitalize—and innovate—on the long-standing tradition of the "devout gaze" in Western Christian piety and practice.[161] It is well known that advances in mathematics and the science of optics in early modernity had altered the significance of seeing as a human and religious experience. The older sort of devout gazing, using "the eyes of faith," was sacramental in structure and scope. It utilized the inner "lens" of faith to overcome the *sensuum defectus* (defect of the senses), permitting the viewer's gaze to "cross the visible" and experience God's saving "countergaze" revealed in sacramental rites. But the telescopic and microscopic lenses that were being perfected during the seventeenth century enhanced and extended the eye's *natural* power of sight, making possible "a 'scientific gaze' which could subvert the 'sacramental gaze.'"[162] These new optical instruments were magnifiers that made use of precisely ground glass to map nature, reveal its hidden reality, register its processes, and measure their results. "It seems certain," writes Bob Scribner, "that more naturalistic representation lessened the power of the gaze and enabled the objectifying glance, creating the emotionally distanced 'cold gaze.' The image could provide information dispassionately, without arousing any sense of personal involvement."[163]

In Scribner's view, this new, "objectifying glance" endorsed the notion that to see is to seize, to take possession and claim ownership of whatever falls within vision's path. The cold gaze of science established a basis for "seeing" that was nonsacramental and didactic. Thus the "devout gaze" of an earlier era became theological, a form of seeing in which "contemplation of the image of Christ crucified," for example, aimed "not so much to involve the viewer emotionally with the image, but to remind him or her of a *doctrine*."[164]

The scientific sharpening of the eye's ability to see nature's "insides" in detail had a perhaps unanticipated impact on painting and religious representation. As we have seen, late mannerist and early baroque painters like Caravaggio reinterpreted biblical stories and religious images in ways that dramatized their naturalness, making them seem almost hyperreal or surreal. But Caravaggio's "surrealism" differed decisively from that of earlier, northern Renaissance artists like Hieronymus Bosch (d. 1516). Bosch had painted obviously fantastic scenes and creatures, making his canvases seem dreamy rather than lifelike. Caravaggio's imaginative forebears were not protosurrealists like Bosch but early mannerists like Pieter Aertsen (1508/9–1575) and his nephew Joachim Beuckelaer (1530–74).[165] These Flemish artists produced works that often assault the viewer's gaze with a profusion of natural objects rendered with quasi-scientific detail and precision. Aertsen's *Meat Stall*, for example, packs still-life elements— sausages, poultry, pig's feet, ham, beef, fish, butter, cheese, pretzels—so densely into the foreground that they seem about to tumble out into the viewer's space; meanwhile, narrative details recede into a background that has to be scrutinized closely (one might say microscopically) if its contents are to be discerned.[166] The narrative program is rather ambiguous, but its significance slowly comes into focus. In the upper right of *The Meat Stall*, the viewer glimpses the open door of a tavern—its floor littered with oyster and mussel shells (popularly perceived as aphrodisiacs)—where a prostitute seems to be soliciting customers. In the upper left, the viewer sees a group of figures in contemporary dress walking through the countryside toward a church dimly visible at the picture's far left. Among them, a woman on a donkey has stopped to give alms to the poor. She is, the viewer slowly realizes, the Virgin Mary, a refugee fleeing with her husband and child to Egypt (Matthew 2.13–15), who "reaches back to give alms of bread to a mendicant boy."[167] The Virgin's act of almsgiving is not part of the biblical record, nor does Aertsen's painting include any of the usual medieval tropes on this scene, such as hovering angels and miraculous disruptions of nature. At the center of the canvas among the still-life objects, meanwhile, rests the head of a butcher's ox, its disturbing open eye staring out at the viewer.[168]

The Flight into Egypt was not one of the fifteen mysteries of the traditional rosary in the early modern era, but it *was* connected to the corona of the Virgin Mary, a form of rosary consisting of sixty-three Aves in remembrance of the number of years Mary was popularly believed to have lived on earth.[169] Aertsen's *Meat Stall* cannot, of course, be construed as belonging to the *Rosenkranzbild* genre. The painting's importance stems rather from its new and challenging optic, for it offers viewers a new way to see the relation between religious image and daily life. It presents an innovative reinterpretation of the relation between faith and world, Christian piety and scientific progress. For at one level, *The Meat Stall* does indeed celebrate material progress in science and agriculture, commerce and marketing—especially as these impacted the production and distribution of food in the Low Countries. Unquestionably, then, one of Aertsen's innovations as an artist was "the emancipation of non-religious themes in painting."[170] For in *The Meat Stall,*

> Aertsen turned a millennium of artistic convention inside out by bringing objects forward to dominate human acts: the picture's vivid display of freshly butchered meat (a subject unthinkable previously in panel painting) all but obscures a tiny background scene of the Flight into Egypt, . . . and the largest person on view is smaller than a sausage. Art historians have granted *The Meat Stall* canonical status as the initiating work in not just one but several genres: market paintings, "inverted" morality pictures, paradoxical encomiums, and—ultimately—the entire field of modern still life.[171]

As early seventeenth-century poet Carel van Mander wrote, Aertsen used "only paint, which he knows how to mix / So that what is smooth appears round and what is flat has relief, / What is dumb speaks and what is dead lives."[172]

In short, Aertsen's canvases exemplified Richeome's "speaking pictures." They were images that redefined the relation between religious image and the Christian's daily life in the world. Keith Moxey observes that instead of being, as altarpieces had been, "an integral part of the ceremonies and functions of the church, elements of ecclesiastical furniture with an ascribed devotional function," the work of Aertsen and Beuckelaer embodied a "new attitude" that "divorced artistic objects from the whole process of religious observance, assigning to them an almost completely secular role."[173] In this, Aertsen and Beuckelaer, though at least nominally Catholic, may have been conceding a point to Calvinist doctrine, which claimed that artists could not and should not attempt to represent God at all. What was needed, Calvin believed, was not a potentially idolatrous "art of the invisible" but an "art of the visible," for "the artistic skills of painting and carving" are "intended for the sensual delight that they afford mankind," and hence the very materialism of art—evident especially in detailed representations of natural objects—makes it a "fit instrument of human pleasure."[174]

Moxey may well be right about Aertsen's implicit concession to a Calvinist understanding of art in relation to Christian faith, but Margaret A.

Sullivan suggests another possible source for paintings like *The Meat Stall*, with its (to us) startling juxtaposition of animal flesh and Mary's act of charity. Her research points to both classical (Pliny the Elder) and humanist (Erasmus) influence on Aertsen's conceptual framework and its embodiment in "excessive and disorderly" portrayals of meat and produce.[175] This framework, she argues, made paintings like *The Meat Stall* "comprehensible to the original viewers."[176] Specifically, it was the "ancient genre of satire—its theory, traditions, literature, long history of exploitation by Christian moralists, and popularity in the Low Countries in the mid-sixteenth century—[that] accounts for Aertsen's new subjects and unique compositions."[177] Pliny the Elder's *Natural History* had already "legitimated low-life painting," and the humanist revival of interest in the Latin and Greek classics made Pliny a popular writer in Northern Europe during the sixteenth century.[178] The difference, of course, was that Pliny himself "says nothing about the meaning of . . . foodstuffs and other low-life subjects"; these objects simply exist for themselves and are "devoid of [ulterior] meaning and associations."[179] But sixteenth-century viewers would have assumed otherwise, since they were "accustomed to assign meaning to objects, even those as unlikely as an eviscerated rabbit or a large peasant shoe."[180] Often these assigned meanings were closely connected to matters of morality or belief (e.g., a skinned rabbit reminded viewers of the radical repentance and renunciation required for growth in faith and devout Christian living).

And that is where the genre of satire comes into play. The Latin word *satura*, Sullivan notes, "had long been exploited by Christian writers, such as Saint Jerome [d. 420], who plundered the [classical] satirists to enliven their moral treatises, sermons, and topical criticism."[181] Christian apologists, however, did not for the most part invoke satire in order to provoke ridicule, for the genre's aim was to present "serious subjects in an entertaining guise."[182] To tell the truth in an appealing way made satire "uniquely qualified to fill a moralizing role," Sullivan notes, and ancient writers often used "the marketplace with its fruit vendors, vegetable sellers, and fishmongers" as a "favorite vantage point."[183] Satire in this moralizing sense was retrieved by influential Christian humanists like Erasmus, who put a positive spin on the Latin phrase *ollas ostentare* (literally, "to show the kitchen pots"). Erasmus's "spirited defense of undignified subjects" like kitchenware helps explain not only how "the genre of satire was understood in the sixteenth century" but also "why Aertsen's unprecedented paintings did not disconcert his viewers."[184] In the context of humanist culture, *The Meat Stall* and similar paintings appealed to a prosperous urban clientele actively "engaged in commerce, civic affairs, the arts, and the professions," yet conscious of the continuing challenge of faith and of the need to practice "virtues of charity and tolerance" (rather than, say, voluntary poverty).[185]

In short, Aertsen's canvases conveyed moral earnestness through the satiric portrayal of objects, persons, and situations. By appealing to the viewer's own consciousness of the bawdy, the excessive, and the everyday, paintings like *The Meat Stall* had the potential to prompt discussion of a broad array of social and religious issues. Like the classical satirists, Aertsen framed social issues "in terms of food, kitchen, and marketplace," relating them to questions about "the decline of morals, the dangers of extravagance and profligate spending, problems of social mobility, the wealthy scorning the poor, virtue as more important than ancestors and inherited wealth, the hypocrisy of friends, and the greed of parasites."[186] In a time of social and religious unrest, sudden economic growth and prosperity, and conspicuous consumption, this way of relating religious faith to visual culture through "speaking pictures" had particular relevance. Images such as those in *The Meat Stall* were significant both because of *what* they represented and because of what they did *not* represent. Sullivan insightfully summarizes the significance of this satiric sort of art:

> By focusing on classical sources and avoiding biblical subjects such as the Last Supper that were literally matters of life and death in the highly charged religious controversies of the time, Aertsen's paintings served a useful social function. Biblical subjects such as Mary and Martha and Christ and the Adultress raise serious moral issues but they were not subjects likely to ignite sectarian animosities or involve the viewers in divisive issues of dogma. The parable of Christ and the Adultress, which warns against casting the first stone, is a plea for tolerance. The story of Mary and Martha raises questions about how a Christian should live, and while contemplation is favored the active life is not condemned. In a time when a person could be burned at the stake for a dissident religious view, or guests could find themselves in deep and dangerous disagreement over a subject such as Christ's descent into Limbo, it was wise to be sensitive to the problem of religious differences and avoid the controversial and disruptive. This point is made most clearly in two [of Aertsen's canvases depicting Martha and Mary, in which] . . . a vase containing lilies—a traditional Marian symbol—is featured prominently in the foreground along with various foodstuffs.[187]

Reinventing the Image of Mary

Thus, while in some situations—such as that of Catholics in England during the sixteenth and seventeenth centuries—the rosary and other Marian devotions may have become defiant emblems of the Old Religion's persistence even in a hostile realm, in other circumstances use of the beads allowed the devout to focus on more peaceful aspects of faith and religious practice. The mysteries of the rosary, after all, drew the praying Christian to biblically warranted scenes (Annunciation; Visitation; Nativity; presentation and finding in the Temple; Christ's trial, passion, death, resurrection, and ascension; the sending of the Spirit) and to basic elements of doctrine (the persons of the Trinity, the uniqueness of God's self-revelation in Christ, Mary's role in the story of salvation) that were widely shared among Catholics and Protestants in the early modern era. Even more controversial mysteries of the rosary such as Mary's assumption and coronation as "Queen of Heaven" were perhaps less threatening in a time when expanded interiority made it increasingly possible for imaginative readers to identify with novelistic plot and character, with heroic (or mock-heroic) stories of appealing human subjects and their fates. It is surely no accident that Cervantes's picaresque novel *Don Quixote* first appeared at precisely this time (in 1605). Nor was it entirely serendipitous that Queen Elizabeth I portrayed herself as a Virgin Mother, for though "bejeweled and painted images of the Virgin Mary had been cast out of churches and monasteries," another "bejeweled and painted image" had been "set up at court."[188]

Traditional stories, moreover, came to be understood as possessing the power to generate new narratives and reinvent old images. As noted earlier, scholars like Lisa McClain contend that among English Catholics in the period between 1559 and 1642, the image of Mary was profoundly reinterpreted under pressure of persecution, with the result that the gentler medieval "Queen of Heaven" became a militant advocate, "a powerful warrior, capable of protecting the souls of those who venerated her through the rosary."[189] Yet Kate Koppelman's research has shown that this bellicose imagery was already well established in fourteenth- and fifteenth-century England, where Mary was seen as "Empresse of Helle," a vengeful, "aggressive and self-willed" advocate, and not merely "a passive font of mercy and grace."[190]

In her complex role as gracious advocate and intrepid avenger, the Virgin Mary thus embodied our potential for "symbolic polyphony," that is, our sense of self as both source of limitless power and desire and root of "overwhelming aggressivity towards self and Other."[191] As medieval English literature testifies, Mary was seen not merely as a refuge to whom one may flee when seeking help or forgiveness but as an accusing judge, "a Mother of God who is chastising, aggressive and commanding."[192] The result of the praying Christian's attempts to relate to such a figure, Koppelman argues, is "devotional ambivalence," contrary emotions and expectations that trouble "both the focus of devotion (in this case the Virgin), and those who look to her for solace."[193] Well before the Reformation or the Elizabethan Settlement, therefore, Mary had become a paradoxical figure in Catholic piety, linking hope and anguish in ways peculiar to her alone. "Her ambivalence, seen in her capacity to induce anguish because of her unpredictability, combines with her divine potential, seen in the hope that her miraculous powers will aid the sinner."[194] She embodied the "ambivalence of sublimity," for even her most dedicated devotees had to ask what might happen if this paragon of perfection were suddenly confronted by the "physical and spiritual disintegration that threaten the lives of ordinary humans."[195] Would the Virgin Mary react as a Mother, mercifully, or as a Sublime Other capable of crushing her suppliants with vituperation and judgment? Praying Catholics were forced to wrestle with the possibility that the "Other who was imagined as virginal, inviolate, immaculate" might in fact be "unpredictable, vengeful, and angry."[196] The complex symbolism surrounding the figure of Mary cannot be fully framed by any single category or essence. Thus, instead of "simplifying Marian devotion by making it predictable and monochromatic," her polyphonic symbolism requires "a more active engagement from the faithful," for "when devotional objects are polyphonous," they become "more worthy of our intimate and engaged attention; they become . . . works in progress, not simply formulaic, passion-less salves."[197]

Perhaps, however, the best examples of how the rosary and the image of Mary were reinterpreted within early modern Catholicism come from the experience of native peoples in "newly discovered" (i.e., newly colonized) parts of the world such as the Americas. Surely the most spectacular and enduring example is the Virgin of Guadalupe, who, as William B. Taylor has noted,

> is represented in many distinct forms including Our Lady of Mercy, Our Lady of the Rosary, Our Lady of the Remedies, the crowned Madonna, Madonna and child, and especially in the joyful and sorrowful events

that connected her life to Christ, including Our Lady of the Immaculate Conception, Our Lady of the Annunciation, Our Lady of the Purification, Our Lady of the Sorrows, and Our Lady of the Assumption.[198]

The story of her appearance at Tepeyac to the Amerindian Juan Diego in 1531 is well known, though the historical facts surrounding that account are not without controversy.[199] Her appearance was marked by several innovative features: she spoke to Juan Diego in the native language, Nahuatl (which already had a history of rich religious imagery among Amerindians), appeared in an indigenous guise (her face is Mexican, though her cloak is European), and focused her revelatory message on themes of compassion, love, and hospitality. Unquestionably, the Virgin of Guadalupe became "a very particular symbol of God's solidarity with the poor and the oppressed of the 'New World,'" a native population that had been savaged by European colonizers "in the name of crown and cross."[200] Likewise, there can be little doubt that she came to be venerated by native Americans as "one of their own who offers compassion . . . a pregnant mother who offers humanity what she carries within her, and, in a mysterious way, she herself has been liberated from the power of evil by the death of Christ on the Cross."[201] Over time, too, national and political symbolism accrued to the Virgin of Guadalupe, as she was linked in colonial Mexico to the struggle for independence.[202]

Anthropologists have sometimes identified Mexican devotion to Guadalupe with the image of a "syncretic goddess" or simply with the "spiritual aspect of protest against the colonial regime."[203] Yet as William Taylor points out, this perspective obscures the fact that Our Lady of Guadalupe has "stood ambiguously for several meanings that were subject to change and that may or may not have moved people to action."[204] Like earlier European images of Mary, Mexico's Guadalupe cannot be forced into a single frame, category, or essence, despite her "truly national status."[205] Indeed, surveying the "proliferation of Marian devotion among individuals, families, social groups, communities, and the nation as a whole," as it developed in Mexico over five centuries, Robert V. Kemper notes that "virtually every week, a fiesta occurs in honor of some manifestation of Mary," while "each year repeats the liturgical cycle for the benefit of the faithful who are thereby reminded of the power of God as expressed through the Virgin."[206]

The "devotional ambivalence" we have discussed is also evident in other Mexican images of the Virgin Mary, many of which have a strongly local character.[207] One such image is the Virgin of the Macana (literally, the "Virgin of the Club"), which is linked to the "rebellion of the Pueblo Indians in New Mexico in 1680" and was "promoted with particular vehemence during the second half of the eighteenth century," at a time of "heightened interest in the pacification of non-Christian Indians by Spanish authorities."[208] The Virgin of the Macana came to be associated with the rosary, as seventeenth- and eighteenth-century portraits and engravings show.[209] These images, whose history and diversity are quite complex, are thus devotional, emphasizing the Virgin's invincible power, but they are also admonitory, for Mary is often depicted *armed*, carrying in her own hands the club (*macana*) that had inflicted injury on her portrait.[210]

As we discussed in the previous chapter, the history of Marian devotion in Mexico and the American Southwest is also linked to Mary of Ágreda, author of the novelistic account of the Virgin Mary's life (*The Mystical City of God*). Persistent rumors held that Sor María had miraculously, through bilocation, visited the Indians living in what is now New Mexico for the purpose of evangelizing and instructing them in the fundamentals of Catholic faith.[211] The rumors were investigated by the Inquisition in Spain, which reported to the Roman Holy Office that their validity, though perhaps doubtful, was an open question; meanwhile, Mary herself was exonerated of any falsification or wrongdoing.[212] Whatever the source of such stories may have been, Mary of Ágreda's own testimony bears witness to her interest in the Christian mission to native populations in North America, though she admits to being unsure whether her involvement in that mission had happened "in the body" or "out of the body."[213] Writing in 1648, many years after the initial controversy over her alleged bilocation had died down, Mary claimed she "had the impression that I gave the Indians some rosaries. I had them with me and I distributed them, and I never saw those rosaries again, I mean not up to the present time."[214] The detail is interesting because by the mid-seventeenth century, rosaries were such an important part of the Catholic devotional repertoire that their use in missionary situations could be taken for granted.

However one may assess the "missionary activity" of Mary of Ágreda, one thing is certain: during the seventeenth century the rosary was rapidly becoming internationalized as a devotion emblematic of early modern Catholic piety. It had become a site of "renegotiation"—a physical object and a set of meditations and prayers through which Catholics could reinterpret their relation to the sacraments (especially the Eucharist); reassess their connection to daily life; refine their understanding of God, self, and world through print and visual media; redefine their understanding of the Virgin Mary's uniqueness; and reconnect prayerfully to the recurrent human experiences of joy and sorrow, gain and loss, birth, death, and rebirth. Like the traveling almsgiver in Aertsen's *Meat Stall*, the figure of Mary could be perceived as powerfully present yet unobtrusive. She could be imagined as a reliable advocate who asks her clients not to withdraw from kitchen or marketplace but to find—among the slaughtered hogs and fat sausages, the squashes and luxuriant cabbages—intimations of immortality.

6

Reading the Beads

Visitors to the northern Indiana campus of the University of Notre Dame usually arrive well equipped with cameras or camcorders. They can often be seen prowling around the perimeter of Notre Dame Stadium (popularly known as "the house that Rockne built," after the legendary football coach), seeking out the best angle for a photo. Others congregate on the south side of the Theodore M. Hesburgh Library near the rectangular reflecting pool to check out "Touchdown Jesus," part of a larger-than-life mosaic that (despite the moniker) actually celebrates Christ's connection with ancient Israel's prophets, priests, and kings. Still others stalk off to the library's west facade to photograph "Number One Moses," a monumental bronze statue of the biblical patriarch created by the Croatian sculptor Ivan Mestrovic (d. 1962). But by far the most popular site on campus is a somewhat secluded spot slightly northwest of the Basilica of the Sacred Heart. There, in every season—rain, snow, or shine—visitors and students gather to pray at the "Grotto," a replica of the renowned shrine to the Virgin Mary in the French town of Lourdes, located in the foothills of the Pyrenees. Nestled among the rocks of Notre Dame's Grotto is a statue of Mary, her hands joined in prayer, a rosary hanging around her right arm. Prayers of every sort are offered at this site—and many young men and women have proposed marriage there—yet the rosary is undoubtedly the Grotto's "prayer of choice" for most Catholic visitors.

Throughout this book we have seen that the most reliable clues for understanding how the rosary and Marian devotion were reframed by early modern Catholics are to be sought not in textual evidence alone (official documents, pronouncements, or treatises) but also in visual representation (e.g., the art of Aertsen, the Carracci, and Caravaggio), in popular print culture (e.g., devotional books like the primer, Richeome's *Pilgrime*, or Mary of Ágreda's *Mystical City of God*), and in those innovative religious movements (e.g., Philip Neri's Oratory) that promoted a "reform of the Tridentine reform." In highlighting these *unofficial* sources that helped remake the rosary for generations of Catholics in Europe—and later in the "New World"—we accept a basic, though not homogeneous, continuity between early modern devotionalism and late medieval "cultures of piety."¹ These latter, though sometimes dissimilar in detail, shared notable qualities, among them a "heightened degree of emotionalism and a preoccupation with the tortured body of Christ and the grief of the Virgin Mary"; they were also "socially shaped and responsive to change."² The distinctive culture of piety that took shape among English-speaking Catholics in the eighteenth and nineteenth centuries influenced attitudes toward liturgy and devotions (the rosary, especially) among Catholics in the United States. The Grotto shrine originally built in the late nineteenth century on the University of Notre Dame campus provides an apt illustration of this process.

Precisely when the rosary became a popular (though not universal) daily devotional practice among devout Catholics is difficult to determine, but its use is already mentioned by the English Jesuit Henry Garnet (or Garnett, 1555–1606):

> euery deuout Catholicke, dailye when he saieth his beades, doth as it were in a booke read and reuerentlye laieth before his eies, Christ our Sauiour incarnat in his Mother, sanctifying John Baptist his holy Precursor, lying in a manger, offered vp to his Father in the Temple, teaching the Doctors, praying in the Garden, cruelly whipped, crowned with thornes, carrying his Crosse, and exalted thereon for our redemption, rising againe, ascending into heauen, sending his holy Spirit and gratious giftes vnto men, taking vp with childly affection his most holy Mother, euen corporally vnto heauen, and exalting and crowning her ouer all his holy Saintes and Angells.³

In other passages, Garnett almost seemed to promote meditation on the mysteries of the rosary as a pious substitute for the scripture and sacraments that traditionally anchored Catholic piety, even though his *Societie of the Rosarie* did provide a brief series of prayers and instructions for private confession and Holy Communion.⁴ Historian John Bossy thus contends that, in contrast to the "social miracle" of a medieval Catholicism whose central defining symbol was the Eucharist, early modern Catholicism—at least in England—emerged as a far more inert, inward-looking, privatized "religion of contemplation . . . formed out of reaction and withdrawal" from the activist faith initially promoted by missionary priests who returned to Britain after 1574.[5] Bossy's point is supported further by evidence we examined in the previous chapter, which illustrated how the rosary was reframed among many recusant English Catholics in quasi-liturgical or sacramental terms, as an alternate "eucharistic site."[6]

In the eighteenth century, nevertheless, publications like Bishop Richard Challoner's *Garden of the Soul* (first edition, 1740) tried to shift English Catholic piety back toward the basics of biblical, liturgical, and sacramental practice. Challoner had subtitled his primer *A Manual of Spiritual Exercises and Instructions for Christians who, (living in the World) aspire to Devotion.*[7] It was thus a work "activist in orientation," teaching Catholics how to spend the day "in the presence of God" while attending to the public business of their lives and vocations in the surrounding society.[8] From the outset, the *Garden* drew attention to the fundamentals of faith and moral life, summarizing Creed and Decalogue while stressing the primacy of scripture and sacraments. Toward the end of his primer, Challoner added instructions for praying the "fifteen mysteries of the Rosary" and the fifteen "petitions" of the medieval "Jesus Psalter."[9] Appended also, under separate pagination, was the full "Office of Our Blessed Lady" in English, with seasonal variations.[10]

Nowhere did Challoner insist that Catholics *must* pray the rosary (or recite Our Lady's Office) daily, yet their inclusion is a sign that Marian piety—so popular in medieval England but largely ignored in the Book of Common Prayer—still survived among early modern English Catholics. It remains true, nevertheless, that *The Garden of the Soul* contained few items that were "specifically Catholic."[11] Its tone was remarkably conciliatory, and it launched no attacks against opposing opinions. Indeed, the *Garden* presaged a genre of devotional works that stressed charity as the "primary obligation on the Christian," a duty "to be exercised within the bounds of the civil community" to which the believer belongs.[12] Far from encouraging a cloistered, hermetic piety, Challoner's primer urged lay Catholics working in the world to lead devout lives rooted in scripture, sacraments, and daily prayer. Its fundamentally peaceful tone portrayed Catholics as loyal to their church's traditions yet as responsible citizens participating in the social and political processes of public life.

In its attention to lay piety and practice and its openness to the surrounding culture, Challoner's work exemplified an "English Catholic Enlightenment" that recalls the spirit of Philip Neri's "Oratorian orbit" and its Christian optimism, which, we have seen, helped "reform the Tridentine reform" during the quarter century between 1585 and 1610. What Mark Goldie has written about the Enlightenment among Scottish Catholics in the last three decades of the eighteenth century may also be said about Challoner's work in England: it was "an irenical and cosmopolitan movement that has parallels in present-day Catholicism but that stands in stark contrast both with the era before it, the age of the militant Counter-Reformation, and the era after it, that of the triumphalist and exclusive sensibility of Victorian Catholicism."[13] Challoner—and Catholic churchmen who followed his views— proposed a piety that sought to make Catholicism's beliefs and worship accessible to its own membership and appealing, as well, to Protestants in a religiously diverse England. They firmly believed that Catholicism had no essential quarrel with culture, that the faithful could be devout and God-centered while holding jobs and serving their neighbors as good citizens in the surrounding world. Piety did not consist in exotic devotions and "extraordinary behaviour, but purity of intention towards God, order and regularity, a concern to 'redeem the time.'"[14] Sanctity, in short, was "perfectly compatible with a "cheerful enjoyment" of one's "situation in the world."[15]

Scarcely more than a century after *The Garden of the Soul* appeared, however, John Henry Newman (by then a convert to the Roman Church) lamented the long *eclipse* of traditional beliefs and practices in England— almost as if Challoner and his primer had never existed or were somehow "insufficiently *Catholic*." In a famous sermon preached at the first provincial synod of Westminster, Newman spoke of a "Second Spring" that began just shortly before the Catholic hierarchy was officially restored in England (1850).[16] Taking his text from the Song of Songs (2.10–12), Newman told the newly reestablished Catholic hierarchy of England:

> Something strange is passing over this land, by the very surprise, by the very commotion, which it excites. . . .
> The past *has* returned, the dead lives. . . . The English Church was, and the English Church was not, and the English Church is once again. . . . It is the coming in of a Second Spring; it is a restoration in the moral world, such as that which yearly takes place in the physical.
>
> Three centuries ago [i.e., ca. 1552], and the Catholic Church, that great creation of God's power, stood in this land in pride of place. . . .
>
> But it was the high decree of heaven, that the majesty of that presence should be blotted out. . . . That old Church in its day became a corpse. . . .

[There was] no longer . . . a Catholic community . . . but a mere hand-
ful of individuals. . . . Here a set of poor Irishmen, coming and going at
harvest time. . . . There, perhaps an elderly person, seen walking in the
streets. . . .

Shall the past be rolled back? Shall the grave open? Shall the Sax-
ons live again to God? . . . The world grows old, but the Church is ever
young. . . . [T]he Church in England has died, and the Church lives
again.[17]

Newman's impassioned sermon, writes historian Mary Heimann, was
"a text rich in poetic license."[18] Not only was it revisionist history; it was
an almost apocalyptic reinterpretation of England's Catholic past, present,
and future. The Roman Church became, in Newman's oratory, the central
character in a drama whose outcome was grandly inevitable. A central
figure in that hoped-for outcome was the Virgin Mary. "One thing I am
sure of," Newman declared, is "that the more the enemy rages against us,
so much the more will the Saints in Heaven plead for us; the more fearful
are our trials from the world, the more present to us will be our Mother
Mary. . . . We shall not be left orphans."[19] Newman's words brought tears
to the eyes of the clergy who first heard it, and for more than a century
his description of a mid-nineteenth-century "Catholic Revival" (a "Second Spring") was accepted as gospel by English Catholic historians,
who believed that the "enlightened" Catholicism of Challoner had been
transformed into a triumphalist *Roman* Catholicism, "more Roman than
Rome" itself.[20] According to this view, Catholics in England turned decisively away from the rather sober, liturgy-and-scripture-centered devotions embodied in Challoner's *Garden* and toward more flamboyant but
ultramontanist (rigid, reactionary) piety imported from Italy and promoted by the papacy. Aspects of this "more Roman than Rome" piety
were expressed in Newman's peroration to the Virgin Mary, which closed
the "Second Spring" sermon:

"Arise, my love, my beautiful one, and come." It is the time for thy Visitation. Arise, Mary, and go forth in thy strength into that north country,
which once was thine own, and take possession of a land which knows
thee not. Arise, Mother of God. . . . Shine on us, dear Lady, with thy
bright countenance, like the sun in his strength, O *stella matutina* [O
morning star], O harbinger of peace, till our year is one perpetual May.
From thy sweet eyes, from thy pure smile, from thy majestic brow, let

ten thousand influences rain down, not to confound or overwhelm, but to persuade, to win over thine enemies. O Mary, my hope, O Mother undefiled, fulfil to us the promise of this Spring. A second temple rises on the ruins of the old. Canterbury has gone its way, and York is gone, and Durham is gone, and Winchester is gone. It was sore to part with them. We clung to the vision of past greatness, and would not believe it could come to nought; but the Church in England has died, and the Church lives again.[21]

Newman's goal in this sermon was to persuade his hearers that the history of Catholicism in post-Reformation England had been a story of steady decline that reached its nadir in the eighteenth century."[22] Only in the 1840s (about the time Newman himself converted to Roman Catholicism!) did the English Catholic community begin to experience a rebirth. Yet Newman's view—though it certainly became "part of the folklore of English Catholicism"—was, in Bossy's opinion, "a piece of tendentious ecclesiastical propaganda."[23] No doubt the Catholic community in England did undergo a momentous transformation during the century-plus between Bishop Challoner's first edition of *The Garden of the Soul* (1740) and Newman's 1852 sermon at the provincial synod of Westminster. No doubt, too, this transformation was not only statistical (from about 80,000 Catholics in 1770 to 750,000 in 1850) but also social, economic, and occupational.[24] Yet in the final analysis, as Bossy asserts, these changes represented "a transformation of the *English* Catholic community," and they could well have happened even in the absence of influence from Rome or the influx of large numbers or Irish immigrants.

Heimann's research into the history of devotions in Victorian England reaches a similar conclusion. "English Catholicism," she writes,

did not in fact become "more Roman than Rome" after the restoration of the hierarchy in 1850. It was Challoner's rather than [Carlo] Bellarmine's catechism which was reissued through the nineteenth and early twentieth centuries, to be memorized by increasing numbers of the faithful; and it was *The Garden of the Soul* rather than the Roman *Raccolta* [a Vatican-approved compendium of prayers] which continued to be used by Catholics living in England, whether for private prayer or in assisting at Mass or Benediction. Furthermore, those extra-liturgical forms which came to be practiced with increasing regularity were devotions which had also been favourites in the recusant tradition: Benediction and the rosary.[25]

English Catholic devotional life, in short, did change "in tone and emphasis" during the nineteenth century and was certainly influenced by Continental sources, including both Italian and French practices, but "it is difficult to justify the common assertion that it became 'Roman,' for all that it became more distinctively Catholic."[26] In short, Challoner's *Garden* had *already* focused the devotional life of Catholics on Benediction and the rosary, more than a century before Newman's "Second Spring." "We should try to say some part of the Rosary every day," Challoner told readers of his manual, for it "is one of the most popular forms of devotion practiced by the faithful throughout the world."[27] Similarly, the *Garden* encouraged Benediction of the Blessed Sacrament (often attached to sung vespers on Sunday afternoon) not only as a way to reaffirm Catholic faith in Christ's presence in the Eucharist but as an opportunity to pray for all the living and the dead, especially the sick.

Propaganda to the contrary, the renascent Catholicism Newman saw unfolding around him in 1852 was in fact "an invigorated *English* recusant tradition, not a Roman one."[28] It was the earlier, native tradition of devotion represented by Challoner that captured the imagination and allegiance of Catholics in England "from the middle of the nineteenth century to the early years of the twentieth."[29] Moreover, the use of devotions that originated in Rome (or elsewhere in Italy) did not necessarily signal that English Catholics regarded them as obligatory because "approved" or "recommended" by the pope. Nor did popular attitudes toward Rome grow noticeably more "papal," despite the language of hymns like Cardinal Wiseman's "God Bless Our Pope."[30] Jennifer Supple has shown, for example, that between 1850 and 1900, Catholics may have sung such tunes with gusto, but they still showed reluctance to contribute money to the "Peter's Pence" collection (taken up annually on the pope's behalf in Catholic parishes).[31] In actual practice, devotion to the pope "as a symbol of holiness and as denominational figurehead was perfectly compatible with a reluctance to wish to have much to do with the bureaucracy and machinery of Rome, still less with the real man who filled the office."[32] It is not at all clear, then, that English Catholic devotional life after 1850 became overwhelmingly ultramontanist, papal, or Roman/Italian.[33]

The Rosary as a Staple of Catholic Devotion

Whatever we may think about Newman's view of English Catholic history in the "Second Spring" sermon, one thing is clear: his words and images were drawn largely from the Bible, the liturgy, and the long history of devotion to Mary among the English. Likening Mary to "the sun in his strength," Newman acclaimed her as *stella matutina* (morning star) and "harbinger of peace."[34] The problem, as we have seen, is that Newman's reading of Marian piety took place within the framework of his larger hermeneutic, namely, that post-Reformation Catholicism in England had lain largely moribund until the 1840s. In this, he ignored the great success of Challoner's *Garden of the Soul*—which not only recommended devotions like the Litany of Loreto, the daily rosary (with meditation on its mysteries), and Benediction of the Blessed Sacrament but also attempted to retrieve the medieval piety linked to the Hours of the Blessed Virgin Mary. Clearly, English Catholics were already well acquainted with their ancient Marian heritage a good century before Newman's proclamation of a "Second Spring."[35]

Thus by the time Newman addressed the newly reestablished Catholic hierarchy in 1852, the rosary was already a staple of Catholic piety. Henry Garnett had recommended praying it daily in the early seventeenth century (advice repeated by Challoner in 1740), and as we saw in the previous chapter, rosaries had become familiar sacred sites—quasi-sacramental spaces—in the lives of recusant English Catholics. It cannot be assumed that the rosary became popular—or was "reintroduced"—in England only as the result of a mid-nineteenth-century ultramontanist revival (Newman's "Second Spring") that had turned its back on the recusant piety of Challoner. Nor is it possible to dismiss the rosary as a merely *popular* devotion, unessential and somewhat at odds with the church's official program of liturgical rites.[36] *The Garden of the Soul* saw no conflict between Catholic liturgy (e.g., Mass, Sunday vespers) and Catholic devotion (e.g., rosary, Benediction). Neither the liturgy nor devotions needed "promotion from Rome" to guarantee their popularity.[37] Both were as popular with the "Garden-of-the-Soul Catholic as for his newer Catholic counterpart," and their appeal was equally strong among working-, middle-, and upper-class Catholics.[38]

Our focus here is the rosary, particularly in its public or communal form. Statistics support a "complementary rather than competitive" relationship between "the growth of Public Rosary and Benediction," at least in English parishes during the late nineteenth and early twentieth centuries.[39] This is not surprising, especially in view of the close connection between rosary and Eucharist that had developed three centuries earlier among Elizabethan Catholics who often reinterpreted the rosary in strongly sacramental terms as a "eucharistic site." Although Cardinal Wiseman may have thought recitation of the rosary needed to be revived because it had become a "devotion . . . little understood, . . . much slighted, even by good people in our country," there is scant evidence to prove his point.[40] The fact of the matter is that the rosary "was included in every reissue of Challoner's spiritual classic, [and] . . . held an honoured place in the old English Catholics' 'penny catechism.'"[41] Its use was promoted by both kinds of English Catholics—those adhering to older, "Garden of the Soul" customs and those fond of newer, ultramontane devotions. "The rosary," Heimann concludes, "hardly divided Catholics from one another."[42]

Turning westward to the other side of the Atlantic, we find similar evidence among Catholics in the United States. Challoner's *Garden* and John Mannock's popular *Poor Man's Catechism* were both known within the American Catholic community before the end of the eighteenth century.[43] And like Challoner, Mannock had recommended devotion to the Virgin Mary through regular recitation of the rosary. Commenting on the petition (or "cry") that concludes the Hail Mary prayer, Mannock's *Catechism* exhorts Christians to

> make this [Mary] your Mother, your powerful advocate to her Son Jesus, by often repeating this *Angelical Prayer* [Hail Mary]: honour her thereby as your pious ancestors ever did before you. . . . Often repeat this prayer when you are in health, against the time, when, through pain and agony, you may not be able: *Holy Mary, Mother of God, pray for us sinners, now and in the hour of our death* [the final petition or "cry" of the Hail Mary]. A prayer so excellent cannot be too often repeated; learn then to say the Rosary, which is composed of the Lord's prayer, and the Hail Mary, and strive to gain the indulgences which are granted to those who undertake that devotion. You have been taught to have a singular love and veneration for the blessed Virgin Mary from your infancy; honour her then through the whole course of your life: every year, on her festivals; every month, with those of the Rosary: every week, on all *Saturdays*; every day, by frequently repeating the *Hail Mary*.[44]

We have seen that Challoner was eager to promote a practical piety that would better integrate Catholics into the surrounding society as good citizens and reliable employees. He therefore urged a sober life of prayer rooted in scripture and liturgy—patterns of devotion that avoided exoticism, enthusiastic excess, or an exaggerated emphasis on externals.[45]

They were also seeking forms of public prayer that might be intelligible, accessible, and appealing to other Christians. *The Poor Man's Catechism* reflected these concerns, as is evident from the careful language it used to describe Catholic devotion to Mary and the saints:

> All our prayers are directed to God, and centre wholly in him; from him alone comes all our help, our health, our happiness; so that, when we invoke the saints or angels, *Holy Mary, Mother of God, pray for us*; *St. Michael, pray for us*; *St. Peter, or Paul, pray for us*; it is not that we expect grace and help from them, as from the author of it, for we know that none but God can give grace and glory; but we hope we may sooner obtain it by their intercession to the throne of mercy than by our own unworthy prayers. When we pray to the saints in heaven, it is only to beg of them to intercede for us; as in like manner we beg those on earth to pray for us; which practice the Scripture recommends in many places. Did not God send Abimeleck to Abraham, to pray for him, because he was a prophet [Genesis 20.7], and the friends of Job, to that patriarch, to pray and offer sacrifice for them, because he was a saint, and more worthy to be heard [Job 42.8]. In this God is honoured, because both their prayers and ours come to him, are centred wholly in him, and granted through the mediation of our Saviour Jesus Christ, our immediate intercessor to the Father.[46]

Present in this text is an astute apologetic that uses biblical citations to defend the traditional Catholic understanding of powerful intercession within the "communion of saints," while stressing *God* as source and center of Christian prayer and Jesus Christ as sole mediator and "immediate intercessor with the Father." Affirmations of this kind seem deliberately crafted to show that the Catholic custom of prayer to Mary and the saints—particularly in devotions like the rosary—was neither unscriptural nor a deviation from the doctrine of God alone as "giver of grace and glory" and unique source of "our help, our health, and our happiness." The emphasis falls on what Catholics have in common with Christians of other denominations, rather than on what separates or divides them.[47]

Like their English counterparts, in short, American Catholics were concerned about fitting into society without losing sight of their distinctive identity and practices. Continuity with the devotional regime of Challoner's *Garden of the Soul* and Mannock's *Poor Man's Catechism* is evident in official manuals of Catholic prayer mandated by the bishops of the United States, especially after the Civil War. The Third Plenary Council of Baltimore (1884), for example, had called for the creation of both a national catechism and a "uniform national prayer book," thereby reflecting the bishops' ongoing concern "for the expression of correct doctrine in the prayer and practice of the community."[48] A printed edition of the *Manual of Prayers*, published in 1889, was very similar in structure and content to Challoner's *Garden*.[49] Most of this *Manual*'s 792 pages were devoted to liturgical rites (Mass and vespers, especially); to scripture (selected psalms, plus the biblical readings assigned to the Masses for Sundays and principal feasts throughout the year); to the other sacraments (baptism, confirmation, penance [confession, reconciliation], marriage, and extreme unction [anointing of the sick]); and to services for particular pastoral occasions (the churching of women after childbirth, burial of the dead). It was, in effect, a one-volume missal, breviary, and *rituale* for lay Catholics.[50]

It is not surprising to find in the American *Manual of Prayers* a pattern of public worship and devotional practice ("lived religion") that strongly resembles Challoner's *Garden*.[51] A section of the manual devoted to the rosary provides explicit instructions not only about how to say the prayer but also about the importance of meditating on the fifteen mysteries.[52] "In order to say the Rosary well," the *Manual* advises, "we should not be satisfied with merely pronouncing the words of the prayers, or with a vague and general reflection on the Mysteries; but we should endeavor to acquire the habit of reciting them with great attention and reverence, at the same time *dwelling in a vivid manner upon the different Mysteries*."[53] The counsel to meditate in a "vivid manner" recalls the use of the spiritual senses and imagination in Ignatius Loyola's *Spiritual Exercises* (a work we discussed earlier).

Meanwhile, the *Manual*'s choice of *liturgical* forms for daily morning (prime) and evening prayer (compline) attests to the primacy of liturgy, even in the lives of lay Catholics. The faithful were encouraged to join "the public prayers of the Church," since there is "always more benefit and comfort to be derived from the Public Offices of the Church than from private devotions, God having ordained that *Communion of prayers* should always have the preference."[54] This is language that anticipated, by almost a century, what the Catholic bishops at the Second Vatican Council said about the priority of liturgy over other forms of Christian prayer.[55] Nevertheless, devotions did find a place in the *Manual of Prayers*, just as they had in Challoner's *Garden of the Soul*.[56] And the American bishops continued to promote the popular devotions of "lived religion"—especially in their more social forms—throughout the nineteenth century. A Catholic Confraternity of the Holy Cross established in Boston in 1805, for instance, promoted devotion to Christ's suffering and death, a theme popular in the late medieval *devotio moderna*.[57] But the group's rules also emphasized "participation in the church's liturgical life, catechetical instruction, mutual support, moral reform, and outreach to the poor."[58] Confraternities like this one thus reflected the communal, parish-centered piety favored by church's hierarchy after the Council of Trent (which we discussed earlier).[59] At the same time, it embodied a notable trend toward "affiliation" within American Catholicism, while providing "an important religious bridge in accommodation to American volunteerism."[60] Often rooted in urban neighborhoods where newly arrived immigrant Catholics clustered, associations that were organized around a devotional focus (e.g., Christ's cross, Mary's rosary) reinforced Catholic identity while addressing social challenges (e.g., poverty, ethnic and racial prejudice). Their purposes, typically, were multiple, embracing "social (mutual aid . . . care of the sick), literary (the promotion of good literature), or devotional (the frequentation of the sacraments, mutual support through prayers)" agendas.[61]

Both print culture and the communal culture of confraternities thus played an important role in the development of American Catholic devotional life. And this was particularly true of the Marian piety associated with the rosary. An early article in the popular magazine *Ave Maria* spoke about the success of sodalities among Catholics in Civil War era America:

> A Sodality, as the word itself makes known, is a collection of persons, be they young or old, and the word, of late days, is only applied to a particular devotion either to the Holy Angels, or to the Immaculate Queen [Mary], or to our Lord Himself. . . . And to witness all this in America! . . . America, where but a short time ago Catholicism was so little known and Catholics so severely used. Most assuredly our Blessed Patroness [Mary] is taking possession of her realm. Her armies are forming; let them all unite, and, with one accord stand ready to obey her least command.[62]

Another article, dealing with the work of the Association of the Perpetual Rosary (begun by French Dominican Father Augustin Chardon in 1858 to promote a continuous recitation of the rosary throughout the world), highlighted the connection between members of this group and the rest of society and church. Praying the rosary, the author argued, has manifold benefits, spiritual and practical: it is "prayer for the multitude that prays no more . . . a source of grace to regenerate the present morbid state of society. . . . It spreads the knowledge of Mary . . . glorifies Mary . . . affords Mary a Guard of Honor to defend her against her enemies . . . defends the Holy Church Militant . . . is a solace to the Church suffering."[63] The Perpetual Rosary, the article concluded, "not only obtains all these precious results by its own proper efficacy, it obtains them in a still greater degree in causing, by its consolidated and regular organization, the practice."[64]

The Rosary as Emblem of American Catholic Identity

The passages just cited are interesting because of their stereoscopic focus. They look outward, to the praying Catholic's relation to the broader welfare of humanity, yet also inward—defensively and even militantly—to the church's mission, the pope's troubles, and Mary's own besieged reputation as advocate and intercessor.

> Mary will not leave unrewarded the honor and glory which the Church on earth has decreed to her. . . . Many souls have a certain presentiment of an era of greatness and prosperity about to rise upon the earth, and which will be the reign of Mary. It is this hope which rejoices the soul of our Holy Father, Pius IX, and which, in the midst of his bitterness, makes him ever full of joy.
>
> Now who does not see how admirable the Perpetual Rosary comes in to harmonize with the hopes of the august Pontiff and of the Church? Does it not lead most naturally to this new era of the glories of Mary in the world?. . .
>
> Oh! who would not take part in this guard of honor of the august Queen of Heaven? Every Christian is a soldier of Jesus Christ. Every Christian may and should be, by this fact alone, a soldier of Mary.[65]

Echoes of Newman's "Second Spring" and of ultramontanist loyalty to the pope can be heard in these words. Indeed, the article in *Ave Maria* pressed the claim that

> the Church is at the present day attacked with violence. One might think that hell was trying to take revenge on Pius the Ninth, and make him

expiate the mortal displeasure occasioned to it by his promulgation of the dogma of the Immaculate Conception [in 1854]. Now, who does not remember that the holy Rosary has saved the Church many times already? . . . Why should it not be destined now to save her again from the perfidious and sacrilegious schemes of all the agents of hell?[66]

Prayerful militancy on the part of "soldiers of Mary" was thus invoked as an antidote to violence against the church, its teachers, and its teachings, for "all can be *armed knights* of Mary, our divine Queen; all can bless her, praise her, with Rosary in hand, and thus defend her worship and avenge her against her enemies, save souls from hell, extend her reign, and obtain new subjects for her empire."[67]

Yet such vast claims about the rosary's efficacy had never been made in Challoner's more sober *Garden of the Soul* or the American bishops' *Manual of Prayers*. The fifteen mysteries of the rosary were presented without commentary in the 1775 edition of the *Garden*, while the *Manual of Prayers* simply invited Catholics to devout meditation on "the sufferings of our Redeemer . . . [and] the exaltation and glory of our Saviour and His Blessed Mother, hoping through the merits of His Passion and her Intercession, to be made partakers of their glory."[68] Militant language was missing, as was any mention of specific promises attached to social, political, or religious outcomes. Other Catholic prayer books contemporary with the 1884 *Manual*—such as an 1882 edition of *The Key of Heaven*, published with approval of New York's Archbishop John McCloskey—were similarly reticent.[69]

A palpable divergence can be discerned, then, between the presentation of the rosary in officially sanctioned sources like the *Manual of Prayers* and in popular print media. Nineteenth-century American prayer books continued to emphasize the basics of Catholic liturgical practice and popular devotion already present in Challoner's *Garden of the Soul* piety and subsequently promoted by the provincial and plenary councils of Baltimore between 1829 and 1884. These basics included Mass and vespers on Sundays and feasts, regular reception of the sacraments, and daily prayer and meditation. At the Third Plenary Council of Baltimore, the American bishops made it clear they regarded the church's liturgy as the indispensable "rule and form of prayer" for Catholics.[70] It insisted that priests "should explain faithfully and clearly the rites and prayers of the Church" by following the injunction given at the twenty-second session of the Council of Trent in 1562, which "has already reminded us that pastors and others having the care of souls frequently explain those things that are read during the Mass" and had also obligated pastors to "piously and prudently explain . . . in the vernacular language, the power, use, and rites of the sacraments."[71] As for the "norm of prayer in general," the American bishops went on to say, "It is obvious that the Roman Breviary is the most perfect of all, since in a wonderful way it combines divine eloquence, writings of the Fathers and sacred hymns in one prayer."[72] In horticultural imagery reminiscent of Challoner's *Garden*, the council urged that in American prayer books "it would be useful to select some of the most precious" prayers and texts of the Roman Missal and Breviary, "so that the liturgy's buds and flowers, like a garden of paradise, might be presented to the minds of readers."[73]

The bishops' goal was to reinforce "an understanding of liturgical prayer as a symbol of the church's juridical authority."[74] This aim reflected a deeper, more fundamental change within American Catholicism in the mid-nineteenth century and represented, as well, "a departure from the course set by John Carroll."[75] John Hughes, archbishop of New York (1850–64), embodied the shift toward "the formation of a Catholic identity characterized by strong social boundaries and internal role distinction between clergy and laity."[76] It was Hughes's view that the basics of Catholic religion required a rigorous emphasis on hierarchical structures, immutable doctrine, and moral discipline. A rapidly growing church composed largely of poor immigrants needed a strong focus that would reinforce Catholic identity within a social and political culture that was often overtly hostile. Joseph Chinnici notes that "Catholics found themselves excluded from most public offices, and Protestants controlled the schools, poor houses, and hospitals."[77] Because Catholics were frequently accused of "causing poverty," they were routinely excluded from full participation in the emerging American economic order based on free-market capitalism.[78]

Archbishop Hughes responded to this situation by insisting that Catholicism possessed "an alternate political economy."[79] This economy countered human nature's inherent selfishness and individualism—embodied, Hughes believed, in the economic system developing in nineteenth-century America—and provided solutions to social problems because it promoted practices of self-examination and mutual responsibility, "restrained passion, arbitrated for the common good, and provided the means by which the human heart could be justified and ennobled."[80]

Joseph Chinnici's research shows how this shift within mid-nineteenth-century American Catholicism impacted the practice of prayer, despite the Third Council of Baltimore's insistence on the primacy of liturgical forms. Archbishop Hughes had developed an understanding of "Catholic political economy" that bound the faithful "closely to the structures, authority, institutions, and doctrines of the church, yet freed [them] to take an active role in society. . . . The moral values Hughes encouraged—obedience to authority, discipline, self-examination—serving the individual Catholic, the church, and society, were designed to further the process of assimilation," while maintaining a firm sense of distinctive Catholic identity.[81] The result was a core of committed lay Catholics for whom prayer was primarily "a contractual arrangement between the believer and God" that could be *expressed through a wide variety of devotions.*[82]

In other words, Hughes had two goals in mind: one was to make it clear (as Challoner had done in England a century earlier) that Catholics were good and reliable *citizens* in a religiously diverse society (*assimilation*); the other was to emphasize Catholic *distinctiveness*, especially in the matter of devotional piety (*identity*). The rosary responded to both goals. On one hand, it was a portable, flexible, vernacular devotion, rooted in basically biblical episodes (the mysteries), and its use could be customized to meet the conditions of Catholics who, like other Americans, had jobs to work and families to support. On the other, the strongly Marian focus of the prayer (rooted in repetitions of the Hail Mary) made the rosary distinctively Catholic. Yet popular devotions, as we have seen, are hard for church authorities to monitor and regulate, especially when their center is the family circle rather than the parish community. Thus, twenty years after Hughes's death, the bishops meeting at the Third Plenary Council of Baltimore acknowledged that the popular devotional "prayers used by the faithful frequently suffer from defects of language and sometimes depart from the path of sound doctrine."[83] In fact, this was a major reason why the council sought, in 1884, to produce a national prayer book based strictly on liturgical sources or devotions that conformed, in both diction and doctrine, to (mainly) Latin exemplars.

Catholic print media did not always embody the council's expressed preference for a piety shaped by "the sacred liturgy's buds and flowers, [its] garden of paradise." While magazines like *Ave Maria* certainly did pay attention to Catholic doctrine, as well as to the church's liturgical feasts and seasons, these had to compete with what were perhaps perceived as more arresting accounts of popular prayer practices and their benefits. For example, the first (1865) volume of *Ave Maria* printed an account of "very edifying incidents" that show "divine sanction" for "the practice of devotion to the Mother of God," based on a letter written in December 1864 by a

Catholic soldier serving in the Union army during the Civil War.[84] On the front lines during a battle near Franklin, Tennessee, the soldier described how his commanding officer had been seriously wounded by Confederate fire but was saved by a scapular he wore in honor of the Virgin Mary.[85] An "officer of the 4th corps," the letter explained, was wounded while driving back the rebel forces: "While he was doing this, a bullet entered on his left; in passing from shoulder to shoulder it tore the flesh all along, except one spot about two inches wide upon which his Scapular rested."[86] The letter writer explained that the office in question had been given the scapular on the previous Easter (1864), without ever suspecting that "it would one day save his life."[87] The scapular, he concluded, had prevented the bullet from severing "the vertebra of the neck, at the head of the spinal column, which, if broken, would [have] cause[d] instant death."[88]

Devotional objects, as we have seen, have often served Catholics as "media of presence" that are believed to protect the owner/wearer/user in perilous circumstances. It was such a perception, probably, that had prompted the martyr John Ogilvie to fling the rosary from the scaffold "as a last souvenir for the Catholics who were near him" when he was executed in 1615.[89] The circumstances of nineteenth-century immigrant Catholics in America may not have been quite as dire, but the appeal of such beliefs persisted. The Civil War soldier's story in *Ave Maria* shows that devotion to Marian media such as scapular or rosary continued to be linked to faith in the Virgin's powerful presence and protection at moments when faith, life, or both were threatened.

Officially approved sources such as the 1889 *Manual of Prayers* avoided mentioning any special claims of protection or privilege associated with Marian media or devotions.[90] Nevertheless, popular devotions—and claims of extraordinary transforming benefits attached to them—proliferated within post–Civil War American Catholicism.[91] The most dominant among these devotions—for example, "the Eucharistic celebration of Forty Hours, Sacred Heart devotion, the rosary, the stations of the cross, the wearing of the scapular"—had an important feature in common: each emphasized "the important of material representation in the religious culture of the period . . . an object with which the believer was actively engaged."[92] The link between Christian piety and visual representation is ancient and long, but as we have seen, that linkage was significantly reframed within early modern Catholicism, partly in response to Protestant objections to the use of religious images, and partly from internal changes within the Catholic community itself. Thus, among nineteenth-century

American Catholics, "use of a sacred representation in a devotional practice occurred within the context of a long polemical literary tradition on material embodiment in both religious and civil life."[93]

Perhaps the most eloquent spokesperson on this matter was James Cardinal Gibbons (1834–1921). His long tenure as archbishop of the primatial see of Baltimore (1878–1921) made him a natural leader within the "liberalizing wing" of American Catholic prelates.[94] Gibbons's *Faith of Our Fathers*, first published in 1876, swiftly became "the most popular apologetical work in the English-speaking world."[95] It combined the characteristics of a traditional catechism (basic instruction about matters of faith, though not in question-and-answer format) with the features of a handbook of apologetics (explanation and defense of Catholic doctrine directed toward non-Catholics). Recent scholarship has also located it within the discourse of "mass-print sentimental culture in nineteenth-century America."[96] Gibbons recognized that Catholicism in the United States could not expand and flourish if it remained "a refuge for impoverished immigrants seeking escape from the pressures of harsh Protestant materialism."[97] Catholics needed to engage in a spirited yet respectful dialogue with their surrounding culture, and *The Faith of Our Fathers* placed in their hands a compendium that encoded the "sentimental/domestic values central to Protestant culture, while at the same time attempting to show the affinity of Catholic teaching for similar notions of family morality."[98]

Two chapters in *The Faith of Our Fathers* are relevant here—those dealing with the Blessed Virgin Mary (chapter 14) and with sacred images (chapter 15).[99] While Gibbons also dealt—as *Challoner* had in *The Garden of the Soul*—with the Mass and other sacraments, his book was "centered on, and invested heavily in, the figure of the nurturing Mother in all her manifestations"; throughout, it "relies on maternal metaphors and symbolism" that depict the church's teaching role as "a distinctively maternal outpouring of love."[100] *The Faith of Our Fathers* did not single out the rosary devotion for explicit discussion, but Gibbons did discuss more general Protestant objections to Catholic prayer addressed to Mary:

> But you will ask: Why do you so often blend together the worship of God and the veneration of the Blessed Virgin? . . . Why do you so often repeat in succession the Lord's prayer and the Angelical salutation [Hail Mary]? Is not this practice calculated to level all distinctions between the Creator and His creature, and to excite the displeasure of a God ever jealous of His glory?[101]

The combined repetition of the Our Father and Hail Mary was of course the most familiar feature of the rosary, so Gibbons's words implicitly endorse and promote the practice. Moreover, Mary's own words in scripture combine praise of God with acknowledgment of her own blessedness: "My soul magnifies the *Lord* . . . behold, from now on all generations will call *me* blessed" (Luke 1.46, 49). "Here," wrote Gibbons, "are the names of Creator and creature interwoven like threads of gold and silver in the same woof, without provoking the jealousy of God. . . . In uniting Mary's praise with that of Jesus we are strictly imitating the sacred Text. We are imitating Joachim, the High Priest, and the people of God in Bethulia, who unite the praises of Judith with the praises of Jehovah [Judith 13.17–20]."[102]

As an apologist, Cardinal Gibbons—like Challoner more than a century earlier—sought to show how faith, prayer, and practice prepared Catholics for full and effective participation in civic life. His chapter titled "Sacred Images" thus argued that the use of material objects in Catholic devotion forms "a continuum with the images, memorials, statues, and material representations that also marked the ordinary life of society."[103] If a family keeps "likenesses of George Washington or Patrick Henry" at home, Gibbons reasoned, those images "cannot fail to exercise a salutary though silent influence on the mind and heart of your child."[104] Gibbons also pointed out that the Council of Trent's decree on sacred images (which we discussed earlier) coincided with the view expressed by the Protestant Leibnitz in his *Systema theologicum*:

> We speak of the honor paid to images, yet this . . . really means that we honor not the senseless thing which is incapable of understanding such honor, but the prototype, which receives honor through its representation, according to the teaching of the Council of Trent. It is in this sense . . . that scholastic writers have spoken of the same worship being paid to the images of Christ as to Christ our Lord himself; for the act which is called the worship of an image is really the worship of Christ Himself . . . the image . . . rendering Him more manifestly present, and raising the mind more actively to the contemplation of Him.[105]

For Gibbons, then, material objects such as statues, paintings, or rosaries provided continuity with "the ordinary life of society"—with its emphasis on inspirational imagery—and at the same time helped to shape "a vision of communal order in private, domestic, and public life."[106] Catholics could use their rosaries (and other material objects of devotion) to engage in society's larger "struggle over the images shaping its public discourse and the minds of its citizens." This helps explain why devotion to Christ's "Holy Face" became so popular among late nineteenth-century American Catholics. His face served to focus prayerful veneration, but it also functioned as "social code."[107] The face, after all, is that part of the human body most obviously "exposed . . . marked with openings towards the world, . . . socially reflective of affective changes in the heart and the emotions, . . . associated with the loss of public honor and its impact on the suffering spirit."[108] In the face of Christ, immigrant Catholics especially could see mirrored their own ambiguous social experience in America. As Christ's noble visage endured scorn and humiliation during the course of his public trial, passion, and execution, so Catholics sometimes registered in their bodies—especially their faces—social "misunderstanding, public ridicule, or . . . loss of prestige."[109] Devotion to the Holy Face gave Catholics not only a meaningful experience of prayer but a "social code" within which to interpret the multiple tensions and anxieties of their personal and communal lives.

The Rosary as Medium of Presence

Nineteenth-century American Catholic devotionalism should be seen, then, in relation to "an ethic of honor and shame that presupposed a society of 'belongingness,'" and not to "the more individualistic economy characteristic of contemporary society."[110] This point is particularly applicable to the rosary as material object, as vocal prayer (recited repetitively), and as a devotion that could be prayed privately or shared with others in public (e.g., prayed together in church before the start of Mass). In America, as elsewhere in the world, the rosary—a way to "pray by hand"—became for Catholics an embodied connection, offering them communion with their religious past in their social present.[111] The deepest human memories, after all, are inscribed on the skin, etched on our bodies. The rituals of private devotion, like those of public worship, are a way of "thinking with the skin" and "remembering with the flesh." For while history, as historian Colleen McDannell has pointed out, may call for "analysis and criticism," human memory is stubbornly "affective and magical."[112] As a result, religious objects such as rosaries or crucifixes serve as powerfully palpable "reminders of significant events, people, moods, and activities by condensing and compressing memory."[113] They are not simply objects of devotion but media of presence and tools of belonging.

It is hardly surprising, then, that among nineteenth- and twentieth-century American Catholics the rosary became not merely popular but ubiquitous. The history of its popularity needs no further discussion here, since it has already been well documented by others.[114] The principal significance of this history, for our discussion, lies in the fact that rosaries often became for Catholics a potent form of intergenerational connection with the faith. Often rosaries were a literal, material link between one generation and another. A deceased Catholic's rosary was often placed in his or her hands during the public viewing and the pre-funeral wake, then removed and given to the heirs prior to burial. Even for Catholics not well known for attendance at church, the rosary could become part of the person's spiritual legacy—as happened with historian Eamon Duffy's Irish grandmother, who was "not a pious woman" and in later life rarely went to church, yet prayed the rosary night after night for members of her family.[115] Even with the arrival of the third millennium, the habit of praying the rosary has not disappeared among American Catholics.[116] Although allegiance to traditional devotions to Mary and the saints—like attendance at Mass—has declined, these practices are still more common among today's Catholics than private Bible reading or group-centered activities such as Bible study programs. It is estimated that about one-fifth of Catholics in the United States still pray the rosary at least once a week.[117] That is still a substantial percentage, given that the overall pattern of "participation in the Catholic community is declining."[118]

A recent book by Garry Wills reinforces the point that the rosary's very *materiality* physically connects those who pray to personal and collective memory:

> The fingers' transit along the beads, if one strips them of fetishistic connections, can help put one in a prayerful mood. . . . There is a kind of tactile memory evoked in their use, helping recall other times of prayer. The British author Eamon Duffy . . . says that the click of rosary beads brings back childhood memories of his grandmother praying through sleepless nights, with her "muttered preamble—This one is for Tom, for Molly, for Lily—as she launched on yet another decade" . . .
>
> There is a natural symbolism in their threaded continuity. I am reminded of the fresco *Good Government* in Siena, in which the citizens hold on to a rope that goes up to the figure of Justice, a sign of linked activity and mutual support. . . . The beads can, indeed, hold us together.[119]

Wills rightly focuses on the rosary's role as "tactile memory" and potential source of social continuity, while other scholars call attention to the riotous complexity of Mary as a religious icon: "It is impossible," writes Robert A. Orsi,

> to tell a simple story about the Virgin Mary. She cannot be held in place by a single attribute—sorrow or delight, purity or compassion—or held accountable for a single social consequence—liberation or oppression, solidarity or fracture. She is not innocent. Her sorrow, for example, has been a source of great consolation to women in their own grief but also a means of disciplining them to understand pain and self-abnegation as their destinies. Mary stands for peace and for divisiveness. She is not solely the creation of theologians or of the masses; she belongs completely neither to her devout nor to culture.[120]

Orsi has touched here on a principal reason why the rosary's mysteries—once limited to fifteen, now expanded to twenty—cover such a wide range of human experience and emotion, from the sublime (Christ's resurrection, Mary's assumption into heaven) to the almost vaudevillian (Mary's visit to Elizabeth, in which a young unmarried woman and her older, formerly sterile cousin compare notes on their pregnancies; the madcap scramble that seems to have accompanied the finding of Jesus in the Temple).[121] In most Marian images, the Virgin does not gaze at us directly but averts her eyes. "She is always," Orsi writes, "refracted through the prism of the needs and fears of the people who approach her and so she is a protean and unstable figure. Because of this instability of meaning, Mary can be the occasion of serious cultural and psychological distress, which in turn provokes more determined efforts to fix her in place. But she continually frustrates these agendas."[122]

For these reasons we have devoted space to discussing the importance of Caravaggio's art as a seminal contribution to the reframing of religious representation generally—and of the figure of Mary specifically—within early modern Catholicism. Not only did Caravaggio rewrite traditional Marian icons in highly original, even startling, ways; he subverted the familiar relationship between viewer and painting. In this, he remained faithful to the radical iconicity of Mary herself, for she "transforms *looking* into a devotional activity" that repels every form of religious voyeurism.[123] The voyeur's "seeing" aims at seizure, a violating intrusion that seeks possession of an object by stealth—making it "mine" without any hint of mutuality. But in Caravaggio's Marian images, mutuality is key. The space uniting viewer and Virgin "becomes an imaginative opening for need, fantasy, desire, like the space between the faces and bodies of children and their caregivers. Devotional space is constituted by the presence of the Madonna and her devout to each other, by the desires of the devout, and by Mary's invitation to them to come to her and her recognition of their needs."[124] One perceives such a transformation of potentially voyeuristic looking into "devotional activity" immediately in paintings like *Madonna di Loreto*.[125] Caravaggio's representation shows nothing of the object viewers would have expected to see—namely, Mary's own house, miraculously transported to the Italian village of Loreto. Instead, the "miracle" viewers see is the faith of simple pilgrims with dirty feet and shabby clothes whose intense gaze brings the "cult statue to life in front of their eyes: Mary is poised on tiptoe with knees crossed, her pose suggesting the weightlessness of an apparition but one so tangible" it casts a shadow on the doorway.[126]

As we have seen, Caravaggio's rewritten Marian icons subverted the distance between viewer and image, thereby altering the experience of looking itself. This new way of looking transforms painted images into "media of presence" and equips viewers with "devotional images and objects" that may be "used to act upon the world, upon others and oneself."[127] This can happen because Marian icons fuse "image and prototype," prompting responses predicated on "the belief that what is represented on an image is actually present, or present in it."[128] In short, visual engagement with icons of Mary are "encounters with presence and they are characterized by the whole range of emotion and behavior that is possible when persons are present to each other in one place."[129]

Rosaries, too, became such media of presence. We may rightly question the modernist assumption that *absence* is ubiquitous because human desire originates solely in experiences of lack and dispossession.[130] As physical objects of material culture, rosaries are not merely souvenirs—empty reminders of an experience (and a person) now vanished or *absent*—but live media perceived as providing believers direct access to Mary's powerful presence. Their very materiality helps "to mark off a sacred domain [of prayer and devotion] as ordered and meaningful."[131] Moreover, the rosary's role as a medium of presence results not from its originality but from its repetitiveness and widespread replication. Replication is, in fact, a "critical aspect of Catholic culture."[132] It is the principal means by which religious practices that might otherwise remain local and ethnic are globalized and

come to embrace "the universality of the supernatural," providing practi-
tioners a means "to participate in a worldwide community that [does] not
recognize the limits of time and space."[133]

A good example of how religious replication can transform material
sites and objects into media of presence is the Grotto of Our Lady of
Lourdes at the University of Notre Dame. Built more than a century ago,
in 1897, the Lourdes Grotto replaced earlier shrines and, as we have seen,
still serves as a focal point of religious life for Notre Dame's Catholic students.[134] As a place of prayer and pilgrimage, the Grotto succeeded not
because of its originality but precisely because it was a reproduction. Similarly, the most frequent prayer offered at this shrine is not innovative but
traditional—the rosary. Critics of art and culture might view the Grotto
as an example of religious fakery, yet among Catholics the "production of
religious replicas was, curiously enough, the production of authenticity."[135]
The Notre Dame Grotto showed that sacredness is migratory—portable,
exportable—and hence cannot be confined to a single spot. One did not
need to visit the French village of Lourdes or bathe in its spring or pray
in its Church of the Holy Rosary (built between 1883 and 1901) to experience Mary's healing presence and power. Creating a replica of its Grotto
on Notre Dame's campus made it clear to Catholics in northern Indiana
"that they were not living in an undefined, wild space but that they were
directly connected to the spiritual centers of Catholicity."[136]

For people of faith, then, authenticity may be established not only
through "direct contact with an original" site or event but also through
the diffusion of the sacred across a variety of locales. By visiting shrines or
their replicas, Catholics "emotionally engaged with the sacred past. They
entered into a series of Catholic stories. It was the engagement with the
material object and the religious narrative that made the shrine 'real.'"[137]
Nevertheless, more often than not Catholics were eager to reproduce the
physical details of an originating site or object as precisely as possible
in their replicas. The accuracy of the reproduction guaranteed that "the
thing being presented as the substitution for something real" could itself
"be treated as real," and could thus "become real."[138] The more realistic
the replica, the more surely it could be perceived as a living medium of
presence offering the faithful an "automatic transition from seeing to em-
pathy and involvement."[139] By engaging in pilgrimage and prayer at a *local*
shrine—a reproduction—the devout could still connect to the practices of
a *global* Catholicism.

Rosaries also partook of such a diffused sacredness. We saw an ear-lier example of this diffusion in that for recusant Catholics in Elizabethan England, rosary beads became—in a church without churches—a sacred site connecting those who held and prayed them to sacramental grace. Circumstances in late nineteenth-century and early twentieth-century America were obviously different from those of late sixteenth-century and early seventeenth-century England, but the sense among Catholics that rosaries are media of presence connecting those who pray to the "treasury of grace" within the "communion of saints" was hardly attenuated. Sig-nificantly, for example, the 1889 *Manual of Prayers*—the national prayer book published by order of the Third Plenary Council of Baltimore—included a "Form of Blessing Rosaries Proper to the Order of Preachers [Dominicans]."[140] Since the eighteenth century, special indulgences had been given to Catholics who recited the rosary using beads blessed by a Dominican priest.[141] And despite their bad reputation among sixteenth-century reformers, indulgences were actually based on the common belief that through prayer, fasting, and action on behalf of others (e.g., visiting the sick or feeding the poor), Christians could connect themselves with "the abundance of God's forgiving love through Jesus" and with "the unity of all Christians in a communion of saints."[142]

From the late fifteenth century onward, indulgences had been attached to recitation of the rosary.[143] Over time, these were expanded under special conditions or for special occasions. Thus, for instance, a "plenary indul-gence" (i.e., a reprieve from any punishment that might still await sinners after their sins are forgiven by the church) was granted those who prayed the rosary daily for a month, provided they also went to confession, re-ceived Holy Communion, and paid a visit to a church or public oratory.[144] (Note here the connection between indulgences, prayer, sacramental activ-ity, and sacred spaces.) As both material object and recited prayer (private or public), the rosary was thus perceived as a privileged site bringing the devout—wherever they were—into direct contact with the communion of saints. In this, one may still detect traces of that "eucharistic" dimension Elizabethan Catholics sometimes ascribed to the rosary. Official Catholic teaching stressed that the believer's bond with the *communio sanctorum* (communion of saints) was effected principally through the *communio sa-cra* (Holy Communion) received at Mass, yet the rosary also possessed quasi-sacramental significance in virtue of its connection with the system of indulgences.[145]

Since the Second Vatican Council, Catholic teaching has stressed the *multiple* presences of Christ among Christians.[146] To say this is also to affirm that multiple *media* of presence are available to people of faith. Christ's presence is experienced not only in public liturgy, sacraments, and prayer but also in "the poor, the sick, and the imprisoned"; in the "pilgrim Church" as it "performs works of mercy"; in evangelization and preaching; in pastoral work and teaching.[147] This more inclusive understanding of how Christ's presence is acknowledged, known, and named among Catholics opens the door to a religious sensibility that finds "sacred reality present in things the devout could manipulate and kiss, wear and decorate, punish and plead with."[148] Such a sensibility does fly in the face of modern views which argue that "presence" can never be in "things" and that representations are precisely *not* what they represent.[149] Yet it is very much in tune with the language and gestures of Christian devotion, as the Vatican's *Directory on Popular Piety and the Liturgy* (2001) recognizes:

> History shows that . . . the life of faith is sustained by the forms and practices of piety, which the faithful have often felt more deeply and actively than the liturgical celebrations. . . . Popular piety is characterized by a great variety and richness of bodily, gestural and symbolic expressions: kissing or touching images, places, relics and sacred objects; pilgrimages, processions, going bare-footed or on one's knees; kneeling and prostrating, wearing medals and badges. These and similar expressions, handed down from parent to child, are direct and simple ways of giving external expression to the heart and to one's commitment to live the Christian life.[150]

The intense tactile, kinetic, visual, and aural engagement that characterizes popular piety suggests that devotional practices or objects (such as the rosary) remain effective media of presence that, though they differ from ritual media (liturgy and sacraments), are still capable of offering people an intense and immediate experience of God's holiness in their lives.

Kitschy Art and Catholic Memory

David Morgan's study *Visual Piety* helps explain why this is so.[151] It has often been assumed that "the aesthetic attitude properly belongs to the urban sophisticate, to the class that enjoys leisure and refinement as the sign of its privilege, in contrast to the uneducated and rural."[152] Concomitant with this attitude—that aesthetic appreciation belongs to connoisseurs of a "higher" socioeconomic class—is the judgment that devotionalism fails to achieve the "disinterestedness" to which religious faith and prayer should ultimately aspire.[153] A passage from Thomas Merton's *Contemplative Prayer* embodies this notion that mature Christian prayer ought to be characterized by a disinterestedness that fuses faith and contemplation with self-transcendence:

> The contemplative . . . accepts the love of God on faith, in defiance of all apparent evidence. This is the necessary condition, for the mystical experience of the reality of God's presence and of his love for us. Only when we are able to "let go" of everything within us, all desire to see, to know, to taste, and to experience the presence of God, do we truly become able to experience that presence with the overwhelming conviction and reality that revolutionize our entire inner life.[154]

Even though Merton never disputed the role of ritual, art, and images in the formation of Christian identity—his father had been a painter, and Merton himself was a Cistercian monk steeped in the daily rites of monastic liturgy—he does seem to place them on a "lower" rung of spiritual development, at least in this text. Whatever their symbolic value as "aids to a devout life," devotions like the rosary, though they may foster the contemplation of Christian mysteries, often seem to lack the "letting go of everything we desire to see, to know, to taste," that is, the pure disinterestedness that distinguishes "the higher forms of contemplative union with God."[155]

Yet such views ignore, distort, or discount the actual experience and recorded witness of many devout Catholics. Orsi's illuminating study of how Catholic women have prayed to Saint Jude (patron saint of hopeless cases) points out that prayer is never a "unidirectional practice"; it is always accompanied by "a reflux of implications, consequences, and entailments for the person praying."[156] By the sheer perseverance and intensity of their prayers to Saint Jude, women united themselves to other people's pain; they "absorbed the anxieties, needs, and distress of others into themselves, into their bodies and hearts. Prayer to Jude rendered them porous; in the practice of the devotion, women dissolved the boundaries of their own subjectivities and lost sight of the difference between themselves and their spouses, parents."[157]

Sometimes, certainly, such a loss of boundaries brought women harm, especially when they ignored their own well-being in order to "help" or protect others (especially wayward husbands) whose behavior was intolerable. Orsi rightly observes that every time "a woman did not tell a distraught friend to leave her alcoholic and abusive husband, protest the treatment she was receiving at work, insist to her children that she needed rest, or stop risking dangerous pregnancies, but instead gave her a prayer card that recalled her to the familiar cycle of sacrifice and submission, she was deepening patterns of women's alienation, surrender and oppression."[158] In such circumstances, unquestionably, Catholic devotions could and did result in sinister consequences, becoming masks of oppression rather than media of divine presence.

On the positive side, however, devotions have often helped people face their own failure, misery, and wretchedness with greater realism. Physical objects like rosaries—which encourage Christians to "pray by hand"—directly engage heart, mind, and body. They are simultaneously material objects, visual stimuli, and media of presence. Far from embodying the "disinterestedness" of prayer, the discourse of such devotions focuses on desire and the body—after the example of Jesus, sweating blood in the Garden of Gethsemane shortly before his arrest and praying, "Abba, Father, all things are possible to you. Take this cup away from me, but not what I will, but what you will" (the first "sorrowful mystery"; see Mark 14.36). Beads slipping one by one through the praying person's fingers are powerful physical incentives to "bring broken bodies to be mended, shattered nerves and sick children to be healed. The body of the believer is explicitly engaged. . . . The transcendence [sought] is deliverance from ailment and anguish. . . . Desire is at the heart of this vision; there is nothing 'disinterested' about it."[159]

The material culture of Christian devotionalism thus bolsters the belief that both awe and desire begin in the body. This conviction was already well in place when the rosary originated in the fourteenth and fifteenth centuries, for in late medieval devotional practices, "the body was the means of participating in the life of God perfectly expressed in Jesus, whose incarnation, suffering, death, and resurrection were the material means of salvation."[160] Devotional images—found, for instance, in fifteenth-century rosary books and in the genre of *Rosenkranzbilder* discussed earlier—reinforced the perception that the human body is a privileged site for "identifying oneself with Christ."[161] In virtue of the mysteries of Christ's incarnation, suffering, and resurrection—mysteries rehearsed whenever the rosary was prayed—the body became "something human between us and God," not only a source of desire but the very embodiment of salvation itself.

Thus, from the late Middle Ages to the twenty-first century, a "variety of sacred acts and objects including the rosary, holy water, scapulars, medals, the Blessed Sacrament, pilgrimage, and icons" became media of presence within what might be called a metaphysics of devotion. Images offer "the iconophile the prospect of sacred presence. In a metaphysics of presence . . . representation harbors the yearning to overcome the difference between sign and referent and join the other to one's own body."[162] Caravaggio's religious paintings, we have seen, embody a metaphysics of devotion that seeks to "shrink the distance" between viewer and image. Although he painted in an early baroque style, Caravaggio capitalized on a tradition whose roots reach back to the medieval *devotio moderna*. His Marian images—painted provocatively, directly from life—were thus at another level quite traditional. With almost embarrassing physical urgency, Caravaggio catapulted Mary and her clients into a shared visual space. Devotees could look upon her precisely because she first looked upon them, accepting with love—and without judgment—their sweat, saliva, sagging diapers, grimy fingernails, and dirty feet. As media of the Madonna's presence to whomever sought her help and protection, Caravaggio's canvases gave new meaning to the phrase "refuge of sinners."[163] Such art reinforced the notion, already present in the later Middle Ages, that the "act of identifying one's sensations with those of a depiction" made the body itself "an organ of knowing"—a "visceral bridge between self and other"; hence the "knowledge the devout sought was the body's knowledge, expressed in the language of enfleshed sensations."[164] In the metaphysics of devotion, the human body became "a powerful organ of religious knowing."[165] Rosary beads, slipping through the fingers one at a time, capitalized on this connection between human body and sacred knowledge.

In the rosary, moreover, Jesus' Mother therefore became "everyone's contemporary."[166] Both visual imagery (e.g., Caravaggio's *Death of the Virgin*) and the mysteries of the rosary made it clear that Mary's life was

> subject to all the vicissitudes and sorrows of human finitude. She aged, she knew loss and loneliness, her hair whitened . . . she was not always, only, the young, slender, beautiful mother. . . . By imagining Mary's history with the emotional discernment born of their own experience, her

devout understood and affirmed that Mary recognized the anxiety, loss, and promise of what was happening to them. She had experienced all of them herself. Through the recitation of the Mysteries, the Blessed Mother and her devout became recognizable to each other.[167]

Not only did the body become a "visceral bridge" uniting Mary and her clients; it also became the deepest source of Catholic memory. For the deepest human memories are buried in the body, borne on breath, blood, and bone. Humans first learn to think with their skins and remember with their bodies. And this holds true especially for Catholics as they grapple with their personal and collective histories. Devotional media such as the rosary "fundamentally formed Catholics['] bodies and imaginations. Devotionalism was the site at which Catholic bodies and architecture, the material and the spiritual, imagination and reality, hope and resignation came together."[168] The loss of such media is thus tantamount to a loss of memory and impedes the construction (and appreciation) of a communal Catholic past.

Yet memory is not photography. Remembering not only registers persons, places, and events but also interprets and reinterprets them as experiences whose impact on our lives is ongoing. Memory is thus neither "a reliable guide to what happened in the past" nor "an infallible map toward the future."[169] It is thus inaccurate to suggest that post–Vatican II Catholicism "lost its memory" by severing (or trying to sever) its ties to the saints in general and to Mary in particular. For one thing, far from eliminating attention to Mary and the saints, postconciliar Catholicism has reasserted the value and importance of personal, prayerful engagement with these great figures of faith. The Vatican's *Directory on Popular Piety and the Liturgy* (n. 197), for example, reaffirms that "the Rosary, or Psalter of the Blessed Virgin Mary, is one of the most excellent prayers to the Mother of God," and that it is "essentially a contemplative prayer" that "encourages the faithful to meditate on the mysteries of the Lord's life." At the same time, the *Directory* seeks to expand the devotional horizons of Catholics, cautioning that loyalty to the rosary should cause the faithful to "discredit or overlook other forms of prayer" or the rich diversity of Marian piety (*Directory*, n. 202).

So instead of seeking to disconnect the church's memory from such devotions, the Catholic bishops at the Second Vatican Council actually "reaffirmed the Council of Trent's counterreformationary endorsement of the veneration of saints and belief in their intercession."[170] In fact, the council's

Dogmatic Constitution on the Church (*Lumen gentium*; 1964) devoted an entire chapter (chapter 8) to the Virgin Mary, reiterating "her place in the Church which is the highest after Christ and also closest to us," and focusing on her role in the history of salvation, her continuing relation to the church, the legitimacy of her cult, and her role as "sign of true hope and comfort for the pilgrim people of God."[171] The same document provided a brief but beautiful account of the mysteries that form the meditative heart of the rosary, linking these to scripture and to Mary's place in Christian liturgies, East and West. Similarly, as we have seen, the *Directory on Popular Piety and the Liturgy* devotes an entire chapter (chap. 5, nn. 183–207) to discussion of the variety and richness of Marian devotions.

Vatican II cannot be accused, then, of denying or diminishing the role of devotions in the embodiment of Catholic memory. The council sought instead to articulate a pastoral strategy that would link devotions—especially those dealing with Mary and the saints—more securely to (1) the biblical sources of the church's faith (*Lumen gentium* 55–59); (2) the uniqueness, "dignity and efficacy of Christ, the One Mediator" between God and humankind (*Lumen gentium* 62); and (3) the rites, prayers, feasts, and seasons of the church's liturgy (*Lumen gentium* 66–67). Postconciliar Catholicism represents not an assault on devotions (and hence on Catholic memory or identity) but rather a search for balance between "false exaggeration" and "too summary an attitude in considering the special dignity of the Mother of God" (*Lumen gentium* 67). In short, when speaking of "the living communion which exists between us and our brothers [and sisters] who are in the glory of heaven," the council, "in keeping with its pastoral preoccupations," sought "to remove or correct any abuses, excesses or defects which may have crept in here and there, and so restore all things that Christ and God be more fully praised" (*Lumen gentium* 51). Authentic veneration of Mary and the saints consists, therefore, "not so much in a multiplicity of external acts, but rather in a more intense practice of our love, whereby, for our own greater good and that of the Church, we seek from the saints example in their way of life, fellowship in their communion, and the help of their intercession" (*Lumen gentium* 51).[172] Devotions are thereby linked to ethics, to the Christian's responsibility toward self and others in the world, and to the "liturgy of the neighbor."[173]

Similar themes were echoed in the *Catechism of the Catholic Church* (1994), particularly in its comments about devotion to the Blessed Virgin Mary and the rosary. While noting that prayerful communion with Mary has been with the church virtually from its inception—the apostles "devoted themselves with one accord to prayer, together with some women, and Mary the mother of Jesus" (Acts 1.14)—the *Catechism* also cautions that "this very special devotion . . . differs essentially from the adoration which is given to the incarnate Word and equally to the Father and the Holy Spirit" (n. 971).[174] It stresses Mary's role as "eschatological icon of the church" (title for n. 972), for she is the same Mother of Jesus mentioned in Acts, who now enjoys, body and soul, the presence of Christ's glory in heaven and "shines forth on earth . . . a sign of certain hope and comfort to the pilgrim people of God" (*Catechism*, n. 972).[175] The *Catechism* (n. 2708) compares devotional practices such as the rosary to the ancient monastic practice of *lectio divina* (a contemplative pondering or mulling over of the scriptures in mind, heart, body, and soul). When reciting the rosary, Christians mobilize their embodied faculties of "thought, imagination, emotion, and desire," focusing them "on the mysteries of Christ" and seeking union with him (*Catechism*, n. 2708).

Catholic Kitsch and the Continuing Appeal of the Rosary

We have seen the continuing appeal of the rosary across historical eras from pre- to postmodern; across gender and generational boundaries; across cultures and social classes; and across a Catholic population often polarized between those on the right and those on the left. Historically, moreover, the practice of using prayer beads connects Catholics globally not only with fellow Christians but also with adherents of other world religions (e.g., Judaism, Hinduism, Buddhism, Islam).[176] A large part of the rosary's popularity may thus be due to its accessibility, to "the simple humanity of the mysteries," each of which points to an experience that all persons who pray may hope to have.[177] Because the mysteries being meditated belong to the whole faith community, the rosary helps those who pray "transcend individual whim" and "breathe, as it were, with the whole body of believers."[178] Further, the rosary is a flexible prayer that lets each person who uses it customize the mysteries to suit his or her own situation in life. "The rosary," Garry Wills remarks, "is not an assignment. . . . The point of having a full course of mysteries to contemplate is simply to provide a framework within which to structure one's reflection. The uses to which one puts that framework can and should differ from person to person."[179]

There are, as well, other ways of interpreting the rosary that link it more closely both to material culture and to the reframing of religious representation that occurred within early modern Catholicism (notably, though not exclusively, in the religious art of Caravaggio). We have explored the rosary as a devotion arising from within "vernacular religion." To speak of vernacularism in this way is not to relegate its practices to a "lowbrow" religious or artistic sensibility. Yet it can hardly be denied that the rosary and the visual images it inspires *have* often been portrayed as "kitschy." Robert C. Solomon points to the "campaign against kitsch" that characterizes much contemporary discourse about philosophical aesthetics, art, and art criticism.[180] He notes that "saccharine religious art," in particular, is commonly criticized as "sweet kitsch," that is, "art (or, to hedge our bets, intended art) that appeals unsubtly and unapologetically to the softer, 'sweeter' sentiments."[181] Catholic "church supply stores" typically abound in kitsch of this kind. Art critic Peter Robb calls it "the dire panoply of standard Catholic iconography," embodied in paintings, statues, and objects (e.g., holy cards, rosaries, devotional books) depicting "nailed hands, rolling eyes, exposed breasts, floating veils, bleeding wounds, cherubs' heads on wings," and offering viewers "a related mix of sex, death, frustration, incest, pain, voyeurism, nymphomania, paedophilia, sadism, repentance."[182]

Robb's unflattering description of "standard Catholic iconography" registers two of the principal objections against sweet kitsch: it is bad *art* that produces bad *ethics*. As sentimentality posing as religious art, it produces "a false . . . carefully edited portrait that limits our vision and restricts our sense of reality."[183] As fraudulent ethics posing as pious image, it provokes emotional excess, promotes immaturity, manipulates viewers, conjures fake feelings, permits uncritical self-indulgence, and blinds its consumers to the truth about themselves and their world.[184] At its worst, kitsch may compromise personal autonomy and lead to violence or cruelty, as the troubled history of how Jews have been depicted in Christian art demonstrates.[185] At best, kitsch is a license for sentimentality, and sentiments have a hard time legitimating their presence in the rarefied precincts of philosophy, aesthetics, and art criticism. In ethics, as in art, sentimentality has become a dirty word, "a term of harsh abuse."[186]

A mainspring of the campaign against kitsch, therefore, is the charge that its images arouse emotion without moving "consumers" to action. A famous example occurs in Milan Kundera's novel *The Unbearable Lightness of Being*:

> Kitsch causes two tears to flow in quick succession. The first tear says: How nice to see children running on the grass!

The second tear says: How nice to be moved, together with all mankind, by children running on the grass!

It is the second tear that makes kitsch kitsch.[187]

In a nutshell, kitsch inspires feelings that go nowhere; it falls short of rous-
ing its consumers to take action and responsibility in the real world. The
sentimental picture of "children running on the grass" fails to motivate
viewers to make generous contributions to UNICEF or seek a solution to
poverty among children in their own neighborhoods. The "second tear"
remains ineffectual, self-indulgent, and superfluous. It is this ethically
moribund side of kitsch that leads many of its critics to complain that
sentimentality actually embodies "flight from, and contempt for, *real* people, by comparison with imaginary ones."[188] Self-indulgent sentimentality
thus "misrepresents the world in order to indulge our feelings."[189] Perhaps
the classic instance is to be found in Dickens's novel *The Old Curiosity
Shop*, where Little Nell is

> a figure who could not exist and was the product of wish-fulfillment—
> a subservient, devoted, totally understanding mixture of child and lover,
> with no wishes of her own. This figure was well-designed to provoke a
> delicious sense of pity and mastery, and to set up further fantasies where
> this feeling could continue. One trouble about this apparently harmless
> pursuit is that it distorts expectations; it can make people unable to deal
> with the real world, and particularly with real girls.[190]

Yet there is another side to kitsch that merits examination, and it is
this aspect that can illumine some of the basic reasons why Marian devotions like the rosary have had such enduring popularity within the
Catholic community. Philosopher Robert C. Solomon points out that it
is "the very nature of an emotion to be engaged, even if only vicariously,
to 'take sides,' sometimes judiciously and sometimes not. Through our
emotions we edit a scene or a situation in such a way that it *matters to
us*, and . . . we are *moved*."[191] Emotions may well be biased—indeed, they
inevitably are—but this does not automatically render them debased or
self-centered. An emotion does not have to make one a Mother Teresa
in order to *matter* or to *make a difference*. Kitsch is indeed "deliberately
designed to . . . move us, by presenting a well-selected and perhaps much-
edited version of some particularly and predictably moving aspect of our
shared experience, including . . . innocent scenes of small children and

our favorite pets playing and religious and other sacred icons."[192] Yet at the same time kitsch reveals something vital and basic about human feeling and human character. The "second tear" that falls when one views a picture of innocent "children running on the grass" does not *have* to be fraudulently self-indulgent. "Need it be said," asks Solomon,

> or are we too cynical to say that some things in life are indeed sweet, some things are dear to us, some things are little and blameless and vulnerable, even if such virtues rarely if ever come unalloyed? And if these qualities provide us with an easy sigh or tear, that only shows how central they are to the very foundations of ethics and character. The work that evokes these emotions may not be great or even good art, but the emotions seem to me to be perfectly sound and feeling them is a virtue and not a vice.[193]

The fundamental soundness of feeling and human emotion is, in fact, a principal reason why the rosary continues to attract devotees. The twenty mysteries attached to this devotion not only map Christ's life and its intimate relation to Mary's but also map human emotions ranging from bitter sorrow, desperation, and unutterable loneliness to surprise, relief, and ecstatic joy. Such emotions are, of course, not "once-in-a-lifetime" events; they are recurrent, repeatable, almost routine. The rosary retrieves this range of human (indeed, humanizing) emotions as key to the experience and understanding of God's self-revelation to humankind in flesh and history. (A similar retrieval is evident in Caravaggio's religious art—as it was also in the Christian optimism of Philip Neri and in reinterpretations of the rosary as a medium of sacramental grace among recusant Catholics in Elizabethan England.) Such emotions make those who pray the rosary vulnerable not only to their human companions (through shared "fellow-feeling") but also to a God who acts in the world in ways that are surprising, not to say preposterous. Meditating on the second "joyful" mystery— the pregnant Mary's visit to her pregnant cousin, Elizabeth—twentieth-century Italian novelist Luigi Santucci noted that it was "the first time the word joy is mentioned in the Gospels":

> Who was [the] first human being to meet Jesus and recognize him? A man of thorny destiny, a belated prophet, a character who seems out of place and without an explanation [John the Baptist]. . . .
>
>   But, John, your somber, lonely life had one moment of joy. In the sunlight you never smiled, but once in the dark urn-like womb, where

neither human threats nor the whistling wind could reach, you experienced a joy you couldn't contain; you encountered a friend enclosed in another womb.

. . . "from the moment your greeting sounded in my ears, the baby kicked for joy in my womb" [cf. Luke 1.44].

This is the first time the word joy is mentioned in the Gospels and we owe it to you, doleful prophet. This is where the good news begins, with this invisible smile in the darkness of a womb.[194]

Perhaps this slightly surreal description of an intrauterine encounter between John and Jesus qualifies as kitsch, yet Santucci's words also remind one of another question: Can visual or literary art

evoke *any* ordinary human emotions without being condemned as kitsch? Is there any room left in our jaded and sophisticated lives for the enjoyment of simple innocence and "sweet" affection? The trumped-up charges against kitsch and sentimentality should disturb us and make us suspicious. These attacks on the most common human sentiments—our reactions to the laughter of a child, or to the death of an infant—go far beyond the rejection of the bad art that evokes them. . . . The fact that we are thus "vulnerable" may make for some very bad art but this should not provoke our embarrassment at experiencing these quite "natural" sentiments ourselves, nor should it excuse the enormous amount of sophistry that is devoted to making fun of and undermining the legitimacy of such emotions.[195]

To argue in favor of the legitimacy of sentiment and emotion in Catholic life is not to ignore the fact that devotions have sometimes been used to evoke or reinforce stereotypical gender roles.[196] Commenting on the liturgical changes within Roman Catholicism following the Second Vatican Council, McDannell argues that popular devotions were largely displaced by a piety "focused on the mass, the Bible, and social outreach."[197] Devotions that had often been prayed in church—for example, communal recitation of the rosary prior to (and during) Mass or Benediction—migrated to the home and the private sphere. By the 1980s, however, "a conservative pope and conservative American public demanded a re-evaluation of traditional Catholic activities," the rosary among them.[198] Yet this process of reinterpreting the rosary did not simply result in a restoration of the (recent or distant) past. Instead, to "redeem rosary-saying as a legitimate

Catholic act," it was first "masculinized" using "the same gendered binary logic that had been expressed a generation earlier."[199] Thus, postconciliar reinterpreters of Catholic devotion, like earlier critics of kitsch, often resorted to a "gendered rhetoric" that linked kitsch to femininity (and the past), while it connected modern piety (and the future) to masculine tropes. The mysteries of the rosary were "masculinized" along Christocentric lines, so that the devotion was no longer "a mindless prayer to Mary" but a "meditation on the Son of Man."[200]

Ironically, this attempt to renew devotion to the rosary by "rescuing" it from the "low" world of kitsch coincided with a movement among historians, sociologists, and art critics to rehabilitate kitsch as a legitimate and important aesthetic sensibility.[201] The "implicit aesthetic, moral and political criteria that served to separate high culture from low, art from kitsch, have been effectively dismantled" in many recent sociological and historical studies, notes Sam Binkley.[202] Kitsch is now widely perceived as a sensibility that "employs the thematics of repetition over innovation, a preference for formulae and conventions over originality and experiment, an appeal to sentimental affirmation over existential probing."[203] For the most part, kitsch spurns creativity as it is usually understood, while it "endorses a repetition of the familiar," grounding it in "an affirmation of the everyday," in a sense of "conventionality," in rhythmic aesthetic forms that firmly embed those who use them in "daily life."[204] The institutions of modern life—art and religion among them—are to a high degree "disembedding institutions . . . that uproot individuals" from comfortable routines and familiar surroundings:

> Modern societies, confronting individuals with unprecedented choices in consumer goods, ethical outlooks and life plans, undermine the security of conventional life with the promise of creative freedom—the freedom to choose oneself through one's own taste expressions—with all the risk and danger this freedom invokes.[205]

Kitsch may be understood as a reaction against such disembeddedness, an attempt to "re-embed" people in practices, images, and institutions that offer participants stability, reassurance, and a strong sense of the familiar, the "tried and true." To that end, Binkley argues, kitsch "aestheticizes repetition" in three basic ways: (1) by creating copies of other cultural products (e.g., "the rustic qualities" of a "vanishing folk tradition"); (2) by making the everyday as appealing as possible (e.g., through "home-bound objects of mundane pleasure"); and (3) by privileging the sentimental through "a joy in feeling itself, whether that feeling is elation, sorrow, or fondness."[206]

In sum, kitsch is "a general corrective to a general modern problem"; it responds to feelings of "existential and personal disembeddedness, loss of assurance in the continuity of life and one's place in the world" brought on by "excessive personal freedom, the uncertainty and the risk of modern social life."[207] Nevertheless, kitsch does have a dark side. As its critics point out, kitsch can become a politically convenient tool of repression among people eager to invert what they perceive as a "bourgeois commitment to openness and innovation."[208] Its surface sweetness and sentimentality may mask a reactionary anti-intellectualism that "carries political implications in its desire for destruction and violence" (as it did, for instance, when the Nazis rose to power in Germany during the early 1930s).[209]

In its more benign guises, however, kitsch "tucks us in" and "fabricates a web of familiarity and comfort."[210] These aspects of a rehabilitated kitsch have begun to attract attention among scholars who study Catholic devotional life. In an imaginative essay on "prayers in plaster and plastic," Robert Westerfelhaus analyzes what he calls the ritual "logic of Catholic kitsch."[211] Ritual interprets communication less as the transmission of messages in space than as the preservation of societies in time. Rites are concerned primarily with enacting shared belief, not with imparting information.[212] Moreover, ritual practices are not concerned exclusively with words and texts; their nonverbal languages include gesture and image. When discussing Catholic piety and devotion to Mary, Westerfelhaus notes that

> kitsch renderings of the Virgin impart little information about her or about the religious tradition to which she belongs. Rather than being a weakness, however, . . . this lack of communicative transmission allows kitsch to bind cult adherents to one another precisely because they need not share a common view, and it enable them to fashion a devotion to the image that simultaneously affirms and challenges the beliefs and practices of orthodox Catholicism.[213]

The rosary does not, of course, challenge these beliefs and practices, even if its more extreme promoters have sometimes made claims for it (and for the Virgin Mary) that are not easily reconciled with the mainstream tenets of Catholic belief.[214] Its preferred mode of communication is not, however, the rational speech of theology and dogma—or even the poetic language of liturgy. Rosaries make use of the "ritual logic of kitsch," with its uncanny capacity to bring together the "sublime and the prosaic" in the "pastiche of everyday life."[215] As material objects, they range from cheap versions made of "glow-in-the-dark" plastic to upscale replicas crafted from precious metals and semiprecious stones. Although the vast majority of rosaries are inexpensive and mass-produced, they form "a vital part of the material culture of Christianity without which many generations of believers could not have practiced their beliefs in the characteristic ways they have."[216] They are as vital to the "record of faith" as the dome of the Basilica of Saint Peter in Rome or the jewel-like Sainte Chapelle in Paris. Indeed, devotional objects and images are so central that it is impossible to understand *how* or *what* Catholics believe in their absence. That is surely the reason why so many small churches and "some of the world's great pilgrimage cathedrals have enshrined thousands of votive *retablos* made from cardboard or tin that pilgrims and parishioners bring to thank Mary or Rita, James or Jude, for their assistance."[217] It is the reason too, I suspect, why artists like Caravaggio could combine, in a single canvas—the *Madonna del Rosario*, for example—the regal figure of Mary handing rosaries to saints and sinners with the sentimental, "kitschy" figure of a kneeling toddler with saggy diapers.

There are, then, fundamental aspects of Catholic belief that can be understood only through the discourse of devotion and the aesthetic sensibility of kitsch. This is a point we have seen in Eamon Duffy's account of his aging grandmother's affection for the rosary.[218] Sleepless and alone in the middle of the night, she would preface each bead with the "muttered preamble—'This one is for Tom, for Henry, for Molly, for Lily.'"[219] Duffy's vignette deftly illustrates the point that there are significant aspects of Catholic belief that can only be detected in "habits of devotion," with their kitschy objects and sometimes slightly askew theologies.

As Christ's Mother has managed to become "everybody's contemporary," then, so too "each generation discovers Mary anew."[220] Often this fresh discovery is actually a *rediscovery*—or, rather, the remaking of a traditional image. Melissa Katz offers some excellent illustrations of how this process works itself out in Catholic devotional art connected with the Virgin Mary. Consider, first, Our Lady of Guadalupe, the early modern image of Mary first revealed to the Mexican peasant Juan Diego in 1531. Katz draws attention to two very different versions of the Guadalupe image. The first, a color pencil drawing by contemporary artist J. Michael Walker, is part of a larger "series known as the *Daily Life of the Virgin of Guada-lupe*, which depicts Mary as a rural indigenous woman ironing her cloak before bed, or eating *Maria*-brand cookies [tea biscuits] while reading letters from her son Jesus, who sends money orders from abroad."[221] The image of Guadalupe ironing her star-studded cloak is entitled *Planchando, Pensando* (*Ironing, Thinking*) and includes on the reverse side this text: "As do so many mothers, the Virgin of Guadalupe tends to the household chores."[222] Also visible, on a wall shelf behind the Virgin, who stands while she irons, is a tiny painting of Saint Joseph holding the infant Jesus. Before it glows a luminous glass votive candle holder.[223] At one level, the sentimentality and domestic humor of *Planchando, Pensando* can be seen as kitschy. Yet the image also remind viewers how deeply icons of Mary are embedded not only in the history of Christian art, East and West, but also in the imagination and prayer life of the working poor, the disenfran-chised, the have-nots—the very people for whom, in 1531, Juan Diego's miraculous image of the Virgin of Guadalupe came as such an unexpected and welcome revelation.

A second and very different use of the Guadalupe image appears in the work of artist Danny Lyon (b. 1942), notably his *Conversation with the Dead*, a series of forty-two black-and-white photographs showing prisoners held by the Texas Department of Corrections in 1967–68.[224] One of Lyon's most arresting and provocative images shows a naked prisoner showering, his back (turned at an angle toward the viewer) tattooed with an image of Our Lady of Guadalupe.[225] This photo reveals that "the decorative functions of Christian imagery, always an undercurrent in popular devotion, have become increasingly apparent as mass production has facilitated the merging of religion and retail."[226] While such popular icons may reflect a tendency to "commodify Mary as well as honor her," they also reveal her continued popularity as a "desirable ally to have on one's side."[227] The Texas prisoner's tattoo epitomizes Mary's journey from the "aloof and perfect queen" of medieval iconography to the "all-forgiving mother . . . defender of the vulnerable, refuge of the marginal, and champion of the lowly."[228] Popular icons like this one do not dishonor but rather "demonstrate Mary's adaptability to the needs of those who need her most."[229] Prisoners—whether incarcerated in Texas or homebound, like Duffy's grandmother, by a self-imposed "infirmity"—are surely among Mary's "neediest cases." Danny Lyon's unforgettable portraits of "real, highly specific individuals within an anonymous prison world" powerfully testify "to the revitalizing effect of basic human concern and the destruction wrought by bureaucracy, ignorance and neglect"; one comes away from them understanding all too well "the unbridgeable abyss between censorship and understanding, between condemnation and compassion."[230]

These reinvented images of Our Lady of Guadalupe illustrate a theme that has persisted throughout out study of the rosary and Marian devotion within early modern Catholicism. Although the works of Walker and Lyon embody multiple messages—artistic, political, decorative, consumerist—their primary purpose seems to be *meditative*. Lyon's prison photos contemplate "the disenfranchised, the poor, the migrants, the homeless, the insane, Chicanos, prisoners, bikers," even as they document the vast dystopia occupied by American institutions of power, where "punishment becomes the ultimate weapon of control," a pervasive "absence" structuring the lives of society's most vulnerable members.[231] These are themes that, mutatis mutandis, also surfaced in our earlier discussions of Caravaggio's art, of Philip Neri's innovative Christian humanism, and of sixteenth- and seventeenth-century rosary confraternities established to provide practical relief to society's desperate and destitute. The rosary, as it was remade in the lives of early modern Catholics, established a radical "democracy" of prayer and mediation based on *need*. It thus appealed across gender and generational boundaries, cultures and social classes, to *all* who were needy—that is, to *everyone*: to the rich and powerful (who need humility, generosity, and compassion); to the troubled (who need comfort and serenity); to the poor (who need food, money, work, and shelter); to the devout (who need to be shaken from composure and self-complacency); to the sinful (who need pardon and forgiveness); to the indifferent (who need passion and a great cause for which to live and die); to the diffident (who need faith and courage); to the sick (who need medicine, health, faithful caregivers, and patient companions).

Thus, no matter how one analyzes its origins, evolution, and contemporary use, the rosary remains a devotion whose center is Mary, the Mother of Jesus, but whose clientele is potentially universal. As a religious icon, Mary is particularly open to what Robert Westerfelhaus calls "kitsch adaptability and multivocality."[232] The widespread variation in "visually rendering the Virgin's image," writes Westerfelhaus,

is accompanied by variations in beliefs and practices associated with devotion to her. In this way, Catholic kitsch differs from most communication defined as ritual. While dissemination of kitsch art serves to perpetuate the image that is the focus of cultic devotion, and is thus instrumental

in maintaining the most important feature of the cult, kitsch does not pro-
mote a shared view of the world but rather allows for multiple views—some
complementary, some conflicting—to exist side by side.[233]

This latter point is especially relevant to the rosary. Of all Western
Catholic devotions it is arguably the most widely diffused and the most
successfully inculturated.[234] Just as the image of Our Lady of Guadalupe
has been adapted to venues as diverse as prisons and upscale art galler-
ies—and to countries as "culturally and geographically removed from
one another as Ethiopia, France, Italy, Japan, Kenya, Poland, Spain, Swe-
den, and the United States"—so the rosary has become a Christian ritual
"code" creating connections (a "democracy of meditation") and attracting
adherents in ways that seem to "transcend time, place, cultures, and even
differences of belief."[235] The rosary's ability to adapt itself to the changing
cultural conditions of diverse times, places, and peoples accounts for its
persistence and continued relevance as a devotional practice.

Consider, for example, the fifth "glorious mystery" of the rosary, Mary's
"coronation" as "Queen of Heaven." This is an "event" for which there
is no explicit biblical evidence, though Catholics have often interpreted
the mysterious figure in Revelation 12.1 (a woman having "on her head
a crown of twelve stars") as an image of Mary, whose offspring, Christ,
tramples the "huge red dragon" (Revelation 12.3), enemy of humankind.[236]
Medieval interpreters routinely assimilated such images to their own sociopolitical experience of queens and kings, courts and courtiers. But one
might also read them in relation to the most memorable "crowned" figure
in the Gospels—Jesus, who wears a circlet of thorns as he trudges toward
Golgotha and certain death. Just as the biblical scenes of Jesus' "triumphal
entry" into Jerusalem during the final week of his life should probably be
read as *parodies* of royalist pretensions and pomposity, so crowns may be
read as *reversals* of the reader's expectations.[237]

To meditate on the mystery of Mary's "coronation" is, then, to remember that she is the same young woman who in Luke's gospel identifies
herself not as royalty but as a negligible "slave-girl" (Luke 1.48).[238] Nevertheless, this lowly "nobody" (unwed and pregnant) becomes the living embodiment of God's mercy to Israel and, indeed, to "*all* who fear
God" (Luke 1.46–55). Preposterously, she claims to make a crucial difference to history, to humanity, and to the very fate of the universe: "From
now on will all ages call me blessed" (Luke 1.48). Imagining this slave
girl crowned "Queen of Heaven" is like imagining Jesus—crowned with

thorns and co-crucified with criminals on the crossbeam of state-sponsored capital punishment—as the ultimate revelation of God's power, wisdom, and divinity.[239] Both images are subversive, transgressive. They invite us to think the unthinkable, to imagine a God who "saves" by refusing to act like God.[240] The mystery's very open-endedness is, perhaps, what makes Mary's crowning as "Queen of Heaven" so appealing and so radically inclusive.

Mary "crowned Queen of Heaven" thus embodies the sheer improbability and subversive comedy of God's choices about *when* (always), *how* (through self-effacement), and *whom* (everyone) to save. By inviting regular reflection on this mystery—and others like it—the rosary brings those who pray to the brink of chaos, because it confronts them with the need to revise radically, every day and with every decade, their preconceptions about how God is named and known in the human world. By reading divine action through the lens of Mary's womanhood and by "imagining Mary's history with the emotional discernment born of their own experience," those who pray the rosary come to recognize how anxiety, loss, grief, joy, hope, and promise belong not only to this world but to the *God* of this world.[241] Through meditation on *her* mysteries—and *theirs*—Mary "and her devout become recognizable to each other"; the rosary became, in effect, the early modern and postmodern equivalent of the medieval book of hours.[242]

If this "book of the rosary" were to be illuminated, as its medieval predecessors were, it would surely include modern icons like J. Michael Walker's *Planchando, Pensando* and Danny Lyon's anonymous prisoner with Our Lady of Guadalupe inscribed on his back. It would need to represent human experience ranging from the kitschy sentimentality of a woman wearing a crown while doing menial household chores to the emotional terror of imprisonment. And it would have to include unexpected pleasure along with harrowing despair. For the former, there is Walker's statement of his own origins as an artist:

> Some thirty-four year ago, an unlikely convergence of good fortune and divine providence dropped me out of the Oklahoma skies and into a remote village in the Sierra Tarahumara of northern México, where I was spiritually and culturally transformed by the light, the landscape, the languages and life, and by the lovely young woman who became my wife, Mimi.

In a very real sense all the artwork I've created since then is a falling-short expression of gratitude for that blessed bump on the head, and an attempt to come to grips with the spiritual essence of our existence.[243]

For the latter, there is James Oles's description of Lyon's tattooed prisoner in the shower:

The men bathe at a processing center for inmates at the beginning of their incarceration; occupying a tight, windowless space, stripped of freedom and clothing, the new prisoners seem trapped, even humiliated. Yet the Virgin of Guadalupe on one young inmate's back, a tattoo frequently seen in Mexican-American and Chicano communities, remains an indelible marker of individuality, and cultural and religious affiliation. . . . [T]he Virgin stabilizes the image, meliorating our rejection of the man as criminal.[244]

As material object and contemplative devotion, the rosary has thus become for many Catholics not only a modern "book of hours" but a sort of panopticon ranging over the whole spectrum of human experience, focused on the life of one woman (Mary), yet lived in myriad existences—"for Christ," wrote Gerard Manley Hopkins, "plays in ten thousand places, / Lovely in limbs, and lovely in eyes not his / To the Father through the features of men's faces."[245]

Conclusion

We fly to your patronage,
O holy Mother of God;
do not despise our petitions in our difficulties,
but deliver us from all dangers, always,
O glorious and blessed Virgin. Amen.

This short petition—dating back to perhaps the third century—is one of the most ancient prayers to the Virgin Mary that we possess.[1] Found in many languages—Greek, Latin, Coptic, Old Slavonic—it came be used in both Eastern and Western Christian liturgies.[2] It is not a prayer that recounts the past but one that seeks immediate assistance in the present and looks forward to delivery "from all dangers, *always*." The compact but intense language of this prayer (usually cited by its Latin title, *Sub tuum praesidium*, literally "under your protection") recalls a comment Eithne Wilkins makes toward the end of her study of "prayer beads and flowers," *The Rose-Garden Game*: the rosary

> is not a mnemonic device in the commonplace sense . . . like the tricks
> we resort to in order to remember people's names and addresses. It is an
> aid to memory in the same way as is the framed photograph of someone
> whose existence, living or dead, we shall not forget, but whose presence
> we wish often to conjure up; or as the image of a saint is, embodying the
> spiritual potency continually invoked into it. The rosary is a memorial
> that can be activated, just as the knot we make in our handkerchief to
> remind ourselves of something [that] must afterwards be activated. . . .
> The thing to be remembered must have been invoked, as it were knotted
> into the material.[3]

As we have seen, the rosary is not only linked—as physical object and contemplative prayer—to Catholic memory; it is also a potent medium of presence. Those who make use of this devotion are not simply trying to recall a past but are celebrating the arrival, the coming-into-presence, of persons and realities (Christ, the Virgin Mary, the major mysteries of salvation) decisive for human life and its future. Our focus has been on the many ways Marian piety, the rosary, and early modern Catholicism itself were reframed—reinterpreted, reinvented—starting in the late sixteenth century, after the Council of Trent. We may speak of *reframing* because history shows that devout attention to Christ's Mother is neither medieval nor modern but is arguably as old as Christianity itself (see, e.g., Acts 1.13–14; John 25–27). It is true, of course, that the Marian rosary, as we have come to know it in the Latin West, originated only during the later Middle Ages (fourteenth through fifteenth centuries). Yet thereafter it became a popular and virtually ubiquitous feature of Catholic prayer and practice and, as we have seen, continues to have a significant place in many people's lives.

As our study draws to a close, it is possible to draw a number of conclusions based on our investigation of historical, devotional, and theological sources. The first of these concerns the rosary's adaptability. Although the structure and basic content of the devotion (repetitions of the Our Father and Hail Mary, meditation on the central mysteries of Christ's and Mary's lives) became well established in the fifteenth century, it still offered devotees considerable freedom and flexibility. The rosary could be prayed individually or in common, in Latin or the vernacular, as private petition or public liturgy. Its counters could be made of precious stones and metals, wood and seed kernels, of knots on a string—or simply of the fingers on one's hands. In times of persecution, it could become a medium of quasi-sacramental presence, as happened among England Catholic recusants after the Elizabethan Settlement deprived them of regular contact with Mass and communion.

Second, the popularity of Ignatius Loyola's *Spiritual Exercises* introduced innovative techniques into the practice of meditating the rosary's mysteries—examples of which we saw in the work of Jesuit writers like Henry Garnett and Louis Richeome. Ignatius had counseled a robust use of the Christian's spiritual senses and a vivid use of imagination when "setting the scene" (*compositio loci*) of biblical events or episodes in the lives of Christ, Mary, and the saints. The possibility of meditating in this way was further enhanced by the expanding interiority and self-awareness of early modern persons, as we noted when examining Mary of Ágreda's novelistic interpretation of Christian narratives in *The Mystical City of God*.

Another source for the early modern reinterpretation of the rosary and Marian piety was political and military. The success of Christian coalition forces at the Battle of Lepanto in 1571—attributed by Pope Pius V to the prayers of the rosary confraternity in Rome—helped reinvigorate the notion (already present in medieval thought) that Mary's militant advocacy would guarantee Catholicism's ultimate triumph over "the infidels" (more specifically, over Islam and the Ottoman Empire). Not only was Lepanto memorialized in dozens of popular early baroque paintings throughout Europe; it also led to the creation of a new liturgical feast, that of the Holy Rosary, which came to be celebrated (and is still observed) by Roman Catholics worldwide. The view that Mary's help could and should be enlisted against the forces of "godlessness" persisted into the twentieth century. Until the changes brought about by the Second Vatican Council (1962–65), "prayers for the conversion of Russia" were regularly recited after Low Mass in Catholic parishes, in response to the 1917 appearances at Fatima, Portugal, where Mary identified herself as "Our Lady of the Rosary."[4]

Our discussion of Mary of Ágreda's work illustrated still another influence that helped reshape the rosary among early modern Catholics— the development of doctrines, specifically those of the Virgin Mary's Assumption and what came to be known as her "Immaculate Conception." Both these doctrines, we have seen, were represented by liturgical feasts in the post-Tridentine *Missale Romanum* of 1570, but neither of them was explicitly defined as Catholic dogma until the nineteenth and twentieth centuries (the Immaculate Conception in 1854; the Assumption of Mary in 1954). Almost certainly the mysteries of the rosary contributed to that doctrinal evolution. The fact that Mary's privileged role in the history of salvation (Annunciation) and her unique destiny after death (assumption into heaven) were among the joyful and glorious mysteries of the rosary— hence an object of frequent, vivid meditation—illustrates the often reciprocal relation between Catholic doctrine and devotion. This is not to say that beliefs about Mary originated in the rosary; rather, that the rosary— by encouraging and embellishing mediation upon her intimate involvement in Christ's birth, death, cross, and resurrection—led Roman Catholics to embrace dogmas that, in the Christian East, for example, have remained objects of liturgical celebration but not of doctrinal definition.

Perhaps, however, the most decisive factor in the reframing of the rosary during the period we have been examining lies in the field of visual culture (including print culture). The tradition of *Rosenkranzbilder* began (as did rosary picture books) not long after the devotion itself developed. Yet we saw in our discussions of Caravaggio's art that important reinterpretations of Mary's place in salvation history and in the daily lives of Christians had begun to emerge in the late sixteenth and early seventeenth centuries. Caravaggio sought to shrink the distance between viewers and the religious subjects he painted. By so doing, he made Mary "everyone's contemporary." Without denying her role as holy Mother of God, Caravaggio managed to make her an appealing woman whom one might well have seen and spoken to in the doorway of an ordinary Roman house. She was not an inaccessible queen crowned with roses and attended by adoring angels but a mother who reached out to prince and pauper, saint and sinner, without rejecting any. In place of artificiality (where holy figures merely "pretend" to be human), Caravaggio proposed a naturalism similar to what Cardinal Gabriele Paleotti had outlined in his *Discorso* on sacred images. Creation itself, in its rich diversity of forms, its splendor and pathos, was the supreme map for Christians hoping to make "the mind's journey into God." Holiness and homeliness, the divine and the daily, God and world, were not competitors but allies.

Thus, while it is sometimes thought that the Counter-Reformation instincts of early modern Catholicism drove a wedge between faith and "action in the world," between private devotion and public liturgy, between secular optimism and religious pessimism ("we have here no lasting city"; Hebrews 13.14), our study suggests otherwise. Devotions like the rosary, for example, did not produce generations of "inward-looking" Catholics who feared or hated the world. We saw, moreover, that the rosary could become not only a medium of presence but a tool of political resistance (for Catholics forced to attend state-sanctioned liturgies in Elizabeth England) and even outright defiance (John Ogilvie, flinging his rosary to the crowd at his execution in 1615). Even in a more peaceful period, Bishop Challoner's popular *Garden of the Soul*, which shaped Catholic spirituality for centuries in both England and the (English-speaking) United States, urged the faithful not to retreat from the world but to prove themselves capable, reasonable, responsible, and prayerful citizens in a religiously plural culture.

In sum, our study reveals that early modern Catholicism was not simply an intransigent, monolithic, authoritarian, "one-size-fits-all" institution whose principal concern was to combat error and defeat enemies. It was often, on the contrary, energetic, innovative, and more open to reform than may at first meet the eye. Devotions like the rosary—portable, exportable, flexible, its mysteries open to multiple interpretations—were quite congenial to believers whose expanding selves were busy exploring an expanding (inner and outer) world. If Mary could become "everyone's contemporary," then Christians themselves might well expect to become "neighbors" to all the world. This early modern conviction—embedded in Philip Neri's "Christian optimism" and reiterated in Richard Challoner's vision of the Christian as a focus of love, service, and unity in the world— reached mature expression in the Second Vatican Council's document "The Church in the Modern World" (n. 43), with which we may conclude:

> They are mistaken who, knowing that we have here no abiding city but seek one which is to come, think that they may therefore shirk their earthly responsibilities. For they are forgetting that by the faith itself they are more obliged than ever to measure up to these duties. . . .
>
> Nor are they any less wide of the mark who think that religion consists in acts of worship alone and in the discharge of certain moral obligations, and who imagine they can plunge themselves into earthly affairs in such a way as to imply that these are altogether divorced from the religious life.
>
> This split between the faith which many profess and their daily lives deserves to be counted among the more serious errors of our age. Long since, the Prophets of the Old Testament fought vehemently against this scandal and even more so did Jesus Christ Himself in the New Testament. . . .
>
> Therefore, let there be no false opposition between professional and social activities on the one part, and religious life on the other. Christians who neglect their temporal duties, jeopardize their eternal salvation.

Far from recommending a retreat from the world, the rosary urged Christians to meditate on precisely those mysteries that make this world a wedding, a new creation where "every tear will be wiped away" (Revelation 21.4), a holy banquet where God and all humanity may meet, feast, and live together in peace.

Notes

NOTES TO INTRODUCTION

1. See Garry Wills, *The Rosary* (New York: Viking, 2005).

2. Jean Delumeau, *Catholicism between Luther and Voltaire: A New View of the Counter-Reformation*, trans. Jeremy Moiser (Philadelphia: Westminster Press, 1977), 30.

3. Cited in ibid.

NOTES TO CHAPTER 1

1. William Forbes-Leith, *Narratives of Scottish Catholics under Mary Stuart and James VI* (Edinburgh: W. Paterson, 1885), 313.

2. See Anne Winston-Allen, *Stories of the Rose: The Making of the Rosary in the Middle Ages* (University Park: Pennsylvania State University Press, 1997), 13–30; 130 (on "Luther's reaction to the mentality of the marketing of the rosary").

3. See John D. Miller, *Beads and Prayers: The Rosary in History and Devotion* (London: Burns and Oates, 2001), 76–86.

4. The mysteries of the rosary came to include five each of the principal "joyful, sorrowful, and glorious" episodes in the lives of Christ and Mary, based mainly in New Testament narratives. They include (1) Gabriel's annunciation to Mary that she would be Jesus' mother; Mary's visit to her cousin Elizabeth; the birth of Jesus; the presentation of the child Jesus in the Jerusalem Temple; and the finding of Jesus in the Temple by Mary and Joseph ("joyful" mysteries); (2) Christ's agony in Gethsemane; his scourging; his crowning with thorns; his carrying of the cross; his crucifixion ("sorrowful" mysteries); and (3) Christ's resurrection; his ascension; the sending of the Holy Spirit on the disciples; Mary's assumption into heaven; Mary's coronation as Queen of Heaven ("glorious" mysteries). To these, Pope John Paul II (d. 2005) added five "luminous" mysteries: Jesus' baptism in the Jordan; the wedding feast at Cana; Jesus' preaching of God's kingdom; Jesus' Transfiguration; the Last Supper (Jesus establishes the Eucharist).

5. See Winston-Allen, *Stories of the Rose*, 111–32. See also the review by Mary S. Skinner, *Speculum* 74:3 (July 1999), 857–59; here, 858.

6. Winston-Allen, *Stories of the Rose*, 126–27.

7. Ibid., 122.

8. Ibid

9. The phrase "Counter-Reformation" suggests a defensive-aggressive reaction against Protestantism and fails to consider the broader, proactive, innovative characteristics of Catholicism in the early modern period. See Michael Mullett, *The Catholic Reformation* (New York: Routledge, 1991), 1. Mullett prefers to speak of the "Catholic Reformation" (ibid., ix). Other scholars prefer the phrase "Catholic revival." See R. Po-chia Hsia, *The World of Catholic Renewal 1540–1770*, 2nd ed., New Approaches to European History, 24 (New York: Cambridge University Press, 2005).

10. See John W. O'Malley, "A Historiographical Frame for the Painting: Recent Interpretations of Early Modern Catholicism," in Franco Mormando, ed., *Saints and Sinners: Caravaggio and the Baroque Image* (Boston: McMullen Museum of Art, Boston College; distributed by University of Chicago Press, 1999), 19–27. O'Malley speaks of "Early Modern" (not "Counter-Reformation") Catholicism because it "is a designation that opens the door to influences other than the Reformation" on the changes Catholicism experienced, especially in the sixteenth and seventeenth centuries (ibid., 24).

11. See John W. O'Malley, *Trent and All That: Renaming Catholicism in the Early Modern Era* (Cambridge: Harvard University Press, 2000), especially 16–71. Jedin's distinction was proposed in his monograph *Katholische Reformation oder Gegensreformation? Ein Versuch zur Klärung der Begriffe nebst einer Jubiläumsbetrachtung über das Trienter Konzil* (Lucerne: Josef Stocker, 1946), 7–8.

12. See Jan Ziolkowski, ed., *Miracles of the Virgin Mary in Verse* (*Miracula sancta dei genitricis Virginis Marie, versifice*), Toronto Medieval Latin Texts 17 (Toronto: Center for Medieval Studies, 1986).

13. See Eamon Duffy, *Marking the Hours: English People and Their Prayers, 1240–1570* (New Haven: Yale University Press, 2006).

14. Hilmar M. Pable, *Conversing with God: Prayer in Erasmus' Pastoral Writings* (Toronto: University of Toronto Press, 1997), 86.

15. See Luther's *Personal Prayer Book* in Gustav K. Wiencke, ed., *Luther's Works*, vol. 28, *Devotional Writings*, II, trans. Martin H. Bertram (Philadelphia: Fortress Press, 1968), 39.

16. Hsia, *World of Catholic Renewal*, 225.

17. Ibid.

18. Ibid. *Devotio moderna* (modern devotion) is the term commonly used for a religious movement that flourished from the late fourteenth to early sixteenth centuries. It focused on the Christian's personal "interior life," placing less emphasis on ritual observances and theological study and blending Christian humanism with a fervent focus on the person of Christ (especially in his suffering). A well-known example of *devotio moderna* is the *Imitation of Christ*, attributed to Thomas à Kempis (1380–1471). The "Oratory of Divine Love" was the source of a new religious community known as the "Theatines," founded in 1524 by Saint

Cajetan (d. 1547) and Gian Pietro Carafa (d. 1559), who became bishop of Chieti ("Theate," hence the order's name) and was later elected Pope Paul IV (1555).

19. See Mullett, *Catholic Reformation*, 1–28. As David M. Luebke writes, use of the Latin word *reformatio* predated Luther and meant many different things to people of his time, "including a restoration of things to their original true form and essence." See "Introduction," in David M. Luebke, ed., *The Counter-Reformation: The Essential Readings* (Oxford: Blackwell, 1999), 5. Significant reform efforts had already emerged within *fifteenth-century* European Catholicism (ibid., 10).

20. The phases were Period 1 (1545–49); Period 2 (1551–52); Period 3 (1562–63). Meetings were held in several Italian cities, not only in Trent. This periodization is accepted in Henricus Denzinger and Adolfus Schönmetzer, eds., *Enchiridion Symbolorum, Definitionum, et Declarationum*, Editio XXXIII, emendata et aucta (Rome: Herder, 1965), 363–64. Hereafter this work is cited as DS, followed by the appropriate paragraph or page number.

21. The term "Protestant" did not at first signify reformers like Luther and his followers but the Holy Roman princes and other imperial authorities who in 1529 "objected to what they perceived as abrogations of their sovereign right to reform religion within their respective territories." Luebke, "Introduction," 5.

22. Mullett, *Catholic Reformation*, 54. On the ambiguous reputation of Marcello Cervini, see William V. Hudon, "Religion and Society in Early Modern Italy: Old Questions, New Insights," *American Historical Review* 101:3 (June 1996): 783–804, especially 795–96.

23. Mullett, *Catholic Reformation*, 54. Throughout much of the sixteenth century, reform of the church was closely linked to reform and restoration of the papacy. See Mullett, *Catholic Reformation*, 11.

24. See Helen Langdon, *Caravaggio: A Life* (New York: Knopf, 1998), 10.

25. See Louis Chatellier, *The Religion of the Poor: Rural Missions in Europe and the Formation of Modern Catholicism, c. 1500–c. 1800*, trans. Brian Pearce (New York: Cambridge University Press, 1997), 12.

26. Ibid.

27. The Oratorians are a men's religious community that began with the Italian "Oratory of Saint Philip Neri," ca. 1575. Further details follow in this paragraph.

28. See Hsia, *World of Catholic Renewal*, 7, 13. Not all ecclesiastics favored autocratic papalism or unlimited authority for the priesthood. A case in point is Gabriele Paleotti, a member of the "Oratorian orbit" and later archbishop of Bologna, whose views will be discussed later in this chapter.

29. Chatellier, *Religion of the Poor*, 12.

30. Hsia, *World of Catholic Renewal*, 224–25.

31. See Delumeau, *Catholicism between Luther and Voltaire*, 61–88. Delumeau also notes (90–91) that respect for the local, indigenous cultures of these peoples was a key aspect of the *successful* Christian missions in those lands.

32. See Chatellier, *Religion of the Poor*, 37–59. See also Hsia, *World of Catholic Renewal*, 6–7.

33. The Capuchins were founded by Matteo di Bassi of Urbino (d. 1552). Their Rule, drawn up in 1529, emphasized simplicity, poverty, personal asceticism, austerity, and contemplative prayer.

34. Chatellier, *Religion of the Poor*, 8.

35. Ibid.

36. Ibid., 10.

37. Ibid.

38. See ibid., 10–11.

39. Hsia, *World of Catholic Renewal*, 7; emphasis added.

40. John Bossy, "The Counter-Reformation and the People of Catholic Europe," *Past and Present*, no. 47 (May 1970): 51–70.

41. Ibid., 52.

42. Ibid., 54.

43. Ibid. Bossy discusses this point in his essay "The Social History of Confession in the Age of the Reformation," *Transactions of the Royal Historical Society*, 5th ser., 25 (1975): 21–38.

44. Bossy, "Social History of Confession," 21.

45. Bossy, "Counter-Reformation and the People of Catholic Europe," 56.

46. This shift contributed toward "laying the foundations of the modern state," as noted by Bossy, "Counter-Reformation and the People of Catholic Europe," 770.

47. Luebke, "Introduction," 9.

48. Pope Pius V's bull *Quo primum* imposed such uniformity in the reformed *Missale Romanum* of 1570. See Manlio Sodi and Achille Maria Triacca, eds., *Missale Romanum editio princeps* (1570), Monumenta Liturgica Concilii Tridentini (Vatican City: Libreria Editrice Vaticana, 1998), 3–4. See also my discussion of *Quo primum* and its consequences in "Reforms, Protestant and Catholic," in Geoffrey Wainwright and Karen B. Westerfield Tucker, eds., *The Oxford History of Christian Worship* (New York: Oxford University Press, 1998), 307–50.

49. See H. Outram Evennett, "Counter-Reformation Spirituality," in Luebke, ed., *The Counter-Reformation: The Essential Readings*, 48–63; here, 49.

50. Ibid., 48.

51. Ibid.

52. Ibid., 49–50. The Council of Constance was convened chiefly to end the late medieval "Great Schism," during which three different prelates (Gregory XIII, Benedict XIII, and John XXIII [not the twentieth-century pope of the same name and number]) all claimed to be the legitimate pope. The solution was to remove all three claimants and elect a new pope (Martin V) upon whom all agreed.

53. Another example of such ambivalence emerged in the career of Gasparo Contarini, a theologian who sought compromise with Lutherans on some issues (e.g., justification) but opposed them on others (e.g., penance and eucharistic doctrine). See William V. Hudon's review of Elisabeth G. Gleason's *Gasparo Contarini: Venice, Rome and Reform*, in *Renaissance Quarterly* 48:3 (Autumn 1995); 623–24; here, 624.

54. See Hudon, "Religion and Society in Early Modern Italy," 795.

55. Anna Beth Rousakis, "From Image of Devotion to Devotional Image: The Changing Role of Art in the Chapel of the *Arciconfraternità della Madonna della Consolazione, detta della Cintura,*" in Christopher Black and Pamela Gravestock, eds., *Early Modern Confraternities in Europe and the Americas: International and Interdisciplinary Perspectives* (Burlington, VT: Ashgate, 2006), 112–28; here, 115.

56. Evennett, "Counter-Reformation Spirituality," 55.

57. See Stephen Greenblatt, *Renaissance Self-Fashioning from More to Shakespeare* (Chicago: University of Chicago Press, 1980), especially 1–9. We will return to the theme of self-fashioning in chapter 4.

58. Evennett, "Counter-Reformation Spirituality," 55.

59. See Greenblatt, *Renaissance Self-Fashioning*, 165–69. "In [Elizabeth's] official spectacles and pageants, everything was calculated to enhance her transformation into an almost magical being, a creature of infinite beauty, wisdom, and power. . . . [E]ven her ordinary public appearances were theatrically impressive." Ibid., 167.

60. Ibid., 9.

61. Ibid.

62. Ibid.

63. Evennett, "Counter-Reformation Spirituality," 61–62.

64. Delumeau, *Catholicism between Luther and Voltaire*, 57, notes that in "the period of Tridentine Catholicism, holiness took steps to alleviate physical misery perhaps more than at any time before."

65. Evennett, "Counter-Reformation Spirituality," 61. See also Delumeau's comments about Jansenist "sacramental rigorism" in *Catholicism between Luther and Voltaire*, 107–8. As Delumeau observes, the term "Jansenism" is notoriously difficult to define with any exactitude; see ibid., 100–128.

66. Evennett, "Counter-Reformation Spirituality," 61.

67. See ibid., 57–60. I discuss the history of eucharistic devotions within Catholicism after Trent in my study *Cult and Controversy: The Worship of the Eucharist Outside Mass* (Collegeville, MN: Liturgical Press, 1982), 164–72, 311–18.

68. See Evennett, "Counter-Reformation Spirituality," 62–63.

69. Herbert Thurston, "Our Popular Devotions. II–The Rosary. V. The Fifteen Mysteries," *The Month* 96 (1900): 620–37; here, 637.

70. Ibid.

71. Ibid.

72. Ibid., 636–37. The doxology is a text ascribing praise and glory to God that is customarily added to the conclusion of a liturgical prayer. Thurston argued that there is little reliable evidence for adding the Gloria Patri to each decade of the rosary prior to the seventeenth century. Evidence for use of the Salve Regina at the conclusion of the rosary's recitation can already be found in the fifteenth century.

73. Evennett, "Counter-Reformation Spirituality," 63.

74. For an English translation of Trent's decree, see Elizabeth Gilmore Holt, ed., *A Documentary History of Art*, 2 vols. (Princeton: Princeton University Press, 1982), 2:62–65.

75. John W. O'Malley, "The Discovery of America and Reform Thought at the Papal Court in the Early Cinquecento," in O'Malley, *Rome and the Renaissance: Studies in Culture and Religion* (London: Variorum Reprints, 1981), 185–200, especially 189.

76. Ibid., 190.

77. Ibid.

78. Paradoxically, as O'Malley notes, Roman pleas for peace and harmony in the universe during the early sixteenth century were often coupled with calls for war against the Turks. By promoting war against the Ottoman Empire, church authorities could divert arms from infighting among Christian princes to a "common enemy," a religious and ethnic outsider, a threatening "other." See ibid.

79. Patrick Hunt, *Caravaggio* (London: Haus, 2004), 156–57.

80. O'Malley, "The Discovery of America and Reform Thought," 194. This notion also led to the conviction that the newly discovered peoples of Asia and America must be evangelized, and that the methods used by missionaries had to correspond to the "destiny and consequent dignity" of those peoples. See ibid., 194–95; cf. 187.

81. Richard P. McBrien, *Lives of the Popes: The Pontiffs from St. Peter to John Paul II* (San Francisco: HarperCollins, 1997), 290.

82. Ibid. McBrien points out that Pius V had originally declared October 7 to be the "feast of Our Lady of Victory"; it was changed by Pius's successor, Gregory XIII (d. 1585), to the "feast of the Most Holy Rosary."

83. For a discussion of the origins and early evolution of the rosary confraternities, see Winston-Allen, *Stories of the Rose*, 24–25, 28–29, 116–22, 127–28.

84. Christopher F. Black, *Italian Confraternities in the Sixteenth Century* (New York: Cambridge University Press, 1989), 103.

85. Ibid.

86. Ibid., 104. Besides the paintings about to be discussed, I will consider other post-Lepanto rosary art in chapter 2.

87. Ibid. Cesari later became the Cavalier d'Arpino and is sometimes referred to under that title.

88. Howard Hibbard, *Caravaggio* (New York: Harper and Row Icon Editions, 1983; reprinted with corrections, 1985), 361. The example Bellori gives probably refers to Caravaggio's *Vase of Flowers*, now lost. See ibid, 10.

89. Ibid., 361.

90. Readers may access an image of Cesari's painting online at http://www.homolaicus.com/arte/cesena/storia.

91. The "Dominican" origin of the rosary was largely disproved more than a century ago by the German Dominican scholar Thomas Esser and by the English Jesuit historian Herbert Thurston. See Thurston's article "Our Popular Devotions, II: The Rosary," *The Month* 96 (1900), 403–18. See also Winston-Allen, *Stories of the Rose*, 13–30. The "Dominic" who in fact is linked to the "life-of-Christ rosary" is the Carthusian Dominic of Prussia (1384–1460), a monk at the Charterhouse in Trier. See Winston-Allen, *Stories of the Rose*, 16–17, 22–26.

92. Hibbard, *Caravaggio*, 317 n. 118 (which begins on p. 316).

93. Ibid. See also Herwarth Röttgen, *Il Cavalier Giuseppe Cesari D'Arpino: Un grande pittore nello splendore della fama e nell'incostanze della fortuna* (Rome: Ugo Bozzi Editore, 2002), 255–56.

94. Hibbard, *Caravaggio*, 317 n. 118.

95. Readers may access an image of Dürer's painting online at http://www.wga.hu. This painting suffered extensive damage and underwent several restorations between 1663 and 1839–41. On the painting's condition—and on what survives of Dürer's original work—see Erwin Panofsky, *The Life and Art of Albrecht Dürer*, with a new introduction by Jeffrey Chipps Smith (Princeton: Princeton University Press, 2005), 109–10.

96. See the note accompanying the painting as reproduced in the Web Gallery of Art at http://www.wga.hu. See also Holt, *Documentary History of Art*, 1:306: "While the graphic media were most congenial to him and his productivity was greatest in these media, Dürer was also a great painter; and the German Renaissance found its first clear expression in his portraits and altarpieces."

97. See the citation in notes that accompany the image of Dürer's *Feast of the Rose Garlands,* at http://www.wgu.hu.

98. On the origins of this genre, see Panofsky, *Life and Art of Albrecht Dürer*, 110–12; see also the image reproduced as figure 157 in "The Illustrations" section (pages unnumbered).

99. Winston-Allen, *Stories of the Rose*, 13–14, 24.

100. Ibid., 24.

101. Ibid. A central figure in the origins of the rosary confraternities was Jakob Sprenger, who launched such a brotherhood in Cologne on September 8, 1475. Sprenger is often identified as the author of *Malleus Maleficarum*, a late medieval treatise that linked witchcraft with female sexuality and was used to defend the practice of witch hunts. See Panofsky, *Life and Art of Albrecht Dürer*, 111.

102. Panofsky, *Life and Art of Albrecht Dürer*, 111.

103. Ibid.

104. Readers may access images of the van Eyck Arnolfini portrait at http:// www.wga.hu. To the left of the painting's famous mirror, we see two sets of beads with tassels. These beads are probably not Marian rosaries but "pater- nosters," medieval prayer beads used to count repetitions of the Lord's Prayer (Paternoster).

105. See Winston-Allen, *Stories of the Rose*, 25, 31–64.

106. Panofsky, *Life and Art of Albrecht Dürer*, 111–12.

107. Readers may access an image of this painting at http://www.sankt-an- dreas.de/kirche/rosenkranzbild.

108. Readers may access an image of this painting at http://www.wga.hu.

109. Cited from the note that accompanies the image of Tiepolo's *The Institu- tion of the Rosary* at the Web site mentioned in note 108, above.

110. See Jean-Luc Marion, "The Blind Man of Siloe," translated by Janine Lan- gan in *Image: A Journal of Religion and the Arts*, no. 29 (Winter 2000–2001): 59–69.

111. Ibid., 65.

112. Ibid., 66.

113. Ibid.

114. Ibid., 68.

115. Langdon, *Caravaggio*, 224–26, 239.

116. An English translation of this decree is available in Holt, *A Documentary History of Art*, 2:62–65.

117. See Holt's prefatory comments, ibid., 2:63.

118. Gabriele Paleotti, *Discorso intorno alle immagini sacre e profane* (1582), ed. Stefano Della Torre, Gian Franco Freguglia, and Carlo Chenis, Monumenta Studia Instrumenta Liturgica (Vatican City: Libreria Editrice Vaticana, 2002).

119. André Wilmart, *Auteurs spirituels et texts dévots du moyen âge latin* (1932; reprint, Paris: Études Augustiniennes, 1971). Wilmart rejected the popu- lar notion that early Christian prayer had been largely liturgical in character and that devotionalism ("private prayers and meditations") emerged only after lay Christians became alienated from the church's official public worship. See Wilmart, *Auteurs spirituels*, 9–10, 13–16. On the relation between early modern Catholic devotionalism and *devotio moderna*, written from a perspective differ- ent from Wilmart's, see Hsia, *World of Catholic Renewal*, 224–26.

120. Wilmart provided an edition of this interesting text in *Auteurs spirituels*, 60–62. Properly speaking, the Creed (e.g., the Apostles' Creed, the Nicene-Con- stantinopolitan Creed) belongs to the liturgy of Christian baptism; it formed the candidates' profession of faith prior to their immersion in the baptismal font. Yet by the late sixth century (589), the Creed was being used at the Eucharist (just before recitation of the Lord's Prayer and communion) in parts of Spain. Two centuries later, Charlemagne introduced the Creed into the liturgy of the royal court at Aachen, and shortly after the beginning of the second millennium, it

spread throughout the West and was adopted at Rome. See Peter G. Cobb, "The Liturgy of the Word in the Early Church," in Cheslyn Jones et al., eds., *The Study of Liturgy*, rev. ed. (New York: Oxford University Press, 1992), 219–29; here, 228.

121. Wilmart, *Auteurs spirituels*, 60; my translation of the author's French.

122. Ibid., 61; my translation of the Latin text.

123. Ibid., 60; my translation of the author's French.

124. Gregory Martin, *Roma Sancta*, ed. George Bruner Parks (Rome: Edizioni di Storia e Letteratura, 1969). Martin lived in Rome from late 1576 to the summer of 1578. See "The Editor's Preface," ix. I have retained the orthography of Martin's original.

125. Martin, *Roma Sancta*, chap. 24, 70–73.

126. Ibid., 70–71.

127. Ibid., 71–72.

128. Ibid., 71, with marginal annotations. The accuracy of Martin's account is supported by other contemporary documents. See Louis Ponnelle and Louis Bordet, *St. Philip Neri and the Roman Society of His Times (1515–1595)*, trans. Ralph Francis Kerr (1932; London: Sheed and Ward, 1979).

129. Ibid., 72; with marginal annotations.

130. See ibid., especially 214–18.

131. Ibid., 214; emphasis in the original.

132. Ibid., 238. On devotion to the rosary among those who belong to "the Rosarie or Societie of our Ladie" at the "English seminarie at Rhemes," see ibid., 115. The Holy Year of 1575 would have been just four years after the Christian forces defeated the Turks at Lepanto in 1571.

133. Ibid., 214–15.

134. See the facsimile edition of the *Missale Romanum editio princeps* (1570), ed. Manlio Sodi and Achille Maria Triacca (publication details in note 48, above), 190–92 [of the facsimile; 246–48 of the editors' numbering]. The solemn intercessions followed the reading of Christ's passion from John's gospel and included prayers for the whole church, as well as for prisoners, pilgrims, the sick, those not in communion with the Church of Rome ("heretics and schismatics"), the Jewish people, and unbelievers ("pagans"). Martin's list of "rosary intentions" follows this liturgical list quite closely, mentioning "pilgrims and trvailers, . . . Catholike armies, . . . Heretikes . . . the sicke . . . the dead . . . the poore . . . the Pope . . . a prelate [bishop], a Prince, such a Cuuntire, such a citie, such an armie," as well as other members of the confraternity.

135. *Roma Sancta*, 216–18.

136. Ibid., 216.

137. An example of a theotokion follows: "It is truly right to bless you, O Theotokos, ever blessed, and most pure, and the Mother of our God: more honorable than the cherubim, incomparably more glorious than the seraphim! Without corruption, you gave birth to God the Word. O true Theotokos, we magnify you!"

138. Martin, *Roma Sancta*, 216. By "our Ladies Mattins," Martin meant vigils and/or lauds of the daily votive office of the Blessed Virgin Mary. Organized on the same pattern as the daily Divine Office (Liturgy of the Hours), the "little office" of Mary contained a full set of prayer hours (matins or vigils, lauds, prime, sext, terce, none, vespers, and compline), using texts praising Mary and her role in the history of salvation. The "Hours of the Blessed Virgin" ("Horae Beatae Mariae Virginis") became a standard part of the medieval Books of Hours in England and elsewhere. See Eamon Duffy, *Marking the Hours*, 4–22.

139. Martin, *Roma Sancta*, 216–27.

140. On the origins of the fifteen mysteries, see Herbert Thurston, "Our Popular Devotions. II–The Rosary; V. The Fifteen Mysteries," *The Month* 96 (1900), 620–37.

141. Martin, *Roma Sancta*, 217.

142. Ibid., 216–27.

143. It is not clear whether Martin had personally applied to enter the Jesuits or was being recruited by them. In any case, he did not join the Society of Jesus. See George Bruner Parks, "The Life and Works of Gregory Martin," in *Roma Sancta*, xiv–xvi. For Martin's account of the activities of Philip Neri and the clergy of the Church of San Girolamo (Saint Jerome) in Rome, see *Roma Sancta*, 73–74.

144. Martin, *Roma Sancta*, 73.

145. Ibid., 74. Ponelle and Bordet, *St. Philip Neri*, 389, note that the "Oratory" in the early stage of its development was not a place but a program or process: "the 'great' Oratory of the afternoon, that Oratory with its four sermons which took place every week-day except Saturday, two and a half hours after the mid-day meal," was characteristically imaginative and improvisatory, especially "during the years between 1570 and 1580," the period described in Martin's *Roma Sancta*.

146. Martin, *Roma Sancta*, 74.

147. Louis Bouyer, *The Roman Socrates: A Portrait of St. Philip Neri*, trans. Michael Day (London: Geoffrey Chapman, 1958). Bouyer also mentions the importance of music in Neri's gatherings; ibid., 54–57.

148. Ibid., 50.

149. Ibid., 39–40, 54–55.

150. Ibid., 39–40. See also Black, *Italian Confraternities in the Sixteenth Century*, 194–96. Neri had started this confraternity while still a layman in the 1540s (ibid., 194).

151. Ibid., 55.

152. For examples, see Ponnelle and Bordet, *St. Philip Neri*, 114–19.

153. Ibid., 116.

154. Ibid.

155. Ibid., 140.

156. Ibid., 140–41.

157. Langdon, *Caravaggio*, 224.

158. Pamela M. Jones, "Federico Borromeo as a Patron of Landscapes and Still Lifes: Christian Optimism in Italy ca. 1600," *Art Bulletin* 70:2 (June 1988), 261–72; here, 270. The phrase "Christian optimism" had been used to describe this moment within Counter-Reformation or early modern Catholicism by A. Dupront, "Autour de Saint Filippo Neri: De l'Optimisme Chrétien," *Mélanges d'Archéologie et d'Histoire* 49 (1932): 219–59.

159. Federico Borromeo (1564–1631) should not be confused with his older cousin Saint Charles Borromeo (1538–84). Both were Catholic prelates, but Federico's approach to the "Counter-Reform" differed from that of Charles.

160. For a discussion of how churchmen in Renaissance Rome tried to retrieve classical Latin rhetoric, see Charles L. Stinger, *The Renaissance in Rome* (1985; Bloomington: Indiana University Press, 1998), 282–91.

161. Ponnelle and Bordet, *St. Philip Neri*, 493.

162. Ibid.

163. Ibid.

164. See the editorial introduction to Gabriele Paleotti, *Discorso intorno alle immagini sacre e profane*, xxx (for the phrase "catechism of images"). See also Pamela M. Jones, "Art Theory as Ideology: Gabriele Paleotti's Hierarchical Notion of Painting's Universality and Reception," in Claire Farago, ed., *Reframing the Renaissance: Visual Culture in Europe and Latin America 1450–1650* (New Haven: Yale University Press, 1995), 127–39. Jones's essay offers valuable insight into Paleotti's work, though she seems mistaken about its publication history (see her 321 n. 1). The *Discorso* first appeared in Italian in 1582, and a Latin version followed, published at Ingolstadt in 1594. See the editorial introduction to the *Discorso*, xiii–xviii.

165. See Giuseppe Fusari, "Introduzione al *Discorso sulle Immagini*," in Paleotti, *Discorso*, xi–xxiv; here, xviii.

166. Ibid., xiv, xviii.

167. For the Latin text, see Charles Borromeo, *Instructionum fabricae et supellectilis ecclesiasticae libri duo*, ed. and trans. Stefano Della Torre and Massimo Marinelli, Monumenta Studia Instrumenta Liturgica, 8 (Vatican City: Libreria Editrice Vaticana, 2000). See also Evelyn Carole Voelker, *Charles Borromeo's Instructiones Fabricae et Supellectilis Ecclesiasticae, 1577: A Translation with Commentary and Analysis* (Ann Arbor, MI: University Microfilms, 1970).

168. For the Latin text, see Borromeo, *Instructionum fabricae* (as in preceding note), c. XVII, 70; my translation.

169. Ibid., c. XVII, 71; my translation.

170. Voelker, *Charles Borromeo's* Instructiones, 233, notes that Borromeo's chapter on sacred pictures and images confronts readers with "the full force of the sixteenth century Counter Reformation tide against the artistic freedom

allowed Renaissance artists," and introduces "strictures [that] would have ruled out most of the work of Michelangelo and Raphael." Voelker points to the example of Paolo Veronese's *Last Supper*, which prompted an investigation by the Inquisition in Venice in 1573. Instead of a traditional "Jesus and the apostles" scene, Veronese had painted a "large and festive canvas" that included "some fifty figures including a cat and dog under the feet of Christ, a blackamoor jester with a parrot on his wrist, and some German mercenaries." (ibid., 233). Veronese got off the hook when the Venetian Inquisitors solved the problem by renaming the work *Feast in the House of Levi* (ibid., 234).

171. Fusari, "Introduzione," in Paleotti, *Discorso*, xix.

172. Ibid., xix–xx. See also Thomas Aquinas, *Summa Theologiae*, Ia Pars, Q. 12, art. 6; Q. 20, art. 1; IIa IIae Pars, Q. 83, art. 3, ad 2um.

173. See Ian Verstegen, "Federico Barocci, Federico Borromeo, and the Oratorian Orbit," *Renaissance Quarterly* 56 (2003): 56–87; here, 57.

174. See Stuart Patrick Lingo, *The Capuchins and the Art of History: Retrospection and Reform in the Arts in Late Renaissance Italy* (Ann Arbor, MI: University Microfilms, 1998), 8.

175. See Constanza Barbieri, "'Invisibilia per visibilia': S. Filippo Neri, le immagini e la contemplazione," in *La Regola et la Fama: San Filippo Neri e l'arte* (Milan: Electa, 1995), 64–79; here, 71; my translation.

176. See ibid., 71.

177. The final four sentences in this paragraph are based on Barbieri's comments; ibid., 71. See also Giuseppe Scavizzi, *Arte e architettura sacra: Cronache e documenti sulla controversia tra riformati e cattolici (1500–1550)* (Reggio Calabria: Casa del libro editrice, 1981), 284–84. Scavizzi gives a table of the scriptural and patristic themes commonly used by Catholic apologists who defend the utility and value of sacred images.

178. For the early history of this renegotiation, see Giuseppe Scavizzi, *The Controversy on Images from Calvin to Baronius*, Toronto Studies in Religion, 14 (New York: P. Lang, 1992).

179. Langdon, *Caravaggio*, 223.

180. Ibid., 223–26, 239–41.

181. Ibid., 224.

182. Ibid., 225.

183. For fifteenth-century examples of this connection between rosary and visual imagery, see Anne Winston-Allen's "The Picture Text and Its 'Readers,'" chap. 2 in *Stories of the Rose*, 31–64.

184. In addition to Anne Winston-Allen's chapter on rosary books, see Herbert Thurston: "Our Popular Devotions: II–The Rosary. IV–The Rosary among the Carthusians," *The Month* 96 (1900): 513–27; Thurston, "Our Popular Devotions: II–The Rosary. V–The Fifteen Mysteries," *The Month* 96 (1900): 620–27.

185. Langdon, *Caravaggio*, 233.

186. Ibid., 225–26.

187. For Trent's rejection of vernacular languages for public worship, see DS 1749: "Even though the Mass contains much instruction for the faithful, it does not seem expedient to the Fathers [i.e., the bishops at the Council] for it to be celebrated indiscriminately in a vernacular language" (my translation). Yet Trent did not prohibit the use of vernacular languages in the Roman Rite *absolutely*. It simply rejected the idea that the liturgy *must* be celebrated *only* in vernacular languages (the position of the Protestant reformers).

188. See Walter Friedlaender, *Caravaggio Studies* (1955; New York: Schocken Books, 1969), 120–30.

189. Ibid., 129.

190. Langdon, *Caravaggio*, 231.

191. Ibid., 226.

192. For a brief history of the Salve Regina, see Herbert Thurston, "The Salve Regina," *The Month* 128 (1918): 248–60; reprinted in Herbert Thurston, *Familiar Prayers: Their Origin and History*, ed. Paul Grosjean (London: Burns Oates, 1953), 115–45. Thurston provides the primitive Latin text of the Salve (116).

193. See Keith P. Luria, "Rural and Village Piety," in Peter Matheson, ed., *Reformation Christianity*, A People's History of Christianity, Vol. 5 (Minneapolis, MN: Fortress Press, 2007), 48–69, especially 60–68.

194. Ibid., 50.

195. John Bossy, *Christianity in the West, 1400–1700* (Oxford: Oxford University Press, 1985), 57–75.

196. Ibid., 57.

197. Luria, "Rural and Village Piety," 49. On the presence of women in rosary confraternities, see ibid., 61.

198. Ibid.

199. Luria's comment (ibid., 61) that "the Rosary fostered an interiorized and individualized spirituality" must be taken with a grain of salt. Bossy points out that participation in religious confraternities, including those associated with the rosary, "encouraged [lay] attendance at mass, augmented stipends, provided for extra masses, rebuilt churches which had fallen down as a result of war or plague." *Christianity in the West*, 63. Luria himself admits the popularity of rosary prayers in parishes helped engage worshipers "in a more active from of worship than that to which they had been accustomed." "Rural and Village Piety," 63.

200. Luria, "Rural and Village Piety," 64.

201. Ibid., 67.

202. Louis Chatellier, *The Europe of the Devout: The Catholic Reformation and the Formation of a New Society*, trans. Jean Birrell (New York: Cambridge University Press, 1989), xi.

203. See Chatellier's "maps of devout Europe," ibid., 25–32.

204. Ibid., xi. Note that fraternities and confraternities have their proximate roots in medieval life. Established to meet the pastoral needs of laypersons or clergy, sometimes both, their purposes were simultaneously religious and convivial. They sought to provide members with material and financial help during times of personal or social crisis (e.g., war, plague, famine, sickness, death). The term "congregation" is commonly used for religious communities of women or men who, particularly after Trent's reforms, made vows (poverty, chastity, obedience) but were not bound to all the restrictions that governed older religious orders (e.g., Benedictine nuns and monks). They were not, for example, bound to public choral chanting of the daily Divine Office, nor were their members strictly cloistered. Sometimes, after Trent, " congregation" was used in a sense synonymous with "confraternity" (such is the case with Chatellier's "Marian congregations"). *Sodalities* were associations established for some explicit religious purpose involving communal action and/or assistance (e.g., caring for the altar or the whole parish church).

205. See ibid., 33–35.

206. Hsia, *World of Catholic Renewal*, 225.

207. Ibid.

208. See Chatellier, *Europe of the Devout*, 217–40.

209. Ibid., 255.

210. Langdon, *Caravaggio*, 224.

211. Chatellier, *Europe of the Devout*, 216. Later he comments: "At the end of the eighteenth century, we begin to see emerge, in certain European countries, the outlines of a specific Catholic society. This society had its elites, whose common features . . . stand out clearly. It had its mass of small men who, in the large towns, lost their heterogeneity and their mobility and began to put down roots. It had its own values and rules, according to which its members led their professional lives, and whose sound basis they, for the most part, recognized. At the heart of the old Christianity, a Catholic society was born, in whose formation the Marian congregations played a major role." Ibid., 239–40.

212. For the quoted phrases, see Bossy, *Christianity in the West*, 59.

NOTES TO CHAPTER 2

1. Readers may view images of the Cappella del Rosario at http://www.kirterion.it/rosario.htm.

2. See Eithne Wilkins, *The Rose-Garden Game: A Tradition of Beads and Flowers* (New York: Herder and Herder / An *Azimuth* Book, 1969), 192. Wilkins points out that this "rope" may not be a string of beads but a "studded thong"–a lifeline? a whip?

3. Ibid., 192.

4. Ibid.; emphasis added.

5. Edward Muir, *Ritual in Early Modern Europe,* 2nd ed., New Approaches to European History, 33 (New York: Cambridge University Press, 2005), 163–251.

6. See examples of Fontana's work at http://www.wga.hu. Carracci's work may be viewed at Google "Images." Carracci's 1582 "Lamentation" (survivors mourning after Christ was taken down from the cross) is in the collection of the Metropolitan Museum of New York and may be viewed online at the Met's "Timeline of Art History."

7. William V. Hudon, "Religion and Society in Early Modern Italy: Old Questions, New Insights," *American Historical Review* 101:3 (June 1996): 783–804; here, 796.

8. Ibid., 783.

9. Ibid., 788.

10. Ibid.

11. Giuseppe Olmi and Paolo Prodi, "Art, Science, and Nature in Bologna *circa* 1600," in *The Age of Correggio and the Carracci: Emilian Painting of the Sixteenth and Seventeenth Centuries,* trans. Robert Erich Wolf (New York: Metropolitan Museum of Art/Cambridge University Press, 1986), 213–35; here 213.

12. Ibid.

13. Ibid., 214.

14. See Nicholas Terpstra, "Apprenticeship in Social Welfare: From Confraternal Charity to Municipal Poor Relief in Early Modern Italy," *Sixteenth Century Journal* 25:1 (1994): 101–20; here, 101.

15. Ibid.

16. Ibid., 215.

17. Ibid. Paleotti himself had graduated from the University of Bologna in 1546 with a doctorate *utriusque juris* (in both civil and canon or church law).

18. Ibid., 219. I have slightly emended what appears to be a faulty Latin citation of the title in Olmi and Prodi's essay.

19. Ibid., 224–25. The admiration between these two men was mutual; Aldrovandi was also influenced by Paleotti.

20. See Gebriele Paleotti, *Discorso intorno alle immagini sacre e profane,* ed. Stefano Della Torre, Gian Franco Freguglia, and Carlo Chenis, Monumenta Studia Instrumenta Liturgica, 25 (Vatican City: Libreria Editrice Vaticana, 2002), bk. II, chap. XXIV, 163–67. A facsimile reprint of the 1582 edition is also available: Gabriele Paleotti, *Discorso intorno alle imagini* [sic] *sacre et profane* (Bologna, 1582), with introduction by Paolo Prodi (Bologna: Arnaldo Forni Editore, 1990). Hereafter, references to the introduction to this latter edition will be cited as Paleotti/Prodi, *Discorso,* followed by the page number (in Roman numerals).

21. Olmi and Prodi, "Art, Science, and Nature," 225.

22. See Paleotti/Prodi, *Discorso,* vii. Prodi also notes the distinctiveness of the *process* by which Paleotti's *Discorso* was produced. It represented, from the beginning, a collaboration among many thinkers rather than the musings of a single writer, and the finished composition resembled a florilegium, or collection of erudite documents.

23. Ibid., vii–viii; my translation.

24. See Paleotti, *Discorso*, bk. I, chap. XII, 44.

25. See ibid., 45–46; emphasis added.

26. See Olmi and Prodi, "Art, Science, and Nature," 226–27. In 1581, Aldrovandi had communicated to Paleotti his views about the utility of pictures for students of the natural sciences and about the potential benefit of images for Christians, citing Paul's notion that "the invisible things of God are known through visible things that have been made" (Romans 1.20). See Paleotti/Prodi, *Discorso*, viii.

27. See Paleotti/Prodi, *Discorso*, ix. See also Olmi and Prodi, "Art, Science, and Nature," 226–29. The three Carracci—Ludovico (1555–1619) and his cousins Agostino (1557–1602) and Annibale (1560–1609)—laid the foundations for a decisive break from the older, mannerist style of painting (imported to Bologna from cities such as Rome) and the beginnings of a vigorous style associated with the baroque, which emphasized dramatic movement and transformation, swirling forms, and high color. See Charles Dempsey, "The Carracci Reform of Painting," in *Age of Correggio and the Carracci*, 237–54.

28. Dempsey, "Carracci Reform of Painting," 244.

29. Ibid. A more accurate translation of "*l'arte che tutto fa, nulla si scopre*" might be: "Real art reveals nothing about itself" or "Art that does everything calls no attention to itself."

30. Ibid.

31. See ibid., 252–53, for discussion of Caravaggio's reaction to Annibale Carracci's painting *Saint Margaret* and its probable influence on the work he was then doing, ca. 1599, on his paintings of Saint Matthew for the Contarelli Chapel in the Church of San Luigi dei Francesi.

32. Ibid., 244.

33. Ibid., 252.

34. Ibid., 253.

35. Ibid.

36. Ibid.

37. Ibid.

38. Ibid.

39. The Litany of Loreto (also known simply as the "Litany of the Blessed Virgin Mary") is a prayer made up of invocations and petitions to which the faithful respond with a repeated phrase (e.g., "Pray for us"). Its first attested use comes from the year 1558, and it was formally approved for public use by Pope Sixtus V in 1587.

40. Arnold Hauser, *Mannerism: The Crisis of the Renaissance and the Origin of Modern Art*, trans. Eric Mosbacher (1965; Cambridge: Belknap Press of Harvard University Press, 1986), 77.

41. Ibid., 76–77.

42. Ibid., 77. When, as Hauser notes, Trent rejected a style that made musical structure more important than the scriptural or liturgical texts, it was reacting against "sensualism."

43. See Paleotti, *Discorso*, book I, chap. XXV.2, 78.

44. The citation is from Augustine's *Confessions*, bk. III, chap. 4, sec. 7; I have translated the Latin of this passage as Paleotti gives it in *Discorso*, bk. I, Chapter XXV.3, 79.

45. Paleotti, *Discorso*, bk. I, chap. XXV.4, 79; my translation.

46. Hauser, *Mannerism*, 77. We know that Paleotti's *Discorso* was an explicit response to Trent because in the 1582 edition, two quotations from its decree on sacred images were cited on the verso of the full title page. See the facsimile in Paleotti/Prodi, *Discorso*, unnumbered second page.

47. Olmi and Prodi, "Art, Science, and Nature," 228.

48. See *Oeuvres Complètes de Saint Francois de Sales*, 4th ed. (Paris: Berche and Tralin, 1879), 13:740–41. This same volume contains the French text of Francis's *L'Introduction à la vie dévote*.

49. Hauser, *Mannerism*, 78.

50. Ibid.

51. See John of the Cross, *The Ascent of Mount Carmel*, in Kieran Kavanaugh, ed., *John of the Cross: Selected Writings* (New York: Paulist Press, 1987), 136.

52. John of the Cross, *The Living Flame of Love* (part of the "Prologue"), in Kavanaugh, *John of the Cross*, 293–94.

53. The phrase "traitor touch" is Walt Whitman's.

54. Hauser, *Mannerism*, 78.

55. Ibid.

56. See David Freedberg, "Johannes Molanus on Provocative Paintings," *Journal of the Warburg and Courtauld Institutes* 34 (1971): 229–45; here, 229.

57. Langdon, *Caravaggio*, 6–7. I would want to qualify Langdon's comment about "the pietistic art of the Counter-Reformation" in light of issues discussed in the first two sections of this chapter.

58. On the "grand narrative" of Christianity and reactions to it, see Lieven Boeve, "Thinking Sacramental Presence in a Postmodern Context: A Playground for Theological renewal," in L. Boeve and L. Leijssen, eds., *Sacramental Presence in a Postmodern Context*, Bibliotheca Ephemeridum Theologicarum Lovaniensium, CLX (Leuven: Peeters, 2001), 3–35, especially 17–23.

59. See Langdon, *Caravaggio*, 5.

60. See discussion in Peter Robb, *M: The Man Who Became Caravaggio* (New York: Henry Holt, 1999), 94–95.

61. Ibid., 95.

62. Hunt, *Caravaggio*, 128, citing Robb, *M: The Man Who Became Caravaggio*, 326.

63. Hunt, *Caravaggio*, 128.

64. Ibid.

65. See Christopher F. Black, *Italian Confraternities in the Sixteenth Century* (New York: Cambridge University Press, 1989), 194–95. See also Louis Ponnelle and Louis Bordet, *St. Philip Neri and the Roman Society of His Times (1515–1595)*, trans. Ralph F. Kerr (1932; London: Sheed and Ward, 1979).

66. The two men knew each other in Rome during the 1530s and 1540s; see Ponnelle and Border, *St. Philip Neri*, 99–105.

67. Ibid., 105–7.

68. Ibid., 101.

69. Ibid., 98. Persiano Rosa (later Neri's confessor) thought "Philip would never have dreamed or thought that there was any place for his insignificant self, or for one of his humour, in the hierarchy of the church."

70. Ibid.

71. Antonio Gallonio, *The Life of St. Philip Neri*, trans. Jerome Bertram (San Francisco: Ignatius Press, 2005), 13.

72. Langdon, *Caravaggio*, 104–13.

73. For the phrase "great swag of knotted red curtain," see Robb, *M: The Man Who Became Caravaggio*, 379. Digital images of Caravaggio's work may be accessed online at http://www.wga.hu/index.html.

74. On Caravaggio's *Death of the Virgin Mary*, see Langdon, *Caravaggio*, 248–51, and Robb, *M: The Man Who Became Caravaggio*, 289–94. On *Madonna del Rosario*, see Langdon, *Caravaggio*, 333–35; Robb, *M: The Man Who Became Caravaggio*, 379–83.

75. Langdon, *Caravaggio*, 334.

76. Ibid., 333.

77. Ibid. The Christian "Holy League" was a coalition formed from Spanish, Venetian, and papal forces, assisted by personnel from the Republic of Genoa, the Duchy of Savoy, the Knights of Malta, and others. This coalition was led by Don John (Don Juan) of Austria, the illegitimate son of Emperor Charles V and half brother of Spain's Philip II.

78. These paintings may be viewed online at the Web Gallery of Art, http://www.wga.hu/index1.html. A painting by Tintoretto was destroyed by fire in 1577. Titian's *Allegory of the Battle of Lepanto* is sometimes called *Phillip II Offering Don Fernando to Victory*.

79. See the information note accompanying this painting at http://www.wga.hu/index1.html.

80. The complex history of Christianity's relationship to Islam is obviously a part of both the background and the foreground of Lepanto.

81. Herbert Thurston, "Rosary," *The Catholic Encyclopedia*, 15 vols. (New York: Robert Appleton, 1912), 13:184–89; here, 189.

82. Ibid. Subsequently, in 1671, Clement X extended the feast of the Holy Rosary to all of Spain. Eventually, in the Roman liturgical calendar this feast

was transferred from the first Sunday of October to the fixed date of October 7, where it is still found.

83. Langdon, *Caravaggio*, 333. Langdon suggests that one reason why *Madonna del Rosario* was never installed in the Neapolitan church of San Domenico, for which it was intended, is that the painting "lacked the celebratory quality of many Rosary altarpieces connected with Lepanto." Ibid., 335.

84. See Robb, *M: The Man Who Became Caravaggio*, 379–80. On the identity of the "black clad white ruffed middle-aged man," see Langdon, *Caravaggio*, 333–35, and 416 n. 18.

85. Benedict Nicolson, "Caravaggio and the Netherlands," *Burlington Magazine* 94, no. 594 (September 1952): 247–52; here, 248.

86. Robb, *M: The Man Who Became Caravaggio*, 265.

87. Langdon, *Caravaggio*, 334–35. See also Christopher F. Black, *Italian Confraternities in the Sixteenth Century* (New York: Cambridge University Press, 1989), 103–4.

88. Black, *Italian Confraternities*, 130, 136.

89. Langdon, *Caravaggio*, 44.

90. Ibid.

91. Black, *Italian Confraternities*, 134–35.

92. Ibid., 136.

93. Ibid.

94. Ibid.

95. Piero Camporesi, *Bread of Dreams: Food and Fantasy in Early Modern Europe*, trans. David Gentilcore (Chicago: University of Chicago Press, 1989), 33.

96. See ibid., 33–34.

97. Ibid., 35.

98. On this point see Black, *Italian Confraternities*, 135–37.

99. See Thorsten Sellin, "The House of Correction for Boys in the Hospice of Saint Michael in Rome," *Journal of the American Institute of Criminal Law and Criminology* 20:4 (February 1930): 533–53; here, 536. Sellin notes that, beginning in 1582, six separate institutions contributed to the creation of this hospice.

100. Langdon, *Caravaggio*, 44–45.

101. See the text of the papal bull *Quamvis infirma* in *Magnum Bullarium Romanum: Bullarium privilegiorum ac diplomatum Romanorum Pontificum Amplissima Collectio* (Rome: Typis Hieronymi Mainardi, 1736; reprint, Graz: Akademische Druk und Verlagsanstalt, 1965), vol. 4, pt. 3, 304–8.

102. Ibid., 306.

103. Ibid.

104. See Sellin, "House of Correction for Boys," 536–37.

105. Langdon, *Caravaggio*, 335.

106. Ibid.

107. Ibid.

108. See Ronald W. Lightbown, *Medieval European Jewellery* (London: Victoria and Albert Museum, 1992), 342–54.

109. Nearly a century earlier (1531), in Mexico this same connection between Mary and the poor became visible in Juan Diego's visions of the Virgin of Guadalupe in Tepeyac, an impoverished area on the outskirts of Mexico City.

110. See Giovanni Baglione, *Le Vite de' Pittori, Scultori et Architetti: Dal Pontificato di Gregorio XIII del 1572 In fino a' tempi di Papa Urbano Ottavo nel 1642*, ed. Jacob Hess and Herwarth Röttgen, 3 vols., Studi e Testi 367–369 (Vatican City: Biblioteca Apostolica Vaticana, in collaboration with Bibliotheca Hertziana, Rome, 1995), 367:137.

111. Robb, *M: The Man Who Became Caravaggio*, 267–68.

112. Ibid., 268. Helen Langdon notes that the sensual details of Mary's appearance should not blind viewers to her other aspects. Like medieval Madonnas, her very size conveys "transcendence." Hence, Mary presents a "deeply ambiguous figure, warm, fleshly (we feel the imprint of her fingers against the child's body), yet with an unreal grace . . . encircled by mysterious light and shade." Langdon, *Caravaggio*, 287.

113. Luigi Santucci, *Meeting Jesus*, trans. Bernard Wall (New York: Herder and Herder, 1971), 154.

114. Robb, *M: The Man Who Became Caravaggio*, 268. Robb notes that Mary's appearance in this painting may have aroused scandal because Caravaggio used a well-known "courtesan" (Maddalena Antognetti/Lena Antonietti) as a model. See ibid., 269–70. See also Hunt, *Caravaggio*, 60–61.

115. Robb, *M: The Man Who Became Caravaggio*, 271.

116. Ibid. Robb claims, with some justification, that "the counter reformation was art's first great age of kitsch—never before had such terrible intensity of feeling found expression in such insanely constricted imagery" (ibid., 180).

117. See, for example, Hunt, *Caravaggio*, 29–52. Hunt highlights Caravaggio's success, despite his "bohemian lifestyle," in attracting influential patrons such as Cardinal Francesco Del Monte.

118. Ibid., 148. In 1607, the *Madonna del Rosario* was apparently bought by a group of Flemish artists that included Peter Paul Rubens. See Robb, *M: The Man Who Became Caravaggio*, 382–83.

119. Robb, *M: The Man Who Became Caravaggio*, 241.

120. See Catherine Puglisi, *Caravaggio* (London: Phaidon, 1998), 192.

121. Ibid. The Latin Vulgate of Genesis 3.15 reads: "Inimicitias ponam inter te et mulierem, et semen tuum et semen illius: ipsa conteret caput tuum, et tu insibidaberis calcaneo eius" (I will place enmity between you [the serpent] and the woman, [and between] your seed and her seed. She will crush your head, and you will lie in ambush for her heel). As Puglisi points out, the Latin mistranslates the Hebrew original.

122. Olmi and Prodi, "Art, Science, and Nature," 225.

123. Ibid., 227. See Carlo Cesare Malvasia's *Felsina pittrice: Vite de' pittori bolognesi*, 2 vols. (1841; reprint, Bologna: Forni, 2004), 1:307–8.

124. See Puglisi, *Caravaggio*, 215. This still life—with its partially decaying objects (rather than idealized nature)—became part of Federico Borromeo's collection in the Pinacoteca Ambrosiana in Milan. Puglisi suggests that the painting evoked for Borromeo a "sacred meaning," since the fruit "celebrated God's creation in their fidelity to nature" (ibid.). Readers may view these works of Caravaggio at www.wga.hu.

125. Robb, *M: The Man Who Became Caravaggio*, 332. Catherine Puglisi concurs: Mary's "stooping pose," she writes, "reveals rather too much breast" (*Caravaggio*, 195).

126. See Langdon, *Caravaggio*, 305.

127. See Puglisi, *Caravaggio*, 195–96.

128. Ibid., 195. Puglisi is quoting Émile Male, *L'art religieux de la fin du XVIe siècle* (Paris: Colin, 1972), 39.

129. Puglisi, *Caravaggio*, 193.

130. See Robb, *M: The Man Who Became Caravaggio*, 332. As Robb points out, not only is Christ nude, but his penis juts forward and is "prominently shadowed on his inner thigh" (ibid., 333).

131. Puglisi, *Caravaggio*, 196.

132. "In his insistence on the human figure and the human drama," writes Puglisi, "Caravaggio came within reach of realizing a classicizing aesthetic, centred on these very concerns since antiquity. . . . Yet his choice of human actors—ordinary individuals whose appearance and behaviour were at odds with the heroic ideal—was irreconcilable with classical principles. Thus, once in the artistic arena of monumental sacred painting, Caravaggio defied its many conventions. Banishing noble protagonists and angelic hosts, lofty architecture and landscapes, he invented anew the grand episodes of sacred history as intimate and fervent dramas enacted by a minimal cast of plebeian players on a near-empty stage" (*Caravaggio*, 196–97).

133. Robb, *M: The Man Who Became Caravaggio*, 201.

134. Holt, *A Documentary History of Art*, 2:65.

135. Robb, *M: The Man Who Became Caravaggio*, 290.

136. The Roman Catholic dogma of Mary's Assumption—that, at the end of her life, Mary was taken body and soul into heaven—was officially defined and promulgated by Pope Pius XII in 1950. The pope declared that "the Immaculate Mother of God, Mary ever Virgin, having completed the course of earthly life, was assumed, body and soul, into heavenly glory." Yet the pope's decree (*Munificentissimus Deus*) left some important issues unresolved. It did not, for example, settle the question of whether Mary actually *died* before her "assumption into heaven."

137. See Stephen Shoemaker, *Ancient Traditions of the Virgin Mary's Dormition and Assumption* (New York: Oxford University Press, 2002).

138. Ibid., 1.

139. Brian E. Daley, trans., *On the Dormition of Mary: Early Patristic Homilies* (Crestwood, NY: St. Vladimir's Seminary Press, 1998), "Introduction," 1–45; here, 6. Chalcedon affirmed Christ as *one divine Person* in *two distinct natures* (divine and human) that are indivisibly and inseparably united without any confusion or change. This means too that Mary must be honored as Theotokos (God-bearer), since to claim she is only Christotokos (Christ-bearer) would imply that Christ's humanity is somehow separable from his divine nature.

140. Daley, "Introduction," *On the Dormition of Mary*, 8–9. "In the half-century that followed the Council of Chalcedon," Daley notes, "the figure of Mary emerged like a comet in Christian devotion and liturgical celebration throughout the world." Ibid., 6.

141. On the circumstances surrounding the commission for *Morte della Vergine*, see Langdon, *Caravaggio*, 246–47.

142. Freedberg, "Johannes Molanus on Provocative Paintings," 229.

143. Holt, *Documentary History of Art*, 2:64.

144. Robb, *M: The Man Who Became Caravaggio*, 79.

145. On the need for closer scrutiny of visual traditions in late medieval and early modern Christianity, see Bob Scribner, "Popular Piety and Modes of Visual Perception in Late-Medieval and Reformation Germany," *Journal of Religious History* 15:4 (December 1989): 448–69. Anne Winston-Allen explores several visual traditions associated with fifteenth- and sixteenth-century rosary books in *Stories of the Rose: The Making of the Rosary in the Middle Ages* (University Park: Pennsylvania State University Press, 1997), 31–64.

146. Robb, *M: The Man Who Became Caravaggio*, 294.

147. In *Madonna del Rosario* and *Madonna dei Pellegrini*, Mary is a young mother; in *Morte della Vergine*, she appears as middle-aged; and in his painting of Jesus' burial (*Deposizione*), she is elderly. (See comments on the *Deposizione* in Puglisi, *Caravaggio*, 173.)

148. Robb, *M: The Man Who Became Caravaggio*, 317.

149. Ibid.

150. On the image of Saint Anne in Caravaggio's *Madonna dei Palafrenieri*, see Puglisi, *Caravaggio*, 195–96.

151. On the pervasive kitschiness of much post-Tridentine Catholic art, see Colleen McDannell, *Material Christianity: Religion and Popular Culture in America* (New Haven: Yale University Press, 1995), 163–97.

152. Robb, *M: The Man Who Became Caravaggio*, 326–27. See also Puglisi, *Caravaggio*, 248.

153. See Puglisi, *Caravaggio*, 183–99.

NOTES TO CHAPTER 3

1. See Christopher Lash, "'Gate of Light': An Ethiopian Hymn to the Blessed Virgin," *Eastern Churches Review* 4, no. 1 (Spring 1972): 36–46; here, 37–38.

2. Ibid., 43.

3. Ibid., 43–44.

4. For the Latin text of this portion of Leo's sermon, see Léon le Grand, *Sermons*, vol. 1; trans. René Dolle, Sources chrétiennes 22 (Paris: Cerf, 1947), 124; my translation.

5. Readers may view these paintings at www.wga.hu.

6. See Catherine Puglisi, *Caravaggio* (London: Phaidon, 1998), 212.

7. Titian's work shows domestic pets playing under the table where the Stranger (Christ) and the two disciples are seated.

8. Puglisi, *Caravaggio*, 213.

9. For an English translation and helpful introduction to the *Spiritual Exercises*, see George E. Ganss, ed., *Ignatius of Loyola: Spiritual Exercises and Selected Works*, Paulist Press Classics of Western Spirituality (New York: Paulist Press, 1991).

10. Ibid., 151; cf. 148–49.

11. Ibid., 151.

12. Ibid., 146.

13. Ibid., 148–49.

14. This Marian altarpiece of Caravaggio's remains in the Cavaletti Chapel of the Church of Sant' Agostino in Rome.

15. The *Index librorum prohibitorum* (*List of Forbidden Books*) was issued by the Roman Congregation of the Inquisition under Pope Paul IV in 1557. Under Pope Pius V, a special Congregation of the Index was created (1571).

16. See Puglisi, *Caravaggio*, 249.

17. The quoted phrase is from the prayer said at all the hours of the Divine Office on the feast of the Lord's circumcision (January 1, also known as the Octave Day of Christmas and, today, as the Solemnity of Mary, Mother of God). See the Latin text in Manlio Sodi and Achille Maria Triacca, eds., *Breviarium Romanum editio princeps* (1568), Monumenta Liturgica Concilii Tridentini (Vatican City: Libreria Editrice Vaticana, 1999), 209 (of the modern edition; 217 in the 1568 edition, of which the modern gives a photostatic facsimile); my translation.

18. Mary's name had already been included in the Roman Eucharistic Prayer (the old "Roman Canon," now called "Eucharistic Prayer I") by the time of Pope Leo the Great (d. 461). Moreover, the celebration of Christ's Nativity in the West included a Marian dimension, as we can tell from homilies by Zeno of Verona (d. 380) and Saint Augustine (d. 430). Liturgical historian Bernard Botte argued that the "first Marian feast of the Roman liturgy" was the one celebrated on January 1, although his thesis is disputed by other scholars. For discussion,

see Georgius Frénaud, "Le culte de Notre Dame dans l'ancienne liturgie latine," in D'Hubert du Manoir, ed., *Maria*, Études sur la sainte vierge, vol. 6 (Paris: Beauchesne, 1961), 157–211. See also Bernard Botte, "Le première fete mariale de la liturgie romaine," *Ephemerides Liturgicae* 47 (1933): 425–30. Botte had argued that the feast of Mary on January 1 (called "Natale S. Mariae") was introduced in Rome sometime between 560 and 590.

19. The Roman "preface" is the variable opening portion of the eucharistic prayer or "canon" (the central prayer of the eucharistic liturgy, which includes Christ's words "this is my body. . ."). The preface was preceded by a dialogue between priest and people ("The Lord be with you / And also with you"; "Lift up your hearts / We lift them up to the Lord," etc.).

20. For the Latin text of this prayer, see Leo Cunibert Mohlberg, ed., *Liber sacramentorum Romanae aeclesiae ordinis anni circuli*, Rerum ecclesiasticarum documenta; Series maior; Fontes, IV (Rome: Herder, 1960),13 n. 51; my translation. This document (known as the "old Gelasian Sacramentary") dates from about 750 c.e. and combines Frankish and Roman elements. The sacramentary is a liturgical book containing the prayers recited by the one who presides at Eucharist (bishop or priest).

21. For the Latin text, see Sodi and Triacca, *Breviarium Romanum editio princeps* (1568), 184 (of the modern edition; 194 of the 1568 edition).

22. See ibid., p. 212 (of the modern edition; 220 of the 1568 edition); my translation.

23. For the Latin text, see Mohlberg, *Liber sacramentorum Romanae aeclesiae*, 184 n. 1246; my translation. The *Communicantes* of the Roman Canon probably dates from the mid-fifth century. The words referring to Mary resemble those found in the anaphora of Saint John Chrysostom. See Anton Hänggi and Irmgard Pahl, eds., *Prex Eucharistica*, Spicilegium Friburgense, 12 (Fribourg, Switzerland: Éditions Universitaries, 1968), 228, 268.

24. See John F. Baldovin, "Eucharistic Prayer," in Paul F. Bradshaw, ed., *The New Westminster Dictionary of Liturgy and Worship* (Louisville: Westminster John Knox Press, 2002), 192–99, especially 196.

25. For the text of this variable *Communicantes*, see Mohlberg, *Liber sacramentorum Romanae aeclesiae*,76 n. 459; my translation.

26. For Latin texts, see ibid., 75 n. 457; my translation.

27. See Antoine Chavasse, *Le sacramentaire Gélasien*, Bibliothèque de Théologie, Serie IV, vol. 1 (Tournai: Desclée, 1958), 97.

28. For further discussion of this point, see Cyrille Vogel, *Medieval Liturgy: An Introduction to the Sources*, trans. and rev. William G. Storey and Niels Rasmussen, NPM Studies in Church Music and Liturgy (Washington, DC: Pastoral Press, 1986), 74. Liturgical texts originally produced in Gaul sometimes did make their way to Rome, since liturgical influences in the Latin West flowed in both directions: from Rome to areas north of the Alps, and vice versa. The liturgical

books of the "Roman" Rite are thus hybrids combining material from multiple sources originating in diverse regions of early medieval Europe.

29. See Antoine Chavasse, *Les ancêtres du Missale Romanum* (1570), Studia Anselmiana, 118; Analecta liturgica, 20 (Rome: Centro Studi S. Anselmo, 1995).

30. See Chavasse, *Le sacramentaire Gélasien*, 375.

31. See ibid., 337, which notes that the titles for the sets of prayers for these feasts are later additions to the old Gelasian Sacramentary.

32. See ibid., 376.

33. Ibid., 376, notes that none of these four Marian feasts are mentioned in the oldest Roman epistolary (the *Comes* of Wurzburg, a book listing New Testament readings to be used at Mass) or the oldest Roman evangelary (book of Gospel readings for Mass), both of which date from about 650. Yet by the end of the seventh century (in the time of Pope Sergius, 687–701), all four Marian feasts seem to have been celebrated in Rome.

34. A sequence is a liturgical hymn or poem sung usually before the "alleluia" chant that precedes the Gospel reading at Mass. The *Stabat mater* has been attributed to several medieval authors, including Innocent III and Jacopo da Tode. The sequence remains an optional text in the post–Vatican II *Missale Romanum* of 1970, but the "Feast of Our Lady of Sorrows" did not enter Roman Catholic liturgical calendars until the eighteenth century and did not become universal until 1814. September 15 was established by Pope Saint Pius X in 1913 as the date for this feast. Notable early modern paintings of the *Mater dolorosa* are those by Titian and El Greco.

35. *MR* 1570 provides special texts only for the four older feasts (February 2, March 25, August 15, September 8). For the feast of Mary's conception, the rubrics of the missal direct the celebrant to use the Mass of Mary's Nativity on September 8. See Sodi and Triacca, *Missale Romanum editio princeps* (1570), 450 (of the modern edition; 6 of the "Proprium Missarum de Sanctis" section of the 1570 edition).

36. For the history of the liturgical books known collectively as the "Gregorian Sacramentary" (named after, but not compiled by, Pope Saint Gregory the Great, d. 604), see Vogel, *Medieval Liturgy*, 79–102. Charlemagne asked for a copy of this book because he wanted to promote "the Roman liturgy in his empire" (ibid., 80).

37. The Latin text of the prayer may be found in Sodi and Triacca, *Missale Romanum editio princeps* (1570), 476 (of the modern edition; 33 of the "Proprium Missarum de Sanctis" of the 1570 edition); my translation.

38. The Latin text of the prayer may be found in ibid., 532 (of the modern edition; 88 of the "Proprium Missarum de Sanctis" of the 1570 edition); my translation.

39. The Latin text of this prayer may be found in ibid., 469 (of the modern edition; 25 of the "Proprium Missarum de Sanctis" of the 1570 edition); my translation.

40. See Edmund Bishop, "The Genius of the Roman Rite," *Liturgica Historica: Papers on the Liturgy and Religious Life of the Western Church* (1918; Oxford: Clarendon Press, 1962, 1–19.

41. This *Ritus servandus* may be found in Sodi and Triacca, *Missale Romanum editio princeps* (1570), 9–22 (of the modern edition; no pagination was given in the original 1570 edition).

42. The Latin text of the most recent version of the *Institutio generalis* (*General Instruction*) may be found in *Missale Romanum; ex decreto sacrosancti oecumenici concilii Vaticani II instauratum, Editio typica teria* (Vatican City: Typis Vaticanis, 2002), 19–86.

43. *MR* 1570 did not technically require the priest to recite the canon *secrete* (inaudibly) or *voce demissa* (with subdued voice). The rubric preceding the part of the canon that follows the *Sanctus* ("Te igitur," etc.) says simply: "Sacerdos extendens et iungens manus, eleuans ad caelum oculos et statim demittens, inclinatus ante altare dicit" (The priest, extending then joining his hands, lifts his eyes toward heaven and immediately lowers them; bowing before the altar, he says). This rubric *could* mean that the priest says the canon at a normal speaking level.

44. See, for example, Virginia Reinburg, "Hearing Lay People's Prayer," in Barbara B. Diefendorf and Carla Hesse, eds., *Culture and Identity in Early Modern Europe (1500–1800): Essays in Honor of Natalie Zemon Davis* (Ann Arbor: University of Michigan Press, 1993), 19–39. See also Reinburg, "Liturgy and the Laity in Late Medieval and Reformation France," *Sixteenth Century Journal* 23:3 (1992): 526–46.

45. Reinburg, "Liturgy and the Laity," 529.

46. Reinburg, "Hearing Lay People's Prayer," 23.

47. Ibid., 23, 24.

48. Ibid., 24.

49. For a similar example from sixteenth-century France, see Kristen B. Neuschel, *Word of Honor: Interpreting Noble Culture in Sixteenth-Century France* (Ithaca: Cornell University Press, 1989), 72–78.

50. Ibid., 188.

51. For the Latin text, see Sodi and Triacca, *Missale Romanum editio princeps* (1570), 3 (of the modern edition; no pagination in the 1570 edition); my translation.

52. For fuller discussion, see Nathan D. Mitchell, "Reforms, Protestant and Catholic," in Geoffrey Wainwright and Karen B. Westerfield Tucker, eds., *The Oxford History of Christian Worship* (New York: Oxford University Press, 2006), 307–50; here, 338.

53. See Walter J. Ong, *Orality and Literacy: The Technologizing of the Word* (New York: Routledge, 1982).

54. Ibid., 49.

55. Ibid.

56. Neuschel, *Word of Honor*, 188.

57. Ibid., 188–89.

58. Ibid., 188.

59. Ibid., 193.

60. Ibid., 191.

61. Ibid.

62. See Robert M. Kingdon, *Church and Society in Reformation Europe* (London: Variorum Reprints, 1985), VIII ("The Control of Morals in Calvin's Geneva"): 3–16.

63. See Reinburg, "Hearing Lay People's Prayer," 27; emphasis in the original.

64. Ibid.

65. See Neuschel's interesting example of a 1562 incident (*Word of Honor*, ix). The episode involved two powerful French nobles, one a captor and the other a prisoner of war. The captor recognized the rank of his prisoner and offered him use of the best bed in his (the captor's) château. The prisoner "declined the offer and insisted that his captor use the bed instead. In the end, sharing the bed became the only honorable alternative."

66. Reinburg, "Hearing Lay People's Prayer," 27.

67. For the Latin text of this prayer, see Vincent Leroquais, *Livres d'heures manuscrits de la bibliothèque nationale*, 2 vols. (Paris: Macon, Protat Frères, 1927), 2:346–47. For an English translation, see Roger S. Wieck, *Time Sanctified: The Book of Hours in Medieval Art and Life* (New York: George Braziller, 1988), 163–64.

68. English translation in Wieck, *Time Sanctified*, 163.

69. Ibid.

70. Ibid., 163–64.

71. On the "joys of Mary" (five, seven, or even more happy events in her life) and their relation to the rosary, see Anne Winston-Allen, *Stories of the Rose* (University Park: Pennsylvania State University Press, 1997), 38–39, 41–43.

72. See André Wilmart, "La prière *O intemerata*," in *Auteurs spirituels et texts dévots du moyen âge latin* (1932; reprint, Paris: Études Augustiniennes, 1971), 474–504; see 488–90 for Latin text of the prayer. For an English translation, see Wieck, *Time Sanctified*, 164.

73. See Virginia Reinburg, "Prayer and the Book of Hours," in Wieck, *Time Sanctified*, 39–44; here, 42.

74. See Reinburg, "Liturgy and the Laity," 546.

75. See Reinburg, "Hearing Lay People's Prayer," 33.

76. See Reinburg, "Liturgy and the Laity," 545.

77. See Reinburg, "Hearing Lay People's Prayer," 34.

78. In addition to the studies of Reinburg, based largely on evidence derived from graphic manuscript illustrations, see Eamon Duffy, "Lay Appropriation of the Sacraments in the Later Middle Ages," *New Blackfriars* 77, no. 899 (December 1995): 53–67.

79. Duffy, "Lay Appropriation of the Sacraments," 56.

80. Ibid., 57.

81. Ibid.

82. The language of "seeing the Lord" was one of the earliest ways Christians used to express what happened at Easter (see, e.g., 1 Corinthians 15.3–8). See also Edward Schillebeeckx, *Jesus: An Experiment in Christology*, trans. Hubert Hoskins (New York: Seabury Press, 1979), 346–79.

83. Puglisi, *Caravaggio*, 154, points out that Contarelli (whose family commissioned the painting) had directed that the apostle be shown near "an isolated altar raised up above three, four, or five steps," wearing "liturgical vestments," and "celebrating the Mass."

84. See ibid., 157, and plate 184.

85. See ibid., 158–59.

86. See Helen Langdon, *Caravaggio: A Life* (New York: Knopf, 1998), 177.

87. Ibid.

88. See Puglisi, *Caravaggio*, 159, for the quoted reference to "tenebrism."

89. Langdon, *Caravaggio: A Life*, 177–78, notes, however, that reports of attacks by Protestants on Catholic priests did circulate in late sixteenth-century Rome.

90. See ibid., 178.

91. Ibid.

92. Reinburg, "Hearing Lay People's Prayer," 34.

93. Neuschel, *Word of Honor*, 191–92.

94. See ibid.

95. Ibid.

96. Ibid. The ancient practice of reading aloud, for example, created a kind of "democracy of readers" based on a shared physical experience that made knowledge audible and hence publicly available to all within earshot.

97. Ibid.

98. Ibid.

99. Ibid., 193. Stephen Greenblatt, *Renaissance Self-Fashioning* (Chicago: University of Chicago Press, 1980), 46, draws attention to earlier medieval precedents (e.g., Bernardine of Siena) for withdrawal into "private space" for purposes of self-scrutiny and introspection.

100. See Georges Bottereau, "Richeome," in M. Viler et al., eds., *Dictionnaire de Spiritualité, Ascétique et Mystique*, 17 vols. (Paris: G. Beauchesne, 1932–95), vol. 13 (1987), cols. 659–63.

101. See ibid., col. 660. Richeome also wrote several anti-Protestant tracts and letters, as well as defenses of the Society of Jesus.

102. See Peter Davidson, "The Jesuit Garden," in John W. O'Malley et al., eds., *The Jesuits II: Cultures, Sciences, and the Arts, 1540–1773* (Toronto: University of Toronto Press, 2006), 86–107; here, 91.

103. See ibid., 91.

104. See Bottereau, "Richeome," col. 662. See also Lewis [*sic*] Richeome, *The Pilgrime of Loreto: Performing His Vow Made to the Glorious Virgin Mary Mother of God*, translated by "E.W." (Paris, 1629; reprinted as vol. 285 of English Recusant Literature, 1558–1640; London: Scolar Press, 1976). I will cite this English translation.

105. See Stephane Van Damme, "Education, Sociability and Written Culture: The Case of the Society of Jesus in France" (Cornell University, Blumenthal Lecture, October 22, 2002), paragraph 20, accessed online at http://dossiersgrihl. revues.org/document on July 24, 2007.

106. See Bottereau, "Richeome," col. 660.

107. Richeome, *Pilgrime*, 1–169.

108. Ibid., 254–446.

109. Ibid., 6. Richeome also explains (ibid., 8) how Mary's house was transported "from Galilee into Sclauonia" in "the yeare 1291," and was thence removed "into Italy in the yeare 1294." This legend is not attested prior to the late fifteenth century, and its historicity is disputed by virtually all scholars today.

110. Richeome lists the fifteen mysteries in an appendix after his discussion of the fortieth day of the pilgrim's journey. Each mystery is presented with an "oblation" and prayer, in the style of the Ignatian *Exercises*. See *Pilgrime*, 449–54.

111. See Bottereau, "Richeome," col. 661; emphasis added.

112. Richeome, *Pilgrime*, 43. I have retained the orthography of the printed edition.

113. Ibid., 44, 47.

114. Ibid., 48.

115. Ibid., 49.

116. Ibid., 48–49.

117. Ibid., 50.

118. Ibid., 53.

119. Ibid., 53–54.

120. Ibid., 54. Richeome explains that the corona is "composed of fifty small beads stringed together, hauing betwixt euery ten a greater one, to distinguish the number, though commonly it hath 63 which is the number of the yeares of our B. Ladyes life. That which we call a Rosary is a triple Chaplet, or Corone, containing 150 beads, stringed, and distinguished after the same fashion" (ibid.). Note three things: the chaplet (corona) itself consists of fifty beads, though "commonly it hath 63," in remembrance of the number of years, according to popular legend, that Mary lived. An appendix at the end of *The Pilgrime of Loreto* begins: "THE CORONE OF B. LADY. The manner of saying the Corone of our B. Lady, consisting of 63 *Aues* & six *Pater noster* in remembrance of the 60 yeares of her life, euery *Pater noster* with the 10 *Aues* are to be sayd and offered in the honour and remembrance of 10 years of her life, and of what she did or suffered in that

272 Notes to Chapter 3

time, with a prayer eyther before or after crauing those graces and vertues, which most did shine in the actions of those yeares" (ibid., 454). For more on these forms of rosary/corona, see Herbert Thurston, "Our Popular Devotions: VI.–The So-Called Bridgettine Rosary," *The Month* 100 (1902): 189–203; Thurston, "The Name of the Rosary," *The Month* 111 (1908); 518; Thurston, "Genuflexions and Aves: A Study in Rosary Origins, Part I," *The Month* 127 (1916): 441–52; and Thurston, "Genuflexions and Aves: A Study in Rosary Origins, Part II," *The Month* 127 (1916): 546–59.

121. Richeome, *Pilgrime*, 54.

122. Ibid., 55.

123. Ibid., 54.

124. Ibid., 55.

125. Puglisi, *Caravaggio*, 276.

126. Richeome, *Pilgrime*, 55.

127. See Hilmar M. Pable, *Conversing with God: Prayer in Erasmus' Pastoral Writings* (Toronto: University of Toronto Press, 1997), 86–88.

128. See John W. O'Malley and Louis A. Perraud, eds., *Collected Works of Erasmus*, vol. 69, *Spiritualia and Pastoralia* (Toronto: University of Toronto Press, 1999). Each work in this volume has its own translator, to be identified when that work is actually cited.

129. See John W. O'Malley, "Introduction," to *Collected Works of Erasmus*, 69:xviii.

130. Ibid. See also Eamon Duffy, *Marking the Hours: English People and Their Prayers, 1240–1570* (New Haven: Yale University Press, 2006), especially 3–22.

131. O'Malley, "Introduction," 69:xviii.

132. Ibid.

133. See F. E. Brightman, "The Bidding of the Bedes," in *The English Rite*, 2 vols. (London: Rivingtons, 1915), 2:1020–45. The word "bede"—Middle English for "bead"—is related to the German verb *beten* (to pray). Later, "bede" was applied to the small spherical objects used for "telling [i.e., counting] the bedes" when praying the rosary or other form of repetitive prayer. To "bid a bede" thus meant to "offer a prayer."

134. Brightman, ibid., 2:1023, notes that originally "bidding the bedes" followed the sermon, but that in England and France "it came to be customary to use it before the sermon. In the English Sarum usage, moreover the bidding was "detached from the sermon altogether and recited under the rood [cross] during the procession."

135. During the Middle Ages, especially in English, French, and German churches, it became customary to include in the Sunday liturgy some vernacular prayers and instructions known as "Prone." Prone permitted greater congregational participation in the liturgy and responded directly to people's practical needs. See Gordon Jeanes, "Bidding Prayer," in Paul Bradshaw, ed., *The New*

Westminster Dictionary of Liturgy and Worship (Louisville: Westminster John Knox Press, 2002), 59–60. The term "Prone" is from the medieval French word for the grill that separated the chancel (or place where public notices were given) from the rest of the church building.

136. See Ulrich S. Leupold, ed., *Luther's Works*, Vol. 23, *Liturgy and Hymns* (Philadelphia: Fortress Press, 1965), "The German Mass and Order of Service, 1526," trans. Augustus Steimle, revised by Ulrich S. Leupold, 53–90; here, 64.

137. Ibid., 66.

138. O'Malley, "Introduction," 69:xviii–xix.

139. See ibid., 69:xix.

140. See Erasmus, "The Lord's Prayer," translated and annotated by John N. Grant, in *Collected Works of Erasmus*, 69:64.

141. See Erasmus, *Prayer of Supplication to Mary, the Virgin Mother, in Time of Trouble* (*Obsecratio ad Virginem Matrem Mariam in rebus adversis*), translated and annotated by John N. Grant, in *Collected Works of Erasmus*, 69:52.

142. Ibid.

143. See Erasmus, *Paean Virgini Matri dicendus* (*Paean in Honour of the Virgin Mother*), translated and annotated by Stephen Ryle, in *Collected Works of Erasmus*, 69:20–38. Significantly, Erasmus uses the Greek term Θεοτόκος (Mother of God) in this work; see Ryle's note 5, p. 21. The Akathist (Greek, ᾽ακάθιστος, "not sitting") hymn is a Greek liturgical composition of twenty-four stanzas in honor of the Virgin Mary, sung standing in the Orthodox Church on Saturday of the fifth week of Lent. The hymn is also used in private prayer and devotion.

144. See ibid., 69:25–31, passim. In relating Mary to the "golden age" and "Diana," Erasmus was appealing to images found in Virgil, Ovid, Catullus, and Horace. See Ryle's notes 24 and 25 on p. 25.

145. See *Virginis Matris apud Lauretum cultae liturgia* (*Liturgy of the Virgin Mother Venerated at Loreto*), translated and annotated by James J. Sheridan, with additional annotation by Erika Rummel and Stephen Ryle, *Collected Works of Erasmus,* 69:83–108.

146. Ibid., 86.

147. Ibid., 86 nn. 1 and 2.

148. Ibid., 86–87.

149. Richeome, *Pilgrime*, 55.

150. An example of Erasmus's humor occurs in his prefatory letter to the *Liturgy of Loreto*; see *Liturgy of the Virgin Mother Venerated at Loreto*, in *Collected Works of Erasmus*, 69:83.

151. See Richeome, *Pilgrime*, the "Epistle Dedicatory" by the English translator.

152. See Davidson, "Jesuit Garden," 93.

153. Richeome, *Pilgrime*, 55–56.

154. See Luke Dysinger, *Psalmody and Prayer in the Writings of Evagrius Ponticus*, Oxford Theological Monographs (New York: Oxford University Press, 2005), 50.

155. Ibid.

156. See Eligius Dekkers, "Were the Early Monks Liturgical?" *Collectanea Cisterciensia* 22 (1960): 120–37.

157. See Robert F. Taft, "Home Communion in the Late Antique East," in Clare V. Johnson, ed., *Ars Liturgiae: Worship, Aesthetics and Praxis. Essays in Honor of Nathan D. Mitchell* (Chicago: Liturgy Training Publications, 2003), 1–25; here, 4.

158. Ibid., 5.

159. See ibid., 7–13.

160. See *The Rule of Benedict*, chaps. 8–20 (for the daily office), in Timothy Fry et al., eds., *RB 1980: The Rule of St. Benedict in Latin and English with Notes* (Collegeville, MN: Liturgical Press, 1980), 202–17. In the *Rule*, the entire 150 psalms were spread over the period of a week, though Benedict was aware that ancient monastic practice required monks to recite the whole psalter each day. See Nathan D. Mitchell, "The Liturgical Code in the Rule of Benedict," ibid., 379–414, especially 410–12.

161. See Taft, "Home Communion," 7.

162. On early monastic Christological interpretations of the psalms, especially in the works of Evagrius Ponticus, see Dysinger, *Psalmody and Prayer*, 152–71.

163. Ibid., 51, 53.

164. Van Damme, "Education, Sociability and Written Culture," pars. 2–3.

165. Ibid., par. 3.

166. Richeome, *Pilgrime*, 172.

167. Ibid., 173–74.

168. For Trent's formula, see Henricus Denzinger and Adolfus Schönmetzer, eds., *Enchiridion Symbolorum*, Editio XXXIII, emendata et aucta (Rome: Herder, 1965), 389 n. 1651.

169. See Sodi and Triacca, *Breviarium Romanum editio princeps* (1568), 487 (of the modern edition; 457 of the 1568 edition). The phrases "substantialiter conuertuntur" (they [i.e., the bread and wine] are substantially converted) and "accidentia . . . sine subiecto" (accidents without a subject) appear in a sermon of Aquinas, used as the fifth reading at the office of vigils (matins). The texts of for the Mass of Corpus Christi in *MR* 1570 (including Aquinas's sequence *Lauda Sion*) avoid using the Aristotelian language of substance and accident. See Sodi and Triacca, *Missale Romanum editio princeps* (1570), 400 (of the modern edition, verso of xxiv in the 1570 edition).

170. Richeome, *Pilgrime*, 163.

171. See John Bossy, *Christianity in the West, 1400–1700* (New York: Oxford University Press, 1985), 57–75.

172. See John Bossy, "The Mass as a Social Institution 1200–1700," *Past and Present*, no. 100 (August 1983): 27–61; here, 58.

173. See ibid.

174. Ibid.

175. Ibid.

176. Ibid., 59.

NOTES TO CHAPTER 4

1. Readers may view Zuccari's Santa Sabina apse mosaic at www.romecity.it/Federicoetaddeozuccari.htm.

2. Readers may view Sassoferrato's painting at campus.udayton.edu/mary/poetry/october02.html.

3. See Eithne Wilkins, *The Rose-Garden Game: A Tradition of Beads and Flowers* (New York: Herder and Herder, 1969), 195. Wilkins is citing the opinion of Noële Maurice-Denis and Robert Boulet.

4. Ibid., 49.

5. See Jeffrey Chipps Smith, *Sensuous Worship: Jesuits and the Art of the Early Catholic Reformation in Germany* (Princeton: Princeton University Press, 2002), especially 35–40.

6. See Kristen B. Neuschel, *Word of Honor: Interpreting Noble Culture in Sixteenth-Century France* (Ithaca: Cornell University Press, 1989), 191–93.

7. Ibid., 193, 191.

8. Ibid., 192.

9. See Stephen Greenblatt, *Renaissance Self-Fashioning: From More to Shakespeare* (Chicago: University of Chicago Press, 1980), 74–114.

10. See Elizabeth Eisenstein, *The Printing Press as an Agent of Change: Communications and Cultural Transformations in Early-Modern Europe*, 2 vols. (New York: Cambridge University Press, 1979), 1:74.

11. Ibid.

12. Ibid., 1:74–75.

13. Ibid., 1:230.

14. See Philippe D'Outreman, *The True Christian Catholique* (1622), trans. John Heigham, English Recusant Literature, 1558–1640, vol. 217 (London: Scolar Press, 1974). I have retrained the English orthography of D'Outreman's (translated) treatise.

15. See James J. O'Donnell, *Augustine: A New Biography* (New York: Ecco/Harper Collins, 2005), 331–32.

16. See D'Outreman, *True Christian Catholique*, 21–22.

17. Ibid., 22.

18. Ibid., 23.

19. Ibid., 24–25.

20. Ibid., 25.

21. Ibid., 19. See also Michel de Montaigne, *The Complete Essays*, trans. M. A. Screech (New York: Penguin Books, 1991), 711.

22. See Eisenstein, *Printing Press as an Agent of Change*, 1:231.

23. See John Bossy, *Christianity in the West, 1400–1700* (New York: Oxford University Press, 1985), 127.

24. See John Bossy, "The Social History of Confession in the Age of the Reformation," *Transactions of the Royal Historical Society*, 5th ser., 25 (1975): 21–38; here, 21; emphasis added.

25. See Jean Delumeau, *Catholicism between Luther and Voltaire: A New View of the Counter-Reformation*, trans. Jeremy Moiser (Philadelphia: Westminster Press, 1977), 166–70.

26. Ibid., 166–67.

27. Ibid., 168.

28. Ibid.

29. Eisenstein, *Printing Press as an Agent of Change*, 1:375 (and n. 248 at the bottom of that page).

30. Ibid.

31. Ibid., 303.

32. Anne Winston-Allen, *Stories of the Rose: The Making of the Rosary in the Middle Ages* (University Park: Pennsylvania State University Press, 1997), 33.

33. Readers may view an image of this painting online at www.wga.hu.

34. Beginning at the bottom, center, of the frame, one may see the following ten scenes: Christ's agony in the garden, his apprehension, his arraignment before Pilate, his flagellation, his carrying the cross, his crucifixion (at the top, center, of the frame), his being taken down from the cross, his burial, the harrowing of hell, and his resurrection.

35. See Erwin Panofsky, *Early Netherlandish Painting*, 2 vols. (Cambridge: Harvard University Press, 1953), 1:203.

36. See Edwin Hall, *The Arnolfini Betrothal: Medieval Marriage and the Enigma of van Eyck's Double Portrait* (Berkeley: University of California Press, 1994), 119. See also Craig Harbison, *Jan van Eyck: The Play of Realism* (London: Reaktion Books, 1991), 79.

37. Hall, *Arnolfini Betrothal*, 119.

38. Ibid. An older mirror image for Mary is the phrase *speculum iustitiae* (mirror of justice), used in the Litany of Loreto, approved for use in public worship by Pope Sixtus V in 1587.

39. Harbison, *Jan van Eyck*, 79.

40. Neuschel, *Word of Honor*, 192.

41. David Aers, "Altars of Power: Reflections on Eamon Duffy's *The Stripping of the Altars: Traditional Religion in England 1400–1580*," *Literature and History*, 3rd ser., 3 (1994): 90–105; here 94.

42. See Louis Chatellier, *The Religion of the Poor*, trans. Brian Pearce (New York: Cambridge University Press, 1997), especially pt. 2, chap. 12, 220–33.

43. See ibid., 220. See also Adolf Adam, *The Liturgical Year: Its History and Its Meaning after the Reform of the Liturgy* (New York: Pueblo, 1981), 174–77.

44. See Chatellier, *Religion of the Poor*, 220–21; Adam, *Liturgical Year*, 174–75.

45. Chatellier, *Religion of the Poor*, 220–21.

46. See Karl Rahner, *Theological Investigations*, vol. 3, trans. Karl-H. Kruger and Boniface Kruger (Baltimore: Helicon Press, 1967), 321–30.

47. Ibid., 322.

48. Ibid., 326–27.

49. See *Enchiridion indulgentiarum: Preces et pia opera* (Vatican City: Vatican Polyglot Press, 1950), 163–65 n. 256. This handbook is a collection of prayers, devotions, and good works for which popes over the centuries have granted indulgences. All such prayers (and the indulgences attached to them) were reviewed, revised, and reformed following the Second Vatican Council. On indulgences and their relation to penance as understood in Catholic tradition, see Karl Rahner and Herbert Vorgrimler, *Theological Dictionary*, trans. Richard Strachan; ed. Cornelius Ernst (New York: Herder and Herder, 1965), 227.

50. For the Latin text, see *Enchiridion indulgentiarum*, 164 n. 256; my translation.

51. See Karl Rahner, "Some Theses for a Theology of Devotion to the Sacred Heart," in *Theological Investigations*, 3:331–52; here, 346.

52. Ibid., 346.

53. Ibid.

54. See Chatellier, *Religion of the Poor*, 220–24.

55. Ibid., 220.

56. See Louis Ponnelle and Louis Bordet, *St. Philip Neri and the Roman Society of His Times (1515–1595)*, trans. Ralph Francis Kerr (London: Sheed and Ward, 1932), 202–3.

57. See Chatellier, *Religion of the Poor*, 201.

58. Ibid.

59. Ibid.

60. Hilmar M. Pabel, "Humanism and Early Modern Catholicism: Erasmus of Rotterdam's *Ars Moriendi*," in Kathleen M. Comerford and Hilmar M Pabel, eds., *Early Modern Catholicism: Essays in Honour of John W. O'Malley, S.J.* (Toronto: University of Toronto Press, 2001), 26–45; here, 29.

61. See John W. O'Malley, "Erasmus and Vatican II: Interpreting the Council," in A. Melloni et al., eds., *Cristianesimo nella storia: Saggi in onore di Giuseppe Alberigo* (Bologna: Società Editrice il Mulino, 1996), 195–211; here, 202–3. See also Pabel, "Humanism and Early Modern Catholicism," 39.

62. See Louis Chatellier, *The Religion of the Devout: The Catholic Reformation and the Formation of a New Society*, trans. Jean Birrell (New York: Cambridge University Press, 1989), 239–52.

63. On these "new practices," see especially ibid., 204–10.

64. See ibid., 209. These Marian Pacts may have been fostered by older Marian congregations that had declined with the early modern development of new religious confraternities of men and women whose focus was on other practices (e.g., the reception of Holy Communion; preparation for a good death; meditation on the passion and wounds of Christ). See ibid., 204–6.

65. Ibid., 209–10.

66. Ibid., 240.

67. See ibid., 252.

68. Ibid., 253.

69. See Neuschel, *Word of Honor*, 191–92.

70. See Chatellier, *Religion of the Devout*, 253; emphasis added.

71. See John W. O'Malley et al., eds., *The Jesuits II: Cultures, Sciences, and the Arts, 1540–1773* (Toronto: University of Toronto Press, 2006).

72. Chatellier, *Religion of the Devout*, 253.

73. See the decree of the Second Vatican Council on the apostolate of laypeople (*Apostolicam actuositatem*; November 18, 1965), in Austin Flannery, ed., *Vatican Council II: The Conciliar and Post Conciliar Documents* (Collegeville, MN: Liturgical Press, 1975), 766–98.

74. See Chatellier, *Religion of the Devout*, 254.

75. See Talal Asad, *Genealogies of Religion: Disciplines and Reasons of Power in Christianity and Islam* (Baltimore: Johns Hopkins University Press, 1993), 78.

76. See Chatellier, *Religion of the Devout*, 255.

77. See ibid., 255.

78. For a short synopsis of how this doctrine developed, see Frederick M. Jelly, "Immaculate Conception," in Joseph A. Komonchak, Mary Collins, and Dermot A. Lane, eds., *The New Dictionary of Theology* (Wilmington, DE: Michael Glazier, 1987), 508–10. The Immaculate Conception was not solemnly defined as a Catholic dogma until Pope Pius IX did so on December 8, 1854. For fuller analysis of the theological significance of this doctrine for Catholics, see Karl Rahner, "The Immaculate Conception," in *Theological Investigations*, vol. 1, trans. Cornelius Ernst (London: Darton, Longman and Todd, 1961), 201–13. As Rahner points out, this dogma does not say that Mary had no need of the grace made available to the world through Christ's victory over sin and death in the events of

his passion and resurrection. Like the rest of humankind, Mary is redeemed and enfolded by the grace of Christ (ibid., 213).

79. See *Summa Theologiae*, IIIa Pars, Q. 27, art. 2, ad 2um.

80. See David M. Petras, "Mary in Eastern Liturgical Tradition," *Liturgical Ministry* 6 (Winter 1997): 11–20; here, 17. The East celebrated the Conception of Mary by Saint Anne on December 9, nine months before the date of the feast of the Birthday of Mary, September 8.

81. Adam, *Liturgical Year*, 213. For more details, see S. J. P. van Dijk, "The Origin of the Latin Feast of the Conception of the Blessed Virgin Mary," *Dublin Review* 228 (1954): 251–67, 428–42.

82. See van Dijk, "Origin of the Latin Feast," 441.

83. See Harbison, *Jan van Eyck*, 79.

84. Ibid., 85.

85. Ibid., 80, 85. For an image of the *Lucca Madonna*, painted ca. 1436, see www.wga.hu.

86. See Neuschel, *Word of Honor*, 202. On Mary of Ágreda, see T. D. Kendrick, *Mary of Agreda: The Life and Legend of a Spanish Nun* (London: Routledge and Kegan Paul, 1967), 94–154.

87. In addition to Kendrick (*Mary of Agreda*), see T. J. Campbell, "Maria de Agreda," in *The Catholic Encyclopedia*, 16 vols. (New York: Appleton, 1913), 1:229–30. See also Joseph Cardinal Hergenröther, *Handbuch der allgemeinen Kirchengeschichte*, ed. J. P. Kirsch, 5th ed., revised; 4 vols. (Freiburg im Breisgau: Herder, 1917), 4:100–103.

88. For the publication history of Mary's works, including *The Mystical City of God*, see Kendrick, *Mary of Agreda*, 159–65.

89. See Hergenröther, *Handbuch der allgemeinen Kirchengeschichte*, 4:103; my translation.

90. Kendrick, *Mary of Agreda*, 81.

91. Ibid.

92. See Henricus Denziger and Adolfus Schönmetzer, eds., *Enchiridion Symbolorum*, Editio XXXIII emendata et aucta (Rome: Herder, 1965), n. 1516. The council referred back to Pope Sixtus IV, whose decree *Cum praeexcelsa* (1477) had affirmed Mary's "wondrous immaculate conception," and whose later constitution *Grave nimis* (1483) approved public solemn liturgical celebrations of Mary's conception. See ibid., nn. 1400, 1425. See also the brief of Pope Alexander VII, "Sollicitudo omnium ecclesiarum" (Solicitude for all the Churches; published in 1661), which reaffirms the propriety of the doctrine of the Immaculate Conception and the Roman Church's celebration of the Feast of the Conception of Mary on December 8 (ibid., nn. 2015–2017).

93. The Missal of 1570 avoided the adjective "immaculate" in reference to Mary's conception. Its rubric for December 8 reads: "In conceptione B. Marie

dicitur Missa de eius Natuitate, que habetur mense Septembris, mutato nomine Natiuitatis in Conceptionem (On the [feast of the] conception of Blessed Mary is said that Mass of her Nativity, which is found in the month of September; the word "Nativity" in those texts is changed to "Conception"). Latin text in Manlio Sodi and Achille Maria Triacca, eds., *Missale Romanum editio princeps* (1570), Monumenta Liturgica Concilii Tridentini (Vatican City: Libreria Vaticana Editrice, 1998), 450 (of the modern edition; p. 6 of the "Proprium Missarum de Sanctis" section of the 1570 edition).

94. See Kendrick, *Mary of Agreda*, 85 (facing page) for a photograph of the title page of the edition published at Madrid in 1670.

95. On the introduction of the theme of the Immaculate Conception into Catholic art before and after Trent, see Rosemary Muir Wright, *Sacred Distance: Representing the Virgin* (New York: Manchester University Press, 2006), ix–xiv, 1–21.

96. See ibid., ix. Muir Wright notes that "the Virgin of the Immaculate Conception" had been "popularized throughout Spain since the early fifteenth century." The diffusion of this image, at least in Spain, happened in tandem with the spread of the rosary as a popular devotion.

97. On the circumstances surrounding Reni's painting, see Muir Wright, *Sacred Distance*, xi. On the establishment of the monastery in which Mary and her mother, Catalina, became novices in January 1619, see Kendrick, *Mary of Agreda*, 7–11. The Conceptionists were a strict branch of Franciscan nuns ("Poor Clares") devoted to promoting the doctrine of the Immaculate Conception. Readers may view an image of Reni's painting online at Google Images. See further Howard Hibbard, "Guido Reni's Painting of the Immaculate Conception," *Metropolitan Museum of Art Bulletin*, n.s., 28:1 (Summer 1969): 19–32.

98. Howard Hibbard notes how earlier painters of the Counter-Reformation era struggled with the best way to depict the Immaculate Conception. The artist-historian Giorgio Vasari recorded his own difficulties dealing with the subject in 1540. See Vasari's text and an image of his painting in Hibbard, "Guido Reni's Painting," 24–25. Vasari, like Reni, invoked the imagery of Revelation 12.1, and the result was "explicit in its theological complexity but . . . confusing as an image" (ibid., 25).

99. See Muir Wright, *Sacred Distance*, xi.

100. See Stanley Gahan, "'The Woman Clothed with the Sun' According to St. Lawrence of Brindisi," *American Ecclesiastical Review* 147 (1962): 395–402. The Capuchins were a strict branch of the Franciscan friars. Lawrence of Brindisi became their vicar general in 1602, the year of Mary of Ágreda's birth, and died in 1619, the year Mary and her mother entered the Conceptionist Franciscan monastery as novices.

101. Cited in Gahan, "'The Woman Clothed with the Sun,'". 399. The quotation is from Lawrence's sermon "On the Nobility of the Virgin Mother of God," translated by Eliot Timlin.

102. Cited in ibid., 400. The quotation is from Lawrence's sermon "The Exaltation of the Virgin Mother of God above Every Creature," translated by Vernon Wagner.

103. See Muir Wright, *Sacred Distance*, xi.

104. Ibid., 18.

105. Ibid., 17.

106. Ibid., 17–18.

107. Hibbard, "Guido Reni's Painting," 19, points out that Reni's own style had been influenced by Caravaggio after he went to Rome, ca. 1599, but that he was "also attracted by antique works and their High Renaissance counterparts."

108. See ibid., xi.

109. Kendrick, *Mary of Agreda*, 82.

110. See Sister Mary of Jesus, *Mystical City of God*, trans. Fiscar Marison (George J. Blatter), 2 vols. (Chicago: Theopolitan, 1902), 1:27. "Presently I saw a most precious veil covering a treasure and my heart burned with desire to see it. . . . Presently the veil fell entirely and my interior eyes saw what I shall not know how to describe in words. I saw a great and mysterious sign in heaven; I saw a Woman, a most beautiful Lady and Queen, crowned with the stars, clothed with the sun, and the moon was at her feet." Hereafter, this work will be cited as *MCG*, followed by volume number and page reference. Chapters 8, 9, and 10 of book 1 offer fuller explanations of Revelation 12.

111. *MCG*, 1:1. Mary mentions, too, that she began revision of *MCG* "on the eighth of December, 1655, on the day of the Immaculate Conception" (ibid., 1:21).

112. Kendrick, *Mary of Agreda*, 85.

113. Sor María explicitly mentions the plan and structure of *MCG* in her introduction to book 1; see *MCG*, 1:19.

114. Kendrick, *Mary of Agreda*, 82.

115. On the history of this work, see I. Backus, "Guillaume Postel, Théodore Bibliander et le 'Protévangile de Jacques,'" *Apocrypha* 6 (1995): 7–65.

116. See, for example, the altarpiece of Saints Joachim and Anne embracing at the Golden Gate outside the walls of Jerusalem. (painted ca. 1500, by the Master of Moulins, Jean Hey) at www.wga.hu.

117. See Kendrick, *Mary of Agreda*, 82–83.

118. See Mary of Agreda, *City of God: The Divine History and Life of the Virgin Mother of God*, trans. Fiscar Marison (George J. Blatter), 3rd ed., abridged (Albuquerque: Corcoran, 1949), 474. This abridged version of *MCG* is the one most commonly available to English readers; it omits many of the repetitions found in the original. Hereafter, this version will be cited as *CG*, followed by page number.

119. *CG* (bk. 6, chap. 2), 483. In this same portion of *CG*, Mary of Ágreda "transcribes" a lengthy prayer the Virgin Mary said to her Son after hearing him predict his impending passion and death. See ibid., 480–81.

120. See *The Life of the Virgin Mary, the Theotokos* (Buena Vista, CO: Holy Apostles Convent/Dormition Skete, 1989), 212. The text is taken from Ephrem's tenth hymn on the Nativity, translated by J. B. Morris in *Nicene and Post-Nicene Fathers of the Christian Church*, 2nd ser., 14 vols. (reprint; Grand Rapids, MI: Eerdmans, 1976), 13:244.

121. See *Life of the Virgin Mary, the Theotokos*, 212; the translation of Ephrem's hymn is from *The Harp of the Spirit*, trans. Sebastian Brock (London: Fellowship of Saints Alban and Sergius, 1975), 68.

122. See *The Life of the Virgin Mary, the Theotokos*, 216; the translation is taken from Romanos's "On the Nativity (Mary and the Magi)", in Marjorie Carpenter, trans., *Kontakia of Romanos, Byzantine Melodist*, 2 vols. (Columbia: University of Missouri Press, 1970), 1:11.

123. See Kendrick, *Mary of Agreda*, 86.

124. See *MCG*, 1:174–75: "In this Conception [of Mary by Anne], although the father [Joachim] was not naturally sterile, yet on account of his age and moderation, his natural powers were in a measure suppressed and weakened; and therefore he was enlivened, restored and enabled to act on his part with entire perfection and with the plenitude of his faculties, proportionately to the sterility of the mother." See also *CG*, 246 (on Mary's visit to Elizabeth): "The fortunate child [John the Baptist], looking through the walls of the maternal womb as through clear glass upon the incarnate Word, and assuming a kneeling posture, adored his Redeemer and Creator, whom he beheld in most holy Mary as if enclosed in a chamber made of the purest crystal."

125. Another example of Sor María's tendency to give readers what her contemporaries perceived as "too much information" about body parts and fluids is her description of Jesus' circumcision. The Virgin Mary is portrayed as requesting Joseph to "procure a crystal or glass vessel for preserving the sacred relic of the Circumcision of the divine Infant," and as carefully catching the "sacred blood" in "some linen cloths." See *CG*, 325.

126. *MCG*, "Introduction," 1:15.

127. Ibid.; emphasis added. In the Clementine Vulgate text of the Bible (published 1592), the text to which Mary alludes is Joel 2.28–29. "Et erit post hæc: effundam spiritum meum super omnem carnem, et prophetabunt filii vestri et filiæ vestrae: senes vestri somnia somniabunt, et juvenes vestri visiones videbunt. Sed et super servos meos et ancillas in diebus illis effundam spiritum meum." This is probably the Latin Bible Mary would have known. In modern Bibles, the second chapter of Joel ends at verse 27. What Mary alludes to is now Joel 3.1–2.

128. See *MCG*, 1:21, where Mary acknowledge that she began "rewriting this history on the eighth of December, 1655."

129. Ibid., 1:15.

130. Ibid., 1:17.

131. See Kendrick, *Mary of Agreda*, 81–82.

132. Neuschel, *Word of Honor*, 194.

133. See Greenblatt, *Renaissance Self-Fashioning*, 1.

134. Ibid.

135. See Dom Gaspar Gorricio de Novara, *Contemplaciones sobre el Rosario de Nuestra Senora Historiadas. Un incunable Sevillano*, ed. and trans. Santiago Cantera Montenegro and Almudena Torrego Casado, Analecta Cartusiana, 195 (Salzburg: Institut für Anglistik und Amerikanistik, Universität Salzburg, 2002).

136. Ibid., 37 (historical introduction written by Santiago Cantera Montenegro).

137. See Kendrick, *Mary of Agreda*, image reproduced facing p. 84.

138. See Dom Gaspar Gorricio de Novara, *Contemplaciones*, 172.

139. See *MCG*, 2:506–15 (bk. 2, chap. 20).

140. Ibid., 510.

141. Kendrick, *Mary of Agreda*, 83.

142. On this point, see Neuschel, *Word of Honor*, 194–95.

143. George E. Ganns, ed., *Ignatius of Loyola: Spiritual Exercises and Selected Works*, Classics of Western Spirituality (New York: Paulist Press, 1991), 141.

144. See Catherine Puglisi, *Caravaggio* (London: Phaidon, 1998), 248–49.

145. See *MCG*, 2:449.

146. See ibid., 2:448–50; *CG*, 324–25.

147. On Renaissance and early modern attention to the sexuality of Christ in religious paintings and preaching, see Leo Steinberg, *The Sexuality of Christ in Renaissance Art and Modern Oblivion*, 2nd ed., rev. and expanded (Chicago: University of Chicago Press, 1996), especially the "Postscript" by John W. O'Malley, 213–16.

148. On these themes in Caravaggio, see Puglisi, *Caravaggio*, 251; in Mary of Ágreda, see *MCG*, 1:23–34, 41–42.

149. Bert Treffers, "The Arts and Craft of Sainthood: New Orders, New Saints, New Altarpieces," in Beverly Louise Brown, ed., *The Genius of Rome, 1592–1623* (London: Royal Academy of Arts, 2001), 340–71; here, 347.

150. Ibid.

151. Ibid.

152. See Richard P. McBrien, *Lives of the Popes: The Pontiffs from St. Peter to John Paul II* (San Francisco: HarperCollins, 1997), 293. See also Bert Treffers, "Il Francesco Hartford del Caravaggio e la Spiritualità Francescana alla fine del XVI. Sec.," *Mitteilungen des kunsthistorischen Instituts in Florenz* 32 (1988): 145–72; here, 154–55.

153. *The Works of Bonaventure*, vol. 1, *Mystical Opuscula*, trans. José de Vinck, 5 vols. (Paterson, NJ: St. Anthony Guild Press, 1960), 1:58 (chap. VII.6). For the Latin text of this passage (based on the Quarcchi edition), see Leon Amoros et al., eds., *Obras de San Buenaventura*, 2 vols. (Madrid: Biblioteca de Autores Cristianos, 1955), 1:632.

154. See Treffers, "Arts and Craft of Sainthood," 347–48. For an image of *Francis in Ecstasy*, see www.wga.hu. The original is at the Wadsworth Atheneum in Hartford.

155. Treffers, "Arts and Craft of Sainthood," 347.

156. See Puglisi, *Caravaggio*, 124.

157. Treffers, "Arts and Craft of Sainthood," 348.

158. Ibid.

159. *MCG*, 2:203.

160. Ibid., 2:204

161. Ibid., 2:205.

162. Treffers, "Arts and Craft of Sainthood," 351.

163. Ibid., 350.

164. Ibid.

165. Ibid.

166. See *MCG*, 2:162–71.

167. Treffers, "Arts and Craft of Sainthood," 353.

168. Treffers, ibid., notes that "Franciscan affective spirituality appears to have been important for St. Filippo Neri" as well. Thus, it is not illogical or unfounded to see both Franciscan mysticism and the "Christian optimism" of the Oratorian orbit at work in Catholic painters like Caravaggio. See further, ibid., 354–55.

169. Neuschel, *Word of Honor*, 194.

170. See Norbert Elias, *The Civilizing Process: Sociogenetic and Psychogenetic Investigations*, trans. Edmund Jephcott, with corrections by the author, rev. ed. (Oxford: Blackwell, 2000), 60–72.

171. See Patrick H. Hutton, "The History of Mentalities: The New Map of Cultural History," *History and Theory* 20 (October, 1981): 237–59.

172. Text cited in Elias, *Civilizing Process*, 122.

173. Ibid.

174. Ibid., 124; Elias is citing a 1672 edition of Antoine de Courtin's *Nouveau traité de civilité*.

175. Ibid., 71. Elias comments that people in Western Europe at this time "stood on a bridge," because "behaviour and the code of behaviour were in motion, but the movement was quite slow."

176. See Greenblatt, *Renaissance Self-Fashioning*, 11–73.

177. See ibid., 47.

178. Ibid.

179. Ibid.

180. Ibid., 31.

181. See ibid., 57. Greenblatt observes that More's writing of *Utopia* was also novelistic; its unity as a work depends "upon its effacement of the hand of the author so as to permit his reintroduction as a fictional character."

182. Neuschel, *Word of Honor*, 194.

183. Ibid., 192.

184. David Warren Sabean, *Power in the Blood: Popular Culture and Village Discourse in Early Modern Germany* (New York: Cambridge University Press, 1984), 53.

185. Ibid.

186. Ibid., 39.

187. Neuschel, *Word of Honor*, 192.

188. See ibid., 193.

189. Greenblatt, *Renaissance Self-Fashioning*, 155–56.

190. Ibid., 156.

191. Ibid.

192. See John T. McNeill and Helena M. Gamer, eds., *Medieval Handbooks of Penance*, Records of Civilization., Sources and Studies, 29 (New York: Columbia University Press, 1938), 315.

193. Ibid.

194. Ibid.

195. Ibid.

196. Ibid.

197. See Greenblatt, *Renaissance Self-Fashioning*, 118.

198. The seven penitential psalms were numbers 6, 32, 38, 51, 102, 130, and 142 (Hebrew numbering; 6, 31, 37, 50, 101, 129, and 142 in the Latin Vulgate numbering).

199. See Bossy, "Social History of Confession in the Age of the Reformation," 37–38. This social universe was still present in early modernity, but its significance was altered. As Greenblatt observes, the penitent's *contrition*, rather than public acts of disclosure and penance, becomes, after Trent, "the central part of the sacrament of penance" (*Renaissance Self-Fashioning*, 118).

200. See John Bossy, "The Counter-Reformation and the People of Catholic Europe," *Past and Present*, no. 47 (May 1970): 51–70; here, 52. This code of religious practice included Sunday Mass; reception of the sacraments (except confirmation) from the hands of the parish priest, "who would baptize, marry, give extreme unction, and bury" each parish member; and at least an annual reception of the Eucharist and the sacrament of penance.

201. See ibid., 58–60.

202. Ibid., 62.

NOTES TO CHAPTER 5

1. Peter M. Lukehart, "Foreword," in Claire Richter Sherman, *Writing on Hands: Memory and Knowledge in Early Modern Europe* (Carlisle, PA: Trout Gallery/Dickinson College, distributed by University of Washington Press, 2001), 7.

2. Martin Kemp. "The Handy Worke of the Incomprehensible Creator," in Richter Sherman, *Writing on Hands*, 22.

3. See Richter Sherman, *Writing on Hands*, 246–47. See also Eamon Duffy, *Marking the Hours: English People and Their Prayers, 1240–1570* (New Haven: Yale University Press, 2006), 6–22.

4. See Michael A. Mullett, *Catholics in Britain and Ireland, 1558–1829*, Social History in Perspective (New York: St. Martin's Press, 1998), 6.

5. Ibid., 7. The Carthusians are a monastic order founded by Saint Bruno (d. 1101) in the late eleventh century. Members of the community live a quasi-solitary life, though they gather for prayer and meals with other monks from time to time. The *devotio moderna* and *Imitation of Christ* have been mentioned earlier in this book.

6. Ibid. The Corpus Christi dramas were plays or pageants held each year on the Feast of Corpus Christ, a celebration first approved in 1264, and kept on the Thursday after Trinity Sunday. The Elizabethan Settlement was Elizabeth I's response to the religious divisions that had arisen in England after the reigns of Edward VI and Mary I. It confirmed the English Church's independence from Rome and established the Book of Common Prayer (originally published in 1549) as its official liturgy. Technically, the settlement comprised two acts: the Act of Supremacy (making the English monarch "supreme governor" of the church in England) and the Act of Uniformity, which replaced the Roman Rite with the liturgy of the Book of Common Prayer.

7. See J. H. Crehan, "Shakespeare and the Sarum Ritual," *The Month*, n.s., 32 (1964): 47–50. Crehan notes the presence of almost verbatim allusions to the prayers used in the late medieval Sarum Rite (one of several local usages in England) in *Midsummer Night's Dream* (possibly produced for the first time ca. 1595).

8. Lisa McClain, "Using What's at Hand: English Catholic Reinterpretations of the Rosary, 1559–1642," *Journal of Religious History* 27:2 (June 2003): 161–76; here, 161.

9. Ibid., 161.

10. See Lisa McClain, "Without Church, Cathedral, or Shrine: The Search for Religious Space among Catholics in England, 1559–1625," *Sixteenth Century Journal* 33:2 (2002): 381–99; here, 381–82. The phrase "Old Religion" refers to an English Catholicism whose identity was shaped less by "doctrinal affirmation or dramas of conscience" than by "a set of ingrained observances which defined and gave meaning to the cycle of the week and the seasons of the year, to birth, marriage and death." See John Bossy, "The Character of Elizabethan Catholicism," *Past and Present* 21 (April 1962): 35–59; here 39.

11. Ibid., 176. McClain notes, "We cannot prove that English Catholics widely accepted" reinterpretations or reconceptualizations of familiar prayers and devotions, though the "continued popularity of the rosary provides an important indicator that it was perceived as satisfying a necessary function, so much so

that English Catholics went to great lengths to transport rosaries, hide them, distribute them, smuggle them, even craft them with their own hands in order to obtain them" (ibid., 165).

12. See ibid., 176. It was common in medieval Catholic theology to speak of "sacraments of desire," by which Christians, unable to participate in the sacramental rite, could obtain its benefits through a spiritual act of desire alone. Aquinas, for example, speaks of the benefits of making an internal, "spiritual communion," even when one cannot be present at Mass, since "one may receive the effect of a sacrament through desire (*in voto*), even if he or she is unable to receive [the consecrated bread and wine] in fact" (*Summa Theologiae*, IIIa Pars, Q. 80, art. 1, ad 3um). On spiritual communion among English Catholics in this period, see, further, Lisa McClain, *Lest We Be Damned: Practical Innovation and Lived Experience among Catholics in Protestant England, 1559–1642*, Religion in History, Society, and Culture (New York: Routledge, 2004), 94–95, 117–21.

13. See McClain, "Using What's at Hand," 164.

14. See John Bucke, *Instructions for the Use of the Beades*, English Recusant Literature, 1558–1640, vol. 77 (Menston, UK: Scolar Press, 1971), 13, 84.

15. McClain, *Lest We Be Damned*, 88. The initial quotation in this sentence is from Bucke, *Instructions for the Use of the Beades*, 4.

16. Elizabeth preferred the title "supreme governor" to "supreme head" of the Church in England, because she exercised her authority through a predominantly lay commission. See David Loades, *Revolution in Religion: The English Reformation 1530–1570*, The Past in Perspective (Cardiff: University of Wales Press, 1992), 88.

17. Mullett, *Catholics in Britain and Ireland*, 9.

18. Ibid., 66.

19. Ibid., 115. Mullett notes that Catholicism in Scotland had been "strongly anchored in the Rosary" and that in the post-Reformation situation, rosaries, "light, portable, inexpensive and concealable," were widely used in the effort to keep the Old Religion alive during the seventeenth and eighteenth centuries.

20. Christopher Haigh, "The Continuity of Catholicism in the English Reformation," *Past and Present* 93 (1981): 37–69; here, 39.

21. Ibid.

22. Loades, *Revolution in Religion*, 53.

23. See Conrad Swan, "The Question of Dissimulation among Elizabethan Catholics," *Canadian Catholic Historical Association Report* 24 (1957): 105–19; accessed online, http://www.umanitoba.ca/colleges/st_pauls/ccha/Back%20Issues/CCHA1957/Swan.htm, November 1, 2007; p. 1 (of 15).

24. McClain, *Lest We Be Damned*, 20.

25. Loades, *Revolution in Religion*, 53, 54. Swan, "Question of Dissimulation," 1, writes: "The [Elizabethan] Settlement was *sui generis* as far as the Reformation as a whole was concerned; and the final break from Rome was . . . rather more

governmental, parliamentary, and political than national, spiritual, and spontane-ous." The term "recusancy" refers to the statutory offense of not complying with the state religion established by the 1559 Settlement.

26. See Bossy, "Character of Elizabethan Catholicism," 39. "Seigneurial Ca-tholicism" refers to the old faith as practiced by wealthier, propertied English men and women.

27. Ibid., 40.

28. See ibid. Bossy notes that composer William Byrd's masses for three, four, and five voices may originally have been performed in such a context. See fur-ther Kerry McCarthy, *Liturgy and Contemplation in Byrd's Gradualia* (New York: Routledge, 2007), 71–110 ("Liturgical Practice and English Catholic Identity").

29. Ibid.

30. Ibid., 41.

31. Ibid.

32. A list prepared for Pope Pius V near the end of 1567 divided the English nobility into three classes: "Catholics," those "favorable to Catholics," and "Prot-estants." The first group ("Catholics") is the largest (thirty-one names), and the first two together far outnumber the fifteen persons listed as Protestants loyal to both the queen and her 1559 Settlement. See Martin Haile, *An Elizabethan Cardi-nal William Allen* (St. Louis: B. Herder, 1914), "Appendix D," 366–67.

33. Loades, *Revolution in Religion*, document IV, iii, 109–10; here, 110.

34. See Mullett, *Catholics in Britain and Ireland*, 8.

35. Ibid.

36. Ibid., 8–9.

37. See ibid., 44.

38. See Bossy, "Character of Elizabethan Catholicism," 43.

39. See ibid., 44–50.

40. See Haile, *Elizabethan Cardinal*, 28–29.

41. See Bossy, "Character of Elizabethan Catholicism," 44. See also Bossy's *The English Catholic Community, 1570–1850* (New York: Oxford University Press, 1976), 12–13.

42. See G. P. Rice, *The Public Speaking of Queen Elizabeth* (New York: Columbia University Press, 1957), 130. The speech, intended for mass distribution and entitled by the editor, "The 'State of the Nation,' 1569," was probably written jointly by Eliza-beth, William Cecil (Lord Burghley), and other influential advisers (ibid., 125).

43. Swan, "Question of Dissimulation among Elizabethan Catholics," 2 (as accessed online). It is possible than some English Catholics who were not op-posed to a vernacular liturgy believed that the pope himself might be willing to recognize the rites of the Book of Common Prayer if Elizabeth were to acknowl-edge his pastoral supremacy over the church. Catholic nonconformity could take either of two forms: *recusants* were Catholics who refused either to attend the services of the Established Church, or to take the Oath of Supremacy, or both;

schismatics ("church-papists") were those who, though Catholic in mind and heart, dissembled and "conformed externally to the legal requirements of attendance at the State Church" (see ibid., 3).

44. The text is found in Haile, *Elizabethan Cardinal*, "Appendix E," 367.

45. See ibid., 101–2.

46. See ibid., 102–3. Thomas Percy, the Earl of Northumberland, was beheaded on August 22, 1572; 300 years later, he was beatified by Pope Leo XIII.

47. See ibid., 100. See also Richard P. McBrien, *Lives of the Popes: The Pontiffs from St. Peter to John Paul II* (San Francisco: HarperCollins, 1997), 280.

48. See Haile, *Elizabethan Cardinal*, 100.

49. Most of the "upper-class" English Catholics, who had not participated in the Northern Rebellion, did not want the papal bull of excommunication to be published. Likewise, the kings of Spain and France refused to allow its publication in any of their dominions, "no one wishing to provoke Elizabeth to enmity" (ibid., 104).

50. See ibid., 105. Felton's wife had been maid of honor to Queen Mary, who, on her deathbed, recommended Lady Felton to Elizabeth. Elizabeth, in turn, "had a great regard for her [Lady Felton], as they had been playmates in childhood, and had given her a special license to keep a priest in her house as long as she lived" (ibid., 105 n. 1).

51. See ibid., 105–6, for the citation from Philip II's letter to Gueran de Spes. Later, Pope Urban VIII (d. 1644) echoed Philip II's doubts about the wisdom of Pius V's course of action. "Wisdom," wrote Urban, "does not teach us to imitate Pius V, or Clement VII, but Paul V who . . . being many times urged by the Spaniards to excommunicate James [I] King of England, never would consent to it" (ibid., 106).

52. Ibid., 106.

53. Swan, "Question of Dissimulation," 4 (of 15, online). Similarly, between 1559 and 1570, many English priests "continued to say Mass in secret while they celebrated the new liturgy in public." See ibid., 3 (of 15, online).

54. Publication of *Regnans in excelsis* certainly precipitated a fresh crisis for English Catholics, but other events (the founding of the expatriate English College at Douai and the flight of Mary, Queen of Scots into England in 1568, and the Northern Rebellion of 1569) also exacerbated the situation. The English College at Douai became the "mother institution" of other seminaries on the European continent (see McClain, *Lest We Be Damned*, 281). For examples of government pressure on institutions like Oxford and Cambridge to rid themselves of "popish trumpery" (Mass books, vessels, and vestments), see Swan, "Question of Dissimulation," 6 (of 15 online).

55. McClain, *Lest We Be Damned*, 21.

56. See Christopher Haigh, "From Monopoly to Minority: Catholicism in Early Modern England," *Transactions of the Royal Historical Society*, 5th ser., 31 (1981): 129–47.

57. See ibid., 133. Haigh notes that throughout the Elizabethan period, English Catholics found access to sacraments quite difficult. Some areas (e.g., Essex, London, the Thames valley) were more plentifully supplied with priests, especially after missionaries began arriving in 1574; but in other locales Catholics may have been able to attend Mass only once or twice a year. Couples had to travel long distances to find a priest to witness their marriage, and fathers of families often had to baptize their children themselves. (Note the documentation Haigh cites in notes 14–15, p. 133).

58. Mullett, *Catholics in Britain and Ireland*, 10. As Mullett indicates, later Catholic historiography took its cue from what Christopher Haigh calls a "partisan, propagandist" version of history promoted by missionary priests (chiefly Jesuits) who arrived in England after 1574—an energetic, innovative contingent of clergy who believed they were replacing the "anaemic, formalist religion" of the Marian priests and bishops with the "vibrant new Catholicism of a devoted minority." Haigh, "From Monopoly to Minority," 129–30, disputes this "propagandist" version of history.

59. See Haigh, "From Monopoly to Minority," 132. Haigh points out that there were whole regions (especially in the north and west of England) that were largely neglected by the missionary priests and Jesuits who infiltrated England from Continental seminaries in the late sixteenth century and later. The missionary priests tended to concentrate their efforts in the south and east and were frequently inclined to attach themselves to wealthier and more socially prominent Catholics (nobles and gentry).

60. See Bossy, *English Catholic Community*, 364.

61. See McClain, *Lest We Be Damned*, 57.

62. Richard Broughton, *A New Manual of Old Christian Catholick Meditations, and Praiers*, English Recusant Literature, 1558–1640, vol. 113 (Menston, UK: Scolar Press, 1972), 25–26. Mullett, *Catholics in Britain and Ireland*, 115, notes how, in mid-seventeenth-century Scotland, the rosary continued to be a common focus of "social gathering for oral prayer," especially when no priest was available.

63. The theological rationale for "sacraments of desire" was based on distinctions between *sacramentum tantum* ("the sacrament alone," the ritual sign and action); *res tantum* ("the reality alone," i.e., the ultimate effect or aim of the sacramental sign and action); and *res et sacramentum* ("the sacrament and reality together," i.e., the simultaneous and efficacious presence of both sacramental sign-action and its intended effect). In the case of the Eucharist, for example, the "sacrament alone" is the ritual action (the celebration Mass); the "reality alone" is the ultimate effect of that celebration—the unity of Christ's Body, the church; and the "reality and sacrament together" are Christ's body and blood, communion in which causes the church's unity. A sacrament received "in desire" (but not in physical fact) would give the Christian the grace and benefits of communion without actually eating and drinking the sacramental signs of Christ's body and blood (the consecrated elements of bread and wine).

64. *The Martyrdom of Polycarp*, XIV.1; translated in Kirsopp Lake, ed., *The Apostolic Fathers*, 2 vols., Loeb Classical Library (1913; Cambridge: Harvard University Press, 1976), 2:331 (Greek text on facing page).

65. See ibid., XIV.1–3; 2:331 (Greek text on facing page).

66. See ibid., XV.2, 2:333 (Greek text on facing page).

67. See McClain, *Lest We Be Damned*, 133.

68. Text cited ibid., 134.

69. Text cited ibid., 135.

70. Ibid.

71. Ibid., 132.

72. See ibid., 90–107.

73. Haigh, "From Monopoly to Minority," 138.

74. See Gregory Martin, *Roma Sancta* (1581), ed. and trans. George Bruner Parks (Rome: Edizioni di Storia e Letteratura, 1969), especially 214–18 (on the Roman confraternity of the rosary and on the method of praying this devotion). Campion became a Jesuit, though Martin did not.

75. See George Bruner Parks, "The Life and Works of Gregory Martin," in *Roma Sancta*, xi–xxxii.

76. Bucke, *Instructions for the Use of the Beades*, title page.

77. Ibid., 14–37. Bucke follows what had by then become the traditional order for meditating on the mysteries of the rosary (joyful, sorrowful, glorious).

78. Ibid., 15–16.

79. See Manlio Sodi and Achille Maria Triacca, eds., *Missale Romanum editio princeps* (1570), Monumenta Liturgica Concilii Tridentini (Vatican City: Libreria Editrice Vaticana, 1998), 283 (of the original pagination; 343 in the edition of Sodi and Triacca). The rubric reads: *Tenens ambabus manibus hostiam, profert verba consecrationis distincte, secrete, et attente* (holding the host in both hands, [the priest] pronounces the words of consecration distinctly, quietly, and attentively). Similar language had been used in John Burckhard's *Ordo Missae*, first published ca. 1502. See J. Wickham Legg, ed., *Tracts on the Mass*, Henry Bradshaw Society, vol. 27 (London: Harrison and Sons, 1904), 156.

80. See Bucke, *Instructions for the Use of the Beades*, 21.

81. See ibid.

82. Ibid., 22.

83. The custom of storing portions of the consecrated eucharistic bread in a tabernacle on or near the main altar of a parish church spread slowly but widely after the Council of Trent. Prior to that time, it was more customary to reserve the sacrament in a pyx (sometimes in the form of a dove) suspended above the altar, or in a "sacrament-house" near the altar.

84. Bucke, *Instructions for the Use of the Beades*, 34–35.

85. Ibid., 34.

86. Ibid., 34–35.

87. A familiar trope in medieval theology held that "from the side of Christ asleep in death on the cross, the church's sacraments poured forth" (*e latere Chrsti dormientis in cruce, fluxerunt ecclesiae sacramenta*). See Thomas Aquinas, *Summa Theologiae*, Ia Pars, Q. 92, art. 3; cf. IIIa Pars, Q. 60, art. 3.

88. McClain, *Lest We Be Damned*, 126.

89. See *The Primer, or Office of the Blessed Virgin Marie, in Latin and English*, English Recusant Literature, vol. 262 (London: Scolar Press, 1975), 213–14 (Latin and English on facing pages).

90. See Bucke, *Instructions for the Use of the Beades*, 49–61, 66–72.

91. See Bossy, *English Catholic Community*, 288–92.

92. Ibid., 289.

93. Ibid.

94. See Nuno Vassallo e Silva, "Art in the Service of God: The Impact of the Society of Jesus on the Decorative Arts in Portugal," in John W. O'Malley et al., eds., *The Jesuits II: Cultures, Sciences, and the Arts 1540–1773* (Toronto: University of Toronto Press, 2006), 182–210; here, 195; emphasis added. The church was built between 1555 and 1573 (ibid., 182).

95. See Bucke, *Instructions for the Use of the Beades*, 21; Garnett, *Societie of the Rosarie*, "The Preface to the Reader," 7. In medieval Catholic liturgy, Wisdom imagery (based on biblical books such as Proverbs, the Book of Wisdom and Sirach [Ecclesiasticus]) had been applied both to the Virgin Mary (on Marian feasts) and to the Eucharist (e.g., the texts used at lauds for the Feast of Corpus Christi).

96. Garnett, *Societie of the Rosarie*, 7. The first antiphon for the first psalm of lauds on Corpus Christi read, "Sapientia aedificavit sibit domum, miscuit vinum, et posuit mensam, alleluia" (Wisdom has built herself a house, mixed wine, and set a table, alleluia). Persons familiar with the liturgy—both clergy and literate laity—would have connected Mary as a figure of Wisdom and with the Wisdom that the Mass of Corpus Christi links to the eucharistic banquet.

97. See Louis Richeome, *The Pilgrime of Loreto*, English Recusant Literature, vol. 285 (London: Scolar Press, 1976), 4, 173.

98. Ibid.

99. See Anne Winston-Allen, *Stories of the Rose: The Making of the Rosary in the Middle Ages* (University Park: Pennsylvania State University Press, 1997), chap. 2, "The Picture Text and Its 'Readers,'" 31–64. The early rosary books were aimed at a population that was largely illiterate, so their printed *images* had greater impact for most "readers" than the *texts* did.

100. See G. L. Barnes, "Laity Formation: The Role of Early English Printed Primers," *Journal of Religious History* 18:2 (December 1994): 139–58. The primers (also spelled "prymers")—which began to appear among educated laity in the early fourteenth century—recycled the contents of the medieval Books of Hours. Compiled as devotional works primarily for use by lay Christians, their contents

were biblical, liturgical, catechetical, and hortatory. Typically, a primer included the Hours of the Blessed Virgin Mary (*horae beatae Mariae Virginis*)—also known as the "Little Office of the Blessed Virgin Mary"; the seven penitential psalms (6, 31, 37, 50, 101, 129, 142, Vulgate numbering); the fifteen gradual psalms (119–133, Vulgate); the Litany of the Saints; and the Office of the Dead (*Dirige* [Direct], so called from the Latin incipit of the first antiphon of the first psalm for the Office of Matins (i.e., vigils, the night office).

101. Ibid., 158.

102. See Edward Burton, ed., *Three Primers Put Forth in the Reign of Henry VIII* (Oxford: University Press, 1834), 335. Bishop Hilsey died in the same year his primer was published (1539), so the title page of the work refers to him as "late bishop of Rochester." See ibid., liv, 305.

103. See ibid., 367.

104. See ibid., 321–22, from Hilsey's "Prologue to the Whole Work."

105. See Hilsey, "Prologue to the Whole Work," in Burton, ed., *Three Primers*, 322.

106. See Barnes, "Laity Formation," 154.

107. See Burton, *Three Primers*, 338–39. For other traditional texts in Hilsey's version of the Hours of Our Lady, see ibid., 341, 343–44, 347, 350, 352–53, 355, 358–60, 368. In *Marking the Hours: English People and Their Prayers, 1240–1570* (New Haven: Yale University Press, 2006), 148, Eamon Duffy mentions Hilsey's "reforming impulse" but fails to take sufficient account of the profoundly *traditional* elements that are also found in Hilsey's 1539 primer. Note also that the notion of Mary as a powerful intercessor (not simply the "sweet gentle maid of Nazareth") was already well established in late medieval and early modern Catholicism in England. This fact qualifies Lisa McClain's claim that "the earlier Mary was often objectified in inanimate metaphors by the church," and that "Mary was rarely portrayed as an actor." See *Lest We Be Damned*, 102.

108. Barnes, "Laity Formation," 157. For Henry VIII's primer, see Burton, *Three Primers*, 437–527.

109. See *The Primer, or Office of the Blessed Virgin Marie* (1599).

110. See ibid., 190–292, 1–160. The separate pagination found in later portions of this primer suggests that it may have incorporated several distinct printed sources that were later collected into a single volume.

111. See Barnes, "Laity Formation," 140.

112. See *The Primer, or Office of the Blessed Virgin Marie*, 217–23.

113. On Joye's work, see Barnes, "Laity Formation," 142–43.

114. See ibid., 142. *[H]ortulus* is a diminutive formed from the Latin noun *hortus* (garden).

115. Challoner (1691–1781) had himself been born of Presbyterian parents but converted to Roman Catholicism while still a child. At fourteen, he went to Douai to study for the priesthood and did not return to England until 1730. He

Notes to Chapter 5

became a bishop in 1741. A 1775 printing of *The Garden of the Soul* is available at the Internet Archive Online, http://www.archive.org/index.php.

116. See *A Manual of Prayers* (1583), English Recusant Literature, 1558–1640, vol. 372 (London: Scolar Press, 1978). The manual includes a table assigning prayers to Mary and the saints twice a week, on Monday and on Saturday (a day long associated with special devotion to the Virgin Mary).

117. See Richard Broughton, *A New Manual of Old Christian Catholick Meditations*, bound with Oliver Almond, *The Uncasing of Heresie* (1624), English Recusant Literature 1558–1640, vol. 113 (Menston, UK: Scolar Press, 1972), 31–41, 58–78.

118. See ibid., 6–7.

119. See ibid., 31–41, 58–78.

120. See McClain, *Lest We Be Damned*, 96. For an example of rosary picture books in England, see F. A. Gasquet, *An English Rosary Book of the 15th Century* (Deovil: Western Chronicle, n.d.; reprinted without pagination from the *Downside Review*).

121. See *The Primer, or Office of the Blessed Virgin Marie* (1599), 204–68. Devotion to the suffering Christ as exemplar of faithful endurance made obvious sense to members of a community whose faith was officially outlawed.

122. By printing a graphic insert ("The Lady Hvngerfordes Meditacions Vpon the Beades") showing how to say the beads, along with woodcuts depicting scenes from the lives of Christ and Mary, Bucke continued the tradition of rosary books that offer visual mnemonics for meditative prayer. See *Instructions for the Use of the Beades*, following pages 87–88.

123. See Barnes, "Laity Formation," 154.

124. See ibid., 144–45; see also Eamon Duffy, *The Stripping of the Altars: Traditional Religion in England 1400–1580* (New Haven: Yale University Press, 1992), 382–83.

125. See Bossy, *English Catholic Community*, 382.

126. See ibid. A 1776 edition of *The Garden of the Soul* published in the American colonies reflected Challoner's sober emphasis on liturgy and the basics of Catholic doctrine. For a modern example based on this late-eighteenth-century edition, see *The Garden of the Soul* (Union City, NJ: John J. Crawley, 1975). It includes "Devotions to Our Lady," beginning with the rosary (see ibid., 168–86). See also the mid-eighteenth-century American edition of *The Garden of the Soul* (New York: D. & J. Sadler, 1856), published with the approval of Archbishop John Hughes of New York; it includes the Office of the Blessed Virgin Mary, plus instructions on the rosary.

127. See Marc R. Forster, "Domestic Devotions and Family Piety in German Catholicism," in Marc R. Forster and Benjamin J. Kaplan, eds., *Piety and Family in Early Modern Europe: Essays in Honour of Steven Ozment* (Burlington, VT: Ashgate, 2005), 97–114; here, 105.

128. This helps explain why parish "rosary devotions" became (and in some places remain) such a staple of Catholic devotional life.

129. Forster, "Domestic Devotions," 107.

130. Ibid.

131. What Marc R. Forster says about Baroque Catholicism in Germany can also be said, with qualifications, about English Catholicism in the era of Challoner's *Garden of the Soul*: it was "public, communal, particularistic, somewhat disorganized, traditional, even conservative," yet it may have provided its adherents with "a wider range of religious opportunities [for both women and men] than more tightly structured Protestant confessions." See ibid., 114.

132. See ibid., 104–5. See also Anna Coreth, *Pietas Austriaca*, trans. William D. Bowman and Anna Maria Leitgeb, Central European Studies (West Lafayette, IN: Purdue University Press, 2004), 45–80.

133. See ibid., 108, 110–11.

134. See Bossy, *English Catholic Community*, 382–83.

135. See Alexandra Walsham, "'Domme Preachers'? Post-Reformation English Catholicism and the Culture of Print," *Past and Present*, no. 168 (August 2000): 72–123; here, 121. Cf. John Bossy's characterization of Elizabethan Catholicism as a "religion of contemplation"; see "Character of Elizabethan Catholicism," 57.

136. See ibid.

137. See Bossy, *English Catholic Community*, 387–90.

138. See Walsham, "'Domme Preachers'?" 121.

139. See ibid., 122.

140. See ibid.

141. See ibid., 115.

142. See ibid., 118.

143. See Louis Richeome, *Holy Pictures of the Mysticall Figures, 1619*, English Recusant Literature, 1558–1640, vol. 250 (London: Scolar Press, 1975).

144. See ibid., A2, "The Printer to the Reader."

145. See ibid.

146. See ibid., B1.

147. See ibid., 2–3.

148. See ibid., 3; emphasis in the original.

149. Ibid.

150. Ibid.

151. See Jean-Luc Marion, "The Blind Man of Siloe," trans. Janine Langan, *Image: A Journal of Religion and the Arts*, no. 29 (Winter 2000–2001): 59–69.

152. Ibid., 66.

153. Richeome, *Holy Pictures of the Mysticall Figures*, 11.

154. Walsham, "'Domme Preachers'?" 118.

155. Ibid., 120. See also the image printed ibid., 119, which shows a 1598 illustrated rosary book that combines text and image as correlated aspects of this devotion.

156. See David Cressy, "Books as Totems in Seventeenth-Century England and New England," *Journal of Library History* 21:1 (Winter 1986): 92–106.

157. See ibid., 92.

158. See Mullett, *Catholics in Britain and Ireland*, 115.

159. See Anne Dillon, "Praying by the Number: The Confraternity of the Rosary and the English Catholic Community, c. 1580–1700," *History* 88, no. 291 (July 2003): 451–71; here, 469.

160. See ibid.

161. On the devout gaze as related to popular piety and visual perception, see Bob Scribner, "Popular Piety and Modes of Visual Perception in Late-Medieval and Reformation Germany," *Journal of Religious History* 15:4 (December 1989): 448–69.

162. See ibid., 464.

163. See ibid.

164. See ibid. See also the printed images, 468; emphasis added.

165. Readers may view the works of the artists discussed here online at http://www.wga.hu.

166. Aertsen's *Meat Stall* is also referred to as *The Butcher Stall* or *Butcher Shop with the Flight into Egypt*.

167. See Charlotte Houghton, "This Was Tomorrow: Pieter Aertsen's *Meat Stall* as Contemporary Art," *Art Bulletin* 86, no. 2 (June 2004): 277–300; here, 287. Earlier, Margaret Sullivan had argued that "scholars are unable to agree on the exact nature of the transaction as the Virgin bends from the saddle toward a small boy." See her "Aertsen's Kitchen and Market Scenes: Audience and Innovation in Northern Art," *Art Bulletin* 81, no. 2 (June 1999): 236–66; here, 251. Houghton supports her own interpretation of this scene by appealing to the impact of "local knowledge" and "local visual culture" on Flemish painting of this period. Mary's "extrabiblical act of charity" appears in three other images, all of them painted "within a few years of Aertsen's picture" ("This Was Tomorrow," 287).

168. See the note on this painting at http://www.wga.hu.

169. See, for example, Garnett, *Societie of the Rosarie*, 78.

170. See the note on Aertsen's later painting, *Peasants by the Hearth*, at http://www.wga.hu. See also Keith P. F. Moxey, *Pieter Aertsen, Joachim Beuckelaer, and the Rise of Secular Painting in the Context of the Reformation* (New York: Garland, 1977), especially 32. Moxey argues that *The Meat Stall* "represents the elevation of a new subject into the repertoire of Western art. Aertsen has turned to the physical context of peasant life itself and found it worthy of representation."

171. See Houghton, "This Was Tomorrow," 277.

172. Cited in Moxey, *Pieter Aertsen*, 33.

173. See ibid., 266–67.

174. See ibid., 165.

175. See Sullivan, "Aertsen's Kitchen," 236.

176. Ibid., 237.

177. Ibid.

178. See ibid., 237, 240–41. Sullivan notes that often, even when the "originality of northern artists" is recognized, it is "generally assumed that the artist was indebted to popular culture and vernacular literature"; the Latin sources "tend to be overlooked even though they comprise the majority of publications in the north." Ibid., 240.

179. See ibid., 241.

180. See ibid.

181. See ibid., 244–45.

182. Ibid., 245.

183. Ibid., 246.

184. See ibid., 247.

185. See ibid., 250, 255.

186. See ibid., 257–58.

187. Ibid., 257.

188. See Stephen Greenblatt, *Renaissance Self-Fashioning* (Chicago: University of Chicago Press, 1980), 168 and 285 n. 24.

189. See McClain, *Lest We Be Damned*, 96.

190. See Kate Koppelman, "Devotional Ambivalence: The Virgin Mary as 'Empresse of Helle,'" *Essays in Medieval Studies* 18 (2001): 67–82; here, 68.

191. See ibid., 69.

192. See ibid., 70. Koppelman cites the medieval "Manuscript Rawlinson Poetry," which pictures Mary as herself a "harrower of hell" who scolds Satan and seizes his power, just as she is liable to accuse human penitents and blame them for "all they have done." See ibid., 70–72, with texts cited and discussed.

193. See ibid., 67.

194. See ibid., 76.

195. See ibid., 73.

196. See ibid., 76.

197. See ibid., 76–77.

198. See William B. Taylor, "The Virgin of Guadalupe in New Spain: An Inquiry into the Social History of Marian Devotion," *American Ethnologist* 14, no. 1 (1987): 9–33; here, 9.

199. On the documentation and controversies concerning the traditional story of the apparition, see Stafford Poole, *Our Lady of Guadalupe: The Origins and Sources of a Mexican National Symbol, 1531–1797* (Tucson: University of Arizona Press, 1995); see also Poole, *The Guadalupan Controversies in Mexico* (Stanford, CA: Stanford University Press, 2006).

200. See Mark Francis, "Building Bridges between Liturgy, Devotionalism, and Popular Religion," *Assembly* 20, no. 2 (April 1994): 636–38; here, 637.

201. Ibid.; Francis is citing Virgilio Elizondo in this quotation.

202. See Taylor, "The Virgin of Guadalupe in New Spain," 10.

203. Ibid., 10.

204. Ibid.

205. See Robert V. Kemper, "Marianismo in Mexico: An Ethnographic Encounter," accessed online, November 23, 2007, at http://faculty.sum.edu/rkemper/anth_3311/anth_3311_Kemper_marianismo_in_mexico.htm.

206. Ibid., 18 (of 21) in the online version cited in the previous note.

207. See Ilona Katzew, "The Virgin of the Macana: Emblem of a Franciscan Predicament in New Spain," *Colonial Latin American Review* 12, no. 2 (2003): 169–98.

208. Ibid., 169. As Katzew explains, the reference to the "club" comes from an account of the rebellion, during which an "Indian Chieftain" entered a house where there was an image of Mary that had been hidden by the Christian faithful. The account also says that the chieftain struck Mary's image on the head with a sharp *macana* that produced a small but permanent scar on her face. See ibid., 174.

209. For an example, see ibid., 177, figure 1 (from a 1761 engraving in the Museo Soumaya, Mexico City). See also ibid., 178, figure 2 (a 1688 engraving from Toledo, which may have been a source of the images produced in Mexico).

210. See ibid., 184, with figure 8 (by an unknown Mexican artist from the second half of the eighteenth century).

211. On the legendary appearances by Mary of Ágreda in the American Southwest, see William H. Donahue, "Mary of Agreda and the Southwest United States," *The Americas* 9, no. 3 (1953): 291–314.

212. See also T. D. Kendrick, *Mary of Ágreda: The Life and Legend of a Spanish Nun* (London: Routledge and Kegan Paul, 1967), 28–45.

213. Ibid., 41–43.

214. Cited in ibid., 43. Mary seems to have meant that after her "visits" to North America, the rosaries formerly in the convent at Ágreda were no longer to be found there (ibid., 44 n. 1). See also ibid., n. 3 ("Sor Maria's Writings), 159–65.

NOTES TO CHAPTER 6

1. See Anne Clark Bartlett and Thomas H. Bestul, eds., *Cultures of Piety: Medieval English Devotional Literature in Translation* (Ithaca: Cornell University Press, 1999), "Introduction," 1–17.

2. Ibid., 2.

3. Henry Garnett, *The Societie of the Rosary*, English Recusant Literature, vol. 112 (Menston, UK: Scolar Press, 1972), 10, 38–39. Garnett mentions all fifteen of the traditional mysteries of the rosary.

4. See ibid., 162–65. Garnett's book is an expanded translation of a work by the Italian Jesuit Lucas Pinelli.

5. See John Bossy, "The Character of Elizabethan Catholicism," *Past and Present*, no. 21 (April 1962): 39–59; here 57.

6. On devotion to Mary as reflected in recusant manuals of prayer, see Patrick L. Malloy, "A Manual of Prayers (1583–1850): A Study of Recusant Devotions" (Ph.D. diss., University of Notre Dame, 1991), 124–33. Challoner's work was a chapter in the ongoing revision of the *Manual*, which first appeared in 1583 and served as the "*vade mecum* of Roman Catholics in England after the Reformation" (ibid., "Abstract," 1).

7. See *The Garden of the Soul* (1775 edition), accessible online at http://www.archive.org/details/a5562827oochaluoft. Unless otherwise indicated, references are to this online edition.

8. See John Bossy, *The English Catholic Community, 1570–1850* (New York: Oxford University Press, 1976), 365.

9. Ibid., 273–317.

10. The appendix containing the Hours of the Virgin Mary is substantial—about 135 pages.

11. Bossy, *English Catholic Community*, 365.

12. Ibid., 365, 380.

13. Mark Goldie, "The Scottish Catholic Enlightenment," *Journal of British Studies* 30:1 (1991): 20–62; here, 22. See also Joseph P. Chinnici, *The English Catholic Enlightenment: John Lingard and the Cisalpine Movement, 1780–1850* (Shepherdstown, WV: Patmos Press, 1980).

14. Bossy, *English Catholic Community*, 379.

15. Ibid.

16. In the Catholic Church's hierarchy, each diocese (administrative unit) has a bishop, and several dioceses within a region constitute an ecclesiastical "province," whose head is an *arch*bishop (or the "metropolitan" of the province). A synod is a meeting of all the bishops of a particular province, called together by the archbishop, who presides. (An individual diocese may also hold a synod, which the bishop and clergy, plus lay representatives, attend). In 1852, the provincial synod of Westminster would have been presided over by Nicholas Cardinal Wiseman, the archbishop of Westminster. Newman's "Second Spring" sermon was preached on July 13, 1852, at Saint Mary's Church, Oscott.

17. Newman's "Second Spring" sermon was accessed online at http://www.newmanreader.org/works/occasions/sermon10.html. The entire sermon occupies eleven pages; quotations here are taken from pp. 3–5, 8–9.

18. Mary Heimann, *Catholic Devotion in Victorian England* (Oxford: Clarendon Press, 1995), 5.

19. Newman, "Second Spring," online version, 10.

20. See Heimann, *Catholic Devotion in Victorian England*, 6.

21. Newman, "The Second Spring," online version, 8.

22. Bossy, *English Catholic Community*, 297.

23. Ibid.

24. See ibid., 298.

25. Heimann, *Catholic Devotion in Victorian England*, 138.

26. Ibid.

27. See *Garden of the Soul*, 290–93.

28. Heimann, *Catholic Devotion in Victorian England*, 137; emphasis added. Later, Heimann writes, "Where the native English Catholic tradition was modified, it seems to have been for reasons which owed little to Roman pronouncements but had more to do with local problems, the need to compete effectively with rival denominations, and the desire to recast traditional piety into the idiom of the day. . . . English Catholicism . . . remained distinct from continental Catholicism" (ibid., 165).

29. Ibid., 165.

30. The first verse of this hymn ran: "Full in the panting heart of Rome, / Beneath the Apostle's crowning dome, / From pilgrims' lips that kiss the ground / Breathes in all tongues one only sound: / 'God bless our Pope, God bless our Pope, / God bless our Pope, the great, the good.'"

31. Jennifer F. Supple, "Ultramontanism in Yorkshire, 1850–1900," *Recusant History* 17, no. 3 (May 1985): 274–86; here, 276.

32. Heimann, *Catholic Devotion in Victorian England*, 139.

33. Heimann, ibid., 141, observes, however, that "English Catholicism" in the nineteenth century "was not only for the English-born." Large numbers of Irish Catholics were also living in England at that time, especially after the 1840s and the Great Famine, and "'English' and 'Irish' Catholics managed to find common spiritual ground which was acceptable to the sensibility of each."

34. Newman's sermon used the Song of Songs 2.10–12 as its basic text. *Stella matutina* was a phrase drawn from the Marian Litany of Loreto, approved for public use by Pope Sixtus V in 1587.

35. See *Garden of the Soul*, 136–42 (Benediction of the Blessed Sacrament); 290–93 (Litany and rosary); appendix (full text of the Hours of the Virgin Mary, with separate pagination).

36. Heimann, *Catholic Devotion in Victorian England*, 39.

37. Ibid., 48–49.

38. Ibid., 51. Heimann bases her assertion on a statistical analysis of the kind and frequency of devotions in Victorian Catholic parishes—material which she presents in appendix I and appendix II of her study.

39. Ibid., 60. "There is no evidence to suggest that the rosary was a devotion which appealed to a different sort of Catholic from one who would attend Benediction" (ibid.).

40. Wiseman's opinion is cited in Edward Norman, *The English Catholic Church in the Nineteenth Century* (Oxford: Clarendon Press, 1984), 142.

41. Heimann, *Catholic Devotion in Victorian England*, 61.

42. Ibid., 60.

43. A set of "Directions on Family Prayer," written in Boston for the Roger Hanley family by the French émigré priest Jean-Louis Cheverus (1768–1836), recommends the use of both these works, especially on Sundays when no priest is available to celebrate Mass. For Cheverus's directions, see Joseph P. Chinnici and Angelyn Dries, eds., *Prayer and Practice in the American Catholic Community*, American Catholic Identities: A Documentary History (Maryknoll, NY: Orbis Books, 2000), 12–13 (document 3). On the history of English Catholic catechisms published between 1550 and 1750, see Geoffrey Scott, "The Poor Man's Catechism," *Recusant History* 27:3 (May 2005): 373–82.

44. *The Poor Man's Catechism, or, The Christian Doctrine Explained* (New York: P. J. Kenedy and Sons, n.d.), 99–100. For an 1815 edition of this *Catechism*, published in the United States, see http://www.books.google.com.

45. Bossy, *English Catholic Community*, 378–79.

46. *Poor Man's Catechism*, 84–85.

47. This is not to deny that, over time, American Catholics became increasingly conscious of their religious difference from Protestants. "To be a Catholic, particularly in Protestant America," Mary Gordon wrote in *Good Boys and Dead Girls* (New York: Viking 1991), "made one an expert at building the limiting, excluding fence," 33.

48. Chinnici and Dries, *Prayer and Practice in the American Catholic Community*, 90–91. The three Plenary Councils of Baltimore (1852, 1866, 1884) were meetings of all the Catholic bishops in the United States (though the Canadian Catholic bishop of Toronto also attended the 1852 meeting). These plenary councils had been preceded by seven "provincial councils" of Baltimore (1829, 1833, 1837, 1840, 1843, 1846, 1849), which included all the bishops within the ecclesiastical "province" of Baltimore—which was then the only province in the United States. Today, all the U.S. Catholic bishops meet annually in November; there is ordinarily a brief summer meeting as well.

49. *A Manual of Prayers for the Use of the Catholic Laity. Prepared and Published by Order of the Third Plenary Council of Baltimore* (New York: Catholic Publications Society, 1888 [copyright date]).

50. The *rituale* (ritual) is a book containing the prayers and scripture texts priests use when administering the sacraments, visiting the sick and dying, burying the dead, distributing Holy Communion outside Mass, or blessing persons, places, or objects. The early modern forebear of the priest's ritual is the post-Tridentine *Rituale Romanum* issued by Pope Paul V in 1614, enlarged in 1752, and revised in 1925. Since the liturgical reforms mandated by the Second Vatican

Council, the rites for each sacrament are often printed in separate books rather than in a single, comprehensive volume.

51. The phrase "lived religion" is used by Paula M. Kane, "Marian Devotion since 1940: Continuity or Casualty?" in James M. O'Toole, ed., *Habits of Devotion: Catholic Religious Practice in Twentieth-Century America* (Ithaca: Cornell University Press, 2004), 89–129; here, 90–91. The phrase "emphasizes the practice of religion embodying at once the contradictory hallmarks of regulation (by some authority) and resistance to regulation" (ibid., 91). See also David D. Hall, ed., *Lived Religion in America* (Princeton: Princeton University Press, 1997), "Introduction."

52. See *Manual of Prayers*, 386–82.

53. Ibid., 369; emphasis added.

54. *Manual of Prayers*, introduction to the liturgy for vespers, 178–79.

55. See the Constitution on the Sacred Liturgy (*Sacrosanctum concilium*), 7: "Every liturgical celebration, because it is an action of Christ the Priest and of his Body, which is the Church, is a sacred action surpassing all others. No other action of the Church can equal its efficacy by the same title and to the same degree"; in Austin Flannery, ed., *Vatican Council II: The Conciliar and Post-Conciliar Documents* (Collegeville, MN: Liturgical Press, 1975), 5.

56. Both Benediction of the Blessed Sacrament and the rosary are found in the *Manual of Prayers*, 220–24, 369–82, as they were in Challoner's *Garden of the Soul*.

57. See Chinnici and Dries, *Prayer and Practice in the American Catholic Community*, 13–17 (document 4). *Manual of Prayers*, 348–67, included forms for the popular devotion known as the Way of the Cross, as well as "The Devotion of the Seven Words on the Cross."

58. Ibid., 13; see also 14–16 (rules 1–13).

59. R. Po-Chia Hsia observes that "Tridentine Catholicism succeeded in the long term not by suppressing 'superstitions,' but by grafting orthodoxy onto traditional and popular religiosity." *The World of Catholic Renewal 1540–1770*, 2nd ed. (New York: Cambridge University Press, 2005), 224–25. Confraternities and sodalities played a prominent role in this process (ibid., 226).

60. Chinnici and Dries, *Prayer and Practice in the American Catholic Community*, 13.

61. Ibid., 63.

62. Cited in ibid., 64–65 (document 22). *Ave Maria* was published at Notre Dame, Indiana, under the auspices of the Congregation of Holy Cross, the priests' group that had founded the University of Notre Dame in 1842. It remained "one of the most popular devotional magazines in American Catholicism for over one hundred years. Begun in 1865 (and ending in 1968), just as communities started to recover from the ravages of the Civil War, its volumes reflected a concern for the course of contemporary society and a revival in practices of prayer" (ibid., 59).

63. See ibid., 59–62 (document 20).

64. Ibid., 61.

65. Ibid., 60.

66. Ibid., 61.

67. Ibid. The image of Catholics as an army of "armed knights" or "soldiers of Mary" continues today in organizations such as the Blue Army (of Fatima), founded in New Jersey by Monsignor Harold V. Colgan and layman John M. Haffert in 1947 to spread devotion to the rosary and promote knowledge about the alleged 1917 apparitions of Mary to three young children in Fatima, Portugal. The apparitions were especially linked to the need for "prayer for the conversion of Russia." See Michael O'Keeffe, "Fatima," in Richard P. McBrien, ed., *The HarperCollins Encyclopedia of Catholicism* (San Francisco: HarperCollins, 1995), 520–21: "In 1930, after a seven-year study, the bishop of Fatima proclaimed the legitimacy of the apparitions and authorized the cult of Our Lady of Fatima," but these remain "private revelations," rather than matters Catholics are obliged to believe and/or practice. For the Blue Army's Web site, see http://www.wafusa.org.

68. *Manual of Prayers*, 368.

69. See *The Key of Heaven, or A Manual of Prayer*, new and improved ed. (New York: P. J. Kenedy, 1882), 395–409. Just before the Marian rosary, this edition of *The Key* printed a "Rosary of the Blessed Name of Jesus," also divided into fifteen mysteries. It appears to be a combination of elements from the Marian rosary, together with material from the medieval "Psalter of Jesus," a version of which was printed in Challoner's *Garden of the Soul*.

70. See *Acta et Decreta Concilii Plenarii Baltimorensis Tertii* (Baltimore: Typis Johannis Murphy et Sociorum, 1886); Titulus VII, "De Doctrina Christiana," nn. 118–22. A portion of this title dealing with prayer books is translated in Chinnici and Dries, *Prayer and Practice in the American Catholic Community*, 92–93 (document 32).

71. See Chinnici and Dries, *Prayer and Practice in the American Catholic Community*, 92.

72. Ibid., 92–93.

73. Ibid., 93.

74. Joseph P. Chinnici, *Living Stones: The History and Structure of Catholic Spiritual Life in the United States* (New York: Macmillan, 1989), 62.

75. Ibid., 56.

76. Ibid.

77. Ibid., 58.

78. Ibid., 58–59.

79. Ibid., 59.

80. Ibid., 61.

81. Ibid., 62; emphasis added.

82. Ibid.

83. Chinnici and Dries, *Prayer and Practice in the American Catholic Community*, 93.

84. See "The Scapular: An Incident of the Late War," *Ave Maria* 1, no. 10 (July 15, 1865): 147.

85. According to legend, the Scapular of Our Lady of Mount Carmel (also called the "brown scapular")—two small patches of cloth connected by cords worn over the head and hanging down on breast and back—was given to Saint Simon Stock in 1251 as a special sign of dedication to Mary. According to popular belief, wearing the scapular protects a person in this life and secures a speedier release from the pains of purgatory (a state of ongoing purification after death) in the next.

86. "The Scapular," *Ave Maria* 1, no. 10 (July 15, 1865): 147.

87. Ibid., 148.

88. Ibid., 147.

89. See Michael A. Mullett, *Catholics in Britain and Ireland, 1558–1829*, Social History in Perspective (New York: St. Martin's Press, 1998), 115. Ogilvie's dying act, Mullett suggests, caused "the Rosary, rather than the Mass" to become "recognised by its foes as the visible expression of Catholic profession" in seventeenth-century Scotland.

90. See *Manual of Prayers*, 368–89, where both rosary and scapular are recommended, without discussion of any singular privileges (such as a secure or speedy release from purgatory) attached to either.

91. See Joseph P. Chinnici, "Deciphering Religious Practice: Material Culture as Social Code in the Nineteenth Century," *U.S. Catholic Historian* 19:3 (2001): 1–19. Chinnici notes that Catholic devotions often promised transforming social, moral, and personal rewards.

92. Ibid., 6, 7.

93. Ibid., 7.

94. See James Emmett Ryan, "Sentimental Catechism: Archbishop James Gibbons, Mass-Print Culture, and American Literary History," *Religion and American Culture* 7:1 (1997): 81–119; here, 90..

95. See Thomas Spalding, "Gibbons, James," in McBrien, *HarperCollins Encyclopedia of Catholicism*, 560 See also James Cardinal Gibbons, *The Faith of Our Fathers: Being a Plain Exposition and Vindication of the Church Founded by Our Lord Jesus Christ*, 92nd ed., revised and enlarged (Baltimore: John Murphy, 1920).

96. Ryan, "Sentimental Catechism," 81.

97. Ibid., 90; Ryan is citing the work of Bonnie G. Smith, *Changing Lives: Women in European History since 1700* (Lexington, MA: Heath, 1989), 178.

98. Ryan, "Sentimental Catechism," 89–90. In line with the historical research of Jay P. Dolan, Ryan notes that Gibbons's catechism succeeded so spectacularly because it soon found a natural marketing ally in the "parish mission movement" that flourished during what Dolan calls the "Catholic Revival." See Jay P. Dolan,

Catholic Revivalism: The American Experience, 1830–1900 (Notre Dame, IN: University of Notre Dame Press, 1978), 86.

99. Gibbons, *Faith of Our Fathers*, 163–209.

100. Ryan, "Sentimental Catechism," 89.

101. Gibbons, *Faith of Our Fathers*, 184.

102. Ibid., 185–86.

103. Chinnici, "Deciphering Religious Practice," 8.

104. Gibbons, *Faith of Our Fathers*, 207.

105. Ibid., 199. Gibbons followed an argument from Gottfried Wilhelm Leibnitz, *Theologicisches System*, ed. Carl Haas (Hildesheim: Georg Olms Verlagsbuchhandlung, 1966; reproduced from the Tübingen edition of 1860), 79–91. Leibniz was commenting on Trent's decree concerning church art.

106. Chinnici, "Deciphering Religious Practice," 8–9.

107. Ibid., 13.

108. Ibid., 14.

109. Ibid., 13.

110. Ibid., 17 n. 44.

111. See Gábor Barna, "The Security of Hope: The Confraternity of the Living Rosary," *Acta Ethnographica Hungarica* 51:3–4 (2006): 345–56.

112. Colleen McDannell, *Material Christianity: Religion and Popular Culture in America* (New Haven: Yale University Press, 1995), 39.

113. Ibid.

114. See, for example, Anne Taves, *The Household of Faith: Roman Catholic Devotions in Mid-Nineteenth-Century America*, Notre Dame Studies in American Catholicism, 7 (Notre Dame, IN: University of Notre Dame Press, 1986). See also Kane, "Marian Devotion since 1940" 89–129. See also McDannell, *Material Christianity*, 132–62 ("Lourdes Water and American Catholicism"), on the role of educational institutions like Notre Dame in promoting Marian piety in nineteenth-century America.

115. See Eamon Duffy, *Faith of Our Fathers: Reflections on Catholic Tradition* (New York: Continuum, 2004), 12.

116. See William V. D'Antonio, James D. Davidson, Dean R. Hoge, and Katherine Meyer, *American Catholics: Gender, Generation, and Commitment* (New York: Rowan and Littlefield/AltaMira Press, 2001), 51–67.

117. See ibid., 59–63, with graphs and statistics.

118. Ibid., 66. The recent (2008) study by the Pew Forum on Religion and Public Life, *U.S. Religious Landscape* Survey, concludes that "Catholicism has experienced the greatest net losses as a result of affiliation change. While nearly one-in-three Americans (31%) were raised in the Catholic faith, today fewer than one in four (24%) describe themselves as Catholic. These losses would have been even more pronounced were it not for the offsetting impact of immigration" (pp. 5–6, "Summary of Key Findings"). This study was accessed online, March 13,

2008, at http://religions.pewforum.org/pdf/report-religious-landscape-study-full.
pdf?sid=ST2008022501236.

119. Garry Wills, *The Rosary* (New York: Viking, 2005), 11.

120. Robert A. Orsi, "The Many Names of the Mother of God," in Melissa R.
Katz, ed., *Divine Mirrors: The Virgin Mary in the Visual Arts* (New York: Oxford
University Press, 2001), 3–18; here, 3–4.

121. On the expansion of the number of mysteries associated with recitation
of the rosary by Pope John Paul II, see Wills, *Rosary*, 8–10. The five "luminous"
mysteries include Christ's baptism, the Marriage at Cana, the Sermon on the
Mount, the Transfiguration, and the Last Supper. "Adding these mysteries," Wills
observes, "breaks with the psalter numerology of the devotion's past history. The
use of three sets of mysteries entailed the saying of 150 Hail Marys in the decades
of the whole—or 100 or 50 if one said two sets or just one. . . . The pope [John
Paul II] has broken those confines now, since the twenty mysteries are not reduc-
ible to the old schema of 150-100-50" (ibid., 9).

122. Orsi, "The Many Names of the Mother of God," 4.

123. For the quoted phrase, see ibid., 5; emphasis added.

124. See ibid.

125. See the discussion of these paintings in chapter 2.

126. Catherina Puglisi, *Caravaggio* (London: Phaidon), 190.

127. Orsi, "The Many Names of the Mother of God," 4.

128. David Freedberg, *The Power of Images: Studies in the History and Theory
of Response* (Chicago: University of Chicago Press, 1989), 30.

129. Orsi, "The Many Names of the Mother of God," 4.

130. Ibid., 6.

131. McDannell, *Material Christianity*, 160.

132. Ibid.

133. Ibid.

134. See ibid., 154–60, for discussion of how the 1897 Grotto came to be built.

135. Ibid., 161.

136. Ibid. Robert Orsi points out that in the nineteenth century, the principal
goal of promoting Marian devotion at Notre Dame—through shrines like the
Grotto and magazines like *Ave Maria*—was not to "Americanize devotionalism"
but "to bring [Catholics in] the United States into the universal church" by linking what was done locally with "modern, Rome-centered, Marian devotions."
See *Thank You, St. Jude: Women's Devotion to the Patron Saint of Hopeless Causes*
(New Haven: Yale University Press, 1996), 29.

137. Ibid.

138. Ibid.

139. Freedberg, *Power of Images*, 200.

140. See *Manual of Prayers*, 369–71.

141. See the official Roman handbook that governed the granting of

indulgences prior to the Second Vatican Council: *Enchiridion Indulgentiarum: Preces et Pia Opera* (Vatican City: Typis Polyglottis Vaticanis, 1950).

142. See Kenan B. Osborne, "Indulgences," in McBrien, *HarperCollins Encyclopedia of Catholicism*, 662–63; here, 662. In 1967, Pope Paul VI reformulated the Roman Catholic doctrine and practices connected with indulgences. The pope "made the use or nonuse of indulgences completely voluntary" (ibid., 663).

143. See *Enchiridion Indulgentiarum*, 268 n. 395, with reference to the 1479 bull (*Ea quae ex fidelium*) of Pope Sixtus IV. These indulgences were renewed at regular intervals, well into the twentieth century.

144. See ibid., 269 n. 395. Note that Pope Paul VI's *Indulgentiarum doctrina* (1967) refined the notion of a "plenary indulgence" by connecting it "with one's deliberate rejection of all sin, even venial" (Osborne, "Indulgences," 663).

145. On the link between "communion of saints" and "Holy Communion," see Josef A. Jungmann, *The Mass of the Roman Rite*, trans. Francis A. Brunner, 2 vols. (1955; Westminster, MD: Christian Classics, 1992), 2:275. As noted earlier, one condition commonly required for receiving a "plenary indulgence" for recitation of the rosary involved receiving communion.

146. See *Sacrosanctum concilium* (*The Constitution on the Sacred Liturgy*; December 4, 1963), n. 7; English translation in *Documents on the Liturgy, 1963–1979: Conciliar, Papal, and Curial Texts* (Collegeville, MN: Liturgical Press, 1982), document 1, pp. 4–27; here, p. 7.

147. See *Mysterium fidei*, the encyclical letter of Pope Paul VI (September 3, 1965), nn. 35–39; English translation in *Documents on the Liturgy, 1963–1979*, document 176, pp. 384–85. See also the *Catechism of the Catholic Church* (1994), n. 1373.

148. See Robert A. Orsi, "'The Infant of Prague's Nightie': The Devotional Origins of Contemporary Catholic Memory," *U.S. Catholic Historian* 21:2 (2003): 1–18; here, 2.

149. See ibid.

150. *Directory on Popular Piety and the Liturgy*, 11, 15. This document is cited from the English translation provided at the Vatican's Web site: http://www.vatican.va.

151. David Morgan, *Visual Piety: A History and Theory of Popular Religious Images* (Berkeley: University of California Press, 1998).

152. Ibid., 29.

153. Morgan, *Visual Piety*, 30, notes that the aesthetic of disinterestedness has often been used to reinforce "the subordination of lower classes and women," though this political agenda is not "all that the disinterested contemplation of art amounts to." One must therefore "be alert to the politics of taste and suspicious of any claim for political neutrality in ranking the disinterested experience of art above the popular reception of images."

154. Thomas Merton, *Contemplative Prayer* (New York: Herder and Herder, 1969), 111.

155. Ibid., 106.
156. Orsi, *Thank You, St. Jude*, 190.
157. Ibid.
158. Ibid., 191.
159. Morgan, *Visual Piety*, 31.
160. Ibid., 61.
161. Ibid.
162. Ibid., 66.
163. The phrase *refugium peccatorum* (refuge of sinners) is from the Litany of Loreto. It also appeared in liturgical prayers that were eventually incorporated into the Roman Missal (in its pre–Vatican II form). See *Enchiridion Indulgentiarum*, nn. 319 (litany) and 438 (missal), pp. 202 and 319. The petition "Pray for us sinners, now and at the hour of our death," also forms the conclusion of the Hail Mary. See also *Missale Romanum: Iuxta typicam vaticanam* (New York: Benziger Brothers, 1942), (177), where it is located among the "Missae propriae quae in aliquibus locis celebrari possunt" (Proper Masses which may be celebrated in certain places) for August 13.
164. Morgan, *Visual Piety*, 66.
165. Ibid.
166. Orsi, "The Many Names of the Mother of God," 13.
167. Ibid.
168. See Orsi, "'The Infant of Prague's Nightie,'" 5–8.
169. Ibid., 18.
170. Morgan, *Visual Piety*, 73.
171. See Flannery, *Vatican Council II*, 413–23.
172. In this passage, the Vatican II explicitly referenced the Council of Trent's decree on sacred images, as well as its decrees on justification and purgatory. See Flannery, *Vatican Council II*, 412 n. 22.
173. See my essay "Theological Principles for an Evaluation and Renewal of Popular Piety," in Peter C. Phan, ed., *Directory on Popular Piety and the Liturgy: Principles and Guidelines: A Commentary* (Collegeville, MN: Liturgical Press, 2005), 59–76.
174. In support of its position, the *Catechism* cites *Lumen gentium* 66.
175. Here the *Catechism* cites *Lumen gentium* 68.
176. See John D. Miller, *Beads and Prayers: The Rosary in History and Devotion* (London: Burns and Oates, 2001), 76–94. For the connection between the rosary as a form of repetitive prayer and the "Judeo-Christian-Islamic way of meditation" known as *baqqesh* (from Hebrew, "seek"), see David Burton Bryan, *A Western Way of Meditation: The Rosary Revisited* (Chicago: Loyola University Press, 1991), 9–12.
177. Bryan, *Western Way of Meditation*, 80–81. Bryan notes that even mysteries that may seem arcane or inaccessible to ordinary people have common

roots in human experience. Thus, for example, the fifth "glorious" mystery—the crowning of Mary as Queen of Heaven—may be understood in light of a desire for self-giving that reaches beyond the grave: "The one who grows old can hope to be allowed to serve even after death" (ibid., 81).

178. Wills, *Rosary*, 10.

179. Ibid.

180. See Robert C. Solomon, "On Kitsch and Sentimentality," *Journal of Aesthetics and Art Criticism* 49:1 (Winter 1991): 1–14; here, 2.

181. Ibid., 1.

182. Peter Robb, *M: The Man Who Became Caravaggio* (New York: Holt, 1999), 326.

183. Solomon, "On Kitsch and Sentimentality," 5.

184. See ibid., 5–12, where Solomon outlines in six headings "what's wrong with kitsch."

185. See, for example, Heinz Schreckenberg, *The Jews in Christian Art: An Illustrated History* (New York: Continuum, 1996); Henry Claman, *Jewish Images in the Christian Church: Art as a Mirror of the Jewish-Christian Conflict, 200–1250* (Macon, GA: Mercer University Press, 2000).

186. Solomon, "On Kitsch and Sentimentality," 2.

187. Milan Kundera, *The Unbearable Lightness of Being*, trans. Michael Henry Heim (New York: Harper and Row, 1984), 251.

188. Mary Midgley, "Brutality and Sentimentality," *Philosophy* 54:209 (1970): 385–89; here, 386; emphasis added.

189. Ibid., 385.

190. Ibid.

191. Solomon, "On Kitsch and Sentimentality," 12.

192. Ibid.

193. Ibid.

194. Luigi Santucci, *Meeting Jesus: A New Way to Christ*, trans. Bernard Wall (New York: Herder and Herder, 1971), 29.

195. Solomon, "On Kitsch and Sentimentality," 13–14.

196. See McDannell, *Material Christianity*, 161–97.

197. Ibid., 185.

198. Ibid.

199. Ibid., 186.

200. Ibid., 186–87, for the phrases in this and the preceding sentence. As McDannell points out, many articles urging a renewal of devotion to the rosary during the 1980s seemed to think that the practice belonged mainly to "pious old women" and had embodied the retrograde, "inward-looking devotionalism of an old, ethnic, feminized Catholicism" (ibid., 187).

201. See Sam Binkley, "Kitsch as a Repetitive System. A Problem for the Theory of Taste Hierarchy," *Journal of Material Culture* 5:2 (2000): 131–52. Binkley

notes that "contemporary sociologists have exposed the myth of cultural hierarchy upon which . . . readings of kitsch [as retrograde, lowbrow] depend as the thinly disguised prejudices of a cultural elitism" (ibid., 132).

202. Ibid., 133.

203. Ibid.

204. Ibid., 134–35.

205. Ibid., 135. Binkley derives the term "disembedding institutions" from the work of Anthony Giddens.

206. Ibid., 142.

207. Ibid., 149.

208. Ibid., 138.

209. Ibid., 141.

210. Ibid., 142.

211. Robert Westerfelhaus, "Prayers in Plaster and Plastic: Catholic Kitsch as Ritual Habit," in Margaret Cormak, ed., *Saints and Their Cults in the Atlantic World* (Columbia: University of South Carolina Press, 2007), 90–110.

212. See ibid., 92–93.

213. Ibid., 93.

214. An example is the title "co-redemptrix" ("co-redeemer") applied to the Virgin Mary. This title raises pastoral and ecumenical difficulties because it seems to compromise the unique place of Christ as "sole Mediator" between God and humankind. The Second Vatican Council avoided the term and insisted in its Constitution on the Church (*Lumen gentium* 62), that Mary's role in the history of salvation is a "subordinate" one. Titles applied to Mary—such as Advocate, Helper, Benefactress, Mediatrix—are to be understood in such a way that they "neither take away from nor add anything to the dignity and efficacy of Christ the one Mediator." These titles have never been officially connected with Mary in the traditional mysteries of the rosary.

215. Morgan, *Visual Piety*, 24.

216. Ibid.

217. Ibid.

218. Duffy, *Faith of our Fathers*, 11–19.

219. Ibid., 12.

220. Melissa R. Katz, "Regarding Mary: Women's Lives Reflected in the Virgin's Image," in *Divine Mirrors*, 19–129; here, 109.

221. Ibid., 107, 109. J. Michael Walker's series *Daily Life of the Virgin of Guadalupe* was exhibited in 2004 at the Fullerton Museum Center (California) and has been shown in other venues across the United States. See http://www.jmichaelwalker.com. For the images of Our Lady of Guadalupe, see http://www.virginguadalupe.com. See also Patricia Leigh Brown, "Saintly Streets Tell a City's Long Tale," *New York Times*, March 9, 2008; "U.S. Section"), accessed April 8, 2008.

222. See the gallery of images at http://www.virginguadalupe.com.

223. This image is reproduced in Katz, "Regarding Mary," 107, and also at http://www.virginguadalupe.com.

224. Danny Lyon, *Conversation with the Dead: An Exhibition of Photographs of Prison Life. With Letters and Drawings by Billy McCune # 122054* (Houston: Institute for the Arts, Rice University, 1970). Several of these photos also appear in Danny Lyon, *Photo, Film 1959–1990* ([Heidelberg]: Edition Braus, 1991), 76–105.

225. See the image reproduced in Lyon, *Photo, Film*, 80. The same image is reproduced in Katz, "Regarding Mary," 108.

226. Katz, "Regarding Mary," 109.

227. Ibid.

228. Ibid.

229. Ibid.

230. Lyon, *Photo, Film*, 76; the words are from Louise and Jonathan Green.

231. Jan-Christopher Horak, "That Danger of Unreason, That Threatening Space of an Absolute Freedom," in Lyon, *Photo, Film*, 106–11; here, 106.

232. Westerfelhaus, "Prayers in Plaster and Plastic," 102.

233. Ibid.; emphasis added.

234. Inculturation, Westerfelhaus ("Prayers in Plaster and Plastic," 103), notes, "is the Catholic theological position that, since potential reception of the Gospel message is implanted in all cultures, the Christian message can and should be given culturally specific expression among different peoples."

235. Ibid., 103, 105.

236. This biblical image is a somewhat exotic one that may have used pre-Christian Jewish sources describing an eschatological conflict between "a woman with child and a dragon." See Adela Yabro Collins, "The Apocalypse (Revelation)," in Raymond Brown et al., eds., *The New Jerome Biblical Commentary* (Englewood Cliffs, NJ: Prentice-Hall, 1990), 996–1016; here, 1008. Collins notes that in the present text of Revelation, the figure of the woman "clothed with the sun and crowned with stars" is probably meant to be "the heavenly Israel, the spouse of God," and, in Christian perspective, the eschatological "new Eve" and "bride of Christ."

237. For Jesus' triumphal entry into Jerusalem, commemorated in the Roman Catholic liturgy on Palm Sunday, see Matthew 21.1–11; Mark 11.1–10; Luke 19.2840; John 12.12–16.

238. "Slave-girl" is the most accurate translation of the Greek word Luke 1.48 uses (δούλη). See the translation of Richmond Lattimore, *The Gospels and the Revelation* (New York: Farrar, Straus and Giroux, 1979), 122.

239. For a more extended development of this theme in postmodern Catholic theology, see Louis-Marie Chauvet, *Symbol and Sacrament*, trans. Patrick Madigan and Madeleine Beaumont (Collegeville, MN: Liturgical Press, 1995), 490–509, 531–33.

240. See ibid., 532, where Chauvet, quoting Walter Kasper, notes that the cross "can be interpreted only as the renunciation by God of God's very self."

241. See Orsi, "Many Names of the Mother of God," 13.

242. Ibid.

243. "Artist's Statement" at http://www.jmichaelwalker.com, accessed April 10, 2008.

244. James Oles, comments on Catalogue Nos. 48A and 48B in Katz, *Divine Mirrors*, 255–56.

245. Gerard Manley Hopkins, "As Kingfishers Catch Fire," in W. H. Gardner, ed., *Poems and Prose* (Baltimore: Penguin Books, 1963), 51.

NOTES TO CONCLUSION

1. See A. Hamman, *Early Christian Prayers*, trans. Walter Mitchell (Chicago: Henry Regnery, 1961), 76.

2. Ibid., 289.

3. Eithne Wilkins, *The Rose-Garden Game* (New York: Herder and Herder, 1969), 198–99.

4. Although eventually approved by church authorities (1930), the events connected with Fatima belong to the category of "private revelations," and Catholics have never been obligated to believe that they actually occurred or that the "messages" entrusted to the children at Fatima are truly the words and thoughts of the Virgin Mary.

Index

Henrietta Maria (queen of England), 106
Henry VIII (king of England), 147, 161
Hergenröther, Joseph (Cardinal), 279n.
   87
Hesse, Carla, 268 n. 44
Hibbard, Howard, 249nn. 88, 92
hierarchy, Catholic, restored in Eng-
   land, 196
Hilsey, John, 173–74, 283n. 107
Hinduism, 224
Holt, Elizabeth Gilmore, 248n. 74,
   249n. 96
Holy Communion (Catholic sacra-
   ment), 18, 107, 109, 112, 117, 126,
   128, 171, 175, 194. *See also* Blessed
   Sacrament; Eucharist(ic); Mass
"Holy Face (of Christ)," devotion to, 212
"Holy League," 260n. 77
Holy Thursday, 149
Hopkins, Gerard Manley, 236
Horace (Roman poet), 106
Horae Beatae Mariae Virginis. See
   Hours of the Blessed Virgin Mary
Horak, Jan-Christopher, 311n. 231
Hortulus animae, 102
Houghton, Charlotte, 296n. 167
Hours of the Blessed Virgin Mary, 9,
   102, 152, 173–74, 177
Hsia, R. Po-chia, 12, 44
Hudon, William V., 247 nn. 54, 55; 257
   n. 7
Hughes, John (archbishop of New
   York), 207
humanism, 36; Christian humanism,
   36, 49, 174, 233
Hunt, Patrick, 61
Hutton, Patrick H., 284n. 171

icon(s), 28, 55, 69, 72, 181; "crossing
   the visible," 55; Mary as, 214; popular, 232; rewritten/rewriting, 40,
   56–76, 215

iconography: Catholic, 50, 225; Marian, 48–56, 121, 214
identity: Catholic, 113, 127, 145, 155,
   205, 219; early modern Catholic,
   127; religious, 113
imagery, Marian, 121, 214–15
images, 73; devotional, 220
imitatio Christi, 30–31
Imitation of Christ (work), 153
Immaculate Conception, 71, 278n. 78;
   279n. 92; discalced nuns of, 138;
   dogma of, 129–30, 239
Index of Forbidden Books, 8, 265 n. 15
indulgence(s), 7, 217, 277n. 49
Innocent I (pope, Saint), 114
intercession (of Mary), 86, 92, 94, 154,
   174, 205
Islam, 11, 145, 224

James (Jacobus) of Voraigne, 95;
   Golden Legend, 95, 134
Jansenists, 18, 123
Jedin, Hubert, 8
John of the Cross (Saint), 57–58; *The
   Ascent of Mount Carmel*, 57; *The
   Living Flame of Love*, 57–58; *Spiri-
   tual Canticle*, 57
Johnson, Clare V., 274n. 157
Jones, Pamela M., 253nn. 158, 164
Joye, George, 175; *Ortulus animae*,
   175, 178
"joys of Mary," 269n. 71
Juan Diego (Saint), 232
Judaism, 224
Jude, Saint, prayers to, 219
Jungmann, Josef A., 307n. 145

Kane, Paula M., 302n. 51
Kasper, Walter (Cardinal), 312n. 240
Katz, Melissa, 231–32
Katzew, Ilona, 298n. 207
Kemp, Martin, 286n. 2

Tiepolo, 27;
Titan (Tiziano Vecellio), 62; *Supper at Emmaus*, 79, 96
transubstantiation, 166
Trent (Council of). *See* Council of Trent
Triacca, Achille Maria, 251n. 134
Triumphant Catholicism, 10, 48; "Church Triumphant," 39
Turk(s), 63, 66, 145; "Turkish menace," 119

University of Notre Dame, 193–94, 216; Basilica of the Sacred Heart, 193; grotto, 193, 216; "Number One Moses," 193; Theodore M. Hesburgh Library, 193; "Touchdown Jesus," 193
Urban VIII (pope), 289n. 51

Van Damme, Stéphane, 108
Vassallo e Silva, Nuno, 292n. 94
vernacular: devotional manuals, 176; "harsh vernacular," 28; languages (Trent's discussion), 41, 255n. 187; vernacularism, 28, 40–42; vernacular religion, 122, 126–27; visual vernacularism, 41
Verstegen, Ian, 39
Vasari, Giorgio, 280n. 100
Vincent, Thomas. *See* Crowther, Arthur
Vinci, Leonardo da, 16, 79; *Last Supper*, 79
Virgil (Roman poet), 106
Virgin Mary, 1, 21–22, 26, 28, 46, 69, 75, 79, 89; Christotokos, 33; as "Empresse of Helle," 188; images of, 39; Mother of God, 32; Mother of the Poor, 42; Queen of Heaven,

188, 234; reinterpretation(s) of, 38; 188–92; Theotokos, 32, 86–87, 140; titles (advocate, helper, benefactress, mediatrix, co-redemptrix), 310n. 214; warrior, 46
Virgin of Guadalupe, 189–90
Virgin of the Macana, 190–91, 298nn. 207–8
Voelker, Evelyn Carole, 253nn. 169, 170
Vogel, Cyrille, 266n. 28

Wainwright, Geoffrey, 268n. 52
Walker, J. Michael, 231–32, 235; *Daily Life of the Virgin of Guadalupe*, 232
Planchando, Pensando (Ironing, Thinking), 232, 235
Walsham, Alexandra, 179–80, 182
Way of the Cross (devotion), 128. *See also* stations of the cross
Westerfelhaus, Robert, 230–31, 233
Westerfield Tucker, Karen B., 268n. 52
Whyte, Thomas, 157–58
Wieck, Roger S., 269n. 67
Wilkins, Eithne, 237; *The Rose-Garden Game*, 237
Wills, Garry, 1, 213, 224
Wilmart, André, 29
Winston-Allen, Anne, 5, 7, 120; *Stories of the Rose*, 5, 21
Wisdom (of God, personified), 110, 121, 172
Wiseman, Nicholas (Cardinal), 199, 201; "God Bless Our Pope," 199
women, 219–20; alienation experienced by, 220
Wright, Rosemary Muir, 280n. 95
Wyatt, Thomas, 148

Zwingli, Ulrich, 8

About the Author

Nathan D. Mitchell is Professor of Theology at the University of Notre Dame, where he is also the Associate Director for the Center for Liturgy. He is the author of *Meeting Mystery: Liturgy, Worship, Sacraments*; *Liturgy and the Social Sciences*; and *Cult and Controversy: The Worship of the Eucharist Outside Mass.*